A BOOK OF

ALGEBRA & CALCULUS
Mathematics Paper – I

For

B.Sc. – I : Semester - I

According to Revised Syllabus (C.G.P.A. Pattern) of
Solapur University, Solapur, w.e.f. June 2014

Prof. ALANDKAR S. J.
M.Sc., M.Phil. B.Ed., Dip. in Comp. Sci.
Head & Associate Professor,
Department of Mathematics & Statistics,
Walchand College of Arts & Science,
Solapur

Prof. DHANSHETTI N. I.
M.Sc., M. Phil.
Head & Associate Professor,
Department of Mathematics,
C. B. Khedgi's College,
Akkalkot, Solapur

Prof. DHONE A. S.
M.Sc.
Head, Department of Mathematics,
Sangameshwar College, Solapur

Prof. MAHIMKAR R. D.
M.Sc.,
Head, Department of Mathematics,
Sangola College, Sangola

N3628

F.Y.B.Sc. ALGEBRA & CALCULUS - MATHEMATICS PAPER - I

First Edition : September 2015 ISBN 978-93-5164-736-2
© : Authors

The text of this publication, or any part thereof, should not be reproduced or transmitted in any form or stored in any computer storage system or device for distribution including photocopy, recording, taping or information retrieval system or reproduced on any disc, tape, perforated media or other information storage device etc., without the written permission of Authors with whom the rights are reserved. Breach of this condition is liable for legal action.

Every effort has been made to avoid errors or omissions in this publication. In spite of this, errors may have crept in. Any mistake, error or discrepancy so noted and shall be brought to our notice shall be taken care of in the next edition. It is notified that neither the publisher nor the authors or seller shall be responsible for any damage or loss of action to any one, of any kind, in any manner, therefrom.

Published By : Printed By :
NIRALI PRAKASHAN Repro Knowledgecast Limited
Abhyudaya Pragati, 1312 Shivaji Nagar, Thane
Off J.M. Road, PUNE - 411005
Tel - (020) 25512336/37/39. Fax - 25511379
Email : niralipune@pragationline.com

DISTRIBUTION CENTERS

PUNE
Nirali Prakashan
119, Budhwar Peth, Jogeshwari Mandir Lane,
Pune - 411002, Maharashtra.
Tel: (020) 24452044, 66022708
Fax : (020) 2445 1538
Email : bookorder@pragationline.com

MUMBAI
Nirali Prakashan
385, S.V.P. Road, Rasdhara Co-op. Hsg.
Society, Girgaum,
Mumbai - 400004, Maharashtra
Tel : (022) 2385 6339 / 2386 9976,
Fax : (022) 2386 9976
Email : niralimumbai@pragationline.com

RETAIL SHOPS

PUNE
Pragati Book Centre
157, Budhwar Peth, Opp. Ratan Talkies,
Pune – 411002, Maharashtra
Tel : 2445 8887 / 6602 2707

Pragati Book Centre
676/B, Budhwar Peth,
Opp. Jogeshwari Mandir,
Pune – 411002, Maharashtra
Tel. : (020) 6601 7784, 2445 2254

PUNE
Pragati Book Centre
Amber Chamber, 28/A, Budhwar Peth,
Appa Balwant Chowk
Pune : 411002, Maharashtra
Tel : (020) 20240335 / 66281669
Email : pbcpune@pragationline.com

PBC Book Sellers and Stationers
152, Budhwar Peth,
Near Jogeshwari Mandir,
Pune – 411002, Maharashtra
Tel : (020) 6609 2463 / 2445 2254

MUMBAI
Pragati Book Corner
Indira Niwas,
111-A Bhavani Shankar Road,
Dadar (W), **Mumbai** – 400028
Tel : (022) 2422 3525 / 6662 5254
Email : pbcmumbai@pragationline.com

DISTRIBUTION BRANCHES

NAGPUR
Pratibha Book Distributors
Above Maratha Mandir, Shop No. 3, First Floor, Rani Zanshi Square, Sitabuldi,
Nagpur 440012, Maharashtra, Tel : (0712) 254 7129

JALGAON
34, V. V. Golani Market, Navi Peth, Jalgaon 425001, Maharashtra,
Tel : (0257) 222 0395, Mob : 94234 91860

KOLHAPUR
New Mahadvar Road, Kedar Plaza, 1st Floor Opp. IDBI Bank
Kolhapur 416 012, Maharashtra. Mob : 9850046155

www.pragationline.com info@pragationline.com

PREFACE

With an immense pleasure, we are presenting the book of Paper - I (Algebra & Calculus) to the F.Y.B.Sc. students of Semester – I (C.G.P.A. Pattern) according to modified syllabus implementing from June 2014 of Solapur University, Solapur. Also we will make an attempt to introduce the series of text books as per the syllabus of B.Sc. Part I, II and III (Mathematics) of each semester.

Main objective of the book is to provide essential and sufficient content of the topics as per the syllabus of Solapur University, Solapur. Also as per the nature of examination papers, we have given multiple choice questions, short questions as well as long questions in the exercise. After each unit or subunit of the chapters, we have included a requisite number of illustrations. B.Sc. - I in the entry point of under-graduate students. At the first step of entry if students get the awareness of the system of syllabus and nature of questions and semesterwise pattern of Solapur University, Solapur, by this book, the students can confidently move forward with first steps and develop his/her knowledge.

Shri Dineshbhai Furia and Shri Jignesh Furia and all the concerned staff of the Nirali Prakashan have provided these text books at the door step of student of Solapur University, Solapur with the assistance of authors who know the needs of the students. Thanks to all of them, special thanks to Mr. Prahakar Nandkile (Marketing Executive, Solapur) for the promotion of this book and Mrs. Anagha Medhekar, Mrs. Anjali Mulye and Mr. Santosh Bare of error free printing and proof reading made by concerned staff. Also thanks to our family members who have kept the patience and given encouragement in all respects.

Valuable suggestions are always welcome from readers and well wishers for the improvement of this book.

Authors

SYLLABUS

SECTION-I : ALGEBRA

1. **Matrices** (10)
   Symmetric and skew symmetric, Elementary transformations, Rank of a matrix (Echelon and Normal form), Characteristic equation of a matrix, Cayley Hamilton theorem and its use in finding the inverse of a matrix.

2. **Linear Equations** (10)
   Applications of matrices to a system of linear (both homogeneous and non-homogeneous) equations. Eigen values and eigen vectors.

3. **Complex Number** (10)
   Modulus and Argument of a complex number, DeMoivre's theorem and its applications, Roots of unity, Roots of complex numbers.

4. **Transcendental Functions** (10)
   Circular functions with their inverses and hyperbolic function of a complex variable along with their inverses.

SECTION-II : CALCULUS

1. **Differentiation** (15)
   Indeterminate forms and L'Hospital's Rule, Successive differentiations, n^{th} derivatives of standard functions, Leibnitz rule. Taylor's theorem and Maclaurin's Theorem (Only Statements). Series expansion of e^x, $\cos x$, $\sin x$, $(1 + x)^n$, $\log(1 + x)$

2. **Function of Two Variables** (10)
   Limit and Continuity of functions of two variables, Partial derivative, Partial derivative of higher orders, Homogeneous functions, Euler's theorem on Homogeneous functions.

3. **Reduction Formulae** (05)
   $\int_0^{\pi/2} \sin^n x \, dx$, $\int_0^{\pi/2} \cos^n x \, dx$, $\int_0^{\pi/2} \sin^n x \cos^m x \, dx$
   (Note that reductions to these forms are not expected)

4. **Vector Calculus** (10)
   Scalar point function, Vector point function, Directional derivative, Gradient, Divergence and Curl and its properties.

CONTENTS

SECTION-I : ALGEBRA

1. Matrices — 1.1 – 1.42

2. Linear Equations — 2.1 – 2.56

3. Complex Number — 3.1 – 3.34

4. Transcendental Functions — 4.1 – 4.26

SECTION-II : CALCULUS

1. Differentiation — 1.1 – 1.64

2. Function of Two Variables — 2.1 – 2.56

3. Reduction Formulae — 3.1 – 3.40

4. Vector Calculus — 4.1 – 4.42

❑❑❑

SECTION-I : ALGEBRA

CHAPTER 1

MATRICES

1.1 INTRODUCTION

The concept of matrix theory was introduced by an English mathematician Arthur Cayley 1858. It is a very useful tool in almost all branches of social and physical sciences. Matrix does not denote a number. The usual rules of algebraic operations are not true in matrix theory.

Matrices are used in Geometry, Statistics, Economics, Sociology, Genetics, Atomic Physics, Engineering, Linear Programming and also in industrial management. The theory of matrices has its origin in the solution of Linear Problems.

Arthur Cayley
(Born in 1821
British Mathematician)

In Std. XII, you have already learned the basic concept of matrix. In this chapter we shall learn finding inverse by using Cayley-Hamilton theorem and solution of a matrix equation.

1.2 MATRIX

Definition : A rectangular arrangement of mn numbers or objects in m rows and n columns is called as matrix of order m × n (read it as m by n). It can be written as

$$A = \begin{bmatrix} a_{11} & a_{12} & \ldots & a_{1n} \\ a_{21} & a_{22} & \ldots & a_{2n} \\ \vdots & \vdots & \vdots & \vdots \\ a_{m1} & a_{m2} & \ldots & a_{mn} \end{bmatrix} \quad \ldots (1)$$

Each entries a_{ij} in this matrix is called an element. The number which lies in i^{th} row and j^{th} column of the matrix is called the (i, j)th element a_{ij}.

Notation : We shall denote a matrix by a capital letters, such as A, B, C, D, ... etc. and their elements by small letters a, b, c, ... or a_{11}, a_{12}, ... etc.

In shorter notation, we shall write equation (1) as

$$A = (a_{ij}) \text{ where, } i = 1, 2, ..., m \text{ and } j = 1, 2, ..., n$$

1.2.1 Types of Matrices

1. Row matrix : A matrix having only one row is called a row matrix (or row vector).

For example, $[1 \ 5 \ 6 \ 9]_{1 \times 4}$.

2. Column matrix : A matrix having only one column is called a column matrix (or column vector).

For example, $\begin{bmatrix} 7 \\ 0 \\ 7 \\ 8 \end{bmatrix}_{4 \times 1}$

3. Square matrix : If the number of rows and columns are equal the matrix is called a square matrix.

For example, $\begin{bmatrix} a_{11} & a_{12} & a_{13} \\ a_{21} & a_{22} & a_{23} \\ a_{31} & a_{32} & a_{33} \end{bmatrix}$ is a square matrix of order 3 × 3 or briefly of order 3.

4. Diagonal matrix : A square matrix in which all non-diagonal elements are zero is called a diagonal matrix.

In short, $D = (d_{ij})$, $d_{ij} = 0$, $\forall \ i \neq j$.

It can also be written in the form

$$D = \text{diag} [d_{11} \ d_{22} \ d_{33} \ ... \ d_{nn}]$$

For example, $\begin{bmatrix} 7 & 0 & 0 \\ 0 & 8 & 0 \\ 0 & 0 & 9 \end{bmatrix}$ or $\begin{bmatrix} 5 & 0 & 0 \\ 0 & 2 & 0 \\ 0 & 0 & 7 \end{bmatrix}$ is a diagonal matrix.

5. Scalar matrix : A diagonal matrix, in which all diagonal elements are equal is called a scalar matrix.

For example, $\begin{bmatrix} 7 & 0 & 0 \\ 0 & 7 & 0 \\ 0 & 0 & 7 \end{bmatrix}$

6. Unit matrix : A scalar matrix, in which all diagonal elements are equal to 1 is called the unit matrix or identity matrix and is denoted by I.

For example, $I_2 = \begin{bmatrix} 1 & 0 \\ 0 & 1 \end{bmatrix}$ and $I_3 = \begin{bmatrix} 1 & 0 & 0 \\ 0 & 1 & 0 \\ 0 & 0 & 1 \end{bmatrix}$ etc.

7. Null matrix : A matrix in which all elements are zero is called a null or zero matrix.

For example, $O_{32} = \begin{bmatrix} 0 & 0 \\ 0 & 0 \\ 0 & 0 \end{bmatrix}$, $O_{23} = \begin{bmatrix} 0 & 0 & 0 \\ 0 & 0 & 0 \end{bmatrix}$ etc.

8. Symmetric matrix : A square matrix $A = (a_{ij})$ is said to be symmetric matrix, if $a_{ij} = a_{ji}$, $\forall$ i and j i.e. if $A = A'$.

For example, $\begin{bmatrix} 1 & 2 & 3 \\ 2 & 4 & 5 \\ 3 & 5 & 6 \end{bmatrix}$ is a symmetric matrix.

9. Skew-symmetric matrix : A square matrix $A = (a_{ij})$ is said to be skew-symmetric, if $a_{ij} = -a_{ji}$, $\forall$ i and j.

i.e. if $A = -A'$.

In a skew-symmetric matrix

$$a_{ii} = -a_{ii}$$

$\Rightarrow \quad 2a_{ii} = 0$

$\Rightarrow \quad a_{ii} = 0$

That is, in skew-symmetric matrix all principal diagonal elements are zero.

For example, $\begin{bmatrix} 0 & 4 & 5 \\ -4 & 0 & -3 \\ -5 & 3 & 0 \end{bmatrix}$ is a skew-symmetric matrix.

10. Trace of a matrix : Let $A = (a_{ij})$ be a square matrix of order n. The trace of A is the sum of the diagonal elements and is denoted as tr(A).

Thus, $\quad tr(A) = a_{11} + a_{22} + \ldots + a_{nn}$

$$= \sum_{i=1}^{n} a_{ii}$$

For example, Let $A = \begin{bmatrix} 5 & 0 & 8 & 4 \\ 1 & 5 & 6 & 9 \\ 5 & 6 & 7 & 7 \\ 7 & 0 & 7 & 8 \end{bmatrix}$

be a square matrix of order four.

Then $\quad$ tr(A) $= 5 + 5 + 7 + 8 = 25$

1.2.2 Algebra of Matrices

1. Addition of matrices : Let $A = (a_{ij})$ and $B = (b_{ij})$ be two matrices of the same order. Then we define the sum of A and B as

$$A + B = (a_{ij} + b_{ij})$$

2. Subtraction of matrices : Let $A = (a_{ij})$ and $B = (b_{ij})$ be two matrices of the same order. Then we define the difference of A and B as

$$A - B = (a_{ij} - b_{ij})$$

3. Scalar multiplication : Let $A = (a_{ij})$ be any matrix and k is any number, we define the product of A by k as

$$Ak = kA = (ka_{ij})$$

4. Multiplication of matrices : Let $A = (a_{ij})$ be a matrix of order $m \times n$ and $B = (b_{jk})$ be a matrix of order $n \times p$, then the product C of A and B can be defined as

$$C = A \cdot B = (C_{ik})$$

where $\quad C_{ik} = \sum_{j=1}^{n} a_{ij} b_{jk}$ and C is a matrix of order $m \times p$.

5. Transpose of a matrix : Let $A = (a_{ij})$ be a matrix of order $m \times n$ the matrix obtained by interchanging rows and columns is called the transpose of A and is denoted by A'.

$$A' = (a_{ji}) \; \forall \; i \text{ and } j.$$

6. Equality of matrices : Two matrices are said to be equal if and only if they are of same order and the corresponding elements are equal. i.e. let $A = (a_{ij})$ and $B = (b_{ij})$ be two matrices of the same order.

Then $A = B$ if and only if $a_{ij} = b_{ij}, \; \forall \; i \text{ and } j$.

7. Idempotent matrix : A square matrix A is called an idempotent matrix if $A^2 = A$.

For example, Let $A = \begin{bmatrix} 2 & -2 & -4 \\ -1 & 3 & 4 \\ 1 & -2 & -3 \end{bmatrix}$, then

$$A^2 = A \cdot A = \begin{bmatrix} 2 & -2 & -4 \\ -1 & 3 & 4 \\ 1 & -2 & -3 \end{bmatrix} \begin{bmatrix} 2 & -2 & -4 \\ -1 & 3 & 4 \\ 1 & -2 & -3 \end{bmatrix}$$

$$= \begin{bmatrix} 2 & -2 & -4 \\ -1 & 3 & 4 \\ 1 & -2 & -3 \end{bmatrix} = A.$$

∴ A is an idempotent matrix.

8. Involuntary matrix : A square matrix A is called an involuntary matrix if $A^2 = I$.

For example : (i) Since $I^2 = I$ always.

∴ Identity matrix is involuntary.

(ii) Let $A = \begin{bmatrix} -1 & 0 \\ -1 & 1 \end{bmatrix}$, then

$$A^2 = A \cdot A = \begin{bmatrix} -1 & 0 \\ -1 & 1 \end{bmatrix} \begin{bmatrix} -1 & 0 \\ -1 & 1 \end{bmatrix}$$

$$= \begin{bmatrix} 1 & 0 \\ 0 & 1 \end{bmatrix} = I$$

∴ A is an involuntary matrix.

9. Nilpotent matrix : A square matrix A is called a nilpotent matrix of index n, if $A^n = O$, where n is the least positive integer.

For example : Let $A = \begin{bmatrix} 2 & 4 \\ -1 & -2 \end{bmatrix}$, then

$$A^2 = A \cdot A = \begin{bmatrix} 2 & 4 \\ -1 & -2 \end{bmatrix} \begin{bmatrix} 2 & 4 \\ -1 & -2 \end{bmatrix}$$

$$= \begin{bmatrix} 0 & 0 \\ 0 & 0 \end{bmatrix}$$

∴ A is a nilpotent matrix of index 2.

10. Singular matrix : A square matrix with determinant zero is called a singular matrix.

11. Elementary matrix : A matrix obtained by taking a single transformation on an identity matrix is called an elementary matrix.

For example : Let $I = \begin{bmatrix} 1 & 0 & 0 \\ 0 & 1 & 0 \\ 0 & 0 & 1 \end{bmatrix}$, then

$\begin{bmatrix} 0 & 1 & 0 \\ 1 & 0 & 0 \\ 0 & 0 & 1 \end{bmatrix}$, $\begin{bmatrix} 1 & 0 & 0 \\ 0 & 0 & 1 \\ 0 & 1 & 0 \end{bmatrix}$ etc. are elementary matrices.

SOLVED EXAMPLES

Example 1.1 : Prove that A is symmetric if and only if A = A'.

Solution : Let $A = (a_{ij})$ be a square matrix of order n.

Then A' must be a square matrix of order n.

Let A be symmetric matrix, then $a_{ij} = a_{ji}$ $\forall$ i and j.

Consider, $(i, j)^{th}$ element of A' = $(j, i)^{th}$ element of A

$\qquad\qquad\qquad\qquad = a_{ji}$

$\qquad\qquad\qquad\qquad = a_{ij}$ $\qquad\qquad$ ($\because$ A is symmetric)

$\qquad\qquad\qquad\qquad = (i, j)^{th}$ element of A

$\therefore \qquad\qquad\qquad$ A' = A

Conversely, suppose that A = A'.

Then A must be a square matrix.

Consider, $\quad a_{ij}$ = the $(i, j)^{th}$ element of A

$\qquad\qquad\quad = $ the $(i, j)^{th}$ element of A' $\qquad\qquad$ ($\because$ A = A')

$\qquad\qquad\quad = $ the $(j, i)^{th}$ element of A

$\qquad\qquad\quad = a_{ji}$

$\therefore \qquad\qquad a_{ij} = a_{ji}$ $\forall$ i and j.

Hence, A is a symmetric matrix.

Example 1.2 : Prove that A is skew-symmetric if and only if. A' = – A.

Solution : Let A be a square matrix of order n.

Then A' is also a square matrix of order n.

Let A be a skew-symmetric matrix, then $a_{ij} = -a_{ji}$ ∀ i and j.

Consider,

The $(i, j)^{th}$ element of A'

$$= (j, i)^{th} \text{ element of A}$$
$$= a_{ji}$$
$$= -a_{ij} \qquad (\because a_{ij} = -a_{ji})$$
$$= \text{the } (i, j)^{th} \text{ element of } (-A)$$

∴   A' = – A

Conversely, suppose that A' = – A.

Then A must be a square matrix.

Consider, the $(i, j)^{th}$ element of A'

$$= \text{the } (i, j)^{th} \text{ element of } (-A) \qquad \ldots \text{(given)}$$
$$= \text{the negative of } (i, j)^{th} \text{ element of A}$$
$$= -a_{ij}$$

∴ $a_{ji} = -a_{ij}$ ∀ i and j.

Hence A is a skew-symmetric matrix.

Example 1.3 : If A and B are symmetric matrices of the same order, prove that AB is symmetric if and only if AB = BA.

Solution : Since A and B are symmetric.

∴   By definition

$$A' = A \text{ and } B' = B \qquad \ldots \text{(i)}$$

Suppose that   AB = BA   … (ii)

Claim : To prove that AB is symmetric.

Consider,   (AB)' = B'A'

$$= BA \qquad (\because \text{ by (i)})$$
$$= AB \qquad (\because \text{ by (ii)})$$

Therefore, AB is a symmetric matrix.

Conversely, suppose AB is symmetric, then

$$(AB)' = AB \qquad \ldots (iii)$$

Claim : To prove that

$$AB = BA$$

Consider, $(AB)' = B'A'$

$$= BA \qquad (\because \text{ by (i)})$$

$$\therefore (AB)' = BA \qquad \ldots (iv)$$

By equation (iii) and (iv), we have

$$AB = BA.$$

Example 1.4 : Let A and B be symmetric matrices of the same order. Prove that AB + BA is symmetric and AB − BA is skew-symmetric.

Solution : Here A and B are symmetric matrices of the same order.

Then $\quad A' = A$ and $B' = B \qquad \ldots (i)$

(a) Consider,

$$(AB + BA)' = (AB)' + (BA)'$$
$$= B'A' + A'B'$$
$$= BA + AB \qquad (\because \text{ by (i)})$$
$$= AB + BA \qquad (\because \text{ By associativity property})$$

Hence AB + BA is symmetric.

(b) Consider,

$$(AB - BA)' = (AB)' - (BA)'$$
$$= B'A' - A'B'$$
$$= BA - AB \qquad (\because \text{ by (i)})$$
$$= -(AB - BA) \qquad (\because \text{ by algebra of matrix})$$

Therefore, AB − BA is skew-symmetric.

Example 1.5 : If A is symmetric and I is an identity matrix of the same order, then prove that $(A + I)(A - I)$ is a symmetric matrix.

Solution : Here A is symmetric and I is an identity matrix of the same order. Then $A' = A$ and $I' = I$ always.

Consider,

$$[(A + I)(A - I)]' = (A - I)'(A + I)'$$
$$= (A' - I')(A' + I')$$
$$= (A' - I)(A' + I) \qquad (\because I' = I)$$
$$= A'^2 - I$$
$$= A^2 - I \qquad (\because A' = A)$$
$$= (A + I)(A - I)$$

Therefore, $(A + I)(A - I)$ is a symmetric matrix.

Example 1.6 : Show that for square matrices A, B of the same order, $AB' + BA'$ is symmetric and $AB' - BA'$ is skew-symmetric.

Solution : Here A, B are square matrices of same order, then A' and B' are also square matrices of same order.

Consider

(a) $(AB' + BA')' = (AB')' + (BA')'$
$$= (B')'A' + (A')'B'$$
$$= BA' + AB'$$
$$= AB' + BA' \qquad (\because \text{by associativity property})$$

Therefore, $AB' + BA'$ is symmetric matrix.

(b) $(AB' - BA')' = (AB')' - (BA')'$
$$= (B')'A' - (A')'B'$$
$$= BA' - AB'$$
$$= -(AB' - BA') \qquad (\because \text{by algebra of matrices})$$

Hence $AB' - BA'$ is a skew-symmetric matrix.

Example 1.7 : Show that every square matrix can be uniquely expressed as the sum of a symmetric and a skew-symmetric matrices.

Solution : Let A, B and C be three square matrices of the same order n.

We know the identity.

$$A = \frac{1}{2}(A + A') + \frac{1}{2}(A - A') \qquad \ldots (i)$$

But $(A + A')' = A' + (A')'$
$= A' + A$
$= A + A'$

$\therefore \quad \dfrac{1}{2}(A + A')' = \dfrac{1}{2}(A + A')$

$\therefore \quad \left[\dfrac{1}{2}(A + A')\right]' = \dfrac{1}{2}(A + A')$

Therefore, $\dfrac{1}{2}(A + A')$ is a symmetric matrix. ... (ii)

Again, $(A - A')' = A' - (A')'$
$= A' - A$
$= -(A - A')$

$\dfrac{1}{2}(A - A')' = -\dfrac{1}{2}(A - A')$

$\therefore \quad \left[\dfrac{1}{2}(A - A')\right]' = -\dfrac{1}{2}(A - A')$

Hence, $\dfrac{1}{2}(A - A')$ is a skew-symmetric matrix. (iii)

From equation (i), (ii) and (iii), A is sum of symmetric and skew-symmetric matrices.

Uniqueness : Let B be a symmetric and C be a skew-symmetric matrix.

Let $\quad A = B + C$ ... (iv)

Then $\quad A' = (B + C)'$
$= B' + C'$
$= B - C \quad$ ... (v) ($\because B' = B$ and $C' = -C$)

Adding equation (iv) and (v), we have

$$A + A' = 2B \Rightarrow B = \dfrac{1}{2}(A + A')$$

Subtracting equation (v) from equation (iv), we get

$$A - A' = 2C \Rightarrow C = \dfrac{1}{2}(A - A')$$

Example 1.8 : Express the following matrix as the sum of a symmetric and a skew-symmetric matrices.

$$\begin{bmatrix} 5 & 4 & 7 \\ 2 & 4 & 6 \\ 3 & 6 & 2 \end{bmatrix}$$

Solution : Let $A = \begin{bmatrix} 5 & 4 & 7 \\ 2 & 4 & 6 \\ 3 & 6 & 2 \end{bmatrix}$

We know the identity

$$A = \frac{1}{2}(A + A') + \frac{1}{2}(A - A') \qquad \ldots \text{(i)}$$

Now, $A' = \begin{bmatrix} 5 & 2 & 3 \\ 4 & 4 & 6 \\ 7 & 6 & 2 \end{bmatrix}$

Adding A and A', we get

$$A + A' = \begin{bmatrix} 5 & 4 & 7 \\ 2 & 4 & 6 \\ 3 & 6 & 2 \end{bmatrix} + \begin{bmatrix} 5 & 2 & 3 \\ 4 & 4 & 6 \\ 7 & 6 & 2 \end{bmatrix}$$

$$= \begin{bmatrix} 10 & 6 & 10 \\ 6 & 8 & 12 \\ 10 & 12 & 14 \end{bmatrix}$$

$\therefore \quad \frac{1}{2}(A + A') = \frac{1}{2}\begin{bmatrix} 10 & 6 & 10 \\ 6 & 8 & 12 \\ 10 & 12 & 14 \end{bmatrix} = \begin{bmatrix} 5 & 3 & 5 \\ 3 & 4 & 6 \\ 5 & 6 & 2 \end{bmatrix} \quad \ldots \text{(ii)}$

which is a symmetric matrix.

Subtracting we get,

$$A - A' = \begin{bmatrix} 5 & 4 & 7 \\ 2 & 4 & 6 \\ 3 & 6 & 2 \end{bmatrix} - \begin{bmatrix} 5 & 2 & 3 \\ 4 & 4 & 6 \\ 7 & 6 & 2 \end{bmatrix}$$

$$= \begin{bmatrix} 0 & 2 & 4 \\ -2 & 0 & 0 \\ -4 & 0 & 0 \end{bmatrix}$$

$$\therefore \quad \frac{1}{2}(A - A') = \frac{1}{2}\begin{bmatrix} 0 & 2 & 4 \\ -2 & 0 & 0 \\ -4 & 0 & 0 \end{bmatrix}$$

$$= \begin{bmatrix} 0 & 1 & 2 \\ -1 & 0 & 0 \\ -2 & 0 & 0 \end{bmatrix} \quad \ldots \text{(iii)}$$

which is a skew symmetric matrix.

From equation (i), (ii) and (iii), we have

$$A = \begin{bmatrix} 5 & 3 & 5 \\ 3 & 4 & 6 \\ 5 & 6 & 2 \end{bmatrix} + \begin{bmatrix} 0 & 1 & 2 \\ -1 & 0 & 0 \\ -2 & 0 & 0 \end{bmatrix}$$

EXERCISE 1.1

1. If A is a symmetric matrix, prove that A'A is a null matrix iff A is a null matrix.

2. If A is a square matrix, prove that :
   (a) A + A' is a symmetric matrix.
   (b) A − A' is a skew-symmetric matrix.

3. If $a_{ij} = i + j$, show that $A = (a_{ij})$ is a symmetric matrix.

4. Prove that a matrix A is symmetric if and only if A = A'.

5. If A and B are symmetric matrices, show that AB' and A'B are both symmetric.

6. Let $A = \begin{bmatrix} 2 & 3 & 4 \\ 1 & 2 & 3 \\ -1 & 1 & 2 \end{bmatrix}$ and $B = \begin{bmatrix} 1 & 3 & 1 \\ 1 & 2 & 1 \\ 2 & 0 & 0 \end{bmatrix}$ be two matrices. Find the elements C_{23}, C_{32} and C_{33} in the product $C = (C_{ij}) = AB$.

7. If A is a square matrix and B = mA + kI, where m and k are scalars, then prove that A and B commute.

8. If A is symmetric, prove that B'AB is also symmetric.

9. Express the following matrices as the sum of a symmetric and a skew-symmetric matrices.

(i) $\begin{bmatrix} 3 & -9 & 7 \\ 0 & 8 & 4 \\ 10 & 2 & 5 \end{bmatrix}$

(ii) $\begin{bmatrix} 4 & -1 & 3 \\ 2 & 5 & 1 \\ 3 & 0 & 6 \end{bmatrix}$

(iii) $\begin{bmatrix} 1 & 3 & 5 \\ -6 & 8 & 3 \\ -4 & 8 & 5 \end{bmatrix}$

(iv) $\begin{bmatrix} 1 & 2 & 4 \\ 7 & 3 & 1 \\ 4 & 1 & 7 \end{bmatrix}$

(v) $\begin{bmatrix} 1 & 2 & 4 \\ 4 & 5 & 6 \\ 7 & 8 & 6 \end{bmatrix}$

(vi) $\begin{bmatrix} 1 & -1 & 2 \\ 4 & 3 & 1 \\ 2 & 5 & -2 \end{bmatrix}$

10. Show that the matrix $\begin{bmatrix} 1 & 1 & 3 \\ 5 & 2 & 6 \\ -2 & -1 & -3 \end{bmatrix}$ is nilpotent and find its index.

11. Show that the matrix $\begin{bmatrix} -5 & -8 & 0 \\ 3 & 5 & 0 \\ 1 & 2 & -1 \end{bmatrix}$ is involuntary.

ANSWERS 1.1

6. $C_{23} = 3$, $C_{32} = -1$ and $C_{33} = 0$.

9. (i) $\begin{bmatrix} 3 & -9/2 & 17/2 \\ -9/2 & 8 & 3 \\ 17/2 & 3 & 5 \end{bmatrix} + \begin{bmatrix} 0 & -9/2 & -3/2 \\ 9/2 & 0 & 1 \\ 3/2 & -1 & 0 \end{bmatrix}$

(ii) $\begin{bmatrix} 4 & 1/2 & 3 \\ 1/2 & 5 & 1/2 \\ 3 & 1/2 & 6 \end{bmatrix} + \begin{bmatrix} 0 & -3/2 & 0 \\ 3/2 & 0 & 1/2 \\ 0 & -1/2 & 0 \end{bmatrix}$

(iii) $\begin{bmatrix} 1 & -3/2 & 1/2 \\ -3/2 & 8 & 11/2 \\ 1/2 & 11/2 & 5 \end{bmatrix} + \begin{bmatrix} 0 & 9/2 & 9/2 \\ -9/2 & 0 & -5/2 \\ -9/2 & 5/2 & 0 \end{bmatrix}$

(iv) $\begin{bmatrix} 1 & 9/2 & 4 \\ 9/2 & 3 & 1 \\ 4 & 1 & 7 \end{bmatrix} + \begin{bmatrix} 0 & -5/2 & 0 \\ 5/2 & 0 & 0 \\ 0 & 0 & 0 \end{bmatrix}$

(v) $\begin{bmatrix} 1 & 3 & 11/2 \\ 3 & 5 & 7 \\ 11/2 & 7 & 6 \end{bmatrix} + \begin{bmatrix} 0 & -1 & -3/2 \\ 1 & 0 & -1 \\ 3/2 & 1 & 0 \end{bmatrix}$

(vi) $\begin{bmatrix} 1 & 3/2 & 2 \\ 3/2 & 3 & 3 \\ 2 & 3 & -2 \end{bmatrix} + \begin{bmatrix} 0 & -5/2 & 0 \\ 5/2 & 0 & -2 \\ 0 & 2 & 0 \end{bmatrix}$

1.3 MINORS AND COFACTORS

Minor : The determinant obtained by deleting the ith row and j^{th} column of an element a_{ij} of $|A|$ is called the minor of the element a_{ij} and is denoted by M_{ij}.

Cofactor : The minor with a proper sign is called a cofactor of an element i.e. the cofactor of an element a_{ij} in $A = (a_{ij})$ is $(-1)^{i+j} \cdot M_{ij}$. It is denoted by A_{ij}.

Thus, $A_{ij} = (-1)^{i+j} \cdot M_{ij}$

1.3.1 Adjoint of a Matrix

The transpose of the matrix of cofactors of A is called the adjoint of A. It is denoted by adj A. i.e. adj $A = (A_{ij})'$.

For example, Let $A = \begin{bmatrix} 1 & 2 & 7 \\ 2 & 1 & 0 \\ 0 & 1 & 3 \end{bmatrix}$

Then, minors are

$M_{11} = \begin{vmatrix} 1 & 0 \\ 1 & 3 \end{vmatrix} = 3 \Rightarrow \therefore$ Cofactors $A_{11} = (-1)^{1+1} M_{11} = 3$

$M_{12} = \begin{vmatrix} 2 & 0 \\ 0 & 3 \end{vmatrix} = 6 \Rightarrow \therefore A_{12} = (-1)^{1+2} M_{12} = -6$

$M_{13} = \begin{vmatrix} 2 & 1 \\ 0 & 1 \end{vmatrix} = 2 \Rightarrow \therefore A_{13} = (-1)^{1+3} M_{13} = +2$

Similarly, $A_{21} = 1$, $A_{22} = 3$, $A_{23} = -1$

$A_{31} = -7$, $A_{32} = 14$, $A_{33} = -3$

$\therefore$ Matrix of cofactors = (A_{ij})

$$= \begin{bmatrix} A_{11} & A_{12} & A_{13} \\ A_{21} & A_{22} & A_{23} \\ A_{31} & A_{32} & A_{33} \end{bmatrix} = \begin{bmatrix} 3 & -6 & 2 \\ 1 & 3 & -1 \\ -7 & 14 & -3 \end{bmatrix}$$

$\therefore$ adj $A = (A_{ij})' = \begin{bmatrix} 3 & 1 & -7 \\ -6 & 3 & 14 \\ 2 & -1 & -2 \end{bmatrix}$

1.4 ELEMENTARY TRANSFORMATION OF A MATRIX

The following operations which refer to rows and columns are known as elementary transformations.

I. Elementary row transformations :

(i) R_{ij} for the interchange of ith and j^{th} rows.

(ii) kR_i for multiplication of the ith row by k.

(iii) $R_i + kR_j$ for addition to the ith row, k times the jth row.

II. Elementary column transformations :

(i) C_{ij} for the interchange of ith and j^{th} columns.

(ii) kC_i for multiplication of the ith column by k.

(iii) $C_i + kC_j$ for addition to the ith column, k times the jth column.

1.4.1 Rank of a Matrix

Definition : The matrix A is said to be of rank r if

(i) There is atleast one non-vanishing minor of order r.

(ii) Every minor of order higher than r vanishes. i.e. of order r + 1 is zero.

It is denoted by $\rho(A)$.

1.4.2 Rank of a Square Matrix

(i) Let A be a square matrix of order n, and $|A| \neq 0$, then its rank is n.

(ii) If $|A| = 0$, then its rank is less than n.

1.4.3 Some Important Results

1. If all minors of a matrix A of order r + 1 are zero, then $\rho(A) \le r$.
2. If a matrix A has a non-zero minor of order r, then $\rho(A) \ge r$.
3. Rank of an identity matrix is its order.
4. Elementary transformations do not alter the rank of a matrix.
5. If A is an m × n matrix of rank r_1 and B is an n × p matrix of rank r_2 such that AB = **O**, then $r_1 + r_2 \le n$.
6. In a square matrix of order n of rank (n − r), the cofactors of the elements of any two parallel rows are proportional.
7. $\rho(AB) \le \min(\rho(A), \rho(B))$.
8. If A' is the transpose of A, then $\rho(A') = \rho(A)$.
9. The rank of a null matrix is zero.
10. The rank of a non-singular matrix of order n is n.

For example,

(i) Let
$$A = \begin{bmatrix} 2 & 3 & 4 \\ 3 & 1 & 2 \\ -1 & 2 & 2 \end{bmatrix}$$

then
$$|A| = \begin{vmatrix} 2 & 3 & 4 \\ 3 & 1 & 2 \\ -1 & 2 & 2 \end{vmatrix} = 0$$

but,
$$M_{33} = \begin{vmatrix} 2 & 3 \\ 3 & 1 \end{vmatrix} = 2 - 9 = -7 \ne 0$$

Therefore, there is a non-zero minor of order two.

Hence, $\rho(A) = 2$

(ii) Let
$$A = \begin{bmatrix} 1 & 2 & 3 \\ 2 & 4 & 6 \\ -3 & -6 & -9 \end{bmatrix}, \text{ then}$$

$$|A| = \begin{vmatrix} 1 & 2 & 3 \\ 2 & 4 & 6 \\ -3 & -6 & -9 \end{vmatrix} = 0$$

Further, $M_{11} = \begin{vmatrix} 4 & 6 \\ -6 & -9 \end{vmatrix} = 0$, $M_{12} = \begin{vmatrix} 2 & 6 \\ -3 & -9 \end{vmatrix} = 0$,

$$M_{21} = \begin{vmatrix} 2 & 3 \\ -6 & -9 \end{vmatrix} = 0 \text{ etc.}$$

Therefore, each of the second order minor is also zero.

As the matrix is non-zero implies $\rho(A) = 1$.

1.4.4 Normal Form of a Matrix

Every non-zero matrix A can be reduced to the form $\left[\begin{array}{c|c} I_r & O \\ \hline O & O \end{array}\right]$ by a sequence of elementary transformations is called the normal form of A.

In this case, $\rho(A)$ = order of I.

Note : Some other forms of a Normal forms are

$\left[\begin{array}{c} I_r \\ \hline O \end{array}\right]$, $[I_r : O]$ and $[I_r]$.

SOLVED EXAMPLES

Example 1.9 : Reduce the following matrix to normal form and find its rank.

$$\begin{bmatrix} 1 & 1 & 1 & -1 \\ 1 & 2 & 3 & 4 \\ 3 & 4 & 5 & 2 \end{bmatrix}$$

Solution : Let $A = \begin{bmatrix} 1 & 1 & 1 & -1 \\ 1 & 2 & 3 & 4 \\ 3 & 4 & 5 & 2 \end{bmatrix}$

$\xrightarrow[R_3 - 3R_1]{R_2 - R_1} \begin{bmatrix} 1 & 1 & 1 & -1 \\ 0 & 1 & 2 & 5 \\ 0 & 1 & 2 & 5 \end{bmatrix}$

$\xrightarrow{R_3 - R_2} \begin{bmatrix} 1 & 1 & 1 & -1 \\ 0 & 1 & 2 & 5 \\ 0 & 0 & 0 & 0 \end{bmatrix}$

$$\xrightarrow[\substack{C_3-C_1\\C_4-C_1}]{C_2-C_1}\begin{bmatrix}1&0&0&0\\0&1&2&5\\0&0&0&0\end{bmatrix}$$

$$\xrightarrow[C_4-5C_2]{C_3-2C_2}\begin{bmatrix}1&0&0&0\\0&1&0&0\\0&0&0&0\end{bmatrix}=\left[\begin{array}{c|c}I_2&O\\\hline O&O\end{array}\right]$$

∴ $\rho(A)$ = Rank of A = order of I_2
     = 2

Example 1.10 : Find the rank of the matrix

$$\begin{bmatrix}6&1&3&8\\4&2&6&-1\\10&3&9&7\\16&4&12&15\end{bmatrix}$$

Solution : Let $A = \begin{bmatrix}6&1&3&8\\4&2&6&-1\\10&3&9&7\\16&4&12&15\end{bmatrix}$

$$\xrightarrow{C_{12}}\begin{bmatrix}1&6&3&8\\2&4&6&-1\\3&10&9&7\\4&16&12&15\end{bmatrix}$$

$$\xrightarrow[\substack{R_3-3R_1\\R_4-4R_1}]{R_2-2R_1}\begin{bmatrix}1&6&3&8\\0&-8&0&-17\\0&-8&0&-17\\0&-8&0&-17\end{bmatrix}$$

$$\xrightarrow[R_4-R_2]{R_3-R_2}\begin{bmatrix}1&6&3&8\\0&-8&0&-17\\0&0&0&0\\0&0&0&0\end{bmatrix}$$

$$\xrightarrow[\substack{C_3 - 3C_1 \\ C_4 - 8C_1}]{C_2 - 6C_1} \begin{bmatrix} 1 & 0 & 0 & 0 \\ 0 & -8 & 0 & -17 \\ 0 & 0 & 0 & 0 \\ 0 & 0 & 0 & 0 \end{bmatrix}$$

$$\xrightarrow{(-1/8)\, C_2} \begin{bmatrix} 1 & 0 & 0 & 0 \\ 0 & 1 & 0 & -17 \\ 0 & 0 & 0 & 0 \\ 0 & 0 & 0 & 0 \end{bmatrix}$$

$$\xrightarrow{C_4 + 17C_2} \begin{bmatrix} 1 & 0 & 0 & 0 \\ 0 & 1 & 0 & 0 \\ 0 & 0 & 0 & 0 \\ 0 & 0 & 0 & 0 \end{bmatrix} = \begin{bmatrix} I_2 & \mathbf{0} \\ \hline \mathbf{0} & \mathbf{0} \end{bmatrix}$$

which is in a normal form.

∴ $\rho(A)$ = rank of A = 2.

Example 1.11 : Find the rank of the matrix.

$$\begin{bmatrix} 1 & 3 & 4 & 5 \\ 1 & 2 & 6 & 7 \\ 1 & 5 & 0 & 10 \end{bmatrix}$$

Solution : Let $A = \begin{bmatrix} 1 & 3 & 4 & 5 \\ 1 & 2 & 6 & 7 \\ 1 & 5 & 0 & 10 \end{bmatrix}$

$$\xrightarrow[R_3 - R_1]{R_2 - R_1} \begin{bmatrix} 1 & 3 & 4 & 5 \\ 0 & -1 & 2 & 2 \\ 0 & 2 & -4 & 5 \end{bmatrix}$$

$$\xrightarrow[\substack{C_3 - 4C_1 \\ C_4 - 5C_1}]{C_2 - 3C_1} \begin{bmatrix} 1 & 0 & 0 & 0 \\ 0 & -1 & 2 & 2 \\ 0 & 2 & -4 & 5 \end{bmatrix}$$

$$\xrightarrow{R_3 + 2R_2} \begin{bmatrix} 1 & 0 & 0 & 0 \\ 0 & -1 & 2 & 2 \\ 0 & 0 & 0 & 1 \end{bmatrix}$$

$$\xrightarrow[C_4 + 2C_2]{C_3 + 2C_1} \begin{bmatrix} 1 & 0 & 0 & 0 \\ 0 & -1 & 0 & 0 \\ 0 & 0 & 0 & 1 \end{bmatrix}$$

$$\xrightarrow[C_{34}]{(-1)C_2} \begin{bmatrix} 1 & 0 & 0 & 0 \\ 0 & 1 & 0 & 0 \\ 0 & 0 & 1 & 0 \end{bmatrix} = [I_3 : \mathbf{O}]$$

which is in normal form.

∴ $\rho(A) = 3$.

1.4.5 Echelon or Canonical or Triangular Form

Any matrix A can be reduced by row transformations to echelon form by the following steps :

(i) If the element a_{11} of A is zero, then use the transformation R_{ij}.

(ii) If $a_{ii} \neq 1$ interchange rows suitably or use $\left(\dfrac{1}{a_{ii}}\right) R_i$ to reduce the element to 1.

(iii) Make all elements below a_{ii} to zero by using $R_j - kR_i$ for all $i < j$ with suitable multiple k.

Remark : If the matrix is in echelon form, then

rank of the matrix = Number of non-zero rows.

Note : Non-zero row is that row which does not contain all the elements zero.

SOLVED EXAMPLES

Example 1.12 : Find the rank of the matrix :

$$\begin{bmatrix} 2 & 3 & -1 & -1 \\ 1 & -1 & -2 & -4 \\ 3 & 1 & 3 & -2 \\ 6 & 3 & 0 & -7 \end{bmatrix}$$

Solution : Let $A = \begin{bmatrix} 2 & 3 & -1 & -1 \\ 1 & -1 & -2 & -4 \\ 3 & 1 & 3 & -2 \\ 6 & 3 & 0 & -7 \end{bmatrix}$

$\xrightarrow{R_{12}} \begin{bmatrix} 1 & -1 & -2 & -4 \\ 2 & 3 & -1 & -1 \\ 3 & 1 & 3 & -2 \\ 6 & 3 & 0 & -7 \end{bmatrix}$

$\xrightarrow[R_4 - 2R_3]{R_2 - 2R_1} \begin{bmatrix} 1 & -1 & -2 & -4 \\ 0 & 5 & 3 & 7 \\ 3 & 1 & 3 & -2 \\ 0 & 1 & -6 & -3 \end{bmatrix}$

$\xrightarrow{R_3 - 3R_1} \begin{bmatrix} 1 & -1 & -2 & -4 \\ 0 & 5 & 3 & 7 \\ 0 & 4 & 9 & 10 \\ 0 & 1 & -6 & -3 \end{bmatrix}$

$\xrightarrow{R_2 - R_3} \begin{bmatrix} 1 & -1 & -2 & -4 \\ 0 & 1 & -6 & -3 \\ 0 & 4 & 9 & 10 \\ 0 & 1 & -6 & -3 \end{bmatrix}$

$\xrightarrow[R_4 - R_2]{R_3 - 4R_2} \begin{bmatrix} 1 & -1 & -2 & -4 \\ 0 & 1 & -6 & -3 \\ 0 & 0 & 33 & 22 \\ 0 & 0 & 0 & 0 \end{bmatrix}$

$\xrightarrow{(1/33) R_3} \begin{bmatrix} 1 & -1 & -2 & -4 \\ 0 & 1 & -6 & -3 \\ 0 & 0 & 1 & 2/3 \\ 0 & 0 & 0 & 0 \end{bmatrix}$

This is in echelon (triangular) form.

∴ $\rho(A)$ = Rank of A = number of non-zero rows = 3.

Example 1.13 : Find the rank of the matrix

$$\begin{bmatrix} 2 & 1 & 1 \\ 2 & 1 & 2 \\ 2 & 1 & 3 \\ -2 & -1 & 4 \end{bmatrix}$$

Solution : Let $A = \begin{bmatrix} 2 & 1 & 1 \\ 2 & 1 & 2 \\ 2 & 1 & 3 \\ -2 & -1 & 4 \end{bmatrix}$

$\xrightarrow[\substack{R_3 - R_1 \\ R_4 + R_1}]{R_2 - R_1} \begin{bmatrix} 2 & 1 & 1 \\ 0 & 0 & 1 \\ 0 & 0 & 2 \\ 0 & 0 & 5 \end{bmatrix}$

$\xrightarrow[R_4 - 5R_2]{R_3 - 2R_2} \begin{bmatrix} 2 & 1 & 1 \\ 0 & 0 & 1 \\ 0 & 0 & 0 \\ 0 & 0 & 0 \end{bmatrix}$

This matrix is the echelon form.

∴ ρ(A) = Number of non-zero rows = 2.

Remark : To determine the rank of matrix $A_{m \times n}$ reduce it to echelon form and if k rows vanishes then the rank of matrix = m − k i.e. number of non-zero rows.

EXERCISE 1.2

1. Reduce the following matrices to their normal form and hence obtain their ranks.

   (i) $\begin{bmatrix} 0 & 1 & 2 & -2 \\ 4 & 0 & 2 & 6 \\ 2 & 1 & 3 & 1 \end{bmatrix}$ (ii) $\begin{bmatrix} 1 & 2 & 3 \\ 3 & 2 & 1 \\ 1 & 3 & 2 \\ 2 & 1 & 3 \end{bmatrix}$

(iii) $\begin{bmatrix} 3 & 1 & 3 & 5 \\ 15 & 8 & 1 & 12 \\ 11 & 5 & 8 & 6 \\ 11 & 8 & 7 & 10 \end{bmatrix}$ (iv) $\begin{bmatrix} 1 & 1 & 1 & 1 \\ 1 & 3 & -2 & 1 \\ 2 & 0 & -3 & 2 \\ 3 & 3 & -3 & 3 \end{bmatrix}$

2. Find the ranks of the following matrices :

(i) $\begin{bmatrix} 2 & 1 & -3 & -6 \\ 3 & -3 & 1 & 2 \\ 1 & 1 & 1 & 2 \end{bmatrix}$ (ii) $\begin{bmatrix} 1 & 3 & 4 & 5 \\ 1 & 2 & 6 & 7 \\ 1 & 5 & 0 & 10 \end{bmatrix}$

(iii) $\begin{bmatrix} 1 & -3 & 2 \\ -3 & 9 & -6 \\ 2 & -6 & 4 \end{bmatrix}$ (iv) $\begin{bmatrix} 4 & 5 & 6 & 7 \\ 9 & 10 & 11 & 12 \\ 10 & 11 & 12 & 13 \\ 18 & 19 & 20 & 21 \end{bmatrix}$

(v) $\begin{bmatrix} -1 & 3 & -4 & 5 \\ -1 & 2 & -6 & 7 \\ -1 & 5 & 0 & 10 \end{bmatrix}$ (vi) $\begin{bmatrix} 2 & 3 & -1 & -2 \\ 3 & 1 & 3 & -2 \\ 6 & 3 & 0 & -8 \\ 1 & -1 & -2 & -4 \end{bmatrix}$

(vi) $\begin{bmatrix} 1 & 2 & 3 \\ 2 & 4 & 7 \\ 3 & 6 & 10 \end{bmatrix}$ (viii) $\begin{bmatrix} 0 & 2 & 1 & 1 \\ 3 & 5 & 1 & 2 \\ 5 & -1 & 2 & 2 \\ 2 & 6 & 5 & 3 \\ 1 & 3 & -3 & -1 \end{bmatrix}$

(ix) $\begin{bmatrix} 6 & 1 & 3 & 8 \\ 4 & 2 & 6 & -1 \\ 10 & 3 & 9 & 7 \\ 16 & 4 & 12 & 15 \end{bmatrix}$ (x) $\begin{bmatrix} 1 & 4 & 3 & 2 \\ 1 & 2 & 3 & 4 \\ 2 & 6 & 7 & 5 \end{bmatrix}$

ANSWERS 1.2

1. (i) $\begin{bmatrix} I_2 & O \\ \hline O & O \end{bmatrix}$ and rank = 2 (ii) $\begin{bmatrix} I_3 \\ \hline O \end{bmatrix}$ and rank = 3

(iii) $[I_4 \mid O]$ and rank = 4 (iv) $\begin{bmatrix} I_3 & O \\ \hline O & O \end{bmatrix}$ and rank = 3.

2. (i) 3, (ii) 3, (iii) 1, (iv) 2, (v) 3, (vi) 3, (vii) 2, (viii) 4, (ix) 2, (x) 3.

1.5 THE CHARACTERISTIC EQUATION OF A MATRIX

Let $A = (a_{ij})$ be a square matrix of order n and λ be any variable.

(a) Characteristic Matrix : The matrix $(A - \lambda I)$ is called the characteristic matrix of A.

(b) Characteristic Polynomial : The determinant $|A - \lambda I|$ is known as the characteristic polynomial.

(c) Characteristic Equation : The equation $|A - \lambda I| = 0$ is known as the characteristic equation.

Remark : (i) Let f(x) be a polynomial given by

$$f(x) = a_0 + a_1 x + a_2 x^2 + \ldots + a_n x^n \text{ then } a_0 I + a_1 A + a_2 A^2 + \ldots + a_n A^n$$

is called the matrix polynomial of A and is denoted as f(A).

(ii) To find the characteristic polynomials a n-square matrix A, either we expand the determinant of $(A - \lambda I_n)$ i.e. $|A - \lambda I_n|$ or we use the following simple formulas of matrices of orders two and three.

(a) Let
$$A = \begin{bmatrix} a_{11} & a_{12} \\ a_{21} & a_{22} \end{bmatrix}$$

Then characteristic polynomial of $A = ch(A) = |A - \lambda I_2|$

$$= \lambda^2 - (a_{11} + a_{22})\lambda + |A|$$
$$= \lambda^2 - tr(a) \cdot \lambda + |A|$$

(b) Let
$$A = \begin{bmatrix} a_{11} & a_{12} & a_{13} \\ a_{21} & a_{22} & a_{23} \\ a_{31} & a_{32} & a_{33} \end{bmatrix}$$

Then $ch(A) = |A - \lambda I_3|$

$$= \lambda^3 - tr(A) + (A_{11} + A_{22} + A_{33})\lambda - |A|$$

where A_{11}, A_{22}, A_{33} are respectively, the cofactors of a_{11}, a_{22}, a_{33}.

1.5.1 Cayley-Hamilton Theorem

Theorem : Every square matrix satisfies its characteristic equation. i.e. if A is a square matrix of order n and $|A - \lambda I| = a_0 + a_1\lambda + a_2\lambda^2 + \ldots + a_n\lambda^n$, then $a_0 I + a_1 A + a_2 A^2 + \ldots + a_n A^n = \mathbf{O}$.

Proof : Let A be a square matrix of order n. Then the elements of $A - \lambda I$ are at most of the first degree in λ. Hence, elements of adj $(A - \lambda I)$ are polynomials in λ of degree $n - 1$ or less.

Let adj $(A - \lambda I) = B_0 + B_1\lambda + B_2\lambda^2 + \ldots + B_{n-1}\lambda^{n-1}$ ... (1)

where $B_0, B_1, \ldots, B_{n-1}$ are matrices of order n.

Since, $A \text{ (adj } A) = |A| I$ ($\because$ Property of adjoint)

$\therefore \quad (A - \lambda I) \text{ adj } (A - \lambda I) = |A - \lambda I| I$

$= (a_0 + a_1\lambda + a_2\lambda^2 + \ldots + a_n\lambda^n) I$

$= (a_0 I + a_1 I \lambda + a_2 I \lambda^2 + \ldots + a_n I \lambda^n$ ... (2)

But $(A - \lambda I) \text{ adj } (A - \lambda I)$

$= (A - \lambda I) [B_0 + B_1\lambda + B_2\lambda^2 + \ldots + B_{n-1}\lambda^{n-1}]$

$= AB_0 + (AB_0 - B_1)\lambda I + (AB_2 - B_1) I\lambda^2 + \ldots - B_{n-1} I\lambda^n$ ... (3)

Equating the coefficients of like powers of λ from equation (2) and (3), we get

$$a_0 I = AB_0$$
$$a_1 I = AB_1 - B_0$$
$$a_2 I = AB_2 - B_1$$
$$\ldots\ldots\ldots\ldots\ldots\ldots\ldots\ldots\ldots$$
$$a_n I = -B_{n-1}$$

Pre-multiplying these equations by $I, A, A^2, \ldots, A^n$ respectively and adding, we get

$$a_0 I = AB_0$$
$$+ a_1 A = A^2 B_1 - AB_0$$
$$+ a_2 A^2 = A^3 B_2 - A^2 B_1$$
$$\vdots \quad \vdots \quad \vdots$$
$$+ a_n A^n = -A^n B_{n-1}$$

Hence, $a_0 I + a_1 A + a_2 A^2 + \ldots + a_n A^n = O$

which proves that A satisfies its characteristic equation.

SOLVED EXAMPLES

Example 1.14 : Find the characteristics of polynomial of

(i) $A = \begin{bmatrix} 1 & 3 \\ 4 & 5 \end{bmatrix}$. Verify Cayley-Hamilton theorem for A.

(ii) $A = \begin{bmatrix} 2 & 1 & 1 \\ 2 & 3 & 2 \\ 3 & 3 & 4 \end{bmatrix}$.

Solution : (i) The diagonal elements are $a_{11} = 1$, $a_{22} = 5$.

$\therefore \quad tr(A) = a_{11} + a_{22} = 1 + 5 = 6$

Now, $\quad |A| = \begin{vmatrix} 1 & 3 \\ 4 & 5 \end{vmatrix} = 5 - 12 = -7$

The characteristic polynomial of A is

$$ch(A) = |A - \lambda I_2|$$
$$= \lambda^2 - tr(A)\lambda + |A|$$
$$= \lambda^2 - (a_{11} + a_{22})\lambda + |A|$$
$$= \lambda^2 - 6\lambda - 7$$

Verification : The characteristic equation is $\lambda^2 - 6\lambda - 7 = 0$.

By Cayley-Hamilton theorem, it is satisfied by A. i.e. $A^2 - 6A - 7I = 0$.

Consider, $A^2 = A \cdot A = \begin{bmatrix} 1 & 3 \\ 4 & 5 \end{bmatrix} \cdot \begin{bmatrix} 1 & 3 \\ 4 & 5 \end{bmatrix} = \begin{bmatrix} 13 & 18 \\ 24 & 32 \end{bmatrix}$

$\therefore \quad A^2 - 6A - 7I = \begin{bmatrix} 13 & 18 \\ 24 & 32 \end{bmatrix} - 6 \begin{bmatrix} 1 & 3 \\ 4 & 5 \end{bmatrix} - 7 \begin{bmatrix} 1 & 0 \\ 0 & 1 \end{bmatrix}$

$= \begin{bmatrix} 13 & 18 \\ 24 & 37 \end{bmatrix} - \begin{bmatrix} 6 & 18 \\ 24 & 30 \end{bmatrix} - \begin{bmatrix} 7 & 0 \\ 0 & 7 \end{bmatrix}$

$= \begin{bmatrix} 13 - 6 - 7 & 18 - 18 - 0 \\ 24 - 24 - 0 & 37 - 30 - 7 \end{bmatrix} = \begin{bmatrix} 0 & 0 \\ 0 & 0 \end{bmatrix}$

$\therefore \quad A^2 - 6A - 7I = 0$

Therefore, the characteristic equation $\lambda^2 - 6\lambda - 7 = 0$ is satisfied by A.

(ii) Here $a_{11} = 2$, $a_{22} = 3$, $a_{33} = 4$

∴ $\quad tr(A) = a_{11} + a_{22} + a_{33} = 2 + 3 + 4 = 9$

Now, $\quad A_{11}$ = Cofactor of a_{11}

$$= (-1)^{1+1} \begin{vmatrix} 3 & 2 \\ 3 & 4 \end{vmatrix} = 12 - 6 = 6$$

A_{22} = Cofactor q a_{22}

$$= (-1)^{2+2} \begin{vmatrix} 2 & 1 \\ 3 & 4 \end{vmatrix} = 8 - 3 = 5$$

A_{33} = Cofactor q a_{33}

$$= (-1)^{3+3} \begin{vmatrix} 2 & 1 \\ 2 & 3 \end{vmatrix} = 6 - 2 = 4$$

Example 1.15 : Verify Cayley-Hamilton theorem for the following matrix A. Also find A^{-1} and A^4.

$$A = \begin{bmatrix} 1 & 1 & 2 \\ 3 & 1 & 1 \\ 2 & 3 & 1 \end{bmatrix}$$

Solution : The characteristics matrix is

$$A - \lambda I = \begin{bmatrix} 1 & 1 & 2 \\ 3 & 1 & 1 \\ 2 & 3 & 1 \end{bmatrix} - \lambda \begin{bmatrix} 1 & 0 & 0 \\ 0 & 1 & 0 \\ 0 & 0 & 1 \end{bmatrix}$$

∴ $\quad A - \lambda I = \begin{bmatrix} 1-\lambda & 1 & 2 \\ 3 & 1-\lambda & 1 \\ 2 & 3 & 1-\lambda \end{bmatrix}$

Now, the characteristic equation is

$$|A - \lambda I| = 0$$

$$\begin{vmatrix} 1-\lambda & 1 & 2 \\ 3 & 1-\lambda & 1 \\ 2 & 3 & 1-\lambda \end{vmatrix} = 0.$$

$(1 - \lambda) [(1 - \lambda)^2 - 3] - 1 [3(1 - \lambda) - 2] + 2 [9 - 2(1 - \lambda)] = 0$

∴ $(1 - \lambda) [1 - 2\lambda + \lambda^2 - 3] - 3 + 3\lambda + 2 + 18 - 4 + 4\lambda = 0$

∴ $(1 - \lambda) [\lambda^2 - 2\lambda - 2] + 7\lambda + 13 = 0$

∴ $\lambda^2 - 2\lambda - 2 - \lambda^3 + 2\lambda^2 + 2\lambda + 7\lambda + 13 = 0$

i.e. $-\lambda^3 + 3\lambda^2 + 7\lambda + 11 = 0$

∴ $\lambda^3 - 3\lambda^2 - 7\lambda - 11 = 0$

To verify that $A^3 - 3A^2 - 7A - 11I = \mathbf{O}$.

Now, $A^2 = \begin{bmatrix} 1 & 1 & 2 \\ 3 & 1 & 1 \\ 2 & 3 & 1 \end{bmatrix} \begin{bmatrix} 1 & 1 & 2 \\ 3 & 1 & 1 \\ 2 & 3 & 1 \end{bmatrix}$

$= \begin{bmatrix} 8 & 8 & 5 \\ 8 & 7 & 8 \\ 13 & 8 & 8 \end{bmatrix}$

and $A^3 = A \cdot A^2 = \begin{bmatrix} 1 & 1 & 2 \\ 3 & 1 & 1 \\ 2 & 3 & 1 \end{bmatrix} \begin{bmatrix} 8 & 8 & 5 \\ 8 & 7 & 8 \\ 13 & 8 & 8 \end{bmatrix}$

$= \begin{bmatrix} 42 & 31 & 29 \\ 45 & 49 & 31 \\ 53 & 45 & 42 \end{bmatrix}$

Consider, $A^3 - 3A^2 - 7A - 11I$

$= \begin{bmatrix} 42 & 31 & 29 \\ 45 & 49 & 31 \\ 53 & 45 & 42 \end{bmatrix} - 3 \begin{bmatrix} 8 & 8 & 5 \\ 8 & 7 & 8 \\ 13 & 8 & 8 \end{bmatrix}$

$- 7 \begin{bmatrix} 1 & 1 & 2 \\ 3 & 1 & 1 \\ 2 & 3 & 1 \end{bmatrix} - 11 \begin{bmatrix} 1 & 0 & 0 \\ 0 & 1 & 0 \\ 0 & 0 & 1 \end{bmatrix}$

∴ $A^3 - 3A^2 - 7A - 11I$

$= \begin{bmatrix} 42 - 24 - 7 - 11 & 31 - 24 - 7 & 29 - 15 - 14 \\ 45 - 24 - 21 & 49 - 21 - 7 - 11 & 31 - 24 - 7 \\ 53 - 39 - 14 & 45 - 24 - 21 & 42 - 24 - 7 - 11 \end{bmatrix}$

$= \begin{bmatrix} 0 & 0 & 0 \\ 0 & 0 & 0 \\ 0 & 0 & 0 \end{bmatrix}$

$\therefore \quad A^3 - 3A^2 - 7A - 11I = \mathbf{O}$ ... (1)

To find A^{-1} : Multiply equation (1) by A^{-1}.

$\therefore \quad A^2 - 3A - 7I - 11A^{-1} = \mathbf{O}$

$\therefore \quad A^2 - 3A - 7I = 11A^{-1}$

i.e. $11A^{-1} = A^2 - 3A - 7I$

$$= \begin{bmatrix} 8 & 8 & 5 \\ 8 & 7 & 8 \\ 13 & 8 & 8 \end{bmatrix} - 3 \begin{bmatrix} 1 & 1 & 2 \\ 3 & 1 & 1 \\ 2 & 3 & 1 \end{bmatrix} - 7 \begin{bmatrix} 1 & 0 & 0 \\ 0 & 1 & 0 \\ 0 & 0 & 1 \end{bmatrix}$$

$$= \begin{bmatrix} -2 & 5 & -1 \\ -1 & -3 & 5 \\ 7 & -1 & -2 \end{bmatrix}$$

$\therefore \qquad A^{-1} = \dfrac{1}{11} \begin{bmatrix} -2 & 5 & -1 \\ -1 & -3 & 5 \\ 7 & -1 & -2 \end{bmatrix}$

To find A^4 : Multiplying equation (1) by A, we get

$A^4 - 3A^3 - 7A^2 - 11A = \mathbf{O}$

$\therefore \quad A^4 = 3A^3 + 7A^2 + 11A$

$$= 3 \begin{bmatrix} 42 & 31 & 29 \\ 45 & 49 & 31 \\ 53 & 45 & 42 \end{bmatrix} + 7 \begin{bmatrix} 8 & 8 & 5 \\ 8 & 7 & 8 \\ 13 & 8 & 8 \end{bmatrix} + 11 \begin{bmatrix} 1 & 1 & 2 \\ 3 & 1 & 1 \\ 2 & 3 & 1 \end{bmatrix}$$

$$= \begin{bmatrix} 193 & 160 & 144 \\ 224 & 207 & 160 \\ 272 & 224 & 193 \end{bmatrix}$$

Example 1.16 : Verify Cayley-Hamilton theorem for the matrix

$$A = \begin{bmatrix} 2 & -1 & 1 \\ -1 & 2 & -1 \\ 1 & -1 & 2 \end{bmatrix}$$

Solution : The characteristics matrix is

$$A - \lambda I = \begin{bmatrix} 2-\lambda & -1 & 1 \\ -1 & 2-\lambda & -1 \\ 1 & -1 & 2-\lambda \end{bmatrix}$$

Therefore, the characteristic equation is given by

$$|A - \lambda I| = 0$$

$$\therefore \quad \begin{vmatrix} 2-\lambda & -1 & 1 \\ -1 & 2-\lambda & -1 \\ 1 & -1 & 2-\lambda \end{vmatrix} = 0$$

$(2-\lambda)[(2-\lambda)^2 - 1] + 1[-2+\lambda+1] + 1[1-2+\lambda] = 0$

$\therefore \quad (2-\lambda)[4 - 4\lambda + \lambda^2 - 1] + \lambda - 1 + \lambda - 1 = 0$

$\therefore \quad (2-\lambda)[\lambda^2 - 4\lambda + 3] + 2\lambda - 2 = 0$

$\therefore \quad (2\lambda^2 - 8\lambda + 6 - \lambda^3 + 4\lambda^2 - 3\lambda + 2\lambda - 2 = 0$

$\therefore \quad -\lambda^3 + 6\lambda^2 - 9\lambda + 4 = 0$ i.e. $\lambda^3 - 6\lambda^2 + 9\lambda - 4 = 0$

$\therefore$ By Cayley-Hamilton theorem. A must satisfy this equation.

i.e. $A^3 - 6A^2 + 9A - 4I = \mathbf{O}$

Verification :

$$A^2 = A \cdot A = \begin{bmatrix} 2 & -1 & 1 \\ -1 & 2 & -1 \\ 1 & -1 & 2 \end{bmatrix} \begin{bmatrix} 2 & -1 & 1 \\ -1 & 2 & -1 \\ 1 & -1 & 2 \end{bmatrix}$$

$$= \begin{bmatrix} 6 & -5 & 5 \\ -5 & 6 & -5 \\ 5 & -5 & 6 \end{bmatrix}$$

and $$A^3 = A \cdot A^2 = \begin{bmatrix} 2 & -1 & 1 \\ -1 & 2 & -1 \\ 1 & -1 & 2 \end{bmatrix} \begin{bmatrix} 6 & -5 & 5 \\ -5 & 6 & -5 \\ 5 & -5 & 6 \end{bmatrix}$$

$$= \begin{bmatrix} 22 & -21 & 21 \\ -21 & 22 & -21 \\ 21 & -21 & 22 \end{bmatrix}$$

Consider, $A^3 - 6A^2 + 9A - 4I$

$$= \begin{bmatrix} 22 & -21 & 21 \\ -21 & 22 & -21 \\ 21 & -21 & 22 \end{bmatrix} - 6 \begin{bmatrix} 6 & -5 & 5 \\ -5 & 6 & -5 \\ 5 & -5 & 6 \end{bmatrix}$$

$$+ 9 \begin{bmatrix} 2 & -1 & 1 \\ -1 & 2 & -1 \\ 1 & -1 & 2 \end{bmatrix} - 4 \begin{bmatrix} 1 & 0 & 0 \\ 0 & 1 & 0 \\ 0 & 0 & 1 \end{bmatrix} = \begin{bmatrix} 0 & 0 & 0 \\ 0 & 0 & 0 \\ 0 & 0 & 0 \end{bmatrix}$$

$\therefore \quad A^3 - 6A^2 + 9A - 4I = \mathbf{O}$

Hence, the theorem is verified.

Example 1.17 : Find the characteristic equation of the matrix

$A = \begin{bmatrix} 1 & 2 & 2 \\ 2 & 1 & 2 \\ 2 & 2 & 1 \end{bmatrix}$ and verify that it is satisfied by A. Also find A^{-1}.

Solution : The characteristic matrix is

$$A - \lambda I = \begin{bmatrix} 1 & 2 & 2 \\ 2 & 1 & 2 \\ 2 & 2 & 1 \end{bmatrix} - \lambda \begin{bmatrix} 1 & 0 & 0 \\ 0 & 1 & 0 \\ 0 & 0 & 1 \end{bmatrix}$$

$$\therefore \quad A - \lambda I = \begin{bmatrix} 1-\lambda & 2 & 2 \\ 2 & 1-\lambda & 2 \\ 2 & 2 & 1-\lambda \end{bmatrix}$$

Therefore, the characteristics equation is given by

$$|A - \lambda I| = 0$$

$$\begin{vmatrix} 1-\lambda & 2 & 2 \\ 2 & 1-\lambda & 2 \\ 2 & 2 & 1-\lambda \end{vmatrix} = 0$$

$(1 - \lambda)[(1 - \lambda)^2 - 4] - 2[2 - 2\lambda - 4] + 2[4 - 2 + 2\lambda] = 0$

∴ $(1 - \lambda)[1 - 2\lambda + \lambda^2 - 4] - 2[-2\lambda - 2] + 2[2 + 2\lambda] = 0$

∴ $(1 - \lambda)[\lambda^2 - 2\lambda - 3] + 4\lambda + 4 + 4 + 4\lambda = 0$

∴ $\lambda^2 - 2\lambda - 3 - \lambda^3 + 2\lambda^2 + 3\lambda + 8\lambda + 8 = 0$

$-\lambda^3 + 3\lambda^3 + 9\lambda + 5 = 0$

i.e. $\lambda^3 - 3\lambda^2 - 9\lambda - 5 = 0$

Cayley-Hamilton theorem states that it is satisfied by A

i.e. $A^3 - 3A^2 - 9A - 5I = \mathbf{O}$.

Verification : Consider

$$A^2 = A \cdot A = \begin{bmatrix} 1 & 2 & 2 \\ 2 & 1 & 2 \\ 2 & 2 & 1 \end{bmatrix} \begin{bmatrix} 1 & 2 & 2 \\ 2 & 1 & 2 \\ 2 & 2 & 1 \end{bmatrix}$$

$$= \begin{bmatrix} 9 & 8 & 8 \\ 8 & 9 & 8 \\ 8 & 8 & 9 \end{bmatrix}$$

and $A^3 = A \cdot A^2 = \begin{bmatrix} 1 & 2 & 2 \\ 2 & 1 & 2 \\ 2 & 2 & 1 \end{bmatrix} \begin{bmatrix} 9 & 8 & 8 \\ 8 & 9 & 8 \\ 8 & 8 & 9 \end{bmatrix}$

$= \begin{bmatrix} 41 & 42 & 42 \\ 42 & 41 & 42 \\ 42 & 42 & 41 \end{bmatrix}$

Now, $A^3 - 3A^2 - 9A - 5I$

$= \begin{bmatrix} 41 & 42 & 42 \\ 42 & 41 & 42 \\ 42 & 42 & 41 \end{bmatrix} - 3 \begin{bmatrix} 9 & 8 & 8 \\ 8 & 9 & 8 \\ 8 & 8 & 9 \end{bmatrix}$

$- 9 \begin{bmatrix} 1 & 2 & 2 \\ 2 & 1 & 2 \\ 2 & 2 & 1 \end{bmatrix} - 5 \begin{bmatrix} 1 & 0 & 0 \\ 0 & 1 & 0 \\ 0 & 0 & 1 \end{bmatrix}$

$= \begin{bmatrix} 41-27-9-5 & 42-24-18 & 42-24-18 \\ 42-24-18 & 41-27-9-5 & 42-24-18 \\ 42-24-18 & 42-24-18 & 41-27-9-5 \end{bmatrix}$

$= \begin{bmatrix} 0 & 0 & 0 \\ 0 & 0 & 0 \\ 0 & 0 & 0 \end{bmatrix} = \mathbf{O}$ i.e. $A^3 - 3A^2 - 9A - 5I = \mathbf{O}$ ... (1)

Therefore, the characteristic equation
$\lambda^3 - 3\lambda^2 - 9\lambda - 5 = 0$ is satisfied by A.

To find A^{-1} : Multiply equation (1) by A^{-1}.

$A^2 - 3A - 9I - 5A^{-1} = \mathbf{O}$

$\therefore \quad 5A^{-1} = A^2 - 3A - 9I$

$\therefore \quad A^{-1} = \frac{1}{5} [A^2 - 3A - 9I]$

$= \frac{1}{5} \left\{ \begin{bmatrix} 9 & 8 & 8 \\ 8 & 9 & 8 \\ 8 & 8 & 9 \end{bmatrix} - 3 \begin{bmatrix} 1 & 2 & 2 \\ 2 & 1 & 2 \\ 2 & 2 & 1 \end{bmatrix} - 9 \begin{bmatrix} 1 & 0 & 0 \\ 0 & 1 & 0 \\ 0 & 0 & 1 \end{bmatrix} \right\}$

$\therefore \quad A^{-1} = \frac{1}{5} \begin{bmatrix} -3 & 2 & 2 \\ 2 & -3 & 2 \\ 2 & 2 & -3 \end{bmatrix}$

Example 1.18 : Find $2A^8 - 3A^5 + A^4 + A^2 - 4I$ where, the matrix

$$A = \begin{bmatrix} 1 & 0 & 2 \\ 0 & -1 & 1 \\ 0 & 1 & 0 \end{bmatrix}$$

Solution : The characteristic matrix is

$$A - \lambda I = \begin{bmatrix} 1 & 0 & 2 \\ 0 & -1 & 1 \\ 0 & 1 & 0 \end{bmatrix} - \lambda \begin{bmatrix} 1 & 0 & 0 \\ 0 & 1 & 0 \\ 0 & 0 & 1 \end{bmatrix}$$

$$\therefore \quad A - \lambda I = \begin{bmatrix} 1-\lambda & 0 & 2 \\ 0 & -1-\lambda & 1 \\ 0 & 1 & -\lambda \end{bmatrix}$$

The characteristic equation is given by
$$|A - \lambda I| = 0$$

$$\therefore \quad \begin{vmatrix} 1-\lambda & 0 & 0 \\ 0 & -1-\lambda & 1 \\ 0 & 1 & -\lambda \end{vmatrix} = 0$$

$\therefore \quad (1 - \lambda)[\lambda(1 + \lambda) - 1] - 0 + 0 = 0$
$\therefore \quad (1 - \lambda)[\lambda + \lambda^2 - 1] = 0$ i.e. $\lambda^3 - 2\lambda + 1 = 0$ ... (1)

By Cayley-Hamilton theorem this is satisfied by
$$A^3 - 2A + I = \mathbf{O}$$

Now dividing the given expression
$2\lambda^8 - 3\lambda^5 + \lambda^4 + \lambda^2 - 4$ by $\lambda^3 - 2\lambda + 1$, we get the remainder
$24\lambda^2 - 37\lambda + 10$ and quotient $2\lambda^5 + 4\lambda^3 - 5\lambda^2 + 9\lambda - 14$

$\therefore \quad 2\lambda^8 - 3\lambda^5 + \lambda^4 + \lambda^2 - 4$
$\quad = (2\lambda^5 + 4\lambda^3 - 5\lambda^2 + 9\lambda - 14)(\lambda^2 - 2\lambda + 1)$
$\quad \quad + 24\lambda^2 - 37\lambda + 10$
$\quad = 24\lambda^2 - 37\lambda + 10$ \quad ($\because$ from equation (1))

$\therefore \quad 2A^8 - 3A^5 + A^4 + A^2 - 4I = 24A^2 - 37A + 10I$

But $\quad A^2 = A \cdot A = \begin{bmatrix} 1 & 0 & 2 \\ 0 & -1 & 1 \\ 0 & 1 & 0 \end{bmatrix} \begin{bmatrix} 1 & 0 & 2 \\ 0 & -1 & 1 \\ 0 & 1 & 0 \end{bmatrix}$

$$= \begin{bmatrix} 1 & 2 & 2 \\ 0 & 2 & -1 \\ 0 & -1 & 1 \end{bmatrix}$$

$$\therefore \quad 2A^8 - 3A^5 + A^4 + A^2 - 4I$$

$$= 24 \begin{bmatrix} 1 & 2 & 2 \\ 0 & 2 & -1 \\ 0 & -1 & 1 \end{bmatrix} - 37 \begin{bmatrix} 1 & 0 & 2 \\ 0 & 1 & 1 \\ 0 & 1 & 0 \end{bmatrix} + 10 \begin{bmatrix} 1 & 0 & 0 \\ 0 & 1 & 0 \\ 0 & 0 & 1 \end{bmatrix}$$

$$= \begin{bmatrix} -3 & 48 & -26 \\ 0 & 95 & -61 \\ 0 & -61 & 34 \end{bmatrix} \qquad \text{... Ans.}$$

EXERCISE 1.3

1. Verify Cayley-Hamilton theorem for the following matrices and hence find the inverse in each case :

(i) $\begin{bmatrix} 2 & 2 & 1 \\ 1 & 3 & 1 \\ 1 & 2 & 2 \end{bmatrix}$
(ii) $\begin{bmatrix} 4 & 3 & -1 \\ 2 & 1 & -2 \\ 1 & 2 & 1 \end{bmatrix}$

(iii) $\begin{bmatrix} 1 & 1 & 3 \\ 1 & 3 & -3 \\ -2 & -4 & -4 \end{bmatrix}$
(iv) $\begin{bmatrix} 2 & -1 & 1 \\ -1 & 2 & -1 \\ 1 & -1 & 2 \end{bmatrix}$

(v) $\begin{bmatrix} 1 & 1 & 2 \\ 3 & 1 & 1 \\ 2 & 3 & 1 \end{bmatrix}$
(vi) $\begin{bmatrix} 1 & 2 & 1 \\ 0 & 1 & -1 \\ 3 & -1 & 1 \end{bmatrix}$

(vii) $\begin{bmatrix} 0 & 1 & 2 \\ 2 & -3 & 0 \\ 1 & 1 & -1 \end{bmatrix}$
(viii) $\begin{bmatrix} 1 & 2 & 7 \\ 2 & 1 & 0 \\ 0 & 1 & 3 \end{bmatrix}$

(ix) $\begin{bmatrix} 1 & 2 & 1 \\ -1 & 0 & 3 \\ 2 & -1 & 1 \end{bmatrix}$
(x) $\begin{bmatrix} 1 & 0 & 2 \\ 0 & 1 & 2 \\ 1 & 2 & 0 \end{bmatrix}$

(xi) $\begin{bmatrix} 1 & -2 & 2 \\ 1 & 2 & 3 \\ 0 & -1 & 2 \end{bmatrix}$

2. Verify the Cayley-Hamilton theorem for the following matrices :

(i) $\begin{bmatrix} 1 & 0 & 0 \\ 1 & 0 & 1 \\ 0 & 1 & 0 \end{bmatrix}$ (ii) $\begin{bmatrix} 2 & 0 & 0 \\ 0 & 1 & 0 \\ 0 & 0 & 1 \end{bmatrix}$

(iii) $\begin{bmatrix} 1 & 1 & 1 \\ 1 & 2 & 1 \\ 3 & 2 & 3 \end{bmatrix}$ (iv) $\begin{bmatrix} 1 & 2 & 4 \\ -1 & 0 & 3 \\ 3 & 1 & -2 \end{bmatrix}$

(v) $\begin{bmatrix} 3 & 1 & 1 \\ -1 & 5 & -1 \\ 1 & -1 & 3 \end{bmatrix}$ (vi) $\begin{bmatrix} 1 & -2 & 3 \\ 2 & 1 & 1 \\ 1 & 0 & -1 \end{bmatrix}$

(vii) $\begin{bmatrix} 3 & 2 & 1 \\ 4 & -1 & 2 \\ -1 & 1 & 3 \end{bmatrix}$ (viii) $\begin{bmatrix} \cos\theta & \sin\theta \\ -\sin\theta & \cos\theta \end{bmatrix}$

3. If $A = \begin{bmatrix} 1 & 1 & 2 \\ 3 & 1 & 1 \\ 2 & 3 & 1 \end{bmatrix}$, find the characteristic equation of matrix A and hence find $2A^8 - 9A^7 - 5A^6 - A^5 + 28A^4 + 14A^3 + 34A^2 - 60A$.

4. If $A = \begin{bmatrix} 2 & -1 \\ 1 & 3 \end{bmatrix}$, show that $A^2 - 5A + 7I = O$ and hence find $A^4 - 4A^3 - A^2 + 2A - 5I$.

5. If $A = \begin{bmatrix} 3 & 1 \\ -1 & 2 \end{bmatrix}$, express $2A^5 - 3A^4 + A^2 - 4I$ as a linear polynomial in A.

6. Given : $A = \begin{bmatrix} 1 & 3 & 7 \\ 4 & 2 & 3 \\ 1 & 2 & 1 \end{bmatrix}$, show that $A^3 - 4A^2 - 20A - 35I = O$ and hence evaluate $A^7 - 4A^6 - 20A^5 - 34A^4 - 4A^3 - 20A^2 - 33A + I$.

7. If $A = \begin{bmatrix} 1 & 4 \\ 2 & 3 \end{bmatrix}$, then express $A^5 - 4A^4 - 7A^3 + 11A^2 - A - 10I$ in terms of A.

8. If $A = \begin{bmatrix} 2 & 1 & 1 \\ 0 & 1 & 0 \\ 1 & 1 & 2 \end{bmatrix}$, find the characteristic equation of matrix A and hence find $A^8 - 5A^7 + 7A^6 - 3A^5 + A^4$.

9. If $A = \begin{bmatrix} 2 & -1 & 1 \\ -1 & 2 & -1 \\ 1 & -1 & 2 \end{bmatrix}$
express $A^6 - 6A^5 + 9A^4 - 2A^3 - 12A^2 + 23A - 9I$ as a linear polynomial in A.

10. Define the term characteristic equation of a matrix.
11. State and prove Cayley-Hamilton theorem.
12. State the echelon form and normal form of a matrix.

ANSWERS 1.3

1. (i) $\dfrac{1}{5}\begin{bmatrix} 4 & -2 & -1 \\ -1 & 3 & -1 \\ -1 & -2 & 4 \end{bmatrix}$ (ii) $\dfrac{1}{11}\begin{bmatrix} 5 & -1 & -7 \\ -4 & 3 & 10 \\ 3 & -5 & -2 \end{bmatrix}$

(iii) $\begin{bmatrix} 3 & 1 & 3/2 \\ -5/4 & -1/4 & -3/4 \\ -1/4 & -1/4 & -1/4 \end{bmatrix}$ (iv) $\begin{bmatrix} 3/4 & 1/4 & -1/4 \\ 1/4 & 3/4 & 1/4 \\ -1/4 & 1/4 & 3/4 \end{bmatrix}$

(v) $\begin{bmatrix} -2/11 & 5/11 & -1/11 \\ -1/11 & -3/11 & 5/11 \\ 7/11 & -1/11 & -2/11 \end{bmatrix}$ (vi) $\begin{bmatrix} 0 & 1/3 & 1/3 \\ 1/3 & 2/9 & -1/9 \\ 1/3 & -7/9 & -1/9 \end{bmatrix}$

(vii) $\begin{bmatrix} 1/4 & 1/4 & 1/2 \\ 1/6 & -1/6 & 1/3 \\ 5/12 & 1/12 & -1/6 \end{bmatrix}$ (viii) $\dfrac{1}{5}\begin{bmatrix} 3 & 1 & -7 \\ -6 & 3 & 14 \\ -2 & -1 & -3 \end{bmatrix}$

(ix) $\begin{bmatrix} 1/6 & -1/6 & 1/3 \\ 7/18 & -1/18 & -2/9 \\ 1/18 & 5/18 & 1/9 \end{bmatrix}$ (x) $\begin{bmatrix} 2/3 & -2/3 & 1/3 \\ -1/3 & 1/3 & 1/3 \\ 1/6 & 1/3 & -1/6 \end{bmatrix}$

(xi) $\dfrac{1}{9}\begin{bmatrix} 7 & 2 & -10 \\ -2 & 2 & -1 \\ -1 & 1 & 4 \end{bmatrix}$

MISCELLANEOUS EXERCISES

I. Theory Questions :

1. Define the terms symmetric and skew-symmetric matrices.
2. Define the terms Idempotent matrix and Nilpotent matrix.
3. Define the terms singular matrix and elementary matrix.
4. Show that for square matrices A, B of the same order, AB' + BA' is symmetric and AB' − BA' is skew-symmetric.
5. Show that every square matrix can be uniquely expressed as the sum of a symmetric and a skew-symmetric matrices.
6. Define the term rank of a matrix.
7. List the elementary row transformations.
8. Define the term normal form of a matrix.
9. Define the term Echelon or canonical form of a matrix.
10. Define the terms characteristic matrix and characteristic equation of a matrix.
11. State and prove Cayley-Hamilton theorem.

II. Numerical Problems :

1. Express the following matrices as the sum of a symmetric and a skew-symmetric matrices.

    (a) $\begin{bmatrix} 1 & 2 & 3 \\ 4 & 5 & 6 \\ 7 & 8 & 9 \end{bmatrix}$
    (b) $\begin{bmatrix} 4 & -1 & 3 \\ 2 & 5 & 1 \\ 3 & 0 & 6 \end{bmatrix}$
    (c) $\begin{bmatrix} 5 & 4 & 7 \\ 2 & 4 & 6 \\ 3 & 6 & 2 \end{bmatrix}$
    (d) $\begin{bmatrix} 1 & \sqrt{2} & 0 \\ \sqrt{2} & -1 & 0 \\ 0 & 0 & 1 \end{bmatrix}$

2. Find the rank of the following matrices :

    (i) $\begin{bmatrix} 2 & -3 & 5 \\ 6 & -9 & 15 \\ 8 & -12 & 20 \end{bmatrix}$
    (ii) $\begin{bmatrix} 1 & 1 & 1 & 1 \\ 3 & 4 & 5 & 2 \\ 2 & 3 & 4 & 0 \end{bmatrix}$

(iii) $\begin{bmatrix} 2 & 3 & -1 & -1 \\ 1 & -1 & -2 & -4 \\ 3 & 1 & 3 & -2 \\ 6 & 3 & 0 & -7 \end{bmatrix}$ (iv) $\begin{bmatrix} 4 & 5 & 6 & 7 \\ 9 & 10 & 11 & 12 \\ 10 & 11 & 12 & 13 \\ 18 & 19 & 20 & 21 \end{bmatrix}$

(v) $\begin{bmatrix} 6 & 1 & 3 & 8 \\ 4 & 2 & 6 & -1 \\ 10 & 3 & 9 & 7 \\ 16 & 4 & 12 & 15 \end{bmatrix}$ (vi) $\begin{bmatrix} 1 & 2 & 3 & 1 \\ 2 & 4 & 3 & 2 \\ 3 & 2 & 1 & 3 \\ 6 & 8 & 7 & 6 \end{bmatrix}$

(vii) $\begin{bmatrix} 0 & 1 & 2 & 1 \\ 1 & 2 & 3 & 2 \\ 3 & 1 & 1 & 3 \end{bmatrix}$

3. Verify the cayley-Hamilton theorem for the following matrices :

(i) $\begin{bmatrix} 1 & 2 & 1 \\ 0 & 1 & -1 \\ 3 & -1 & 1 \end{bmatrix}$ (ii) $\begin{bmatrix} 1 & 2 & 1 \\ -1 & 0 & 3 \\ 2 & -1 & 1 \end{bmatrix}$

(iii) $\begin{bmatrix} 1 & 0 & 2 \\ 0 & 2 & 1 \\ 2 & 0 & 3 \end{bmatrix}$ (iv) $\begin{bmatrix} 2 & 2 & 1 \\ 1 & 3 & 1 \\ 1 & 2 & 2 \end{bmatrix}$

(v) $\begin{bmatrix} 1 & 1 & 0 \\ 0 & 0 & 1 \\ 2 & 1 & -2 \end{bmatrix}$

4. Using Cayley-Hamilton theorem find A^{-1}.

(i) $\begin{bmatrix} 1 & 1 & 3 \\ 1 & 3 & -3 \\ -2 & -4 & -4 \end{bmatrix}$ (ii) $\begin{bmatrix} 1 & 1 & -2 \\ -1 & 2 & 1 \\ 0 & 1 & -1 \end{bmatrix}$

(iii) $\begin{bmatrix} 1 & 1 & 2 \\ 3 & 1 & 1 \\ 2 & 3 & 1 \end{bmatrix}$ (iv) $\begin{bmatrix} 2 & -1 & 1 \\ -1 & 2 & -1 \\ 1 & -1 & 2 \end{bmatrix}$

5. If $A = \begin{bmatrix} 1 & 4 \\ 2 & 3 \end{bmatrix}$, express $A^5 - 4A^4 - 7A^3 + 11A^2 - A - 10I$ as a linear polynomial.

6. Verify Cayley-Hamilton theorem for the matrix $\begin{bmatrix} 1 & 2 & 3 \\ 2 & -1 & 4 \\ 3 & 1 & -2 \end{bmatrix}$.

   Hence find A^{-1} and A^4.

7. Find the value of p for which the following matrix will have (i) rank 1, (ii) rank 2, (iii) rank 3.

$$\begin{bmatrix} 3 & P & P \\ P & 3 & P \\ P & P & 3 \end{bmatrix}$$

ANSWERS

1. (a) $\begin{bmatrix} 1 & 3 & 5 \\ 3 & 5 & 7 \\ 5 & 7 & 9 \end{bmatrix} + \begin{bmatrix} 0 & -1 & -2 \\ 1 & 0 & -1 \\ 2 & 1 & 0 \end{bmatrix}$

   (b) $\begin{bmatrix} 4 & \frac{1}{2} & 3 \\ \frac{1}{2} & 5 & \frac{1}{2} \\ 3 & \frac{1}{2} & 6 \end{bmatrix} + \begin{bmatrix} 0 & -\frac{3}{2} & 0 \\ \frac{3}{2} & 0 & \frac{1}{2} \\ 0 & -\frac{1}{2} & 0 \end{bmatrix}$

   (c) $\begin{bmatrix} 5 & 3 & 5 \\ 3 & 4 & 6 \\ 5 & 6 & 2 \end{bmatrix} + \begin{bmatrix} 0 & 1 & 2 \\ -1 & 0 & 0 \\ -2 & 0 & 0 \end{bmatrix}$

2. (i) 1, (ii) 2, (iii) 3, (iv) 2, (v) 2, (vi) 3, (vii) 3.

4. (i) $\frac{1}{4}\begin{bmatrix} 12 & 4 & 6 \\ -5 & -1 & -3 \\ -1 & -1 & -1 \end{bmatrix}$ (ii) $\frac{1}{2}\begin{bmatrix} 3 & 1 & -5 \\ 1 & 1 & -1 \\ 1 & 1 & -3 \end{bmatrix}$

(iii) $\begin{bmatrix} 1 & 3 & 7 \\ 4 & 2 & 3 \\ 1 & 2 & 1 \end{bmatrix}$ (iv) $\dfrac{1}{4}\begin{bmatrix} 3 & 1 & -1 \\ 1 & 3 & 1 \\ -1 & 1 & 3 \end{bmatrix}$

5. $A + 5I$.

6. $\dfrac{1}{40}\begin{bmatrix} -3 & 5 & 11 \\ 14 & -10 & 2 \\ 5 & 5 & -5 \end{bmatrix}$; $\begin{bmatrix} 248 & 101 & 218 \\ 272 & 109 & 50 \\ 104 & 98 & 204 \end{bmatrix}$

7. $P = 3$; rank = 1, $2p^3 - 9p^2 + 27 \neq 0$; rank $A = 3$, $P \neq 3$; rank $A = 2$.

III. Multiple Choice Questions :

1. If $A_\alpha = \begin{bmatrix} \cos\alpha & \sin\alpha \\ -\sin\alpha & \cos\alpha \end{bmatrix}$, then which of the following is true

   (a) $A_\alpha A_\beta = A_{\alpha+\beta}$ (b) $A_\alpha A_\beta = A_{\alpha-\beta}$
   (c) $A_\alpha A_\beta = A_{\beta-\alpha}$ (d) none of these

2. If $A = \begin{bmatrix} 1 & 2 \\ 4 & -3 \end{bmatrix}$, then $A^3 = \ldots$

   (a) $\begin{bmatrix} 9 & -4 \\ -8 & 17 \end{bmatrix}$ (b) $\begin{bmatrix} 15 & -21 \\ 10 & -3 \end{bmatrix}$

   (c) $\begin{bmatrix} -7 & 30 \\ 60 & -67 \end{bmatrix}$ (d) $\begin{bmatrix} 7 & 30 \\ 60 & 37 \end{bmatrix}$

3. If $A = \begin{bmatrix} 0 & 1 \\ -1 & 0 \end{bmatrix}$ such that $(\alpha I + \beta A)^2 = A$ then which of the following is true

   (a) $\alpha = \beta$ (b) $\alpha = -\beta$
   (c) $\alpha = \dfrac{1}{\beta}$ (d) $\alpha = \beta^2$

4. If the non-singular matrix A is symmetric then A^{-1} is ……
   (a) also symmetric   (b) skew-symmetric
   (c) Hermitian   (d) none of these

5. The characteristic polynomial of the matrix $\begin{bmatrix} 1 & 2 \\ 3 & 4 \end{bmatrix}$ is ……

   (a) $\lambda^2 - 5\lambda - 2$ (b) λ^2
   (c) λ^3 (d) $\lambda^2 + 5\lambda - 2$

6. The rank of the matrix $\begin{bmatrix} 2 & 1 & 1 \\ 2 & 1 & 2 \\ 2 & 1 & 3 \\ -2 & -1 & 4 \end{bmatrix}$ is ...

   (a) 3   (b) 1
   (c) 2   (d) 4

7. If $A = \begin{bmatrix} 1 & 2 & 0 \\ 3 & -1 & 4 \end{bmatrix}$, then the matrix AA' is ......

   (a) $\begin{bmatrix} 1 & 2 \\ 3 & 0 \end{bmatrix}$ (b) $\begin{bmatrix} 5 & 0 \\ 1 & 12 \end{bmatrix}$
   (c) $\begin{bmatrix} 3 & 1 \\ 1 & 14 \end{bmatrix}$ (d) $\begin{bmatrix} 5 & 1 \\ 1 & 26 \end{bmatrix}$

8. A square matrix $A = (a_{ij})$ is called symmetric matrix if for all i and j ...

   (a) $a_{ij} = a_{ji}$ (b) $a_{ij} = a_{ji}^2$
   (c) $a_{ij} = -a_{ij}$ (d) $a_{ij} = -a_{ji}$

9. If A and B are symmetric matrices then AB is symmetric if ......

   (a) $AB = (AB)^{-1}$ (b) AB = – BA
   (c) AB = BA   (d) none of these

10. If A is square matrix then the matrix A + A' is ....

    (a) symmetric   (b) skew-symmetric
    (c) elementary   (d) none of these

11. If A is a square matrix then the matrix A – A' is ......

    (a) symmetric   (b) skew-symmetric
    (c) elementary   (d) unitary

12. The inverse of the matrix is $\begin{bmatrix} 2 & 1 \\ 0 & 4 \end{bmatrix}$ ......

    (a) $\begin{bmatrix} 1/2 & 0 \\ 1/8 & 1/4 \end{bmatrix}$ (b) $\begin{bmatrix} 1/2 & 0 \\ -1/8 & 1/4 \end{bmatrix}$
    (c) $\begin{bmatrix} 1/2 & -1/8 \\ 0 & 1/4 \end{bmatrix}$ (d) $\begin{bmatrix} -1/2 & 1/8 \\ 0 & -1/4 \end{bmatrix}$

13. If A is an n × n matrix of rank (n – 1), then its adjoint is of rank …
    (a) 1
    (b) 0
    (c) n
    (d) 2

14. A matrix A is invertible if and only if ……
    (a) |A| = 0
    (b) |A| ≠ 0
    (c) A = A'
    (d) $A^2 = I$

15. If A is any matrix, then AA' and A'A are ……
    (a) symmetric
    (b) skew-symmetric
    (c) conjugate
    (d) none of these

16. For a matrix $A = \begin{bmatrix} P & O \\ O & Q \end{bmatrix}$ where P and Q are submatrices, Rank A = ……
    (a) rank P
    (b) rank (PQ)
    (c) rank Q
    (d) rank P + rank Q

17. If $a_{ij} = i - j$, then the matrix $A = (a_{ij})$ is ……
    (a) symmetric
    (b) skew-symmetric
    (c) conjugate
    (d) involuntary

18. A square matrix A is called an idempotent matrix if ……
    (a) $A^2 = A$
    (b) $A^2 = I$
    (c) $A^T = A$
    (d) $A^n = O$

19. A square matrix A is said to be an involutory matrix if ……
    (a) $A^2 = A$
    (b) $A^2 = I$
    (c) $A \cdot A^T = I$
    (d) $A^n = O$

20. The index of nilpotent matrix $\begin{bmatrix} ab & b^2 \\ -a^2 & -ab \end{bmatrix}$ is ……
    (a) 0
    (b) 1
    (c) 2
    (d) 3

ANSWERS

1. (a)	2. (c)	3. (b)	4. (a)	5. (a)	6. (c)	7. (d)	8. (a)
9. (c)	10. (a)	11. (b)	12. (c)	13. (a)	14. (b)	15. (a)	16. (d)
17. (b)	18. (a)	19. (b)	20. (c)				

2
CHAPTER

LINEAR EQUATIONS

2.1 INTRODUCTION

It was Prof. Wassily Leontif in 1949 introduced the concept of linear equations in Economics and Engineering. Since the equations involving huge amount of data are usually linear. i.e. they are described by systems of linear equations. One of the most frequent applications of matrices to various fields in engineering and social sciences arises from the need to solve a system of linear equations.

Prof. Dr. Wassily Leontief

The process of solving a system of linear equations by reducing it to (echelon form requires the writing of a number of equivalent system) triangular form is a tedious work. The amount of labor work involved in this process is minimised by using a matrix rotation form.

2.2 SYSTEM OF LINEAR EQUATIONS

A system of linear equations is a collections of one or more linear equations involving the same variables – say $x_1, x_2, \ldots, x_n$.

For example,
$$2x - 3y + 4z = -4$$
$$x + z = 0$$

Since the solution of the system is the list of values satisfying each equation of the system. The problem of solving two linear equations in two variables is similar to find the point of intersection of given two lines.

For example, consider the problem.

$$x + 2y = 1$$
$$x - 3y = -4$$

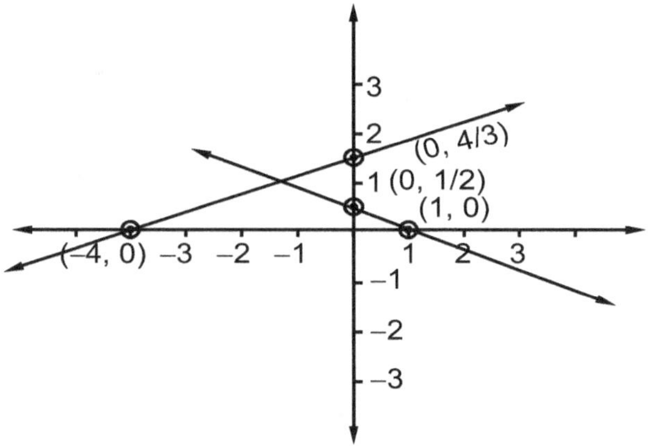

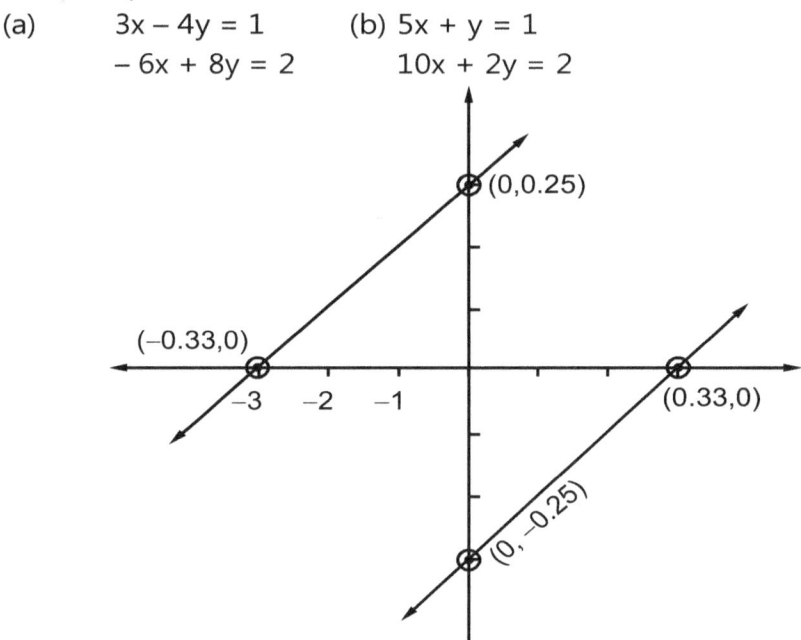

Fig. 2.1 : Exactly one solution

Here the two given lines intersecting at a single point, so the system has exactly one solution. But it is not necessary that the two lines intersect at a single point, they may be parallel or coincide.

For example,

(a) $3x - 4y = 1$ (b) $5x + y = 1$
          $-6x + 8y = 2$ $10x + 2y = 2$

Fig. 2.2 : (a) No solution

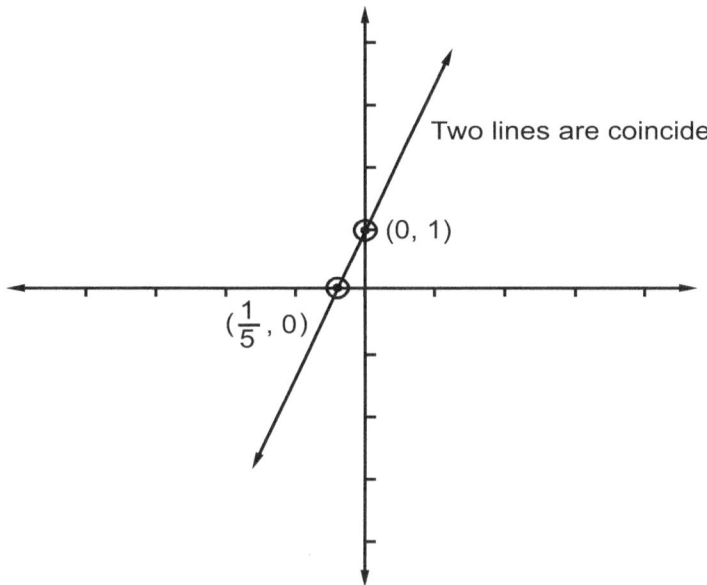

Fig. 2.2 : (b) Infinite number of solutions

Thus the system of linear equations has either.
1. exactly one solution or
2. infinitely many solutions or
3. no solution.

2.2.1 Types of Linear Equations

1. Consistent : A system of equations having one or more solution is said to be consistent.

For example, The system 2.1 and 2.2 (b) given above are consistent.

2. Inconsistent : A system of equations having no solution is said to be inconsistent.

For example, the system 2.2 (a) given above is inconsistent.

2.3 SYSTEM OF HOMOGENEOUS LINEAR EQUATIONS

Consider the following system of m homogeneous linear equations in n unknowns say $x_1, x_2, ..., x_n$.

$$\left.\begin{array}{l} a_{11}x_1 + a_{12}x_2 + a_{13}x_3 + ... + a_{1n}x_n = 0 \\ a_{21}x_1 + a_{22}x_2 + a_{23}x_3 + ... + a_{2n}x_n = 0 \\ \quad\quad\quad\quad\quad\quad\quad\quad\quad\quad................................ \\ a_{m1}x_1 + a_{m2}x_2 + a_{m3}x_3 + ... + a_{mn}x_n = 0 \end{array}\right\} \quad ... (1)$$

In matrix form these equations can be written as
$$AX = O \qquad \ldots (2)$$

where,
$$A = \begin{bmatrix} a_{11} & a_{12} & \ldots & a_{1n} \\ a_{21} & a_{22} & \ldots & a_{2n} \\ \ldots & \ldots & \ldots & \ldots \\ a_{m1} & a_{m2} & \ldots & a_{mn} \end{bmatrix}$$

is called the coefficient matrix of the system.

and $\quad X = (x_1, x_2, \ldots, x_n)'$, $O = (0, 0, 0, \ldots, 0)'$

are called matrix of unknowns and zero matrix respectively.

$$\text{The matrix } [A, O] = \begin{bmatrix} a_{11} & a_{12} & \ldots & a_{1n} & : & 0 \\ a_{21} & a_{22} & \ldots & a_{2n} & : & 0 \\ \ldots & \ldots & \ldots & \ldots & : & \ldots \\ a_{m1} & a_{m2} & \ldots & a_{mn} & : & 0 \end{bmatrix}$$

is called the augmented matrix of the system.

Here the coefficient and the augmented matrices will have the same rank. Hence a system of homogeneous linear equation is consistent always. Obvious solutions of system of equations (1) are
$$x_1 = 0 = x_2 = \ldots = x_n \text{ when } |A| \neq 0.$$

This is called a trivial or zero solution.

For a non-zero solutions, the necessary and sufficient condition is $|A| = 0$.

2.3.1 Nature of the General Solution

Let $AX = O$ be denotes the system of homogeneous m linear equations in n variables. Then A will be matrix of order $m \times n$.

Let $\rho(A)$ will be r.

Case I : $\quad \rho(A) = r = n$

In this case the number of parameters or the number of independent solutions $= n - r = 0$. Hence there is a unique solution $X = O$ i.e. $x_1 = x_2 = \ldots x_n = 0$. This is called a trivial or zero solution.

Case II : $\quad \rho(A) = r < n$

Here the number of parameters or the number of independent solutions $= n - r$.

2.3.2 Chart of Nature of Solution

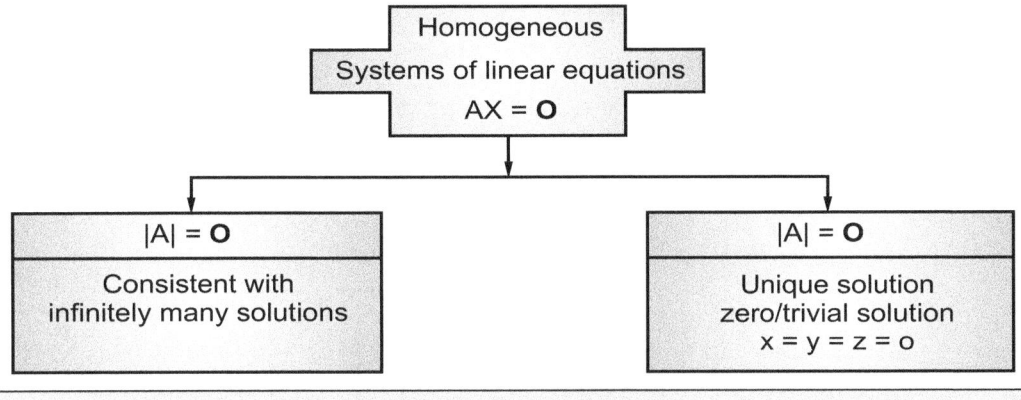

SOLVED EXAMPLES

Example 2.1 : Solve :

$$x - y + z = 0$$
$$x + 2y - z = 0$$
$$2x + y + 3z = 0$$

Solution : The system of equations can be written as

$$\begin{bmatrix} 1 & -1 & 1 \\ 1 & 2 & -1 \\ 2 & 1 & 3 \end{bmatrix} \begin{bmatrix} x \\ y \\ z \end{bmatrix} = \begin{bmatrix} 0 \\ 0 \\ 0 \end{bmatrix}$$

$$\xrightarrow[R_3 - 2R_1]{R_2 - R_1} \begin{bmatrix} 1 & -1 & 1 \\ 0 & 3 & -2 \\ 0 & 3 & 1 \end{bmatrix} \begin{bmatrix} x \\ y \\ z \end{bmatrix} = \begin{bmatrix} 0 \\ 0 \\ 0 \end{bmatrix}$$

$$\xrightarrow{R_3 - R_2} \begin{bmatrix} 1 & -1 & 1 \\ 0 & 3 & -2 \\ 0 & 0 & 3 \end{bmatrix} \begin{bmatrix} x \\ y \\ z \end{bmatrix} = \begin{bmatrix} 0 \\ 0 \\ 0 \end{bmatrix}$$

Here below the diagonal elements all elements are zeros.

∴ This is in triangular form i.e. in echelon form.

∴ Rank of A = ρ(A) = r = 3 and the number of variables = n = 3.

∴ $\qquad r = n$

Hence the equations have only trivial solutions $x = y = z = 0$.

Example 2.2 : Solve :
$$x + y + z = 0$$
$$2x + 5y + 6z = 0$$

Solution : The system of equations can be written as

$$\begin{bmatrix} 1 & 1 & 1 \\ 2 & 5 & 6 \end{bmatrix} \begin{bmatrix} x \\ y \\ z \end{bmatrix} = \begin{bmatrix} 0 \\ 0 \\ 0 \end{bmatrix}$$

$$\xrightarrow{R_2 - 2R_1} \begin{bmatrix} 1 & 1 & 1 \\ 0 & 3 & 4 \end{bmatrix} \begin{bmatrix} x \\ y \\ z \end{bmatrix} = \begin{bmatrix} 0 \\ 0 \\ 0 \end{bmatrix}$$

∴ $\quad x + y + z = 0$ ... (1)
$\quad\quad 3y + 4z = 0$ ... (2)

The rank of A = r = 2 and the number of variables = n = 3.

∴ r < n. The system has therefore non-trivial solutions.

∴ The number of parameters = n − r = 3 − 2 = 1.

Putting z = t, we get from equation (2)
$$3y + 4t = 0 \Rightarrow y = -4t/3$$

Now from equation (1),
$$x - \frac{4t}{3} + t = 0 \Rightarrow x = t/3$$

∴ The solutions are $x = t/3$, $y = -\frac{4t}{3}$ and $z = t$.

Example 2.3 : Solve :
$$x + y - z + t = 0$$
$$x - y + 2z - t = 0$$
$$3x + y + t = 0$$

Solution : In matrix form, we have

$$\begin{bmatrix} 1 & 1 & -1 & 1 \\ 1 & -1 & 2 & -1 \\ 3 & 1 & 0 & 1 \end{bmatrix} \begin{bmatrix} x \\ y \\ z \\ t \end{bmatrix} = \begin{bmatrix} 0 \\ 0 \\ 0 \end{bmatrix}$$

$$\xrightarrow[R_3 - 3R_1]{R_2 - R_1} \begin{bmatrix} 1 & 1 & -1 & 1 \\ 0 & -2 & 3 & -2 \\ 0 & -2 & 3 & -2 \end{bmatrix} \begin{bmatrix} x \\ y \\ z \\ t \end{bmatrix} = \begin{bmatrix} 0 \\ 0 \\ 0 \end{bmatrix}$$

$$\xrightarrow{R_3 - R_2} \begin{bmatrix} 1 & 1 & -1 & 1 \\ 0 & -2 & 3 & -2 \\ 0 & 0 & 0 & 0 \end{bmatrix} \begin{bmatrix} x \\ y \\ z \\ t \end{bmatrix} = \begin{bmatrix} 0 \\ 0 \\ 0 \end{bmatrix} \qquad \ldots (1)$$

∴ The coefficient matrix is in echelon form.

∴ $\quad \rho(A) = r =$ number of non-zero rows

$\qquad = 2$ and $n = 4$

∴ $\qquad r < n \Rightarrow$ The system has infinite solutions.

∴ The number of parameters $= n - r = 4 - 2 = 2$.

Equation (1) becomes

$\qquad x + y - z + t = 0 \qquad \ldots (2)$

$\qquad - 2y + 3z - 2t = 0 \qquad \ldots (3)$

Putting $z = k_1$ and $t = k_2$.

∴ Equation (3) $\quad \Rightarrow - 2y + 3k_1 - 2k_2 = 0$

$\qquad\qquad\qquad \Rightarrow - 2y = - 3k_1 + 2k_2$

$\qquad\qquad\qquad \Rightarrow y = \dfrac{3k_1}{2} - k_2$

Substituting these in equation (2), we get

$\qquad x + \dfrac{3}{2} k_1 - k_2 - k_1 + k_2 = 0$

∴ $\qquad x + \dfrac{k_1}{2} = 0$

∴ $\qquad x = - \dfrac{k_1}{2}$

∴ The solution are

$\qquad x = - \dfrac{k_1}{2}, \; y = \dfrac{3k_1}{2} - k_2, \; z = k_1 \text{ and } t = k_2$

where k_1 and k_2 are parameters.

Example 2.4 : Solve :
$$7x + y - 2z = 0$$
$$x + 5y - 4z = 0$$
$$3x - 2y + z = 0$$
$$2x - 7y + 5z = 0$$

Solution : The system of equations can be written as

$$\begin{bmatrix} 7 & 1 & -2 \\ 1 & 5 & -4 \\ 3 & -2 & 1 \\ 2 & -7 & 5 \end{bmatrix} \begin{bmatrix} x \\ y \\ z \end{bmatrix} = \begin{bmatrix} 0 \\ 0 \\ 0 \\ 0 \end{bmatrix}$$

$\xrightarrow{R_{12}}$
$$\begin{bmatrix} 1 & 5 & -4 \\ 7 & 1 & -2 \\ 3 & -2 & 1 \\ 2 & -7 & 5 \end{bmatrix} \begin{bmatrix} x \\ y \\ z \end{bmatrix} = \begin{bmatrix} 0 \\ 0 \\ 0 \\ 0 \end{bmatrix}$$

$\xrightarrow[R_4 - 2R_1]{\substack{R_2 - 7R_1 \\ R_3 - 3R_1}}$
$$\begin{bmatrix} 1 & 5 & -4 \\ 0 & -34 & 26 \\ 0 & -17 & 13 \\ 0 & -17 & 13 \end{bmatrix} \begin{bmatrix} x \\ y \\ z \end{bmatrix} = \begin{bmatrix} 0 \\ 0 \\ 0 \\ 0 \end{bmatrix}$$

$\xrightarrow[R_4 - R_3]{(1/2) R_2}$
$$\begin{bmatrix} 1 & 5 & -4 \\ 0 & -17 & 13 \\ 0 & -17 & 13 \\ 0 & 0 & 0 \end{bmatrix} \begin{bmatrix} x \\ y \\ z \end{bmatrix} = \begin{bmatrix} 0 \\ 0 \\ 0 \\ 0 \end{bmatrix}$$

$\xrightarrow{R_3 - R_2}$
$$\begin{bmatrix} 1 & 5 & -4 \\ 0 & -17 & 13 \\ 0 & 0 & 0 \\ 0 & 0 & 0 \end{bmatrix} \begin{bmatrix} x \\ y \\ z \end{bmatrix} = \begin{bmatrix} 0 \\ 0 \\ 0 \\ 0 \end{bmatrix} \quad \ldots (1)$$

∴ The rank of the coefficient matrix = r = ρ(A).
= number of non-zero rows
= 2 but n = number of variables = 3.

∴ ρ(A) = r < n. The system has infinite number of solutions.

∴ The number of parameters = n − r = 3 − 2 = 1.

From equation (1), we write

$$x + 5y - 4z = 0 \quad \ldots (2)$$
$$-17y + 13z = 0 \quad \ldots (3)$$

Putting $z = t$ in equation (3), we get

$$-17y + 13t = 0$$
$$\Rightarrow y = \frac{13t}{17}$$

Again from equation (2),

$$x + \frac{65t}{17} - 4t = 0$$

$$\therefore \quad x + \frac{65t - 68t}{17} = 0$$

$$\therefore \quad x - \frac{3t}{17} = 0$$

$$\therefore \quad x = \frac{3t}{17}$$

∴ The solutions are

$$x = \frac{3t}{17}, \ y = \frac{13t}{17} \text{ and } z = t \text{ where, t is a parameters.}$$

Example 2.5 : Determine the values of λ for which the following equations possess a non-trivial solution and obtain these solutions for the real values of λ.

$$3x_1 + x_2 - \lambda x_3 = 0$$
$$4x_1 - 2x_2 - 3x_3 = 0$$
$$2\lambda x_1 + 4x_2 + \lambda x_3 = 0$$

Solution : The system of equations can be written as

$$\begin{bmatrix} 3 & 1 & -\lambda \\ 4 & -2 & -3 \\ 2\lambda & 4 & \lambda \end{bmatrix} \begin{bmatrix} x_1 \\ x_2 \\ x_3 \end{bmatrix} = \begin{bmatrix} 0 \\ 0 \\ 0 \end{bmatrix} \quad \ldots (I)$$

The system of equations has non-trivial solutions if the rank of coefficient matrix is less than number of unknowns.

i.e. $\rho(A) = r < n = 3$.

For this, the determinant of the coefficient matrix A must be zero.

i.e. $|A| = 0$

$$\therefore \quad \begin{vmatrix} 3 & 1 & -\lambda \\ 4 & -2 & -3 \\ 2\lambda & 4 & \lambda \end{vmatrix} = 0$$

$\therefore \quad 3(-2\lambda + 12) - 1(4\lambda + 6\lambda) - \lambda(16 + 4\lambda) = 0$

$\therefore \quad -6\lambda + 36 - 10\lambda - 16\lambda - 4\lambda^2 = 0$

$\therefore \quad -4\lambda^2 - 32\lambda + 36 = 0 \quad \text{i.e.} \quad \lambda^2 + 8\lambda - 9 = 0$

$\therefore \quad (\lambda + 9)(\lambda - 1) = 0$

$\therefore \quad \lambda = -9, 1.$

Hence, the real values of λ for which the given system of equations will have a non-zero solution are $-9, 1$.

Case I : For $\lambda = -9$, equation (I) becomes.

$$\begin{bmatrix} 3 & 1 & 9 \\ 4 & -2 & -3 \\ -18 & 4 & -9 \end{bmatrix} \begin{bmatrix} x_1 \\ x_2 \\ x_3 \end{bmatrix} = \begin{bmatrix} 0 \\ 0 \\ 0 \end{bmatrix}$$

$$\xrightarrow[R_3 + 6R_1]{R_2 - R_1} \begin{bmatrix} 3 & 1 & 9 \\ 1 & -3 & -12 \\ 0 & 10 & 45 \end{bmatrix} \begin{bmatrix} x_1 \\ x_2 \\ x_3 \end{bmatrix} = \begin{bmatrix} 0 \\ 0 \\ 0 \end{bmatrix}$$

$$\xrightarrow{R_{12}} \begin{bmatrix} 1 & -3 & -12 \\ 3 & 1 & 9 \\ 0 & 10 & 45 \end{bmatrix} \begin{bmatrix} x_1 \\ x_2 \\ x_3 \end{bmatrix} = \begin{bmatrix} 0 \\ 0 \\ 0 \end{bmatrix}$$

$$\xrightarrow{R_2 - 3R_1} \begin{bmatrix} 1 & -3 & -12 \\ 0 & 10 & 45 \\ 0 & 10 & 45 \end{bmatrix} \begin{bmatrix} x_1 \\ x_2 \\ x_3 \end{bmatrix} = \begin{bmatrix} 0 \\ 0 \\ 0 \end{bmatrix}$$

$$\xrightarrow{R_3 - R_2} \begin{bmatrix} 1 & -3 & -12 \\ 0 & 10 & 45 \\ 0 & 0 & 0 \end{bmatrix} \begin{bmatrix} x_1 \\ x_2 \\ x_3 \end{bmatrix} = \begin{bmatrix} 0 \\ 0 \\ 0 \end{bmatrix}$$

$$\xrightarrow{(1/5) R_2} \begin{bmatrix} 1 & -3 & -12 \\ 0 & 2 & 9 \\ 0 & 0 & 0 \end{bmatrix} \begin{bmatrix} x_1 \\ x_2 \\ x_3 \end{bmatrix} = \begin{bmatrix} 0 \\ 0 \\ 0 \end{bmatrix} \quad \ldots \text{(II)}$$

∴ The rank of the coefficient matrix A = ρ(A)
= r = number of non-zero rows
= 2
But n = number of unknowns = 3
∴ ρ(A) = r < n

Therefore, the system has infinite solutions.

∴ The number of parameters = n − r = 3 − 2 = 1.

From equation (II), we write,

$$x_1 - 3x_2 - 12x_3 = 0 \qquad \ldots (i)$$
$$2x_2 + 9x_3 = 0 \qquad \ldots (ii)$$

Putting $x_3 = t$ in equation (ii), we get

$$2x_2 + 9t = 0$$

∴ $$x_2 = -\frac{9}{2}t$$

Again from equation (i)

$$x_1 + \frac{27t}{2} - 12t = 0$$

∴ $$x_1 + \frac{3t}{2} = 0$$

∴ $$x_1 = -\frac{3t}{2}$$

∴ The solutions are $x_1 = -\frac{3t}{2}$, $x_2 = -\frac{9t}{2}$ and $x_3 = t$ where t is a parameter.

Case II : For $\lambda = +1$, the system (I) becomes.

$$\begin{bmatrix} 3 & 1 & -1 \\ 4 & -2 & -3 \\ 2 & 4 & 1 \end{bmatrix} \begin{bmatrix} x_1 \\ x_2 \\ x_3 \end{bmatrix} = \begin{bmatrix} 0 \\ 0 \\ 0 \end{bmatrix}$$

$$\xrightarrow{R_1 - R_3} \begin{bmatrix} 1 & -3 & -2 \\ 4 & -2 & -3 \\ 2 & 4 & 1 \end{bmatrix} \begin{bmatrix} x_1 \\ x_2 \\ x_3 \end{bmatrix} = \begin{bmatrix} 0 \\ 0 \\ 0 \end{bmatrix}$$

$$\xrightarrow[R_3 - 2R_1]{R_2 - 4R_1} \begin{bmatrix} 1 & -3 & -2 \\ 0 & 10 & 5 \\ 0 & 10 & 5 \end{bmatrix} \begin{bmatrix} x_1 \\ x_2 \\ x_3 \end{bmatrix} = \begin{bmatrix} 0 \\ 0 \\ 0 \end{bmatrix}$$

$$\xrightarrow{R_3 - R_2} \begin{bmatrix} 1 & -3 & -2 \\ 0 & 10 & 5 \\ 0 & 0 & 0 \end{bmatrix} \begin{bmatrix} x_1 \\ x_2 \\ x_3 \end{bmatrix} = \begin{bmatrix} 0 \\ 0 \\ 0 \end{bmatrix}$$

$$\xrightarrow{(1/5) R_2} \begin{bmatrix} 1 & -3 & -2 \\ 0 & 2 & 1 \\ 0 & 0 & 0 \end{bmatrix} \begin{bmatrix} x_1 \\ x_2 \\ x_3 \end{bmatrix} = \begin{bmatrix} 0 \\ 0 \\ 0 \end{bmatrix} \quad \ldots \text{(III)}$$

Therefore, the rank of the coefficient matrix
$$= \rho(A) = r = \text{number of non-zero rows}$$
$$= 02$$
But $n = $ number of unknowns
$$= 3$$
$\therefore \quad \rho(A) = r < n$

$\therefore$ The system has infinite number of solutions.

The number of parameters $= n - r = 3 - 2 = 1$

Now from equation (III), we write,
$$x_1 - 3x_2 - 2x_3 = 0 \quad \ldots \text{(iii)}$$
$$2x_2 + x_3 = 0 \quad \ldots \text{(iv)}$$

Putting $x_2 = k$ in equation (iv), we get
$$2k + x_3 = 0 \implies x_3 = -2k$$

$\therefore$ Equation (iii) gives
$$x_1 - 3k + 4k = 0$$
$\therefore \quad x_1 = -k$

Hence, the solutions are $x_1 = -k$, $x_2 = k$, $x_3 = -2k$ where, k is a parameter.

Example 2.6 : For what values of λ the following equations have non-zero solutions.
$$\lambda x_1 - x_2 - x_3 = 0$$
$$-x_1 + \lambda x_2 - x_3 = 0$$
$$-x_1 - x_2 + \lambda x_3 = 0$$

Solution : The system of equations can be written as
$$\begin{bmatrix} \lambda & -1 & -1 \\ -1 & \lambda & -1 \\ -1 & -1 & \lambda \end{bmatrix} \begin{bmatrix} x_1 \\ x_2 \\ x_3 \end{bmatrix} = \begin{bmatrix} 0 \\ 0 \\ 0 \end{bmatrix}$$

The system has non-zero solution if r < n = 3.

For this its determinant must be zero.

i.e. $|A| = 0$

$$\begin{vmatrix} \lambda & -1 & -1 \\ -1 & \lambda & -1 \\ -1 & -1 & \lambda \end{vmatrix} = 0$$

$\lambda(\lambda^2 - 1) + 1(-\lambda - 1) - 1(1 + \lambda) = 0$

i.e. $\lambda^3 - \lambda - \lambda - 1 - 1 - \lambda = 0$

∴ $\lambda^3 - 3\lambda - 2 = 0$

∴ $(\lambda + 1)(\lambda^2 - \lambda - 2) = 0$

$(\lambda + 1)(\lambda + 1)(\lambda - 2) = 0$

∴ $\lambda = -1, 2$.

Hence, the given system has non-zero solution for $\lambda = -1, 2$.

EXERCISE 2.1

I. Solve the following equations :

1. $3x + 4y - z - 6w = 0$, $2x + 3y - 2z - 3w = 0$
   $2x + y - 14z - 9w = 0$, $x + 3y + 13z + 3w = 0$
2. $3x + 2z + 2w = 0$, $-x + 7y + 4z + 9w = 0$
   $7x - 7y - 5w = 0$
3. $x + 2y + 3z = 0$, $2x + 3y + z = 0$
   $4x + 5y + 4z = 0$, $x + y - 2z = 0$
4. $2x_1 - x_2 + 3x_3 = 0$, $3x_1 + 2x_2 + x_3 = 0$, $x_1 - 4x_2 + 5x_3 = 0$
5. $2x + 5y + 6z = 0$, $x - 2y + 3z = 0$
6. $x + 3y - 2z = 0$, $2x - y + 4z = 0$, $x - 11y + 14z = 0$
7. $x_1 + x_2 + 3x_3 = 0$, $x_1 - x_2 + x_3 = 0$, $x_1 - 2x_2 = 0$, $x_1 - x_2 + x_3 = 0$
8. $x_1 + 2x_2 + 3x_3 = 0$, $2x_1 + x_2 + 4x_3 = 0$, $5x_1 - 6x_2 + 2x_3 = 0$
9. $x + 2z - 2w = 0$, $2x - y - w = 0$, $x + 2z - w = 0$, $4x - y + 3z - w = 0$
10. $4x + 2y + z + 3w = 0$, $6x + 3y + 4z + 7w = 0$, $2x + y + w = 0$
11. $3x_1 + 4x_2 - x_3 - 6x_4 = 0$, $2x_1 + 3x_2 + 2x_3 - 3x_4 = 0$
    $2x_1 + x_2 - 14x_3 - 9x_4 = 0$, $x_1 + 3x_2 + 13x_3 + 3x_4 = 0$

II. Find the values of λ for which the following equations has a non-zero solution :

(i) $(3\lambda - 8)x + 3y + 3z = 0$
$3x + (3\lambda - 8)y + 3z = 0$
$3x + 3y + (3\lambda - 8)z = 0$

(ii) $2x + 3y - 2z = 0$
$3x - y + 3z = 0$
$7x + \lambda y - z = 0$

(iii) $x_1 + \lambda x_2 + 2x_3 = 0$
$2x_1 + x_2 - x_3 = 0$
$4x_1 + 2x_2 - 5x_3 = 0$

III. Determine the values of λ for which following sets of equations possess a non-trivial solution and obtain these solutions for the real values of λ.

(i) $(1 - \lambda)x_1 + 2x_2 + 3x_3 = 0$
$3x_1 + (1 - \lambda)x_2 + 2x_3 = 0$
$2x_1 + 3x_2 + (1 - \lambda)x_3 = 0$

(ii) $x + 4y + 2z = 0$
$4x + 9y + z = 0$
$\lambda x + 3y + \lambda z = 0$

(iii) $2x_1 - 2x_2 + x_3 = \lambda x_1$
$2x_1 - 3x_2 + 2x_3 = \lambda x_2$
$-x_1 + 2x_2 = \lambda x_3$

IV. Show that the system of equations :
$$x + z = 0$$
$$y + z = 0$$
$$z + w = 0$$
$$w + x = 0 \text{ has only a trivial solution.}$$

ANSWERS 2.1

I. 1. $x = 6k$, $y = -3k$, $z = 0$, $w = k$, where k is a parameter.

2. $x = -\frac{2}{3}(t_1 + t_2)$, $y = -\frac{1}{21}(29t_1 + 14t_2)$, $z = t_2$, $w = t_1$, where t_1 and t_2 are parameters.

3. Trivial solution $x = y = z = 0$.

4. $x_1 = -t$, $x_2 = t$ and $x_3 = t$ where t is a parameter.
5. $x = -t$, $y = 0$, $z = t$ where t is a parameter.
6. $x = -\dfrac{10t}{7}$, $y = \dfrac{8t}{7}$, $z = t$ where t is a parameter.
7. $x_1 = -2t$, $x_2 = -t$, $x_3 = t$ where t is a parameter.
8. Trivial solution $x_1 = 0 = x_2 = x_3$.
9. Trivial solution $x = y = z = w = 0$.
10. $x = t_2$, $y = -2t_2 - t_1$, $z = -t_1$ and $w = t_1$ where t_1 and t_2 are parameters.
11. $x = 11t_1 + 6t_2$, $y = -8t_1 - 3t_2$, $z = t_1$, $w = t_2$ where t_1 and t_2 are parameters.

II.
(i) $\lambda = 2/3,\ 11/3$
(ii) $\lambda = 5$
(iii) $\lambda = 1/2$

III.
(i) $\lambda = 6;\ x_1 = x_2 = x_3 = t$
(ii) $\lambda = 1;\ x = 2t,\ y = -t,\ z = t$
(iii) $\lambda = 1;\ x_1 = 2t_2 - t_1,\ x_2 = t_2,\ z = t_1$
$\lambda = -3;\ x_1 = t,\ x_2 = -2t,\ x_3 = t$.

2.4 NON-HOMOGENEOUS SYSTEM OF LINEAR EQUATIONS

Consider the system of m linear equations in n unknowns.

$$\left.\begin{array}{l} a_{11}x_1 + a_{12}x_2 + a_{13}x_3 + \ldots + a_{1n}x_n = b_1 \\ a_{21}x_1 + a_{22}x_2 + a_{23}x_3 + \ldots + a_{2n}x_n = b_2 \\ a_{31}x_1 + a_{32}x_2 + a_{33}x_3 + \ldots + a_{3n}x_n = b_3 \\ \ldots\ldots\ldots\ldots\ldots\ldots\ldots\ldots\ldots\ldots\ldots\ldots\ldots\ldots \\ a_{m1}x_1 + a_{m2}x_2 + a_{m3}x_3 + \ldots + a_{mn}x_n = b_m \end{array}\right\} \quad \ldots (1)$$

The matrix equation of a system (1) is

$$AX = B$$

where
$$A = \begin{bmatrix} a_{11} & a_{12} & \ldots & a_{1n} \\ a_{21} & a_{22} & \ldots & a_{2n} \\ \ldots & \ldots & \ldots & \ldots \\ a_{m1} & a_{m2} & \ldots & a_{mn} \end{bmatrix}$$

is called the coefficient matrix of the system.

and $X = (x_1, x_2, \ldots, x_n)'$, $B = (b_1, b_2, \ldots, b_m)'$

are respectively called matrix of unknowns and column of constants.

$$\text{The matrix } [A, B] = \begin{bmatrix} a_{11} & a_{12} & \ldots & a_{1n} & : & b_1 \\ a_{21} & a_{22} & \ldots & a_{2n} & : & b_2 \\ \ldots & \ldots & \ldots & \ldots & & \ldots \\ a_{m1} & a_{m2} & \ldots & a_{mn} & : & b_m \end{bmatrix} \quad \ldots (2)$$

is called the augmented matrix of the system.

2.4.1 Some Important Results

1. If $\rho(A) < \rho([A, B])$, then the equations $AX = B$ are inconsistent.
2. If $\rho(A) = \rho([A, B])$, then the equations $AX = B$ are consistent.

2.4.2 Nature of the General Solution

Consider the system (1) of (2.4). Then the coefficient matrix A will be of order $m \times n$. Let $\rho(A) = r$ and $\rho([A, B]) = r_1$ be their ranks.

Case I : Consistent equations : If $r = r_1$

(a) **Unique solution :** $r = r_1 = n$ where, n = number of unknowns.

(b) **Infinite solution :** $r = r_1$, $r < n$.

Here the number of parameters or the number of independent solutions = $n - r$.

Case II : Inconsistent equations : If $r \neq r_1$ ($r < r_1$).

2.4.3 Chart of Nature of Solution

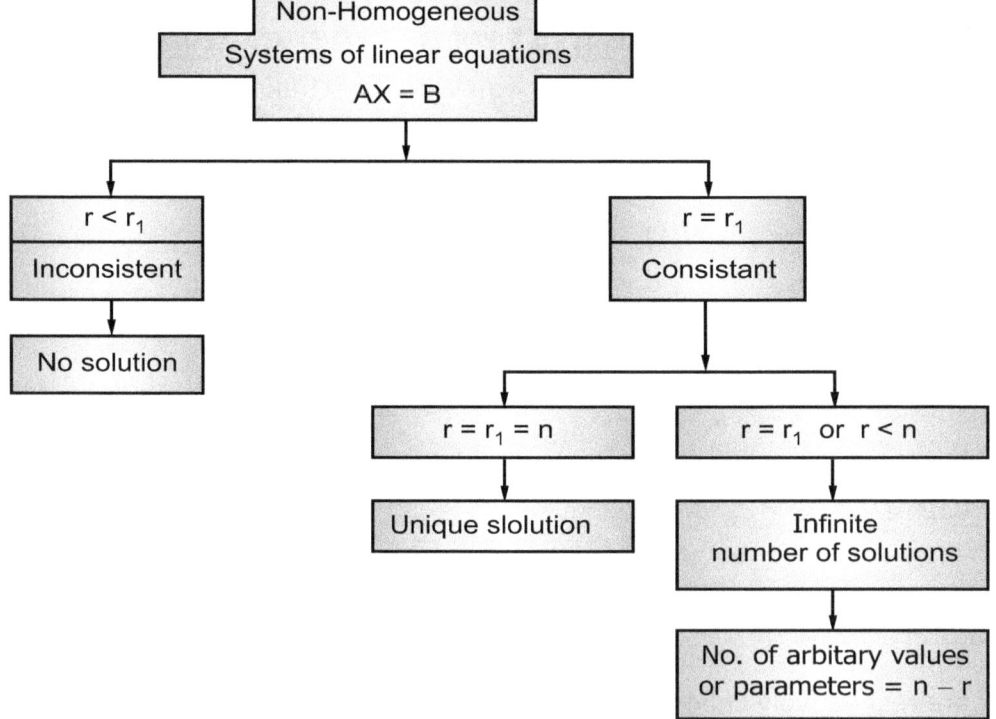

2.4.4 Procedure To Test Consistency

(i) Write the system in matrix form AX = B, where A is a matrix of order m × n.

(ii) Write the coefficient matrix A and the augmented matrix [A, B].

(iii) Reduce the system AX = B in echelon/triangular form by using row transformations only.

(iv) Find the rank of A and [A, B] say r and r_1 respectively and noting rank of matrix is equal number of non-zero rows in (iii).

(v) Rewrite (iii) as a set of linear equations.

(vi) Use the above nature of the general solution or chart of nature of solution.

SOLVED EXAMPLES

Example 2.7 : Test for consistency

$$2x + 6y = -11$$
$$6x + 20y - 6z = 3$$
$$6y - 18z = -1$$

Solution : The matrix equation of the given system is

$$\begin{bmatrix} 2 & 6 & 0 \\ 6 & 20 & -6 \\ 0 & 6 & -18 \end{bmatrix} \begin{bmatrix} x \\ y \\ z \end{bmatrix} = \begin{bmatrix} -11 \\ -3 \\ -1 \end{bmatrix}$$

$\xrightarrow{R_2 - 3R_1}$ $\begin{bmatrix} 2 & 6 & 0 \\ 0 & 2 & -6 \\ 0 & 6 & -18 \end{bmatrix} \begin{bmatrix} x \\ y \\ z \end{bmatrix} = \begin{bmatrix} -11 \\ 30 \\ -1 \end{bmatrix}$

$\xrightarrow{R_3 - 3R_2}$ $\begin{bmatrix} 2 & 6 & 0 \\ 0 & 2 & -6 \\ 0 & 0 & 0 \end{bmatrix} \begin{bmatrix} x \\ y \\ z \end{bmatrix} = \begin{bmatrix} -11 \\ 30 \\ -91 \end{bmatrix}$

This is in echelon/triangular form.

Here, $A = \begin{bmatrix} 2 & 6 & 0 \\ 0 & 2 & -6 \\ 0 & 0 & 0 \end{bmatrix}$ and $[A, B] = \begin{bmatrix} 2 & 6 & 0 & : & -11 \\ 0 & 2 & -6 & : & 30 \\ 0 & 0 & 0 & : & -91 \end{bmatrix}$

∴ $\rho(A)$ = number of non-zero rows in A
    = 2

and $\rho([A, B])$ = number of non-zero rows in augment matrix [A, B]
= 3

∴ $\rho(A) < \rho([A, B])$

∴ The system is inconsistent.

Example 2.8 : Find the augmented matrix [A, B] of the following system and reduce it to echelon form

$$x + y + 3z = 1$$
$$2x + 3y - z = 3$$
$$5x + 7y + z = 7$$

Solution : Here, the augmented matrix [A, B] is

$$= \begin{bmatrix} 1 & 1 & 3 & : & 1 \\ 2 & 3 & -1 & : & 3 \\ 5 & 7 & 1 & : & 7 \end{bmatrix}$$

$$\xrightarrow[R_3 - 5R_1]{R_2 - 2R_1} \begin{bmatrix} 1 & 1 & 3 & : & 1 \\ 0 & 1 & -7 & : & 1 \\ 0 & 2 & -14 & : & 2 \end{bmatrix}$$

$$\xrightarrow{R_3 - 2R_1} \begin{bmatrix} 1 & 1 & 3 & : & 1 \\ 0 & 1 & -7 & : & 1 \\ 0 & 0 & 0 & : & 0 \end{bmatrix}$$

This is in echelon form.

Example 2.9 : Test for consistency and solve :

$$x - 2y = 5$$
$$2x + 3y = 3$$
$$3x + 2y = 7$$

Solution : The matrix equation of the given system is

$$\begin{bmatrix} 1 & -2 \\ 2 & 3 \\ 3 & 2 \end{bmatrix} \begin{bmatrix} x \\ y \end{bmatrix} = \begin{bmatrix} 5 \\ 3 \\ 7 \end{bmatrix}$$

$$\xrightarrow[R_3 - 3R_1]{R_2 - 2R_1} \begin{bmatrix} 1 & -2 \\ 0 & 7 \\ 0 & 8 \end{bmatrix} \begin{bmatrix} x \\ y \end{bmatrix} = \begin{bmatrix} 5 \\ -7 \\ -8 \end{bmatrix}$$

$$\xrightarrow[(1/8) R_3]{(1/7) R_2} \begin{bmatrix} 1 & -2 \\ 0 & 1 \\ 0 & 1 \end{bmatrix} \begin{bmatrix} x \\ y \end{bmatrix} = \begin{bmatrix} 5 \\ -1 \\ -1 \end{bmatrix}$$

$$\xrightarrow{R_3 - R_2} \begin{bmatrix} 1 & -2 \\ 0 & 1 \\ 0 & 0 \end{bmatrix} \begin{bmatrix} x \\ y \end{bmatrix} = \begin{bmatrix} 5 \\ -1 \\ 0 \end{bmatrix} \quad \ldots (i)$$

This is in echelon form.

Here, $A = \begin{bmatrix} 1 & -2 \\ 0 & 1 \\ 0 & 0 \end{bmatrix}$ and $[A, B] = \begin{bmatrix} 1 & -2 & : & 5 \\ 0 & 1 & : & -1 \\ 0 & 0 & : & 0 \end{bmatrix}$

∴ $\rho(A) = r = 2$ and $\rho([A, B]) = 2 = r_1$

∴ $r = r_1$

Therefore, the system is consistent.

Further, $r = n$ where 'n' is number of unknowns.

Hence, the system has unique solution.

Now, from equation (i)

$$x - 2y = 5$$
$$y = -1$$

∴ $x - 2(-1) = 5$

∴ $x + 2 = 5$

∴ $x = 3$

∴ The solution is $x = 3, y = -1$.

Example 2.10 : Show that the following equations are consistent and solve them.

$$x + y + z + w = 1$$
$$2x - y + z - 2w = 2$$
$$3x + 2y - z - w = 3$$

Solution : The matrix equation of the given system is

$$\begin{bmatrix} 1 & 1 & 1 & 1 \\ 2 & -1 & 1 & -2 \\ 3 & 2 & -1 & -1 \end{bmatrix} \begin{bmatrix} x \\ y \\ z \\ w \end{bmatrix} = \begin{bmatrix} 1 \\ 2 \\ 3 \end{bmatrix}$$

$$\xrightarrow[R_3 - 3R_1]{R_2 - 2R_1} \begin{bmatrix} 1 & 1 & 1 & 1 \\ 0 & -3 & -1 & -4 \\ 0 & -1 & -4 & -4 \end{bmatrix} \begin{bmatrix} x \\ y \\ z \\ w \end{bmatrix} = \begin{bmatrix} 1 \\ 0 \\ 0 \end{bmatrix}$$

$$\xrightarrow[R_{23}]{(-1)R_2 \text{ and } (-1)R_3} \begin{bmatrix} 1 & 1 & 1 & 1 \\ 0 & 1 & 4 & 4 \\ 0 & 3 & 1 & 4 \end{bmatrix} \begin{bmatrix} x \\ y \\ z \\ w \end{bmatrix} = \begin{bmatrix} 1 \\ 0 \\ 0 \end{bmatrix}$$

$$\xrightarrow{R_3 - 3R_2} \begin{bmatrix} 1 & 1 & 1 & 1 \\ 0 & 1 & 4 & 4 \\ 0 & 0 & -11 & -8 \end{bmatrix} \begin{bmatrix} x \\ y \\ z \\ w \end{bmatrix} = \begin{bmatrix} 1 \\ 0 \\ 0 \end{bmatrix} \quad \ldots \text{(i)}$$

This is in echelon form.

Here, coefficient matrix $A = \begin{bmatrix} 1 & 1 & 1 & 1 \\ 0 & 1 & 4 & 4 \\ 0 & 0 & -11 & -8 \end{bmatrix}$

and augmented matrix = $[A, B] = \begin{bmatrix} 1 & 1 & 1 & 1 & : & 1 \\ 0 & 1 & 4 & 4 & : & 0 \\ 0 & 0 & -11 & -8 & : & 0 \end{bmatrix}$

∴ $\rho(A) = r = 3$

and $\rho[A, B] = r_1 = 3$

∴ $\rho(A) = r = r_1 = \rho[A, B]$

Therefore, the system is consistent.

But $\quad n = $ number of unknowns $= 4$

∴ $\quad r < n$

∴ Number of parameters $= n - r = 4 - 3 = 1$

Again from equation (1)

$x + y + z + w = 1$ ... (ii)

$y + 4z + 4w = 0$ ... (iii)

$-11z - 8w = 0$ ... (iv)

Putting w = t in equation (iv), we get

$$-11z = 0 + 8t \Rightarrow z = -\frac{7t}{11}$$

Equation (iii) gives

$$y - \frac{4}{11}(0 + 8t) + 4t = 0 \Rightarrow y - \frac{32t}{11} + 4t = 0$$

$$\therefore y = -\frac{12t}{11}$$

Substituting these in equation (ii), we get

$$x = 1 + \frac{9t}{11}$$

∴ The solutions are $x = \frac{1}{11}(11 + 9t)$, $y = -\frac{12t}{11}$

$z = -\frac{8t}{11}$ and w = t where t is a parameter.

Example 2.11 : Solve :

$$4x - 5y - 2z - 2 = 0$$
$$5x - 4y + 2z + 2 = 0$$
$$2x + 2y + 8z - 1 = 0$$

Solution : Rewriting the given system

$$2x + 2y + 8z = 1$$
$$4x - 5y - 2z = 2$$
$$5x - 4y + 2z = -2$$

The matrix equation of this system is

$$\begin{bmatrix} 2 & 2 & 8 \\ 4 & -5 & -2 \\ 5 & -4 & 2 \end{bmatrix} \begin{bmatrix} x \\ y \\ z \end{bmatrix} = \begin{bmatrix} 1 \\ 2 \\ -2 \end{bmatrix}$$

$$\xrightarrow{R_3 - R_2} \begin{bmatrix} 2 & 2 & 8 \\ 4 & -5 & -2 \\ 1 & 1 & 4 \end{bmatrix} \begin{bmatrix} x \\ y \\ z \end{bmatrix} = \begin{bmatrix} 1 \\ 2 \\ -4 \end{bmatrix}$$

$$\xrightarrow[R_1 - 2R_3]{R_2 - 4R_3} \begin{bmatrix} 0 & 0 & 0 \\ 0 & -9 & -18 \\ 1 & 1 & 4 \end{bmatrix} \begin{bmatrix} x \\ y \\ z \end{bmatrix} = \begin{bmatrix} 9 \\ 18 \\ -4 \end{bmatrix}$$

Therefore, $\rho(A) = 2$ and $\rho([A, B]) = 3$

∴ $\rho(A) < \rho([A, B])$ i.e. $r < r_1$

Hence, the system is inconsistent.

Example 2.12 : Discuss the solution of the system of equations :

$$x + y + z = 6$$
$$2x + y + 3z = 13$$
$$5x + 2y + z = 12$$

Solution : The matrix equation of the given system is

$$\begin{bmatrix} 1 & 1 & 1 \\ 2 & 1 & 3 \\ 5 & 2 & 1 \end{bmatrix} \begin{bmatrix} x \\ y \\ z \end{bmatrix} = \begin{bmatrix} 6 \\ 13 \\ 12 \end{bmatrix}$$

$$\xrightarrow{\substack{R_2 - 2R_1 \\ R_3 - 5R_1}} \begin{bmatrix} 1 & 1 & 1 \\ 0 & -1 & 1 \\ 0 & -3 & -4 \end{bmatrix} \begin{bmatrix} x \\ y \\ z \end{bmatrix} = \begin{bmatrix} 6 \\ 1 \\ -18 \end{bmatrix}$$

$$\xrightarrow{R_3 - 3R_2} \begin{bmatrix} 1 & 1 & 1 \\ 0 & -1 & 1 \\ 0 & 0 & -7 \end{bmatrix} \begin{bmatrix} x \\ y \\ z \end{bmatrix} = \begin{bmatrix} 6 \\ 1 \\ -21 \end{bmatrix} \quad \ldots \text{(i)}$$

This is in echelon form.

∴ $\rho(A) = r = 3$ and $\rho([A, B]) = 3 = r_1$

∴ $r = r_1$

Therefore, system is consistent.

Further, n = number of variables
= 3

∴ r = n

∴ The system has unique solution.

From equation (i), we write

$$x + y + z = 6 \quad \ldots \text{(ii)}$$
$$-y + z = 1 \quad \ldots \text{(iii)}$$
$$-7z = -21 \quad \ldots \text{(iv)}$$

Equation (iv) $\Rightarrow z = 3$

∴ Equation (iii) becomes

$$-y + 3 = 1 \Rightarrow y = 2$$

Substituting these equation (ii), we get,
$$x = 1$$
∴ The solution is
$$x = 1, y = 2, z = 3.$$

Example 2.13 : Test for consistency and solve :
$$x_1 - 2x_2 + x_3 - x_4 = -1$$
$$3x_1 - 2x_3 + 3x_4 = 4$$
$$5x_1 - 4x_2 + x_4 = 2$$

Solution : The matrix equation of the given system is

$$\begin{bmatrix} 1 & -2 & 1 & -1 \\ 3 & 0 & -2 & 3 \\ 5 & -4 & 0 & 1 \end{bmatrix} \begin{bmatrix} x_1 \\ x_2 \\ x_3 \\ x_4 \end{bmatrix} = \begin{bmatrix} -1 \\ 4 \\ 2 \end{bmatrix}$$

$\xrightarrow{\begin{subarray}{l} R_2 - 3R_1 \\ R_3 - 5R_1 \end{subarray}}$ $\begin{bmatrix} 1 & -2 & 1 & -1 \\ 0 & 6 & -5 & 6 \\ 0 & 6 & -5 & 6 \end{bmatrix} \begin{bmatrix} x_1 \\ x_2 \\ x_3 \\ x_4 \end{bmatrix} = \begin{bmatrix} -1 \\ 7 \\ 7 \end{bmatrix}$

$\xrightarrow{R_3 - R_2}$ $\begin{bmatrix} 1 & -2 & 1 & -1 \\ 0 & 6 & -5 & 6 \\ 0 & 0 & 0 & 0 \end{bmatrix} \begin{bmatrix} x_1 \\ x_2 \\ x_3 \\ x_4 \end{bmatrix} = \begin{bmatrix} -1 \\ 7 \\ 0 \end{bmatrix}$

Clearly, $\rho(A) = \rho[A, B] = 02 = r$

But n = number of unknowns
$$= 4$$

∴ The number of parameters = $n - r = 4 - 2 = 2$.

From the above system, we have
$$x_1 - 2x_2 + x_3 - x_4 = -1 \quad \ldots (i)$$
$$6x_2 - 5x_3 + 6x_4 = 7 \quad \ldots (ii)$$

Putting $x_3 = t_1$ and $x_4 = t_2$ in equation (ii), we get
$$x_2 = \frac{5t_1}{6} - t_2 + \frac{7}{6}$$

Substituting these in equation (i), we get

$$x_1 = \frac{2t_1}{3} - t_2 + \frac{4}{3}$$

∴ The solutions are

$$x_1 = \frac{2t_1}{3} - t_2 + \frac{4}{3}, \quad x_2 = \frac{5t_1}{6} - t_2 + \frac{7}{6}, \quad x_3 = t_1 \text{ and } x_4 = t_2$$

where, t_1 and t_2 are parameters.

Example 2.14 : For what values of η, the equations :

$$x + 2y + z = 3$$
$$x + y + z = \eta$$
$$3x + y + 3z = \eta^2$$

have a solution and solve them completely in each case.

Solution : The matrix equation of the given system is

$$\begin{bmatrix} 1 & 2 & 1 \\ 1 & 1 & 1 \\ 3 & 1 & 3 \end{bmatrix} \begin{bmatrix} x \\ y \\ z \end{bmatrix} = \begin{bmatrix} 3 \\ \eta \\ \eta^2 \end{bmatrix}$$

$$\xrightarrow[R_3 - 3R_1]{R_2 - R_1} \begin{bmatrix} 1 & 2 & 1 \\ 0 & -1 & 0 \\ 0 & -5 & 0 \end{bmatrix} \begin{bmatrix} x \\ y \\ z \end{bmatrix} = \begin{bmatrix} 3 \\ \eta - 3 \\ \eta^2 - 9 \end{bmatrix}$$

$$\xrightarrow{R_3 - 5R_2} \begin{bmatrix} 1 & 2 & 1 \\ 0 & -1 & 0 \\ 0 & 0 & 0 \end{bmatrix} \begin{bmatrix} x \\ y \\ z \end{bmatrix} = \begin{bmatrix} 3 \\ \eta - 3 \\ \eta^2 - 5\eta + 6 \end{bmatrix} \quad \ldots \text{(I)}$$

∴ The system is consistent if $\rho(A) = \rho([A, B])$.

For this $\eta^2 - 5\eta + 6$ must be zero.

∴ $\eta^2 - 5\eta + 6 = 0$

$\Rightarrow (\eta - 3)(\eta - 2) = 0$

∴ $\eta = 2, 3$.

Case I : For $\eta = 2$, equation (I) becomes

$$\begin{bmatrix} 1 & 2 & 1 \\ 0 & -1 & 0 \\ 0 & 0 & 0 \end{bmatrix} \begin{bmatrix} x \\ y \\ z \end{bmatrix} = \begin{bmatrix} 3 \\ -1 \\ 0 \end{bmatrix} \quad \ldots \text{(II)}$$

Here, $\rho(A) = \rho([A, B]) = r = 2$
and n = number of unknowns = 3
∴ $r < n$
∴ The system has infinite solutions.
The number of parameters = $n - r = 1$.
From equation (II),
$$x + 2y + z = 3 \qquad \ldots \text{(i)}$$
$$+ y = + 1 \qquad \ldots \text{(ii)}$$
From equation (i) and (ii), we have
$$x + z = 1$$
Putting $z = t$, we get
$$x = 1 - t$$
∴ The solutions are
$x = 1 - t$, $y = 1$ and $z = t$, where t is a parameter.

Case II : For $\eta = 3$, equation (I) becomes
$$\begin{bmatrix} 1 & 2 & 1 \\ 0 & -1 & 0 \\ 0 & 0 & 0 \end{bmatrix} \begin{bmatrix} x \\ y \\ z \end{bmatrix} = \begin{bmatrix} 3 \\ 0 \\ 0 \end{bmatrix} \qquad \ldots \text{(iii)}$$

∴ $\rho(A) = \rho([A, B]) = r = 2$
and $n = 3$.
∴ $r < n \Rightarrow$ the system has infinite number of solutions number of parameters = $n - r = 1$.
From equation (iii),
$$x + 2y + z = 3 \qquad \ldots \text{(iv)}$$
$$-y = 0 \Rightarrow y = 0$$
∴ $x + z = 0$ (From (iv))
∴ $x + z = 3$
Putting $z = t$, we have
$$x = 3 - t.$$
∴ The solutions are $x = 3 - t$, $y = 0$, $z = t$, where t is a parameters.

Example 2.15 : For what values of λ will the following system of equations fail to have a unique solution ? Will the system have any solutions for these values of λ ?
$$\lambda x + y + z = 1$$
$$x + \lambda y + z = 1$$
$$x + y + \lambda z = -2$$

Solution : The matrix equation of the given system is

$$\begin{bmatrix} \lambda & 1 & 1 \\ 1 & \lambda & 1 \\ 1 & 1 & \lambda \end{bmatrix} \begin{bmatrix} x \\ y \\ z \end{bmatrix} = \begin{bmatrix} 1 \\ 1 \\ -2 \end{bmatrix} \qquad \ldots \text{(I)}$$

Since the system will have no unique solution if

$$|A| = 0 \Rightarrow \begin{vmatrix} \lambda & 1 & 1 \\ 1 & \lambda & 1 \\ 1 & 1 & \lambda \end{vmatrix} = 0$$

∴ $\lambda(\lambda^2 - 1) - 1(\lambda - 1) + 1(1 - \lambda) = 0$

i.e. $\lambda^3 - 3\lambda + 2 = 0$

∴ $(\lambda - 1)^2 (\lambda + 2) = 0$

∴ $\lambda = 1, 1, -2$.

Case I : For $\lambda = 1$, equation (I) becomes

$$\begin{bmatrix} 1 & 1 & 1 \\ 1 & 1 & 1 \\ 1 & 1 & 1 \end{bmatrix} \begin{bmatrix} x \\ y \\ z \end{bmatrix} = \begin{bmatrix} 1 \\ 1 \\ -2 \end{bmatrix}$$

$$\xrightarrow[R_3 - R_1]{R_2 - R_1} \begin{bmatrix} 1 & 1 & 1 \\ 0 & 0 & 0 \\ 0 & 0 & 0 \end{bmatrix} \begin{bmatrix} x \\ y \\ z \end{bmatrix} = \begin{bmatrix} 1 \\ 0 \\ -3 \end{bmatrix}$$

∴ $\rho(A) \neq \rho([A, B])$

∴ The system is inconsistent.

Case II : For $\lambda = -2$, equation (I) becomes,

$$\begin{bmatrix} -2 & 1 & 1 \\ 1 & -2 & 1 \\ 1 & 1 & -2 \end{bmatrix} \begin{bmatrix} x \\ y \\ z \end{bmatrix} = \begin{bmatrix} 1 \\ 1 \\ -2 \end{bmatrix}$$

$$\xrightarrow{R_{13}} \begin{bmatrix} 1 & 1 & -2 \\ 1 & -2 & 1 \\ -2 & 1 & 1 \end{bmatrix} \begin{bmatrix} x \\ y \\ z \end{bmatrix} = \begin{bmatrix} -2 \\ 1 \\ 1 \end{bmatrix}$$

$$\xrightarrow[R_3 + 2R_1]{R_2 - R_1} \begin{bmatrix} 1 & 1 & -2 \\ 0 & -3 & 3 \\ 0 & 3 & -3 \end{bmatrix} \begin{bmatrix} x \\ y \\ z \end{bmatrix} = \begin{bmatrix} -2 \\ 3 \\ -3 \end{bmatrix}$$

$$\xrightarrow{R_3 + R_2} \begin{bmatrix} 1 & 1 & -2 \\ 0 & -3 & 3 \\ 0 & 0 & 0 \end{bmatrix} \begin{bmatrix} x \\ y \\ z \end{bmatrix} = \begin{bmatrix} -2 \\ 3 \\ 0 \end{bmatrix}$$

$$\xrightarrow{(1/3) R_2} \begin{bmatrix} 1 & 1 & -2 \\ 0 & -1 & 1 \\ 0 & 0 & 0 \end{bmatrix} \begin{bmatrix} x \\ y \\ z \end{bmatrix} = \begin{bmatrix} -2 \\ 1 \\ 0 \end{bmatrix} \quad \ldots \text{(II)}$$

Here $\rho(A) = \rho[A, B] = r = 2$

and $n = 3$.

$\therefore$ $r < n \Rightarrow$ system has infinite solutions.

Number of parameters = $n - r = 1$.

From (II), we write

$$x + y - 2z = -2 \quad \ldots \text{(III)}$$
$$-y + z = 1 \quad \ldots \text{(IV)}$$

Putting $y = t$ in (IV), we get

$\therefore \quad z = 1 + t$

Putting these values in equation (III), we have

$$x + t - 2 - 2t = -2$$

$\therefore \quad x - t = 0$

$\therefore \quad x = t$

$\therefore$ The solutions are $x = t$, $y = t$ and $z = 1 + t$ where t is a parameter.

Example 2.16 : Investigate for what values of λ and μ, the following system of equations :

$2x + 3y + 5z = 9$, $7x + 3y - 2z = 8$, $2x + 3y + \lambda z = \mu$ will have (i) no solution, (ii) a unique solution, (iii) infinite number of solutions.

Solution : The matrix equation of the given system is

$$\begin{bmatrix} 2 & 3 & 5 \\ 7 & 3 & -2 \\ 2 & 3 & \lambda \end{bmatrix} \begin{bmatrix} x \\ y \\ z \end{bmatrix} = \begin{bmatrix} 9 \\ 8 \\ \mu \end{bmatrix}$$

$$\xrightarrow[R_3 - R_1]{R_2 - 3R_1} \begin{bmatrix} 2 & 3 & 5 \\ 1 & -6 & -17 \\ 0 & 0 & \lambda - 5 \end{bmatrix} \begin{bmatrix} x \\ y \\ z \end{bmatrix} = \begin{bmatrix} 9 \\ -19 \\ \mu - 9 \end{bmatrix}$$

(i) If $\lambda = 5$ and $\mu \neq 9$, then $\rho(A) = 2 = r$ and $\rho([A, B]) = r_1 = 3$.

∴ $r < r_1$ ⇒ The system has no solution.

(ii) The system has unique solution if $|A| \neq 0$ (i.e. $\rho(A) = r = n = 3$).

This requires $\lambda - 5 \neq 0$.

∴ $\lambda \neq 5$.

Thus, if $\lambda \neq 5$ the system has unique solution for any μ.

(iii) If $\lambda = 5$ then the above system becomes.

$$\begin{bmatrix} 2 & 3 & 5 \\ 1 & -6 & -17 \\ 0 & 0 & 0 \end{bmatrix} \begin{bmatrix} x \\ y \\ z \end{bmatrix} = \begin{bmatrix} 9 \\ -19 \\ \mu - 9 \end{bmatrix}$$

∴ $\rho(A) = 2$ but $\rho([A, B])$ will be 2 if $\mu - 9 = 0$.

∴ The system is consistent and will possess infinite solutions if $\lambda = 5$ and $\mu = 9$.

EXERCISE 2.2

1. Test for consistency the following systems of equations and if possible solve completely in each case.

1. $x + 2y + 3z = 3$
   $2x + 3y + 8z = 4$
   $5x + 8y + 19z = 11$

2. $x + 2y + 3z = 14$
   $3x + y + 2z = 11$
   $2x + 3y + z = 11$

3. $2x_1 - x_2 - 4x_3 = 2$
   $4x_1 - 2x_2 - 6x_3 = 5$
   $6x_1 - 3x_2 - 8x_3 = 8$

4. $x - 3y - 2z = 6$
   $2x - 4y - 3z = 8$
   $-3x + 6y + 8z = -5$

5. $x_1 + 2x_2 + x_3 - 3 = 0$
   $2x_1 + 5x_2 - x_3 + 4 = 0$
   $3x_1 - 2x_2 - x_3 - 5 = 0$

6. $x_1 + 2x_2 - x_3 = 3$
   $3x_1 - x_2 + 2x_3 = 1$
   $2x_1 - 2x_2 + 3x_3 = 2$
   $x_1 - x_2 + x_3 = -1$

7. $x_1 + x_2 + 3x_3 = 1$
   $2x_1 + 3x_2 - x_3 = 3$
   $5x_1 + 7x_2 + x_3 = 7$

8. $x + 2y - 3z + 4w = 2$
   $2x + 5y - 3z + w = 1$
   $5x + 12y - 7z + 6w = 3$

9. $5x + 3y + 7z = 4$
   $3x + 26y + 2z = 9$
   $7x + 2y + 10z = 5$

10. $x_1 + 2x_2 + 3x_3 = 1$
    $x_1 + 3x_2 + 6x_3 = 3$
    $2x_1 + 6x_2 + 13x_3 = 5$

11. $x + 2y - 3z = 2$
    $2x + 3y + z = 4$
    $3x + 4y + 5z = 8$

12. $x_1 + 3x_2 - 2x_3 + 5x_4 = 4$
    $2x_1 + 8x_2 - x_3 + 9x_4 = 9$
    $3x_1 + 5x_2 - 12x_3 + 17x_4 = 7$

13. $x - y + z = 1$
    $2x - 2y + 4z = 4$
    $x - y + 3z = 3$

14. $x + 3y - z = 4$
    $2x + y + z = 7$
    $2x - 4y + 4z = 6$
    $3x + 4y = 11$

15. $2x - y + z = 4$
    $3x - y + z = 6$
    $4x - y + 2z = 7$
    $+ x - y + z = -9$

16. $x + y + z = 1$
    $x + 2y + 3z = 4$
    $x + 3y + 5z = 7$
    $x + 4y + 7z = 10$

17. $2x_1 - 3x_2 + 7x_3 = 5$
    $3x_1 + x_2 - 3x_3 = 13$
    $2x_1 + 19x_2 - 47x_3 = 32$

18. $2x + y + 5z = 4$
    $3x - 2y + 2z = 2$
    $5x - 8y - 4z = 1$

19. $x - y + 2z + w = 2$
    $3x + 2y + w = 1$
    $4x + y + 2z + 2w = 3$

2. For what value of λ the equations :
    $x + y + 4z = 1$
    $x + 2y - 2z = 1$
    $\lambda x + y + z = 1$ will have a unique solution.

3. For what value of λ the equations :
    $x + 2y + z = 2$
    $\lambda x + 3y - z = 1$
    $\lambda x - y - 2z = 1$ fail to have a unique solution ?

4. Show that the following systems of equations are inconsistent.
    1. $x_1 + x_2 + 2x_3 = 4$
       $2x_1 + 3x_2 + 6x_3 = 10$
       $3x_1 + 6x_2 + 10x_3 = 17$
    2. $x + y + z + 3 = 0$
       $3x + y - 2z + 2 = 0$
       $2x + 4y + 7z - 7 = 0$
    3. $4x - 5y - 2z - 2 = 0$
       $5x - 4y + 2z + 2 = 0$
       $2x + 2y + 8z - 1 = 0$
    4. $x_1 - 2x_2 + 3x_3 = 2$
       $2x_1 - 3x_2 + 8x_3 = 7$
       $3x_1 - 4x_2 + 13x_3 = 8$
    5. $2x + 6y = -11,\ 6x + 20y - 6z = -3,\ 6y - 18z = -1.$

5. For what values of η, the equations :

$$x + y + z = 1$$
$$2x + y - 4z = \eta$$
$$4x + 5y + 10z = \eta^2$$

have a solution and solve them completely in each case.

6. Investigate for what values of λ and μ, the following systems of equations :

$$x + y + z = 6$$
$$x + 2y + 3z = 10$$
$$x + 2y + \lambda z = \mu$$

will have (i) no solution, (ii) a unique solution and (iii) an infinity of solutions.

7. Short answer questions :

(a) Discuss the nature of solution of homogeneous system of m equations in n unknowns.

(b) Define the terms consistency and inconsistency.

(c) Discuss the consistency of non-homogeneous system of m linear equations in n unknowns.

ANSWERS 2.2

1.
1. $x = 1 - 5t$, $y = 2t + 2$, $z = t$.
2. $x = 1$, $y = 2$, $z = 3$.
3. $x = t$, $y = 2t - 4$, $z = 1/2$.
4. $x = 1$, $y = -3$, $z = 2$.
5. $x_1 = 2$, $x_2 = -1$, $x_3 = 3$.
6. $x_1 = -1$, $x_2 = 4$, $x_3 = 4$.
7. $x_1 = -10t$, $x_2 = 1 + 7t$, $x_3 = t$.
8. Inconsistent.
9. $x = \frac{1}{11}(7 - 16t)$, $y = \frac{1}{11}(3 + t)$, $z = t$.
10. $x_1 = -6$, $x_2 = 5$, $x_3 = -1$.
11. Inconsistent.
12. No solution.

13. $x = t, y = t, z = 1$.
14. $x = \dfrac{1}{5}(17 - 4t), y = \dfrac{1}{5}(1 + 3t), z = t$.
15. No solution.
16. $x = t - 2, y = 3 - 2t, z = t$.
17. Inconsistent.
18. Inconsistent.
19. $x = 1 - \dfrac{4t_1}{5} - \dfrac{3t_2}{5}, y = \dfrac{6t_1}{5} + \dfrac{2t_2}{5} - 1, z = t_1, w = t_2$.

2. $\lambda \neq \dfrac{7}{10}$

3. $\lambda = -\dfrac{7}{2}$

5. $\lambda = 2, -3$
   $\lambda = 2 : x = 1 - 7t, y = -6t, z = t$
   $\lambda = -3 : x = -4 + 5t, y = 5 - 6t, z = t$.

6. (i) No solution if $\lambda = 3$ and $\mu \neq 10$.
   (ii) Unique solution if $\lambda \neq 3$ and μ may be any value.
   (iii) Infinite solutions if $\lambda = 3$ and $\mu = 10$.

2.5 EIGENVALUES AND EIGENVECTORS

As we have already studied (discussed) the terms characteristic matrix, characteristic polynomial and characteristic equation in chapter I of a square matrix of order n. These terms are used to find the eigenvalues and eigenvectors.

Definition : If A is a square matrix of order n, then the values of λ for which the equation $AX = \lambda X$ or $(A - \lambda I) X = 0$. ... (1)

has non-trivial solutions are called the eigenvalues of A. Eigenvalues are also called proper values or characteristic roots or Latent roots.

Definition : If λ is an eigenvalue, then the non-zero vector X satisfying (1), is called the eigenvector of A. Eigenvectors are also called characteristic vector or latent vectors or proper vectors.

Remark : The equations $(A - \lambda I) X = O$ will have a non-zero solution if and only if $|A - \lambda I| = 0$ i.e. if and only if, λ is a root of the characteristic equation of A.

Trace of a square matrix :

Let $A = (a_{ij})$ be a square matrix of order n then

$$\text{Trace } A = a_{11} + a_{22} + \ldots + a_{nn} = \sum_{i=1}^{n} a_{ii}$$

2.5.1 Some Important Results

1. If λ is an eigenvalue of the matrix A, then
   (i) λ^m is an eigenvalue of A^m.
   (ii) $k\lambda$ is an eigenvalue of kA, where k is a scalar.
   (iii) $f(\lambda)$ is an eigenvalue of polynomial f(A).
   (iv) λ is also an eigenvalue of A'.
   (v) $1/\lambda$ is an eigenvalue of A^{-1}, if $|A| \neq 0$.
2. $\lambda = 0$ is an eigenvalue of the matrix A if and only if A is singular i.e. $|A| = 0$.
3. The eignevalues of a triangular matrix are its diagonal elements.
4. The sum of the eigenvalues of a square matrix of order n is equal to the trace of the matrix.
5. The product of the eigenvalues of a square matrix of order n is equal to the determinant of the matrix.
6. Any square matrix A and its transpose A' have the same eignevalues.

SOLVED EXAMPLES

Example 2.17 : Is $\begin{bmatrix} 1 \\ 4 \end{bmatrix}$ an eigenvector of $\begin{bmatrix} -3 & 1 \\ -3 & 8 \end{bmatrix}$?

Solution : Let $A = \begin{bmatrix} -3 & 1 \\ -3 & 8 \end{bmatrix}$ and $X = \begin{bmatrix} 1 \\ 4 \end{bmatrix}$

Consider, $AX = \begin{bmatrix} -3 & 1 \\ -3 & 8 \end{bmatrix} \begin{bmatrix} 1 \\ 4 \end{bmatrix}$

$= \begin{bmatrix} -3 + 4 \\ -3 + 32 \end{bmatrix} = \begin{bmatrix} 1 \\ 29 \end{bmatrix}$

$\neq \lambda \begin{bmatrix} 1 \\ 4 \end{bmatrix}$

$\therefore X = \begin{bmatrix} 1 \\ 4 \end{bmatrix}$ is not an eigenvector of A, because AX is not a multiple of X.

Example 2.18 : Is $\begin{bmatrix} 6 \\ -5 \end{bmatrix}$ an eigenvector of $\begin{bmatrix} 1 & 6 \\ 5 & 2 \end{bmatrix}$?

If so, find the eigenvalue.

Solution : Let $A = \begin{bmatrix} 1 & 6 \\ 5 & 2 \end{bmatrix}$ and $X = \begin{bmatrix} 6 \\ -5 \end{bmatrix}$

Consider, $AX = \begin{bmatrix} 1 & 6 \\ 5 & 2 \end{bmatrix} \begin{bmatrix} 6 \\ -5 \end{bmatrix} = \begin{bmatrix} -24 \\ 20 \end{bmatrix}$

$$= -4 \begin{bmatrix} 6 \\ -5 \end{bmatrix} = -4X$$

$\therefore \quad AX = -4X$

$\therefore \quad X = \begin{bmatrix} 6 \\ -5 \end{bmatrix}$ is an eigenvector of $A = \begin{bmatrix} 1 & 6 \\ 5 & 2 \end{bmatrix}$ and $\lambda = -4$ is the eigenvalue of A.

Example 2.19 : Show that 7 is an eigenvalue of $\begin{bmatrix} 1 & 6 \\ 5 & 2 \end{bmatrix}$ and find the corresponding eigenvector.

Solution : The number 7 is an eigenvalue of A if and only if the equation $AX = 7X$ has a non-zero solution. ... (1)

But equation (1) is euivalent to $(A - 7I) X = 0$.

i.e. $\left(\begin{bmatrix} 1 & 6 \\ 5 & 2 \end{bmatrix} - 7 \begin{bmatrix} 1 & 0 \\ 0 & 1 \end{bmatrix} \right) \begin{bmatrix} x \\ y \end{bmatrix} = \begin{bmatrix} 0 \\ 0 \end{bmatrix}$

$\therefore \begin{bmatrix} -6 & 6 \\ 5 & -5 \end{bmatrix} \begin{bmatrix} x \\ y \end{bmatrix} = \begin{bmatrix} 0 \\ 0 \end{bmatrix}$

$\xrightarrow{\substack{(1/6) R_1 \\ (1/5) R_2}} \begin{bmatrix} -1 & 1 \\ 1 & -1 \end{bmatrix} \begin{bmatrix} x \\ y \end{bmatrix} = \begin{bmatrix} 0 \\ 0 \end{bmatrix}$

$\xrightarrow{R_2 + R_1} \begin{bmatrix} -1 & 1 \\ 0 & 0 \end{bmatrix} \begin{bmatrix} x \\ y \end{bmatrix} = \begin{bmatrix} 0 \\ 0 \end{bmatrix}$

$\therefore \quad \rho((A - 7I)) = 1 = r$
But $\quad n = $ Number of unknowns $= 2$
Clearly $\quad r < n$.

$\therefore$ The system has non-trivial solution and number of free variables (parameters) $= n - r = 1$.

From above equation, we write $-x + y = 0$.
putting $y = t$, we get
$$x = t$$

∴ The general solution is $\begin{bmatrix} x \\ y \end{bmatrix} = \begin{bmatrix} t \\ t \end{bmatrix} = t \begin{bmatrix} 1 \\ 1 \end{bmatrix}$

Hence, 7 is an eigenvalue and $\begin{bmatrix} 1 \\ 1 \end{bmatrix}$ is the corresponding eigenvector.

Example 2.20 : Is 5 an eigenvalue of $\begin{bmatrix} 6 & -3 & 1 \\ 3 & 0 & 5 \\ 2 & 2 & 6 \end{bmatrix}$?

Solution : Let $A = \begin{bmatrix} 6 & -3 & 1 \\ 3 & 0 & 5 \\ 2 & 2 & 6 \end{bmatrix}$ and $\lambda = 5$.

The scalar 5 is an eigenvalue of A if and only if $(A - 5I) X = O$ has a non-trivial solution.

Consider $(A - 5I) X = O$

∴ $\left(\begin{bmatrix} 6 & -3 & 1 \\ 3 & 0 & 5 \\ 2 & 2 & 6 \end{bmatrix} - 5 \begin{bmatrix} 1 & 0 & 0 \\ 0 & 1 & 0 \\ 0 & 0 & 1 \end{bmatrix} \right) \begin{bmatrix} x \\ y \\ z \end{bmatrix} = \begin{bmatrix} 0 \\ 0 \\ 0 \end{bmatrix}$

i.e. $\begin{bmatrix} 1 & -3 & 1 \\ 3 & -5 & 5 \\ 2 & 2 & 1 \end{bmatrix} \begin{bmatrix} x \\ y \\ z \end{bmatrix} = \begin{bmatrix} 0 \\ 0 \\ 0 \end{bmatrix}$

$\xrightarrow{\underset{R_3 - 2R_1}{R_2 - 3R_1}}$ $\begin{bmatrix} 1 & -3 & 1 \\ 0 & 4 & 2 \\ 0 & 8 & -1 \end{bmatrix} \begin{bmatrix} x \\ y \\ z \end{bmatrix} = \begin{bmatrix} 0 \\ 0 \\ 0 \end{bmatrix}$

$\xrightarrow{R_3 - 2R_2}$ $\begin{bmatrix} 1 & -3 & 1 \\ 0 & 4 & 2 \\ 0 & 0 & -5 \end{bmatrix} \begin{bmatrix} x \\ y \\ z \end{bmatrix} = \begin{bmatrix} 0 \\ 0 \\ 0 \end{bmatrix}$

∴ $\rho(A - 5I) = r = 3$ but n = number of variables = 3.

∴ $r = n \Rightarrow$ The system has unique solution means it has no free variables. Thus, as $|A - 5I| \neq 0$, it is an invertible matrix, which means that 5 is not an eigenvalue of A.

Example 2.21 : Find the eigenvalues of $A = \begin{bmatrix} 2 & 3 \\ 3 & -6 \end{bmatrix}$.

Solution : Here, $A = \begin{bmatrix} 2 & 3 \\ 3 & -6 \end{bmatrix}$.

The characteristic equation of A is given by
$$|A - \lambda I| = 0$$
$$\left| \begin{bmatrix} 2 & 3 \\ 3 & -6 \end{bmatrix} - \lambda \begin{bmatrix} 1 & 0 \\ 0 & 1 \end{bmatrix} \right| = 0$$

$\therefore \begin{vmatrix} 2 - \lambda & 3 \\ 3 & -6 - \lambda \end{vmatrix} = 0$

$\therefore (2 - \lambda)(-6 - \lambda) - 9 = 0$

i.e. $-(2 - \lambda)(6 + \lambda) - 9 = 0$

$\therefore (2 - \lambda)(6 + \lambda) + 9 = 0$

$\therefore -\lambda^2 - 4\lambda + 21 = 0$

i.e. $\lambda^2 + 4\lambda - 21 = 0$

$\therefore (\lambda + 7)(\lambda - 3) = 0$

$\therefore \lambda = -7, 3$.

The eigenvalues of A are $-7, 3$.

Example 2.22 : If $A = \begin{bmatrix} 3 & 0 & 0 \\ 0 & 3 & \sqrt{2} \\ 0 & \sqrt{2} & 2 \end{bmatrix}$, then find the eigenvalues of A and $A^3 + A + 2I$.

Solution : The characteristic equation of A is
$$|A - \lambda I| = 0$$
$$\begin{vmatrix} 3 - \lambda & 0 & 0 \\ 0 & 3 - \lambda & \sqrt{2} \\ 0 & \sqrt{2} & 2 - \lambda \end{vmatrix} = 0$$

$\therefore (3 - \lambda)[(3 - \lambda)(2 - \lambda) - 2] - 0 + 0 = 0$

i.e. $(3 - \lambda)[\lambda^2 - 5\lambda + 4] = 0$

$\therefore (3 - \lambda)(\lambda - 1)(\lambda - 4) = 0$

Therefore the eigenvalues of A are 1, 3, 4.

Eigenvalues of $A^3 = 1^3, 3^3, 4^3 = 1, 27, 64$.

Eigenvalues of $A = 1, 3, 4$.

∴ Eigenvalues of $f(A) = A^3 + A + 2I$

First eigenvalue $= f(1) = 1 + 1 + 2 = 4$

Second eigenvalue $= f(3) = 27 + 3 + 2 = 32$

Third eigenvalue $= f(4) = 64 + 4 + 2 = 70$

∴ The required eigenvalues are 1, 3, 4 and 4, 32, 70.

Example 2.23 : If X is an eigenvector for A corresponding to λ, then find A^3X.

Solution : Let X be an eigenvector of A corresponding to λ, then we have

$$AX = \lambda X \qquad \ldots (i)$$

Premultiplying both sides by A, we get

$$AAX = A\lambda X$$

∴ $$A^2X = \lambda AX$$

$$= \lambda \lambda X \qquad \text{(by (i))}$$

$$= \lambda^2 X$$

Again, premultiply by A

$$AA^2X = A\lambda^2 X$$

$$A^3X = \lambda^2 AX = \lambda^2 \lambda X \qquad \text{(by (i))}$$

∴ $$A^3X = \lambda^3 X$$

Example 2.24 : Find the eigenvalues and eigenvectors of the matrix

$$A = \begin{bmatrix} 1 & 1 & 1 \\ 1 & 2 & 1 \\ 3 & 2 & 3 \end{bmatrix}$$

Solution : The characteristic equation of the matrix A is given by

$$|A - \lambda I| = 0$$

i.e. $$\left| \begin{bmatrix} 1 & 1 & 1 \\ 1 & 2 & 1 \\ 3 & 2 & 3 \end{bmatrix} - \lambda \begin{bmatrix} 1 & 0 & 0 \\ 0 & 1 & 0 \\ 0 & 0 & 1 \end{bmatrix} \right| = 0$$

$$\therefore \quad \begin{vmatrix} 1-\lambda & 1 & 1 \\ 1 & 2-\lambda & 1 \\ 3 & 2 & 3-\lambda \end{vmatrix} = 0$$

$\therefore \quad (1-\lambda)[(2-\lambda)(3-\lambda) - 2] - 1[3-\lambda-3] + 1[2-3)] = 0$

$\therefore \quad (1-\lambda)[\lambda^2 - 5\lambda + 4] + \lambda + 2 + 3\lambda - 6 = 0$

$\therefore \quad \lambda^2 - 5\lambda + 4 - \lambda^3 + 5\lambda^2 - 4\lambda + 4\lambda - 4 = 0$

i.e. $-\lambda^3 + 6\lambda^2 - 5\lambda = 0$

$\therefore \quad \lambda^3 - 6\lambda^2 + 5\lambda = 0$

$\lambda(\lambda^2 - 6\lambda + 5) = 0$

$\therefore \quad \lambda(\lambda - 1)(\lambda - 5) = 0$

$\therefore \quad \lambda = 0, 1, 5.$

Therefore, the eigenvalues are $\lambda_1 = 0$, $\lambda_2 = 1$, $\lambda_3 = 5$.

Case I: For $\lambda_1 = 0$, the corresponding eigenvector is given by

$$(A - \lambda_1 I) X = \mathbf{O}$$

i.e. $\left(\begin{bmatrix} 1 & 1 & 1 \\ 1 & 2 & 1 \\ 3 & 2-\lambda & 3-\lambda \end{bmatrix} - 0 \begin{bmatrix} 0 & 0 & 0 \\ 0 & 0 & 0 \\ 0 & 0 & 0 \end{bmatrix} \right) \begin{bmatrix} x \\ y \\ z \end{bmatrix} = \begin{bmatrix} 0 \\ 0 \\ 0 \end{bmatrix}$

$$\begin{bmatrix} 1 & 1 & 1 \\ 1 & 2 & 1 \\ 3 & 2 & 3 \end{bmatrix} \begin{bmatrix} x \\ y \\ z \end{bmatrix} = \begin{bmatrix} 0 \\ 0 \\ 0 \end{bmatrix}$$

$\xrightarrow{\begin{array}{c} R_2 - R_1 \\ R_3 - R_1 \end{array}} \begin{bmatrix} 1 & 1 & 1 \\ 0 & 1 & 0 \\ 0 & -1 & 0 \end{bmatrix} \begin{bmatrix} x \\ y \\ z \end{bmatrix} = \begin{bmatrix} 0 \\ 0 \\ 0 \end{bmatrix}$

$\xrightarrow{R_3 + R_2} \begin{bmatrix} 1 & 1 & 1 \\ 0 & 1 & 0 \\ 0 & 0 & 0 \end{bmatrix} \begin{bmatrix} x \\ y \\ z \end{bmatrix} = \begin{bmatrix} 0 \\ 0 \\ 0 \end{bmatrix}$

$\therefore \quad x + y + z = 0$

$y = 0$

$\therefore \quad x + z = 0$

Putting $z = t$, we get

$x = -t$

Therefore, the general solution is

$$X = \begin{bmatrix} x \\ y \end{bmatrix} = \begin{bmatrix} -t \\ 0 \\ t \end{bmatrix} = t \begin{bmatrix} -1 \\ 0 \\ 1 \end{bmatrix}$$

Hence, the corresponding eigenvector is

$$X_1 = \begin{bmatrix} -1 \\ 0 \\ 1 \end{bmatrix}$$

Case II : For $\lambda_2 = 1$, the corresponding eigenvector is given by

$$(A - \lambda_2 I) X = O$$

$$\therefore \begin{bmatrix} 0 & 1 & 1 \\ 1 & 1 & 1 \\ 3 & 2 & 2 \end{bmatrix} \begin{bmatrix} x \\ y \\ z \end{bmatrix} = \begin{bmatrix} 0 \\ 0 \\ 0 \end{bmatrix}$$

$$\xrightarrow{R_{12}} \begin{bmatrix} 1 & 1 & 1 \\ 0 & 1 & 1 \\ 3 & 2 & 2 \end{bmatrix} \begin{bmatrix} x \\ y \\ z \end{bmatrix} = \begin{bmatrix} 0 \\ 0 \\ 0 \end{bmatrix}$$

$$\xrightarrow{R_3 - 3R_1} \begin{bmatrix} 1 & 1 & 1 \\ 0 & 1 & 1 \\ 0 & -1 & -1 \end{bmatrix} \begin{bmatrix} x \\ y \\ z \end{bmatrix} = \begin{bmatrix} 0 \\ 0 \\ 0 \end{bmatrix}$$

$$\xrightarrow{R_3 + R_2} \begin{bmatrix} 1 & 1 & 1 \\ 0 & 1 & 1 \\ 0 & 0 & 0 \end{bmatrix} \begin{bmatrix} x \\ y \\ z \end{bmatrix} = \begin{bmatrix} 0 \\ 0 \\ 0 \end{bmatrix}$$

$\therefore \qquad x + y + z = 0$

$\qquad y + z = 0 \Rightarrow y = -z$ and $x = 0$.

$\therefore$ There is only one free variable and putting $z = t$, we get

$$y = -t$$

There is only one free variable and putting $z = t$, we get

$$y = -t$$

$\therefore$ The solution is $x = 0, y = -t, z = t$.

i.e. $[0, -t, t]' = t [0, -1, 1]'$

$\therefore$ The corresponding vector is $\begin{bmatrix} 0 \\ -1 \\ 1 \end{bmatrix} = X_2$.

Case III : $\lambda_3 = 5$. The corresponding eigenvector is given by

$$(A - \lambda_3 I) X = O$$

i.e. $\begin{bmatrix} -4 & 1 & 1 \\ 1 & -3 & 1 \\ 3 & 2 & -2 \end{bmatrix} \begin{bmatrix} x \\ y \\ z \end{bmatrix} = \begin{bmatrix} 0 \\ 0 \\ 0 \end{bmatrix}$

$\xrightarrow{R_{12}}$ $\begin{bmatrix} 1 & -3 & 1 \\ -4 & 1 & 1 \\ 3 & 2 & -2 \end{bmatrix} \begin{bmatrix} x \\ y \\ z \end{bmatrix} = \begin{bmatrix} 0 \\ 0 \\ 0 \end{bmatrix}$

$\xrightarrow[R_3 - 3R_1]{R_2 + 4R_1}$ $\begin{bmatrix} 1 & -3 & 1 \\ 0 & -11 & 5 \\ 0 & 11 & -5 \end{bmatrix} \begin{bmatrix} x \\ y \\ z \end{bmatrix} = \begin{bmatrix} 0 \\ 0 \\ 0 \end{bmatrix}$

$\xrightarrow{R_3 + R_2}$ $\begin{bmatrix} 1 & -3 & 1 \\ 0 & -11 & 5 \\ 0 & 0 & 0 \end{bmatrix} \begin{bmatrix} x \\ y \\ z \end{bmatrix} = \begin{bmatrix} 0 \\ 0 \\ 0 \end{bmatrix}$

i.e. $x - 3y + z = 0$
$-11y + 5z = 0$

∴ $\rho(A - \lambda_3 I) = r = 2$ and $n = 3$.

∴ $r < n \Rightarrow$ The system has non-trivial solution.

Number of arbitrary values/free variables $= n - r = 1$.

Putting $z = t$, we get
$$-11y + 5t = 0$$

∴ $y = \dfrac{5t}{11}$

and $x = \dfrac{4t}{11}$

Therefore, the solution is

$$X = \begin{bmatrix} x \\ y \\ z \end{bmatrix} = \begin{bmatrix} \dfrac{4t}{11} \\ \dfrac{5t}{11} \\ t \end{bmatrix} = \dfrac{t}{11} \begin{bmatrix} 4 \\ 5 \\ 11 \end{bmatrix}$$

Hence, the corresponding eigenvector is
$$X_3 = \begin{bmatrix} 4 \\ 5 \\ 11 \end{bmatrix}$$

Example 2.25 : Find the eigenvalues and eigenvectors of the matrix
$$A = \begin{bmatrix} 2 & -2 & 2 \\ 1 & 1 & 1 \\ 1 & 3 & -1 \end{bmatrix}$$

Solution : The characteristic equation of the matrix is given by
$$|A - \lambda I| = 0$$

i.e.
$$\begin{vmatrix} 2-\lambda & -2 & 2 \\ 1 & 1-\lambda & 1 \\ 1 & 3 & -1-\lambda \end{vmatrix} = 0$$

∴ $(2 - \lambda) [-(1 + \lambda)(1 - \lambda) - 3] + 2[-1 - \lambda - 1] + 2[3 - (1 - \lambda)] = 0$

i.e. $-(2 - \lambda)[1 - \lambda^2 + 3] - 2(2 + \lambda) + 2(2 + \lambda) = 0$

∴ $-(2 - \lambda)[1 - \lambda^2 + 3] = 0$

i.e. $8 - 2\lambda^2 - 4\lambda + \lambda^3 = 0$

i.e. $\lambda^3 - 2\lambda^2 - 4\lambda + 8 = 0$

∴ $\lambda^2(\lambda - 2) - 4(\lambda - 2) = 0$

∴ $(\lambda - 2)(\lambda^2 - 4) = 0$

i.e. $(\lambda - 2)(\lambda - 2)(\lambda + 2) = 0$

∴ $(\lambda - 2)^2 (\lambda + 2) = 0$

∴ $\lambda = 2, 2, -2$.

The eigenvalues are $\lambda_1 = 2$, $\lambda_2 = 2$ and $\lambda_3 = -2$.

Case : For $\lambda_1 = \lambda_2 = 2$ (twice).

This is a double root.

The corresponding characteristic vector is given by
$$(A - \lambda I) X = O$$

i.e.
$$\begin{bmatrix} 0 & -2 & 2 \\ 1 & -1 & 1 \\ 1 & 3 & -3 \end{bmatrix} \begin{bmatrix} x \\ y \\ z \end{bmatrix} = \begin{bmatrix} 0 \\ 0 \\ 0 \end{bmatrix}$$

$$\xrightarrow{R_{12}} \begin{bmatrix} 1 & -1 & 1 \\ 0 & -2 & 2 \\ 1 & 3 & -3 \end{bmatrix} \begin{bmatrix} x \\ y \\ z \end{bmatrix} = \begin{bmatrix} 0 \\ 0 \\ 0 \end{bmatrix}$$

$$\xrightarrow{R_3 - R_1} \begin{bmatrix} 1 & -1 & 1 \\ 0 & -2 & 2 \\ 0 & 4 & -4 \end{bmatrix} \begin{bmatrix} x \\ y \\ z \end{bmatrix} = \begin{bmatrix} 0 \\ 0 \\ 0 \end{bmatrix}$$

$$\xrightarrow{R_3 + 2R_2} \begin{bmatrix} 1 & -1 & 1 \\ 0 & -2 & 2 \\ 0 & 0 & 0 \end{bmatrix} \begin{bmatrix} x \\ y \\ z \end{bmatrix} = \begin{bmatrix} 0 \\ 0 \\ 0 \end{bmatrix}$$

$$\xrightarrow{(1/2) R_2} \begin{bmatrix} 1 & -1 & 1 \\ 0 & -1 & 1 \\ 0 & 0 & 0 \end{bmatrix} \begin{bmatrix} x \\ y \\ z \end{bmatrix} = \begin{bmatrix} 0 \\ 0 \\ 0 \end{bmatrix}$$

i.e. $\quad x - y + z = 0$
$\quad\quad\quad -y + z = 0$

∴ There is only one free variable.

Putting $z = t$, we get
$\quad y = t$ and $x = 0$.

∴ The solution is $= \begin{bmatrix} x \\ y \\ z \end{bmatrix} = \begin{bmatrix} 0 \\ t \\ t \end{bmatrix} = t \begin{bmatrix} 0 \\ 1 \\ 1 \end{bmatrix}$

∴ The corresponding eigenvector is $X_1 = X_2 = \begin{bmatrix} 0 \\ 1 \\ 1 \end{bmatrix}$.

Case II : $\lambda_3 = -2$, the corresponding eigenvector is given by
$\quad\quad (A - \lambda_3 I) X = \mathbf{O}$

i.e. $\begin{bmatrix} 4 & -2 & 2 \\ 1 & 3 & 1 \\ 1 & 3 & 1 \end{bmatrix} \begin{bmatrix} x \\ y \\ z \end{bmatrix} = \begin{bmatrix} 0 \\ 0 \\ 0 \end{bmatrix}$

$\xrightarrow{R_3 - R_2} \begin{bmatrix} 4 & -2 & 2 \\ 1 & 3 & 1 \\ 0 & 0 & 0 \end{bmatrix} \begin{bmatrix} x \\ y \\ z \end{bmatrix} = \begin{bmatrix} 0 \\ 0 \\ 0 \end{bmatrix}$

$$\xrightarrow{R_{12}} \begin{bmatrix} 1 & 3 & 1 \\ 4 & -2 & 2 \\ 0 & 0 & 0 \end{bmatrix} \begin{bmatrix} x \\ y \\ z \end{bmatrix} = \begin{bmatrix} 0 \\ 0 \\ 0 \end{bmatrix}$$

$$\xrightarrow{R_2 - 4R_1} \begin{bmatrix} 1 & 3 & 1 \\ 0 & -14 & -2 \\ 0 & 0 & 0 \end{bmatrix} \begin{bmatrix} x \\ y \\ z \end{bmatrix} = \begin{bmatrix} 0 \\ 0 \\ 0 \end{bmatrix}$$

i.e. $\quad x + 3y + z = 0$

$\quad -14y - 2z = 0 \Rightarrow 7y + z = 0$

$\therefore \quad y = -\dfrac{z}{7}$

Putting $z = t$, we get

$\quad y = \dfrac{t}{7}$ and $x = \dfrac{4t}{7}$, where t is a parameter.

$\therefore$ The solution is $= \begin{bmatrix} x \\ y \\ z \end{bmatrix} = \begin{bmatrix} \dfrac{4t}{7} \\ -\dfrac{t}{7} \\ t \end{bmatrix} = \dfrac{t}{7} \begin{bmatrix} 4 \\ -1 \\ 7 \end{bmatrix}$

$\therefore$ The eigenvector is $X_3 = \begin{bmatrix} 4 \\ -1 \\ 7 \end{bmatrix}$.

Example 2.26 : Find the eigenvectors of the symmetric matrix

$$A = \begin{bmatrix} 2 & -1 & 1 \\ -1 & 2 & -1 \\ 1 & -1 & 2 \end{bmatrix}$$

Solution : The characteristic equation of the given matrix is

$\quad |A - \lambda I| = 0$

i.e. $\begin{vmatrix} 2-\lambda & -1 & 1 \\ -1 & 2-\lambda & -1 \\ 1 & -1 & 2-\lambda \end{vmatrix} = 0$

$\therefore \quad (2-\lambda)[(2-\lambda)^2 - 1] + 1[-2 + \lambda + 1] + 1[1 - 2 + \lambda] = 0$

On simplifying we get,
$$\lambda^3 - 6\lambda^2 + 9\lambda - 4 = 0$$
$\therefore \quad \lambda^3 - \lambda^2 - 5\lambda^2 + 5\lambda + 4\lambda - 4 = 0$
$\quad \lambda^2(\lambda - 1) - 5\lambda(\lambda - 1) + 4(\lambda - 1) = 0$
i.e. $(\lambda - 1)(\lambda^2 - 5\lambda + 4) = 0$
$\therefore \quad (\lambda - 1)(\lambda - 1)(\lambda - 4) = 0$
$\therefore \quad \lambda = 1, 1, 4.$
$\therefore \quad$ The eigenvalues are 1, 1, 4.

Case I : $\lambda_1 = 1$ (twice).

This is double root.

The corresponding eigenvector is given by
$$(A - \lambda_1 I) X = O$$

i.e. $\begin{bmatrix} 1 & -1 & 1 \\ -1 & 1 & -1 \\ 1 & -1 & 1 \end{bmatrix} \begin{bmatrix} x \\ y \\ z \end{bmatrix} = \begin{bmatrix} 0 \\ 0 \\ 0 \end{bmatrix}$

$\xrightarrow[R_3 - R_1]{R_2 + R_1} \begin{bmatrix} 1 & -1 & 1 \\ 0 & 0 & 0 \\ 0 & 0 & 0 \end{bmatrix} \begin{bmatrix} x \\ y \\ z \end{bmatrix} = \begin{bmatrix} 0 \\ 0 \\ 0 \end{bmatrix}$

i.e. $\quad x - y + z = 0$

Clearly there are two arbitrary values or free variables.

Putting $y = t_1$ and $z = t_2$, we get
$$x = t_1 - t_2$$

$\therefore \quad$ The solution is

$$X = \begin{bmatrix} x \\ y \\ z \end{bmatrix} = \begin{bmatrix} t_1 - t_2 \\ t_1 \\ t_2 \end{bmatrix} = \begin{bmatrix} t_1 - t_2 \\ t_1 + 0t_2 \\ 0t_1 + t_2 \end{bmatrix}$$

$$= \begin{bmatrix} t_1 \\ t_1 \\ 0t_1 \end{bmatrix} + \begin{bmatrix} -t_2 \\ 0t_2 \\ t_2 \end{bmatrix}$$

$$= t_1 \begin{bmatrix} 1 \\ 1 \\ 0 \end{bmatrix} + t_2 \begin{bmatrix} -1 \\ 0 \\ 1 \end{bmatrix}$$

Therefore, there are two eigenvectors corresponding to the double root $\lambda_1 = \lambda_2 = 1$.

$$X_1 = \begin{bmatrix} 1 \\ 1 \\ 0 \end{bmatrix} \text{ and } X_2 = \begin{bmatrix} -1 \\ 0 \\ 1 \end{bmatrix}$$

Case II : For $\lambda_3 = 4$, the corresonding eigenvector is given by
$$(A - \lambda_3 I) X = O$$

i.e. $\begin{bmatrix} -2 & -1 & 1 \\ -1 & -2 & -1 \\ 1 & -1 & -2 \end{bmatrix} \begin{bmatrix} x \\ y \\ z \end{bmatrix} = \begin{bmatrix} 0 \\ 0 \\ 0 \end{bmatrix}$

$\xrightarrow[(-1) R_2]{R_{13}}$ $\begin{bmatrix} 1 & -1 & -2 \\ 1 & 2 & 1 \\ -2 & -1 & 1 \end{bmatrix} \begin{bmatrix} x \\ y \\ z \end{bmatrix} = \begin{bmatrix} 0 \\ 0 \\ 0 \end{bmatrix}$

$\xrightarrow[R_3 + 2R_1]{R_2 - R_1}$ $\begin{bmatrix} 1 & -1 & -2 \\ 0 & 3 & 3 \\ 0 & -3 & -3 \end{bmatrix} \begin{bmatrix} x \\ y \\ z \end{bmatrix} = \begin{bmatrix} 0 \\ 0 \\ 0 \end{bmatrix}$

$\xrightarrow{R_3 + R_2}$ $\begin{bmatrix} 1 & -1 & -2 \\ 0 & 3 & 3 \\ 0 & 0 & 0 \end{bmatrix} \begin{bmatrix} x \\ y \\ z \end{bmatrix} = \begin{bmatrix} 0 \\ 0 \\ 0 \end{bmatrix}$

i.e. $\quad x - y - 2z = 0$
$\quad\quad 3y + 3z = 0$

Here $\quad \rho(A - \lambda_3 I) = 2 = r$ and $n = 3$.
$\therefore\;$ Number of parameters or arbitrary values $= n - r = 1$.
Putting $z = t$, we get,
$$y = -t$$
and hence $\quad x = t$

$\therefore\;$ The solution is $X = \begin{bmatrix} x \\ y \\ z \end{bmatrix} = \begin{bmatrix} t \\ -t \\ t \end{bmatrix} = t \begin{bmatrix} 1 \\ -1 \\ 1 \end{bmatrix}$

$\therefore\;$ The corresponding eigenvector is
$$X_3 = \begin{bmatrix} 1 \\ -1 \\ 1 \end{bmatrix}.$$

Example 2.27 : Find the eigenvectors of the matrix

$$A = \begin{bmatrix} 1 & 2 & 3 \\ 0 & 2 & 3 \\ 0 & 0 & 2 \end{bmatrix}$$

Solution : Since the given matrix A is in triangular form.

Therefore, their eigenvalues are its diagonal elements.

Hence, the eigenvalues are $\lambda_1 = 1, \lambda_2 = 2, \lambda_3 = 2$.

Case I : For $\lambda_1 = 1$, the corresponding eigenvector is given by

$$(A - \lambda_1 I) X = \mathbf{O}$$

i.e. $\left(\begin{bmatrix} 1 & 2 & 3 \\ 0 & 2 & 3 \\ 0 & 0 & 2 \end{bmatrix} - 1 \begin{bmatrix} 1 & 0 & 0 \\ 0 & 1 & 0 \\ 0 & 0 & 1 \end{bmatrix} \right) \begin{bmatrix} x \\ y \\ z \end{bmatrix} = \begin{bmatrix} 0 \\ 0 \\ 0 \end{bmatrix}$

$$\rightarrow \begin{bmatrix} 0 & 2 & 3 \\ 0 & 1 & 3 \\ 0 & 0 & 2 \end{bmatrix} \begin{bmatrix} x \\ y \\ z \end{bmatrix} = \begin{bmatrix} 0 \\ 0 \\ 0 \end{bmatrix}$$

$\xrightarrow{(1/2) R_3} \begin{bmatrix} 0 & 2 & 3 \\ 0 & 1 & 3 \\ 0 & 0 & 1 \end{bmatrix} \begin{bmatrix} x \\ y \\ z \end{bmatrix} = \begin{bmatrix} 0 \\ 0 \\ 0 \end{bmatrix}$

$\xrightarrow{R_1 - R_3} \begin{bmatrix} 0 & 2 & 2 \\ 0 & 1 & 3 \\ 0 & 0 & 1 \end{bmatrix} \begin{bmatrix} x \\ y \\ z \end{bmatrix} = \begin{bmatrix} 0 \\ 0 \\ 0 \end{bmatrix}$

∴ $\quad 2y + 2z = 0$

$\quad\quad y + 3z = 0$

$\quad\quad\quad\quad z = 0$

Clearly $y = 0$ and x is free variable.

∴ The solution is $X = [t\ 0\ 0]' = t\ [1\ 0\ 0]'$.

Hence, the corresponding eignevector is

$$X_1 = \begin{bmatrix} 1 \\ 0 \\ 0 \end{bmatrix}.$$

Case II : $\lambda_2 = \lambda_3 = 2$ (twice).

The corresponding eigenvector is given by
$$(A - \lambda_2 I) X = O$$

i.e. $\begin{bmatrix} -1 & 2 & 3 \\ 0 & 0 & 3 \\ 0 & 0 & 0 \end{bmatrix} \begin{bmatrix} x \\ y \\ z \end{bmatrix} = \begin{bmatrix} 0 \\ 0 \\ 0 \end{bmatrix}$

i.e. $z = 0$ and $-x + 2y + 3z = 0$

gives $-x + 2y = 0$.

Therefore, there is only one free variable say $y = t$.

Then $x = 2t$.

The solution is $X = [2t \ t \ 0]' = t [2 \ 1 \ 0]'$.

The corresponding eigenvector is

$$X_3 = \begin{bmatrix} 2 \\ 1 \\ 0 \end{bmatrix}.$$

Hence there is only one eigenvector corresponding to this double root.

2.6 SOME IMPORTANT PROPERTIES

1. Prove that eigenvalues of a matrix A and its transpose A' are same.

Proof : The characteristic equation of square matrix A of order n is
$$|A - \lambda I| = 0$$

Taking transpose both sides, we get
$$|A' - \lambda I| = 0$$

This is the characteristic equation of A'.

Noting that $|A| = |A'|$, the result follows.

2. Show that 0 is an eigenvalue of a matrix if and only if the matrix is singular. i.e. $|A| = 0$.

Proof : Let A be a square matrix of order n. Then the characteristic equation of matrix A is given by
$$|A - \lambda I| = 0$$

If $\lambda = 0$, then $|A| = 0$.

i.e. A is singular.

Further if matrix A is singular i.e. $|A| = 0$.

Then $\quad |A - \lambda I| = 0 \Rightarrow |A| - \lambda |I| = 0$

i.e. $\quad 0 - \lambda \cdot 1 = 0$

$\therefore \quad \lambda = 0$

3. If λ is an eigenvalue of a matrix A then show that $1/\lambda$ is the eigenvalue of A^{-1}.

Proof : Let A be a square matrix of order n such that $|A| \neq 0$.

Let X be the eigenvector corresponding to eigenvalue λ, then

$$AX = \lambda X$$

Premultiplying by A^{-1}, we get

$$A^{-1}AX = A^{-1}\lambda X$$

i.e. $\quad IX = \lambda A^{-1}X$

$\therefore \quad \dfrac{1}{\lambda} X = A^{-1}X$

$\therefore \quad \dfrac{1}{\lambda}$ is the eigenvalue of A^{-1}.

4. Show that the eigenvalues of an idempotent matrix are either zero or unity.

Proof : Let A be an idempotent matrix and λ be its eigenvalue. Then

$$A^2 = A \text{ and } AX = \lambda X \qquad \ldots (1)$$

Premultiply by A

$\therefore \quad A(AX) = A\lambda X = \lambda(AX)$

i.e. $\quad A^2 X = \lambda \cdot \lambda X$ $\qquad$ by (1)

$\therefore \quad AX = \lambda^2 X \qquad \ldots (2)$

From equation (1) and (2),

$$\lambda^2 X = \lambda X$$

i.e. $\quad (\lambda^2 - \lambda) X = 0$

$\Rightarrow \quad \lambda^2 - \lambda = 0$

$\Rightarrow \quad \lambda(\lambda - 1) = 0$

$\therefore \quad \lambda = 0$ or 1.

5. If λ is an eigenvalue of A then prove that λ^n is an eigenvalue of A^n.

Proof : Let λ be an eigenvalue of A, then

$$AX = \lambda X \qquad \ldots (1)$$

Premultiply by A, we get

$$A^2 X = A\lambda X = \lambda AX = \lambda\lambda X = \lambda^2 X \qquad \text{by (1)}$$

Again multiply by A, we get

$$A(A^2 X) = A(\lambda^2 X) = \lambda^2 AX$$

$$\therefore \qquad A^3 X = \lambda^2 \lambda X = \lambda^3 X \qquad \text{by (1)}$$

$\therefore$ In general, $A^n X = \lambda^n X$

The result follows.

6. Prove that the sum of the eigenvalues of a square matrix of order m is equal to the trace of the matrix.

Proof : Let $A = (a_{ij})$ be a square matrix of order m.

Let $\lambda_1, \lambda_2, \ldots, \lambda_m$ be the eigenvalues of A. Then the characteristic equation of A is

$$|A - \lambda I| = 0$$

On expanding this determinant interms of the elements of its diagonal terms, we have

$$0 = |A - \lambda I| = \lambda^m - \lambda^{m-1} \cdot \sum_{i=1}^{m} a_{ii} + \lambda^{m-2} \left[\sum_{i \neq j = 1}^{m} \begin{vmatrix} a_{ii} & a_{ij} \\ a_{ji} & a_{jj} \end{vmatrix} \right] + \ldots$$

$$+ \ldots + (-1)^{m-1} \begin{vmatrix} a_{11} & a_{12} & \ldots & a_{1m} \\ a_{21} & a_{22} & \ldots & a_{2m} \\ \ldots & \ldots & \ldots & \ldots \\ a_{m1} & a_{m2} & \ldots & a_{mm} \end{vmatrix}$$

Hence, $\qquad \sum_{i=1}^{m} \lambda_i = \sum_{i=1}^{m} a_{ii} = \text{Trace } A$

EXERCISE 2.3

1. Find the eigenvalues and eigenvectors of the following matrices :

(i) $\begin{bmatrix} 1 & 4 \\ 3 & 2 \end{bmatrix}$

(ii) $\begin{bmatrix} 5 & 0 & 1 \\ 0 & -2 & 0 \\ 1 & 0 & 5 \end{bmatrix}$

(iii) $\begin{bmatrix} 3 & 1 \\ 6 & 2 \end{bmatrix}$
(iv) $\begin{bmatrix} 0 & 1 & 1 \\ 1 & 0 & 1 \\ 1 & 1 & 0 \end{bmatrix}$

(v) $\begin{bmatrix} 1 & 0 & -1 \\ 1 & 2 & 1 \\ 2 & 2 & 3 \end{bmatrix}$
(vi) $\begin{bmatrix} 1 & 1 & 3 \\ 1 & 5 & 1 \\ 3 & 1 & 1 \end{bmatrix}$

(vii) $\begin{bmatrix} 2 & 0 & 1 \\ 0 & 3 & 0 \\ 1 & 0 & 2 \end{bmatrix}$
(viii) $\begin{bmatrix} 3 & 1 & 4 \\ 0 & 2 & 6 \\ 0 & 0 & 5 \end{bmatrix}$

(ix) $\begin{bmatrix} 4 & 3 \\ 2 & 9 \end{bmatrix}$
(x) $\begin{bmatrix} 2 & 0 & 1 \\ 0 & 2 & 0 \\ 1 & 0 & 2 \end{bmatrix}$

(xi) $\begin{bmatrix} 3 & 2 & 4 \\ 2 & 0 & 2 \\ 4 & 2 & 3 \end{bmatrix}$
(xii) $\begin{bmatrix} 0 & -1 \\ 1 & 0 \end{bmatrix}$

2. Show that '2' is an eigenvalue of $\begin{bmatrix} 3 & 2 \\ 3 & 8 \end{bmatrix}$.

3. Show that -2 is an eigenvalue of $\begin{bmatrix} 7 & 3 \\ 3 & -1 \end{bmatrix}$.

4. Short answer questions :

(i) Is $\begin{bmatrix} 1 \\ -2 \\ 1 \end{bmatrix}$ an eigenvector of $\begin{bmatrix} 3 & 0 & 7 \\ 3 & 3 & 7 \\ 5 & 6 & 5 \end{bmatrix}$?

(ii) Define the terms eigenvalues and eigenvectors.

(iii) Prove that the eigenvalues of a square matrix A and its transpose are the same.

(iv) If A is an idempotent matrix then show that the eigenvalues of A is either 0 or 1.

(v) If λ is an eigenvalue of A then show that $\dfrac{1}{\lambda}$ is an eigenvalue of A^{-1}.

5. Find the characteristic equation of the following matrices :

(a) $\begin{bmatrix} 1 & -4 \\ 4 & 2 \end{bmatrix}$
(b) $\begin{bmatrix} 5 & 3 \\ 3 & 5 \end{bmatrix}$

(c) $\begin{bmatrix} 2 & 1 \\ -1 & 4 \end{bmatrix}$
(d) $\begin{bmatrix} 3 & 2 & 4 \\ 2 & 0 & 2 \\ 4 & 2 & 3 \end{bmatrix}$

6. Find the eigenvalues of the following matrices :

(a) $\begin{bmatrix} 0 & -1 \\ 1 & 0 \end{bmatrix}$
(b) $\begin{bmatrix} 4 & 1 & -1 \\ 2 & 5 & -2 \\ 1 & 1 & 2 \end{bmatrix}$
(c) $\begin{bmatrix} 1 & -1 & 2 \\ 0 & 1 & 0 \\ 1 & 2 & 1 \end{bmatrix}$

ANSWERS (2.3)

1. (i) $\lambda = -2, 5$ and $\begin{bmatrix} 4 \\ -3 \end{bmatrix}, \begin{bmatrix} 1 \\ -1 \end{bmatrix}$.

(ii) $\lambda = 2, 4, 6;$ $\begin{bmatrix} 0 \\ 1 \\ 0 \end{bmatrix}, \begin{bmatrix} -1 \\ 0 \\ 1 \end{bmatrix}$ and $\begin{bmatrix} 1 \\ 0 \\ 1 \end{bmatrix}$

(iii) $\lambda = 0, 5;$ $\begin{bmatrix} 1 \\ -3 \end{bmatrix}$ and $\begin{bmatrix} 1 \\ 2 \end{bmatrix}$

(iv) $\lambda = -1, -1, 2;$ $\begin{bmatrix} -1 \\ 1 \\ 0 \end{bmatrix}, \begin{bmatrix} -1 \\ 0 \\ 1 \end{bmatrix}, \begin{bmatrix} 1 \\ 1 \\ 1 \end{bmatrix}$

(v) $\lambda = 1, 2, 3;$ $\begin{bmatrix} 1 \\ -1 \\ 0 \end{bmatrix}, \begin{bmatrix} 2 \\ -1 \\ -2 \end{bmatrix}, \begin{bmatrix} 1 \\ -1 \\ -2 \end{bmatrix}$

(vi) $\lambda = 6, 3, -2;$ $\begin{bmatrix} 1 \\ 2 \\ 1 \end{bmatrix}, \begin{bmatrix} 1 \\ -1 \\ 1 \end{bmatrix}$ and $\begin{bmatrix} 1 \\ 2 \\ 1 \end{bmatrix}$

(vii) $\lambda = 3, 3, 1;$ $\begin{bmatrix} 1 \\ 1 \\ 1 \end{bmatrix}, \begin{bmatrix} 1 \\ -2 \\ 1 \end{bmatrix}$ and $\begin{bmatrix} 1 \\ 0 \\ -1 \end{bmatrix}$

(viii) $\lambda = 2, 3, 5;$ $\begin{bmatrix} 1 \\ -1 \\ 0 \end{bmatrix}, \begin{bmatrix} 1 \\ 0 \\ 0 \end{bmatrix}$ and $\begin{bmatrix} 3 \\ 2 \\ 1 \end{bmatrix}$

(ix) $\lambda = 3, 10;$ $\begin{bmatrix} -3 \\ 1 \end{bmatrix}$ and $\begin{bmatrix} 1 \\ 2 \end{bmatrix}$

(x) $\lambda = 1, 2, 3;$ $\begin{bmatrix} 1 \\ -1 \\ 0 \end{bmatrix}, \begin{bmatrix} 0 \\ 1 \\ 0 \end{bmatrix}$ and $\begin{bmatrix} 1 \\ 0 \\ 1 \end{bmatrix}$

(xi) $\lambda = i, -i;$ $\begin{bmatrix} i \\ 1 \end{bmatrix}$ and $\begin{bmatrix} -i \\ 1 \end{bmatrix}$.

2. Yes

3. Yes

4. (i) No

5. (a) $\lambda^2 - 3\lambda + 18 = 0$, (b) $\lambda^2 - 10\lambda - 15 = 0$, (c) $\lambda^2 - 6\lambda + 9 = 0$

(d) $\lambda^3 - 6\lambda^2 - 15\lambda - 8 = 0$

6. (a) $\pm i$ (b) 3, 3, 5 (c) $1, 1 \pm \sqrt{2}$

MISCELLANEOUS EXERCISES

I. Theory Questions :

1. Define the terms consistency and inconsistency.
2. Discuss the nature of solution of non-homogeneous system of m linear equation in n unknowns.
3. Define the terms eigen values and eigen vectors of a matrix.
4. If λ is an eigen value of a matrix then prove that λ^m in an eigen value of A^m.
5. Prove that $\lambda = 0$ is an eigen value of the matrix A if any only if A is singular.
6. Prove that the matrices A and A' have the same eigen values.
7. If $\lambda_1, \lambda_2, \ldots, \lambda_n$ are the eigen values of A then prove that $\dfrac{1}{\lambda_1}, \dfrac{1}{\lambda_2}, \ldots, \dfrac{1}{\lambda_n}$ are the eigen values of A^{-1}.

II. Numerical Problems :

(A) Test for consistency and hence solve :

(i) $x + 2y + 3z = 0,$ $2x + 3y + z = 0$
$4x + 5y + 4z = 0,$ $x + 2y - 2z = 0$

(ii) $x + y + 2z = 0,$ $x + 2y + 3z = 0$
$x + 3y + 4z = 0,$ $3x + 4y + 7z = 0$

(iii) $x - 2y + 3z = 0,$ $2x + 5y + 6z = 0$

(B) For what values of λ, the following system of equations possesses a non-trivial solution ? Obtain the general solution in each case.

$3x + y - \lambda z = 0, \; 4x - 2y - 3z = 0, \; 2\lambda x + 4y - \lambda z = 0$

(C) (a) $2x + 3y = -2, \; 2x + y = 1, \; 3x + 2y = 1$

(b) $2x_1 - 3x_2 + 7x_3 = 5, \; 3x_1 + x_2 - 3x_3 = 13, \; 2x_1 + 19x_2 - 47x_3 = 32$

(c) $x + 2y + 3z = 1, \; 2x + 5y + 3z = 6, \; x + 8z = -6$

(d) $x_1 + x_2 + x_3 = 4, \; x_1 - x_2 + x_3 = 0, \; 2x_1 - x_2 + x_3 = 1$

(e) $x + y + z = 6, \; x - y + 2z = 5, \; 3x + y + z = 8, \; 2x - 2y + 3z = 7$

(f) $x + y + z = 6, \; x + 2y + 3z = 14, \; x + 4y + 7z = 30$

(g) $x + y + z = -3, \; 3x + y - 2z = -2, \; 2x + 4y + 7z = 7$

(h) $2x + 2y - 2z = 1, \; 4x + 4y - z = 2, \; 6x + 6y + 2z = 3$

(i) $x + y + 4z = 6, \; 3x + 2y - 2z = 9, \; 5x + y + 2z = 13$

(j) $x + y = 1, \; 2x + 3y = 1, \; 5x - y = 11.$

(D) Investigate for what value of λ the following system of equations :

$\lambda x + 2y - 2z = 1, \; 4x + 2\lambda y - z = 2, \; 6x + 6y + \lambda z = 3$ have infinity solutions ?

(E) Investigate for what values of λ and μ, the following system of equations :

$2x + 3y + 5z = 9, \; 7x + 3y - 2z = 8, \; 2x + 3y + \lambda z = \mu$ will have (i) no solution (ii) a unique solution, (iii) infinite number of solutions.

(F) Find the eigen values and eigen vectors of the following matrices :

(i) $\begin{bmatrix} 8 & -6 & 2 \\ -6 & 7 & -4 \\ 2 & -4 & 3 \end{bmatrix}$ (ii) $\begin{bmatrix} 6 & -2 & 2 \\ -2 & 3 & -1 \\ 2 & -1 & 3 \end{bmatrix}$ (iii) $\begin{bmatrix} 4 & 6 & 6 \\ 1 & 3 & 2 \\ -1 & -5 & -2 \end{bmatrix}$

(iv) $\begin{bmatrix} \cos\theta & -\sin\theta \\ \sin\theta & \cos\theta \end{bmatrix}$ (v) $\begin{bmatrix} 2 & 0 & 1 \\ 0 & 2 & 0 \\ 1 & 0 & 2 \end{bmatrix}$ (vi) $\begin{bmatrix} -2 & -1 \\ 5 & 4 \end{bmatrix}$

(vii) $\begin{bmatrix} 3 & -4 \\ 2 & -6 \end{bmatrix}$ (viii) $\begin{bmatrix} 2 & 2 \\ 13 & \end{bmatrix}$

ANSWERS

(A) (i) $x = y = z = 0$
(ii) $x = t, \ y = t, \ z = -t$
(iii) $x = -3t, \ y = 0, \ z = t$

(B) $\lambda = 1, -9$
For $\lambda = 1$; $x = -t, \ y = t, \ z = -2t$
For $\lambda = -9$; $x = -3t, \ y = -9t, \ z = 2t$

(C) (a) Inconsistent
(b) Inconsistent
(c) $x = 1, \ y = 2, \ z = -1$
(d) $x_1 = 1, \ x_2 = 2, \ x_3 = 1$
(e) $x = 1, \ y = 2, \ z = 3$
(f) $x = t - 2, \ y = 8 - 2t, \ z = t$
(g) Inconsistent
(h) $x = \dfrac{1}{2} - t, \ y = t, \ z = 0$
(i) $x = 2, \ y = 2, \ z = \dfrac{1}{2}$
(j) $x = 2, \ y = -1$

(D) $\lambda = 2$; $x = \dfrac{1}{2} - t, \ y = t, \ z = 0$

(E) (i) $\lambda = 5$ and $\mu \neq 9$
(ii) $\lambda \neq 5$ and for any λ.
(iii) $\lambda = 5, \ \mu = 9$

(F) (i) $\lambda = 0, 3, 15$;
For $\lambda_1 = 0$; $X_1 = [1, 2, 2]'$
For $\lambda_2 = 3$; $X_2 = [2, 1, -2]'$
For $\lambda_3 = 15$; $X_3 = [2, -2, 1]'$

(i) $\lambda = 2, 2, 8$

For $\lambda_1 = \lambda_2 = 2$ double root; $X_1 = [1, 2, 0]'$ and $X_2 [1, 0, -2]'$
For $\lambda_2 = 8$; $X_3 = [2, -1, 1]'$.

(iii) $\lambda = 1, 2, 2$.

    For $\lambda_1 = 1$; $X_1 = [4, 1, -3]'$
    For $\lambda_2 = \lambda_3 = 2$; $X_1 = X_3 = [3, 1, -2]'$

(iv) $\lambda = e^{i\theta}, e^{-i\theta}$

    For $\lambda_1 = e^{i\theta}$; $X_1 = [i, 1]'$
    For $\lambda_2 = e^{-i\theta}$; $X_2 = [i, -1]$

(v) $\lambda = 1, 2, 3$

    For $\lambda_1 = 1$; $X_1 = [1, 0, -1]'$
    For $\lambda_2 = 2$; $X_2 = [0, 1, 0]'$
    For $\lambda_3 = 3$; $X_3 = [1, 0, 1]'$

(vi) $\lambda = -1, 3$

    For $\lambda = -1$, $X_1 = [-1, 1]$
    For $\lambda = 3$, $X_2 = \{-1/5, 1]'$

(vii) $\lambda = 2, -5$,

    For $\lambda = 2$, $X_1 = [4, 1]'$
    For $\lambda = -5$, $X_2 = [1, 2]'$

(viii) $\lambda = 1, 4$

    For $\lambda = 1$, $X_1 = [2, -1]'$
    For $\lambda = 4$, $X_2 = [1, 1]'$

III. Multiple Choice Questions :

Select the correct alternative for each of the following :

1. A matrix A is symmetric if ......
   (a) $A = -A'$ (b) $A = A'$
   (c) $A^2 = A$ (d) $A^2 = I$

2. The system of equations $x - 2y = -1$ and $-x + 3y = 3$ has ......
   (a) unique solution   (b) infinite solution
   (c) no solution   (d) none of these

3. If the eigenvalues of $\begin{bmatrix} 8 & -6 & 2 \\ -6 & 7 & -4 \\ 2 & -4 & 3 \end{bmatrix}$ are 3 and 15, then the third eigenvalue is ......
   (a) 1   (b) -1
   (c) 0   (d) 3

4. The eigenvalues of the matrix $\begin{bmatrix} 1 & 2 & 3 \\ 0 & 2 & 5 \\ 0 & 0 & 3 \end{bmatrix}$ are ......

   (a) 1, 2, 3 (b) 0, 1, 2
   (c) 3, 5, 7 (d) 0, 2, 5

5. Matrix $\begin{bmatrix} \lambda & 2 \\ 1 & \lambda - 1 \end{bmatrix}$ is singular for λ = ...

   (a) 1, 2 (b) 1, −2
   (c) 2, −1 (d) −1, −2

6. The eigenvalues of $A = \begin{bmatrix} 0.5 & -0.6 \\ 0.75 & 1.1 \end{bmatrix}$ are roots of the equation ...

   (a) $\lambda^2 + 1.6\lambda + 1 = 0$ (b) $\lambda^2 - 1.6\lambda + 1 = 0$
   (c) $\lambda^2 - 1.6\lambda - 1 = 0$ (d) $\lambda^2 - \lambda - 1 = 0$

7. If λ is an eigenvalue of an invertible matrix A, then the eigenvalue of A^{-1} is ......

   (a) λ (b) $-\lambda$
   (c) λ^2 (d) λ^{-1}

8. The eigenvector of $\begin{bmatrix} 1 & 6 \\ 5 & 2 \end{bmatrix}$ is ......

   (a) $\begin{bmatrix} -5 \\ 6 \end{bmatrix}$ (b) $\begin{bmatrix} 6 \\ -5 \end{bmatrix}$
   (c) $\begin{bmatrix} 3 \\ -2 \end{bmatrix}$ (d) $\begin{bmatrix} -2 \\ 3 \end{bmatrix}$

9. If −2 and 5 are eigenvalues of $A = \begin{bmatrix} 1 & 4 \\ 3 & 2 \end{bmatrix}$ then the trace of A = ...

   (a) −10 (b) 10
   (c) 3 (d) −3

10. The product of eigenvalues of a square matrix A is ......
    (a) 0
    (b) 1
    (c) non-zero
    (d) |A|

11. If λ is an eigenvalue of A, then it is an eigen value of B, only if B = ...
    (a) A or A^T
    (b) A^2
    (c) A^{-1}
    (d) none of these

ANSWERS

1. (b)	2. (a)	3. (c)	4. (a)	5. (c)	6. (b)	7. (d)	8. (b)
9. (c)	10. (d)	11. (a)					

3
CHAPTER

COMPLEX NUMBER

Birth date : Born on 18th of July 1806.

Birthname : Jean Robert Argand.

Birthplace : Paris

Nationality : Swiss

Jean-Robert Argand

    Jean-Robert Argand was an amateur mathematician born in Paris. Argand is famed for his geometrical interpretation of the complex numbers where i is interpreted as a rotation through 90°. The concept of the modulus of a complex number is also due to Argand but Cauchy, who used the term later, is usually credited as the originator this concept. The Argand diagram is taught to most school children who are studying Mathematics and Argand's name will live on in the history of Mathematics through this important concept.

3.1 INTRODUCTION

    Whenever collection of something occurs it paves the way to the concept of number. Collection is the attitude of human being by birth. This concept gives birth to the natural numbers. When we made an attempt to solve the algebraic equations by considering operations such as addition, subtraction, multiplication and division, number system is flourished with integers, rationals and irrationals. Eventually, a real number system is developed which we used in our day-to-day life. Equations of the type $x^2 + a^2 = 0$, $a > 0$ does not obtained the solution in real number system since square of every real number is positive. Hence there is a need to develop new system by introducing the concept of imaginary unit, namely $i = \sqrt{-1}$. Any number of the form 'ib', for real b, is known as an imaginary number.

Diagrammatic representation of the system of numbers is as follows :

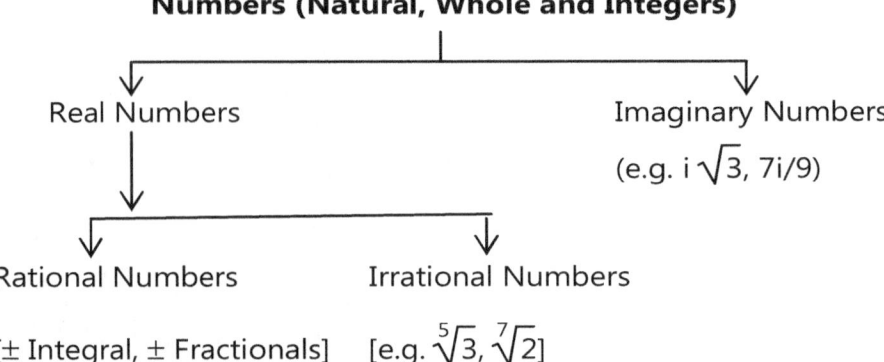

3.2 COMPLEX NUMBER

Oftenly we come across a square root of negative number as part of the values for the roots of algebraic equations.

For example, in equation $x^2 + 2x + 2 = 0$, roots are $x = \dfrac{-2 \pm \sqrt{4-8}}{2} = -1 + i$. Hence there is a needed to introduce a new number system to be developed of the form $a + ib$, where a, b are real numbers and $i = \sqrt{-1}$ is an imaginary unit and we called it as complex number.

3.2.1 Definition

A number $a + ib$, which is the combination of real and imaginary numbers is known as complex number where a, b are real numbers and $i = \sqrt{-1}$ is an imaginary unit.

If $z = a + ib$ is a complex number, then a is known as a real part of z, denoted as Re (z) and b is known as an imaginary part of z, denoted as Im (z). Note that b is the coefficient of i and the imaginary number is ib.

3.2.2 Equality of Complex Numbers

Two complex numbers are said to be equal if their real and imaginary parts are equal.

Let $a_1 + ib_1 = a_2 + ib_2$

∴ $(a_1 - a_2) = i(b_2 - b_1)$

Squaring both sides, we get

$(a_1 - a_2)^2 = i^2(b_2 - b_1)^2 = -(b_2 - b_1)^2$ $(\because i^2 = -1)$

∴ $(a_1 - a_2)^2 + (b_2 - b_1)^2 = 0$

It will satisfy only if, $a_1 - a_2 = 0$ and $b_2 - b_1 = 0$.

∴ $a_1 = a_2$ and $b_1 = b_2$. Hence the proof.

3.2.3 Graphical Representation of a Complex Number

For better understanding of the real number system we use real line as its graphical representation. Similarly, J. R. Argand suggested that complex numbers can be represented by points in a plane.

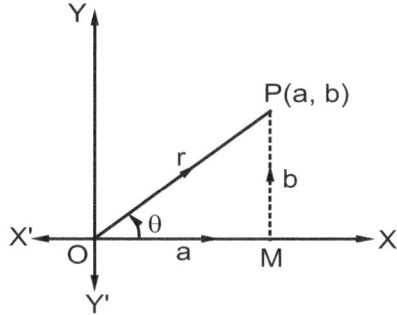

Fig. 3.1

Consider X-axis as real part of complex number and Y-axis as imaginary part of complex number with O as origin. Then a complex number $z = a + ib$ is a point $P(a, b)$ in the plane as shown in Fig. 3.1.

Also, its polar relations are

$$z = a + ib = r(\cos\theta + i\sin\theta) \qquad \ldots (3.1)$$
$$r = d(OP) = \sqrt{a^2 + b^2} \qquad \ldots (3.2)$$

and

$$\theta = \tan^{-1}\left(\frac{b}{a}\right) \qquad \ldots (3.3)$$

In vector notation form

$$\overline{OP} = \overline{OM} + \overline{MP} = a + ib \quad \text{(vector form)} \ldots (3.3\text{ a})$$

where, $\overline{OM}$ and $\overline{MP}$ are vectors of magnitude a and b.

3.3 MODULUS AND ARGUMENT OF A COMPLEX NUMBER

Let P(a, b) be a point in complex plane as shown in Fig. 3.1, which represents a complex number z = a + ib. Take OP = r and m $\angle$ XOP = θ. Then a = r cos θ, b = r sin θ.

Modulus of a complex number : A quantity r of a complex number z = a + ib is known as the modulus of a complex number z and is represented as

$$|z| = r = |a + ib| = \sqrt{a^2 + b^2} \qquad \ldots (3.4)$$

Amplitude or argument of a complex number : A quantity θ of a complex number z = a + ib is known as the amplitude or argument of a complex number z and is represented by in short as

$$\arg z \text{ or } \operatorname{ampl} z = \theta = \tan^{-1}\left(\frac{b}{a}\right) \qquad \ldots (3.5)$$

Note that OP will be same for multiples of rotations of 2π in either anticlockwise or clockwise direction. Hence general polar form of z = a + ib is z = r [cos (2nπ + θ) + i sin (2nπ + θ)] where n = 0, ± 1, ± 2, ... Here 2nπ + θ is known as general amplitude of z and θ which lies between – π and π is known as principal value of amplitude of z or argument of z.

3.3.1 Algebra of Complex Number

I. Addition and Subtraction :

Let $z_1 = a_1 + ib_1$ and $z_2 = a_2 + ib_2$ be two complex numbers.

Then $\quad z_1 + z_2 = (a_1 \pm a_2) + i (b_1 \pm b_2) \qquad \ldots (3.6)$

For example, let $z_1 = 3 - 2i$, $z_2 = -4 - 5i$ be two complex numbers.

Then $\quad z_1 + z_2 = (3 + (-4)) + ((-2) + (-5)) i = -1 - 7i$

and $\quad z_1 - z_2 = (3 - (-4)) + ((-2) - (-5)) i = 7 + 3i$

II. Multiplication :

Let $z_1 = a_1 + ib_1$ and $z_2 = a_2 + ib_2$ be two complex numbers.

Then $\quad z_1 \cdot z_2 = (a_1 + ib_1) \cdot (a_2 + ib_2)$

$\qquad \qquad = a_1 a_2 + i a_1 b_2 + i b_1 a_2 + i^2 b_1 b_2$

$\qquad \qquad = (a_1 a_2 - b_1 b_2) + i (a_1 b_2 + a_2 b_1)$ where $i^2 = -1$

Thus $\quad z_1 \cdot z_2 = (a_1 a_2 - b_1 b_2) + i (a_1 b_2 + a_2 b_1) \qquad \ldots (3.7)$

III. Division :

Let $z_1 = a_1 + ib_1$ and $z_2 = a_2 + ib_2$ be two complex numbers.

Then $\dfrac{z_1}{z_2} = \dfrac{a_1 + ib_1}{a_2 + ib_2}$

To separate real and imaginary parts multiply numerator and denominator by $a_2 - ib_2$ (i.e. conjugate of denominator $a_2 + ib_2$).

$$\dfrac{z_1}{z_2} = \dfrac{a_1 + ib_1}{a_2 + ib_2} \cdot \dfrac{a_2 - ib_2}{a_2 - ib_2}$$

$$= \dfrac{a_1 a_2 - i a_1 b_2 + i a_2 b_2 - i^2 b_1 b_2}{a_2^2 - i^2 b_2^2}$$

$$= \dfrac{(a_1 a_2 + b_1 b_2) + i(a_2 b_1 - a_1 b_2)}{a_2^2 + b_2^2} \qquad (\because i^2 = -1)$$

Thus, $\dfrac{z_1}{z_2} = \dfrac{(a_1 a_2 + b_1 b_2)}{(a_2^2 + b_2^2)} + i \dfrac{(a_2 b_1 - a_1 b_2)}{(a_2^2 + b_2^2)}$ ... (3.8)

Now we see that if n is any real number, one of the values of $(\cos \theta + i \sin \theta)^n$ is $\cos(n\theta) + i \sin(n\theta)$. De Moivre's states this theorem as.

3.4 DE MOIVRE'S THEOREM

Abraham De Moivre was a French-born mathematician who pioneered the development of analytic geometry and the theory of probability. States that for any complex number (and in particular, for any real number) x and integer n it holds that

$(\cos x + i \sin x)^n = \cos(nx) + i \sin(nx)$

While the formula was named after De Moivre, he never explicitly stated it in his works. The formula is important because it connects complex numbers (i stands for the imaginary unit ($i^2 = -1$)) and trigonometry. The expression $\cos x + i \sin x$ is sometimes abbreviated to cis x.

Abraham de Moivre

1667-1754

Statement : For any rational number n, one of the value of $(\cos \theta + i \sin \theta)^n$ is $\cos(n\theta) + i \sin(n\theta)$.

i.e. $(\cos \theta + i \sin \theta)^n = \cos n\theta + i \sin n\theta$

Proof : Consider the following cases :

(i) n as a non-negative integer.

(ii) n as a negative integer.

(iii) n as a fraction.

Case (i) : Let n be any non-negative integer.

Consider,

$(\cos \theta_1 + i \sin \theta_1)(\cos \theta_2 + i \sin \theta_2) = [\cos \theta_1 \cos \theta_2 - \sin \theta_1 \sin \theta_2]$
$\qquad + i [\sin \theta_1 \cos \theta_2 + \cos \theta_1 \sin \theta_2]$

$= \cos(\theta_1 + \theta_2) + i \sin(\theta_1 + \theta_2)$

Similarly we can prove that

$(\cos \theta_1 + i \sin \theta_1)(\cos \theta_2 + \sin \theta_2) \cdot (\cos \theta_3 + i \sin \theta_3)$

$= \cos(\theta_1 + \theta_2 + \theta_3) + i \sin(\theta_1 + \theta_2 + \theta_3)$

Continuing in this way we can prove that :

$(\cos \theta_1 + i \sin \theta_1)(\cos \theta_2 + i \sin \theta_2) \ldots (\cos \theta_n + i \sin \theta_n)$

$= \cos(\theta_1 + \theta_2 + \ldots + \theta_n) + i \sin(\theta_1 + \theta_2 + \ldots + \theta_n)$

Putting $\theta_1 = \theta_2 = \theta_3 = \ldots = \theta_n = \theta$, we get

$(\cos \theta + i \sin \theta)^n = \cos n\theta + i \sin n\theta$

Thus the theorem is true for any non-negative integer.

Case (ii) : Let n be a negative integer.

Take $n = -m$, where m is a positive integer.

$(\cos \theta + i \sin \theta)^n = (\cos \theta + i \sin \theta)^{-m}$

$= \dfrac{1}{(\cos \theta + i \sin \theta)^m}$

$= \dfrac{1}{\cos(m\theta) + i \sin(m\theta)} \qquad$ using case (i)

$$= \frac{\cos(m\theta) - i\sin(m\theta)}{((\cos m\theta) + i\sin(m\theta))(\cos(m\theta) - i\sin(m\theta))}$$

$$= \frac{\cos(m\theta) - i\sin(m\theta)}{\cos^2(m\theta) + \sin^2(m\theta)}$$

$$= \cos(m\theta) - i\sin(m\theta)$$

$$= \cos[(-m)\theta] + i\sin[(-m)\theta]$$

$$[\because \cos(-\theta) = \cos(\theta)]$$

$$= \cos(n\theta) + i\sin(n\theta)$$

Case (iii) : Let n be a fraction :

Take $n = \frac{p}{q}$, where p, q are positive or negative integers.

From equation (i) and (ii), we have

$$\left[\cos\left(\frac{\theta}{q}\right) + i\sin\left(\frac{\theta}{q}\right)\right]^q = \cos\theta + i\sin\theta$$

$$\therefore \quad (\cos\theta + i\sin\theta)^{1/q} = \cos\left(\frac{\theta}{q}\right) + i\sin\left(\frac{\theta}{q}\right)$$

$$(\cos\theta + i\sin\theta)^n = (\cos\theta + i\sin\theta)^{p/q}$$

$$= [(\cos\theta + i\sin\theta)^{1/q}]^p$$

$$= \left(\cos\left(\frac{\theta}{q}\right) + i\sin\left(\frac{\theta}{q}\right)\right)^p$$

$$= \cos\left(\frac{p\theta}{q}\right) + i\sin\left(\frac{p\theta}{q}\right)$$

$$= \cos(n\theta) + i\sin(n\theta), \text{ where } n = \frac{p}{q}$$

Thus,

$$(\cos\theta + i\sin\theta)^n = \cos(n\theta) + i\sin(n\theta)$$

Corollary 1 : If $z = \cos\theta + i\sin\theta$ then $1/z = \cos\theta - i\sin\theta$.

Proof : $z = \cos\theta + i\sin\theta$

$$\therefore \quad \frac{1}{z} = z^{-1} = (\cos\theta + i\sin\theta)^{-1}$$

$$= \cos(-\theta) + i\sin(-\theta)$$

$$\therefore \quad \frac{1}{z} = \cos\theta - i\sin\theta$$

Corollary 2 : If $z = \cos\theta + i\sin\theta$ then
$$z^n + z^{-n} = 2\cos n\theta \text{ and } z^n - z^n = 2i\sin n\theta$$

Proof : $z = \cos\theta + i\sin\theta$

Then $z^n = \cos n\theta + i\sin n\theta$

and $z^{-n} = \cos n\theta - i\sin n\theta$

∴ $z^n + z^{-n} = 2\cos n\theta$

and $z^n - z^n = 2i\sin n\theta$

Remark :

1. DeMoivre's theorem holds even when n is any real number.
2. In general $(\sin\theta + i\cos\theta)^n \neq \sin n\theta + i\cos n\theta$.
3. In general $(\cos\theta + i\sin\phi)^n \neq \cos n\theta + i\sin n\phi$.

SOLVED EXAMPLES

Example 3.1 : Simplify : $\dfrac{(\cos 7\theta + i\sin 7\theta)^5 (\cos 3\theta - i\sin 3\theta)^{2/3}}{\left(\cos\dfrac{4\theta}{5} + i\sin\dfrac{4\theta}{5}\right)^{3/8} \left(\cos\dfrac{5\theta}{9} - i\sin\dfrac{5\theta}{9}\right)^{18}}$

Solution : Here,

$(\cos 7\theta + i\sin 7\theta)^5 = ((\cos\theta + i\sin\theta)^7)^5 = (\cos\theta + i\sin\theta)^{35}$

$(\cos 3\theta - i\sin 3\theta)^{2/3} = (\cos(-3)\theta + i\sin(-3)\theta)^{2/3}$

$= (\cos\theta + i\sin\theta)^{(-3)\cdot\left(\frac{2}{3}\right)} = (\cos\theta + i\sin\theta)^{-2}$

$\left(\cos\dfrac{4\theta}{5} + i\sin\dfrac{4\theta}{5}\right)^{3/8} = [(\cos\theta + i\sin\theta)^{4/5}]^{3/8} = (\cos\theta + i\sin\theta)^{3/10}$

$\left(\cos\dfrac{5\theta}{9} - i\sin\dfrac{5\theta}{9}\right)^{18} = \left[\cos\left(\dfrac{-5}{9}\right)\theta + i\sin\left(\dfrac{-5}{9}\right)\theta\right]^{18}$

$= (\cos\theta + i\sin\theta)^{18\left(\frac{-5}{9}\right)} = (\cos\theta + i\sin\theta)^{-10}$

∴ We have

Expression $= \dfrac{(\cos\theta + i\sin\theta)^{35} (\cos\theta + i\sin\theta)^{-2}}{(\cos\theta + i\sin\theta)^{3/10} (\cos\theta + i\sin\theta)^{-10}}$

$= (\cos\theta + i\sin\theta)^{35 - 2 + \frac{3}{10} - 10}$

$$= (\cos \theta + i \sin \theta)^{23 + \frac{3}{10}}$$

$$= (\cos \theta + i \sin \theta)^{\frac{233}{10}}$$

$$= \cos\left(\frac{233}{10}\theta\right) + i \sin\left(\frac{233}{10}\theta\right)$$

Note :

(i) $(\cos \theta + i \sin \phi)^n \ne \cos(n\theta) + i \sin(n\phi)$

For example,

$(\cos(30) + i \sin(60))^2 \ne \cos(60) + i \sin(120)$

Since, L.H.S. $= \left[\frac{\sqrt{3}}{2}(1+i)\right]^2 = \frac{3}{4}(1 - 1 + 2i) = \frac{3i}{2}$

R.H.S. $= \frac{1}{2} + \frac{\sqrt{3}}{2}i = \frac{1}{2}(1 + \sqrt{3}\,i)$

(ii) $(\sin \theta + i \cos \theta)^n \ne \sin(n\theta) + i \cos(n\theta)$

For example, Taking $\theta = 30$ and $n = 2$.

We have L.H.S. $= \left(\frac{(1 + \sqrt{3}\,i)}{2}\right)^2$

$$= \frac{1 - 3 + 2\sqrt{3}\,i}{4} = \frac{-2 + 2\sqrt{3}\,i}{4} = \frac{-1}{2} + \frac{u\sqrt{3}}{2}$$

R.H.S. $= \frac{\sqrt{3}}{2} + \frac{i}{2} = \frac{1}{2}(\sqrt{3} + i)$

$\therefore$ L.H.S. $\ne$ R.H.S.

But

$$(\sin \theta + i \cos \theta)^n = \left[\cos\left(\frac{\pi}{2} - \theta\right) + i \sin\left(\frac{\pi}{2} - \theta\right)\right]^n$$

$$= \cos\left[n\left(\frac{\pi}{2} - \theta\right)\right] + i \sin\left[n\left(\frac{\pi}{2} - \theta\right)\right]$$

Example 3.2 : If $2 \cos \theta = x + \frac{1}{x}$, then show that $x^n + \frac{1}{x^n} = 2 \cos n\theta$ and $x^n - \frac{1}{x^n} = 2i \sin n\theta$.

Solution : Given : $x + \dfrac{1}{x} = 2\cos\theta \Rightarrow x^2 - (2\cos\theta)x + 1 = 0$, a quadratic equation. $\therefore x^2 - 2x\cos\theta + \cos^2\theta = -1 + \cos^2\theta$

$\Rightarrow (x - \cos\theta)^2 = -1 + \cos^2\theta = -(1 - \cos^2\theta) = -\sin^2\theta = i^2\sin^2\theta$

$\Rightarrow (x - \cos\theta) = \pm i\sin\theta$

$\Rightarrow x = \cos\theta \pm i\sin\theta$

$\Rightarrow x^n = (\cos\theta + i\sin\theta)^n = \cos n\theta + i\sin n\theta$.

Using De Moivre's theorem.

If $x^n = \cos n\theta + i\sin n\theta$

So $x^{-n} = (\cos\theta + i\sin\theta)^{-n} = \cos n\theta - i\sin n\theta$

$\therefore \quad x^n + x^{-n} = 2\cos n\theta \text{ and } x^n - x^{-n} = 2i\sin(n\theta)$

Example 3.3 : Separate given complex number into real and imaginary parts.

(i) $z = \sqrt{i}$.

Solution : We have,

$$i = 0 + i \cdot 1 = r\cos\theta + ir\sin\theta$$

Equating real and imaginary parts from either side, we get

$$r\cos\theta = 0, \quad r\sin\theta = 1$$

$\Rightarrow r^2(\cos^2\theta + \sin^2\theta) = 0^2 + 1^2 \Rightarrow r^2 = 1^2 \Rightarrow r = 1$

Equations $\cos\theta = 0, \sin\theta = 1 \Rightarrow \theta = \dfrac{\pi}{2}$

$\therefore \quad i = \cos\left(\dfrac{\pi}{2}\right) + i\sin\left(\dfrac{\pi}{2}\right)$

$\therefore \quad z = \sqrt{i} = \left(\cos\left(\dfrac{\pi}{2}\right) + i\sin\left(\dfrac{\pi}{2}\right)\right)^{1/2}$

$\quad = \cos\left(\dfrac{\pi}{4}\right) + i\sin\left(\dfrac{\pi}{4}\right)$

Using De Moivre's theorem,

Thus, $\text{Re}(z) = \cos\left(\dfrac{\pi}{4}\right) = \dfrac{1}{\sqrt{2}}$

$\text{Im}(z) = \sin\left(\dfrac{\pi}{4}\right) = \dfrac{1}{\sqrt{2}}$

(ii) $z = (i)^i$

We know, $i = \cos\left(\dfrac{\pi}{2}\right) + i\sin\left(\dfrac{\pi}{2}\right) = e^{i\pi/2}$

By Euler's formula.

∴ $z = (i)^i = (e^{i\pi/2})^i = e^{-\pi/2} = e^{-\pi/2} \cdot 1 + i(0)$

Thus $\text{Re}(z) = e^{-\pi/2}, \ \text{Im}(z) = 0$

(iii) $z = \tan^{-1}(x + iy)$

Let $z = \tan^{-1}(x + iy) = p + iq \Rightarrow \tan(p + iq) = x + iy$

So its complex conjugate

$\tan^{-1}(x - iy) = p - iq \Rightarrow \tan(p - iq) = x - iy$

We have, $\tan(2p) = \tan[(p + iq) + (p - iq)]$

$= \dfrac{\tan(p + iq) + \tan(p - iq)}{1 - \tan(p + iq)\tan(p - iq)}$

$= \dfrac{(x + iy) + (x - iy)}{1 - (x + iy)(x - iy)}$

$= \dfrac{2x}{1 - x^2 - y^2}$

∴ $p = \dfrac{1}{2}\tan^{-1}\left(\dfrac{2x}{1 - x^2 - y^2}\right)$

Similarly, $\tan(2iq) = \tan[(p + iq) - (p - iq)]$

$= \dfrac{\tan(p + iq) - \tan(p - iq)}{1 + \tan(p + iq)\tan(p - iq)}$

$= \dfrac{(x + iy) - (x - iy)}{1 + (x + iy)(x - iy)} = \dfrac{2iy}{1 + x^2 + y^2}$

But $\tan(2iq) = i\tanh(2q)$

∴ $\tanh(2q) = \dfrac{2y}{1 + x^2 + y^2} \Rightarrow q = \dfrac{1}{2}\tanh^{-1}\left(\dfrac{2y}{1 + x^2 + y^2}\right)$

Thus, $\text{Re}(x) = \dfrac{1}{2}\tan^{-1}\left(\dfrac{2x}{1 - x^2 - y^2}\right)$

$\text{Im}(z) = \dfrac{1}{2}\tanh^{-1}\left(\dfrac{2y}{1 + x^2 + y^2}\right)$

Example 3.4 : Show that :

$$(1 + \cos\theta + i\sin\theta)^n + (1 + \cos\theta - i\sin\theta)^n = 2^{n+1} \cos^n\left(\frac{\theta}{2}\right) \cos\left(\frac{n\theta}{2}\right)$$

Solution : Consider

$$\text{L.H.S.} = (1 + \cos\theta + i\sin\theta)^n + (1 + \cos\theta - i\sin\theta)^n$$

Put $\quad 1 + \cos\theta = 2\cos^2\frac{\theta}{2}$ and $\sin\theta = 2\sin\frac{\theta}{2}\cos\frac{\theta}{2}$

$$= \left[2\cos^2\frac{\theta}{2} + i\,2\sin\frac{\theta}{2}\cos\frac{\theta}{2}\right]^n + \left[2\cos^2\frac{\theta}{2} - i\,2\sin\frac{\theta}{2}\cos\frac{\theta}{2}\right]^n$$

$$= 2^n \cos^n\left(\frac{\theta}{2}\right) \left\{ \left[\cos\frac{\theta}{2} + i\sin\frac{\theta}{2}\right]^n + \left[\cos\frac{\theta}{2} - i\sin\frac{\theta}{2}\right]^n \right\}$$

Applying De Moivre's theorem,

$$= 2^n \cos^n\left(\frac{\theta}{2}\right) \left\{ \cos\left(\frac{n\theta}{2}\right) + i\sin\left(\frac{n\theta}{2}\right) + \cos\left(\frac{n\theta}{2}\right) - i\sin\left(\frac{n\theta}{2}\right) \right\}$$

$$= 2^{n+1} \cos^n\left(\frac{n\theta}{2}\right) \cos\left(\frac{n\theta}{2}\right) = \text{R.H.S.}$$

Example 3.5 : If p and q are roots of the equation $x^2 - 2x + 4 = 0$, then show that $p^n + q^n = 2^{n+1} \cos\left(\frac{n\pi}{3}\right)$. Hence deduce that $p^6 + q^6 = 128$.

Solution : Given equation : $x^2 - 2x + 4 = 0$ is quadratic. Hence its roots are $x = \frac{2 \pm \sqrt{4-16}}{2} = 1 \pm \sqrt{3}\,i$. Take $p = 1 + \sqrt{3}\,i,\ q = 1 - \sqrt{3}\,i$.

Here, $\quad p = 1 + \sqrt{3}\,i = 2\left(\frac{1}{2} + \frac{\sqrt{3}}{2}i\right)$

$$= 2\left(\cos\frac{\pi}{3} + i\sin\frac{\pi}{3}\right)$$

$$q = 1 - \sqrt{3}\,i = 2\left(\frac{1}{2} - \frac{\sqrt{3}}{2}i\right) = 2\left(\cos\frac{\pi}{3} - i\sin\frac{\pi}{3}\right)$$

$$\therefore \quad p^n + q^n = \left[2\left(\cos\frac{\pi}{3} + \sin\frac{\pi}{3}\right)\right]^n + \left[2\left(\cos\frac{\pi}{3} - i\sin\frac{\pi}{3}\right)\right]^n$$

$$= 2^n\left[\cos\frac{n\pi}{3} + i\sin\frac{n\pi}{3} + \cos\frac{n\pi}{3} - i\sin\frac{n\pi}{3}\right]$$

$$= 2^n\left(2\cos\frac{n\pi}{3}\right) = 2^{n+1}\cos\frac{n\pi}{3}$$

by De Moivre's theorem

For $n = 6$, $\quad p^6 + q^6 = 2^{6+1}\cos\left(\frac{6\pi}{3}\right) = 2^7\cos(2\pi) = 128$

Example 3.6 : Prove that :

$$\left(\frac{1 + \sin\theta + i\cos\theta}{1 + \sin\theta - i\cos\theta}\right)^n = \cos\left[\frac{n\pi}{2} - n\theta\right] + i\sin\left[\frac{n\pi}{2} - n\theta\right]$$

Solution : We have,

$(\sin\theta + i\cos\theta)(\sin\theta - i\cos\theta) = \sin^2\theta - i^2\cos^2\theta = \sin^2\theta + \cos^2\theta = 1$

Therefore, $\quad$ L.H.S. $= \left(\frac{1 + \sin\theta + i\cos\theta}{1 + \sin\theta - i\cos\theta}\right)^n$

$$= \left[\frac{(\sin\theta + i\cos\theta)(\sin\theta - i\cos\theta) + (\sin\theta + i\cos\theta)}{1 + \sin\theta - i\cos\theta}\right]^n$$

$$= \left[\frac{(\sin\theta + i\cos\theta)(\sin\theta - i\cos\theta + 1)}{(1 + \sin\theta - i\cos\theta)}\right]^n = (\sin\theta + i\cos\theta)^n$$

$$= \left[\cos\left(\frac{\pi}{2} - \theta\right) + i\sin\left(\frac{\pi}{2} - \theta\right)\right]^n = \cos\left[\frac{n\pi}{2} - n\theta\right] + i\sin\left[\frac{n\pi}{2} - n\theta\right]$$

$= $ R.H.S. $\hfill$ by De Moivre's theorem

Example 3.7 : If $2\cos\theta = x + \frac{1}{x}$ then show that $x^n + \frac{1}{x^n} = 2\cos n\theta$.

Solution : $\quad x + \frac{1}{x} = 2\cos\theta$

$\therefore \quad x^2 - 2\cos\theta x + 1 = 0 \hfill \ldots (i)$

$\therefore \quad (x - \cos\theta)^2 = x^2 - 2\cos\theta x + \cos^2\theta$

$= -1 + \cos^2\theta \hfill$ by (i)

$= -\sin^2\theta$

$$\therefore \quad (x - \cos\theta)^2 = i^2 \sin^2\theta$$
$$\therefore \quad x - \cos\theta = \pm i \sin\theta$$
$$\therefore \quad x = \cos\theta \pm i \sin\theta$$

Let us,
$$x = \cos\theta + i \sin\theta$$
$$\therefore \quad x^n = (\cos\theta + i \sin\theta)^n = \cos n\theta + i \sin n\theta$$
and
$$x^{-n} = (\cos\theta + i \sin\theta)^{-n}$$
$$x^{-n} = \cos n\theta - i \sin n\theta$$
$$\therefore \quad x^n + x^{-n} = (\cos n\theta + i \sin n\theta) + (\cos n\theta - i \sin n\theta)$$
$$= 2\cos n\theta$$
$$\therefore \quad x^n + \frac{1}{x^n} = 2\cos n\theta$$

EXERCISE (3.1)

1. Simplify :

   (a) $\dfrac{(\cos 5\theta - i \sin 5\theta)^2 (\cos 7\theta + i \sin 7\theta)^{-3}}{(\cos 4\theta - i \sin 4\theta)^3 (\cos\theta + i \sin\theta)^5}$

   (b) $\dfrac{(\cos 2\theta - i \sin 2\theta)^7 (\cos 3\theta + i \sin 3\theta)^{-5}}{(\cos 4\theta + i \sin 4\theta)^{12} (\cos 5\theta - i \sin 5\theta)^{-6}}$

   (c) $\dfrac{(\sin p + i \cos p)^4}{(\sin q - i \cos q)^5}$

   (d) $\left(\dfrac{1 + \sin\left(\frac{\pi}{8}\right) + i \cos\left(\frac{\pi}{8}\right)}{1 + \sin\left(\frac{\pi}{8}\right) - i \cos\left(\frac{\pi}{8}\right)} \right)^8$

   (e) $(1 + \cos\theta + i \sin\theta)^n + (1 + \cos\theta - i \sin\theta)^n$

   (f) $\dfrac{(\cos\theta + i \sin\theta)^4}{(\cos\theta - i \sin\theta)^5}$

   (g) $\dfrac{(\cos 2\theta + i \sin 2\theta)^{3/2} (\cos\theta - i \sin\theta)^3}{(\cos 3\theta - i \sin 3\theta)^2 (\cos 5\theta - i \sin 5\theta)^{2/5}}$

   (h) Find the value of $\left(\sin\dfrac{\pi}{6} + i \cos\dfrac{\pi}{6} \right)^7$.

   (i) For any positive value show that :
   $$(1 + i)^n + (1 - i)^n = 2^{\left(\frac{n+2}{2}\right)} \cdot \cos\left(\frac{n\pi}{4}\right)$$
   and hence find the value of $(1 + i)^4 + (1 - i)^4$.

(j) If $x + \dfrac{1}{x} = 2\cos\alpha$ and $y + \dfrac{1}{y} = 2\cos\beta$. Prove that :

$$x^m \cdot y^n + \dfrac{1}{x^m \cdot y^n} = 2\cos(m\alpha + n\beta).$$

(k) If α and β are roots of the equation $x^2 - 2\sqrt{3}\,x + 4 = 0$, prove that : $\alpha^3 + \beta^3 = 0$.

2. Prove that :

(a) $(3+4i)^{2/3} + (3-4i)^{2/3} = 2(5)^{2/3}\cos\left[\dfrac{2}{3}\tan^{-1}\dfrac{4}{3}\right]$

(b) $(1+\sqrt{3}\,i)^6 + (1-\sqrt{3}\,i)^6 = -2^6$

3. (a) Prove that $(1+i\sqrt{3})^8 + (1-i\sqrt{3})^8 = -2^8$.

(b) If $x_k = \cos\left(\dfrac{\pi}{2^k}\right) + i\sin\left(\dfrac{\pi}{2^k}\right)$. Prove that $x_1 \cdot x_2 \cdot x_3 \ldots = -1$.

ANSWERS (3.1)

1. (a) 1   (b) $\cos 11\theta - i\sin 11\theta$

(c) $-\sin(4p+5q) - i\cos(4p+5q)$

(d) -1 (e) $2^{n+1}\cos^n\left(\dfrac{\theta}{2}\right)\cos\left(\dfrac{n\theta}{2}\right)$

(f) $\cos 9\theta + i\sin 9\theta$ (g) $\cos 8\theta + i\sin 8\theta$

(h) $\dfrac{1}{2} + \dfrac{\sqrt{3}}{2}i$ (i) -8

(j) -1

3.5 ROOTS OF A COMPLEX NUMBER

For positive integer q, complex number $(a+ib)^{1/q}$ has q roots and we claim that these q roots are distinct and can be arranged in geometrical progression.

Theorem : If q is any positive integer then $(\cos\theta + i\sin\theta)^{1/q}$ has exactly q distinct values which can be arranged in geometrical progression.

Proof : Using De Moivre's theorem, we say that one of the value of $(\cos\theta + i\sin\theta)^{1/q}$ is $\cos\dfrac{\theta}{q} + i\sin\dfrac{\theta}{q}$.

Due to periodic nature of $\cos\theta$ and $\sin\theta$, we have

$$\cos\theta = \cos(2n\pi + \theta)$$

and $\sin\theta = \sin(2n\pi + \theta)$, for positive n.

Hence,

$$(\cos\theta + i\sin\theta)^{1/q} = [\cos(2n\pi + \theta) + i\sin(2n\pi + \theta)]^{1/q}$$

$$= \cos\left(\frac{2n\pi + \theta}{q}\right) + i\sin\left(\frac{2n\pi + \theta}{q}\right)$$

where, $n = 0, 1, 2, \ldots (q-1)$.

Following are the q distinct roots for $n = 0, 1, 2, \ldots (q-1)$.

$$\cos\left(\frac{\theta}{q}\right) + i\sin\left(\frac{\theta}{q}\right), \qquad \text{for } n = 0$$

$$\cos\left(\frac{2\pi + \theta}{q}\right) + i\sin\left(\frac{2\pi + \theta}{q}\right), \qquad \text{for } n = 1$$

$$\cos\left(\frac{2\pi(q-1) + \theta}{q}\right) + i\sin\left(\frac{2\pi(q-1) + \theta}{q}\right), \qquad \text{for } n = q-1$$

Note that for $n > q-1$ we get same values as that of above roots but may not be in sequence.

Further if we denote these roots as $z_0, z_1, \ldots, z_{q-1}$ then we can easily observed that they forms an geometric progression.

Procedure to find q distinct roots of $(a + ib)^{1/q}$.

Step 1 : Express $(a + ib)$ in polar form i.e. $r(\cos\theta + i\sin\theta)$.

Step 2 : Take general value of θ as $2n\pi + \theta$, since $\cos\theta$, $\sin\theta$ are periodic.

Step 3 : Apply De Moivre's theorem.

Step 4 : Putting $n = 0, 1, 2, \ldots (q-1)$ we get q distinct roots. Remember that complex roots always exist in its conjugate pairs.

Roots of complex number x + iy :

Let $z = x + iy$, then its polar form be $z = r(\cos\theta + i\sin\theta)$, where $r = \sqrt{x^2 + y^2}$ and $\theta = \tan^{-1}\left(\frac{y}{x}\right)$.

∴ $z = r\{\cos(2k\pi + \theta) + i\sin(2k\pi + \theta)\}$

Then $z^{1/n} = r^{1/n}\{\cos(2k\pi + \theta) + i\sin(2k\pi + \theta)\}^{1/n}$

i.e. $z^{1/n} = r^{1/n}\left\{\cos\left(\dfrac{2k\pi + \theta}{n}\right) + i\sin\left(\dfrac{2k\pi + \theta}{n}\right)\right\}$

Putting $k = 1, 2, 3, \ldots, n-1$, we get n distinct n^{th} roots of unity.

Working rule to find the n distinct roots of $(x + iy)^{1/q}$:

Step-I : Express $x + iy$ in a polar form i.e. of the form $r(\cos\theta + i\sin\theta)$

Step-II : Add $2k\pi$ to the angle.

Step-III : Apply De Moivre's theorem.

Step-IV : The required n^{th} roots are obtained from step-III by giving n values to k as $k = 0, 1, 2, \ldots, n-1$.

SOLVED EXAMPLES

Example 3.7 : Find all values of (i) $(-1)^{1/3}$, (ii) $(1)^{1/5}$, (iii) $(\sqrt{3} + i)^{1/3}$, (iv) $(1 + i)^{1/3}$.

Solution : (i) $(-1)^{1/3}$

We know that $\cos\pi = -1$, $\sin\pi = 0$.

$-1 = -1 + 0i$
$= \cos\pi + i\sin\pi$
$= \cos(2k\pi + \pi) + i\sin(2k\pi + \pi)$,

By generalization.

∴ $(-1)^{1/3} = [\cos(2k+1)\pi + i\sin(2k+1)\pi]^{1/3}$

∴ $(-1)^{1/3} = \cos\left(\dfrac{2k+1}{3}\right)\pi + i\sin\left(\dfrac{2k+1}{3}\right)\pi$

... De Moivre's theroem

Put $k = 0, 1$, we get,

$z_0 = \cos\dfrac{\pi}{3} + i\sin\dfrac{\pi}{3} = \dfrac{1}{2} + \dfrac{i\sqrt{3}}{2}$

$z_1 = \cos\pi + i\sin\pi = -1$

$z_2 = \cos\dfrac{5\pi}{3} + i\sin\dfrac{5\pi}{3} = \dfrac{1}{2} - \dfrac{i\sqrt{3}}{2}$

(ii) $(1)^{1/5}$

$\therefore \quad 1 = \cos 0 + i \sin 0$

$\therefore \quad 1 = \cos(2k\pi + 0) + i \sin(2k\pi + 0)$

$\therefore \quad 1 = \cos(2k\pi) + i \sin(2k\pi)$

$\therefore \quad (1)^{1/5} = (\cos 2k\pi + i \sin 2k\pi)^{1/5}$

$\therefore \quad (1)^{1/5} = \cos\left(\dfrac{2k\pi}{5}\right) + i \sin\left(\dfrac{2k\pi}{5}\right)$

Put $k = 0, 1, 2, 3, 4$ we get five roots of unity as,

$$z_0 = \cos 0 + i \sin 0 = 1$$

$$z_1 = \cos \dfrac{2\pi}{5} + i \sin \dfrac{2\pi}{5}$$

$$z_2 = \cos \dfrac{4\pi}{5} + i \sin \dfrac{4\pi}{5}$$

$$z_3 = \cos \dfrac{6\pi}{5} + i \sin \dfrac{6\pi}{5}$$

$$z_4 = \cos \dfrac{8\pi}{5} + i \sin \dfrac{8\pi}{5}$$

(iii) $(\sqrt{3} + i)^{1/3}$

$$z = x + iy = \sqrt{3} + i$$

Equating real and imaginary parts.

$\therefore \quad x = \sqrt{3}, \quad y = 1$

Polar from of z is $z = r(\cos \theta + i \sin \theta)$ where,

$r \cos \theta = \sqrt{3}$, $r \sin \theta = 1$ $\therefore r^2 = 3 + 1 = 4 \Rightarrow r = 2$.

and $\quad \theta = \tan^{-1}\left(\dfrac{y}{x}\right)$

$\therefore \quad \theta = \tan^{-1}\left(\dfrac{1}{\sqrt{3}}\right)$

$\therefore \quad \theta = \dfrac{\pi}{6}$

$\therefore \quad z = 2\left(\cos \dfrac{\pi}{6} + i \sin \dfrac{\pi}{6}\right)$

$$\therefore \quad z = 2\left[\cos\left(2k\pi + \frac{\pi}{6}\right) + i\sin\left(2k\pi + \frac{\pi}{6}\right)\right]$$

$$\therefore \quad z^{1/3} = 2^{1/3}\left[\cos\left(2k\pi + \frac{\pi}{6}\right) + i\sin\left(2k\pi + \frac{\pi}{6}\right)\right]^{1/3}$$

$$\therefore \quad z^{1/3} = 2^{1/3}\left[\cos\left(\frac{12k+1}{6}\right)\pi + i\sin\left(\frac{12k+1}{6}\right)\pi\right]^{1/3}$$

$$\therefore \quad z^{1/3} = 2^{1/3}\left[\cos\left(\frac{12k+1}{18}\right)\pi + i\sin\left(\frac{12k+1}{18}\right)\pi\right]$$

Put $k = 0, 1, 2$ we get three roots of the given complex number.

$$z_0 = 2^{1/3}\left[\cos\frac{\pi}{18} + i\sin\frac{\pi}{18}\right]$$

$$z_1 = 2^{1/3}\left[\cos\frac{13\pi}{18} + i\sin\frac{13\pi}{18}\right]$$

$$= 2^{1/3}\left[\frac{-\cos 5\pi}{18} + i\sin\frac{5\pi}{18}\right]$$

$$z_2 = 2^{1/3}\left[\cos\frac{25\pi}{18} + i\sin\frac{25\pi}{18}\right]$$

$$z_2 = 2^{1/3}\left[\cos\left(\frac{18\pi + 7\pi}{18}\right) + i\sin\left(\frac{8\pi + 7\pi}{18}\right)\right]$$

$$= -2^{1/3}\left[+\cos\frac{7\pi}{18} + i\sin\frac{7\pi}{18}\right]$$

Since $\cos(\pi + \theta) = -\cos\theta, \sin(\pi + \theta) = -\sin\theta$

(iv) $(1 + i)^{1/3}$

Let $\quad z = x + iy = 1 + i$

$\therefore \quad x = 1, y = 1$

$\quad r = \sqrt{x^2 + y^2}$

$\therefore \quad r = \sqrt{2}$

$\quad \theta = \tan^{-1}\left(\frac{y}{x}\right)$

$\therefore \quad \theta = \tan^{-1}(1)$

$\therefore \quad \theta = 45° = \frac{\pi}{4}$

Polar form is $z = r(\cos\theta + i\sin\theta)$

$$z = \sqrt{2}\left(\cos\frac{\pi}{4} + i\sin\frac{\pi}{4}\right)$$

$$z = \sqrt{2}\left[\cos\left(2k\pi + \frac{\pi}{4}\right) + i\sin\left(2k\pi + \frac{\pi}{4}\right)\right]$$

$$z^{1/3} = (\sqrt{2})^{1/3}\left[\cos\left(\frac{8k\pi + \pi}{4}\right) + i\sin\left(\frac{8k\pi + \pi}{4}\right)\right]^{1/3}$$

$$z^{1/3} = (2)^{1/6}\left[\cos\frac{(8k+1)}{12}\pi + i\sin\frac{(3k+1)}{12}\pi\right]$$

Putt $k = 0, 1, 2$.

$$\therefore \quad z_0 = (2)^{1/6}\left[\cos\frac{\pi}{12} + i\sin\frac{\pi}{12}\right]$$

$$\therefore \quad z_1 = (2)^{1/6}\left[\cos\frac{9\pi}{12} + i\sin\frac{9\pi}{12}\right]$$

$$= 2^{1/6}\left[\cos\frac{3\pi}{4} + i\sin\frac{3\pi}{4}\right]$$

$$z_2 = (2)^{1/6}\left[\cos\frac{17\pi}{12} + i\sin\frac{17\pi}{12}\right]$$

$$= 2^{1/6}\left[\cos\left(\frac{12\pi + 5\pi}{12}\right) + i\sin\left(\frac{12\pi + 5\pi}{12}\right)\right]$$

$$= -2^{1/6}\left[\cos\left(\frac{5\pi}{12}\right) + i\sin\left(\frac{5\pi}{12}\right)\right]$$

Example 3.8 : Find all values of $x^7 - x^4 + x^3 - 1 = 0$.

Solution : Given equation is $x^7 - x^4 + x^3 - 1 = 0$.

$\therefore \quad x^4(x^3 - 1) + 1(x^3 - 1) = 0$

$\therefore \quad (x^4 + 1)(x^3 - 1) = 0$

$\therefore \quad x^4 + 1 = 0$ or $x^3 - 1 = 0$

$\therefore \quad x = (-1)^{1/4}$ or $x = (1)^{1/3}$

Now, $\quad 1 = \cos 0 + i\sin 0 \quad$ (Since $\cos 0 = 1$ and $\sin 0 = 0$

$\quad\quad\quad 1 = \cos 2k\pi + i\sin 2k\pi \quad\quad\quad$ by generalization)

$$(1)^{1/3} = (\cos 2k\pi + i \sin 2k\pi)^{1/3}$$

$$\therefore \quad (1)^{1/3} = \cos\left(\frac{2k\pi}{3}\right) + i \sin\left(\frac{2k\pi}{3}\right)$$

using De Moivre's Theorem

$$\alpha_1 = \cos 0° + i \sin 0° = 1$$

$$\alpha_2 = \cos \frac{2\pi}{3} + i \sin \frac{2\pi}{3} = \frac{-1 + i\sqrt{3}}{2}$$

$$\alpha_3 = \cos \frac{4\pi}{3} + i \sin \frac{4\pi}{3} = \frac{-1 - i\sqrt{3}}{2}$$

Similarly, $\quad -1 = \cos \pi + i \sin \pi$

$\therefore \quad -1 = \cos(2k\pi + \pi) + i \sin(2k\pi + \pi)$

By generalization.

$$\therefore \quad (-1)^{1/4} = [\cos(2k+1)\pi + i \sin(2k+\pi)]^{1/4}$$

$$\therefore \quad (-1)^{1/4} = \cos \frac{(2k+1)}{4}\pi + i \sin \frac{(2k+1)}{4}\pi$$

Put k = 0, 1, 2, 3.

$$\beta_1 = \cos \frac{\pi}{4} + i \sin \frac{\pi}{4} = \frac{1+i}{\sqrt{2}}$$

$$\beta_2 = \cos \frac{3\pi}{4} + i \sin \frac{3\pi}{4} = \frac{-1+i}{\sqrt{2}}$$

$$\beta_3 = \cos \frac{5\pi}{4} + i \sin \frac{5\pi}{4} = \frac{-1-i}{\sqrt{2}}$$

$$\beta_4 = \cos \frac{7\pi}{4} + i \sin \frac{7\pi}{4} = \frac{1-i}{\sqrt{2}}$$

$\therefore$ Required roots are $\frac{-1 \pm i\sqrt{3}}{2}, \pm \frac{(1+i)}{\sqrt{2}}, \pm \frac{(1-i)}{\sqrt{2}}$

Example 3.9 : Solve : $x^6 + x^5 + x^4 + x^3 + x^2 + x + 1 = 0$.

Solution : Given equation : $x^6 + x^5 + x^4 + x^3 + x^2 + x + 1 = 0$.

Multiplying both sides by $(x - 1)$.

$$(x - 1)(x^6 + x^5 + x^4 + x^3 + x^2 + x + 1) = 0$$

$$x^7 + x^6 + x^5 + x^4 + x^3 + x^2 - x^6 - x^5 - x^4 - x^3 - x^2 - x^1 - x - 1 = 0$$

$\therefore \qquad x^7 - 1 = 0$

$\therefore \qquad x = (1)^{1/7}$

$\therefore \qquad 1 = \cos 0 + i \sin 0$

$\therefore \qquad 1 = \cos(2k\pi) + i \sin(2k\pi) \qquad$ by generalization

By generalization.

$\therefore \qquad (1)^{1/7} = [\cos 2k\pi + i \sin 2k\pi]^{1/7}$

$\therefore \qquad (1)^{1/7} = \cos\left(\dfrac{2k\pi}{7}\right) + i \sin\left(\dfrac{2k\pi}{7}\right)$

using De Moivre's theorem

Put $k = 0, 1, 2, 3, 4, 5, 6$.

$$z_0 = \cos 0 + i \sin 0 = 1$$

$$z_1 = \cos \dfrac{2\pi}{7} + i \sin \dfrac{2\pi}{7}$$

$$z_2 = \cos \dfrac{4\pi}{7} + i \sin \dfrac{4\pi}{7}$$

$$z_3 = \cos \dfrac{6\pi}{7} + i \sin \dfrac{6\pi}{7}$$

$$z_4 = \cos \dfrac{8\pi}{7} + i \sin \dfrac{8\pi}{7}$$

$$z_5 = \cos \dfrac{10\pi}{7} + i \sin \dfrac{10\pi}{7}$$

$$z_6 = \cos \dfrac{12\pi}{7} + i \sin \dfrac{12\pi}{7}$$

Example 3.10 : Evaluate $\int \cos^4 \theta \, d\theta$.

Solution : Let $x = \cos \theta + i \sin \theta$

$\dfrac{1}{x} = \cos \theta - i \sin \theta$

$$\therefore \qquad x + \frac{1}{x} = 2\cos\theta \Rightarrow \cos\theta = \frac{1}{2}(x + x^{-1})$$

Now, $\qquad \cos^4\theta = \frac{1}{2^4}(x + x^{-1})^4$

$= \frac{1}{2^4}\{{}^4C_0 x^4 (x^{-1})^0 + {}^4C_1 x^3 (x^{-1})^1 + {}^4C_2 x^2 (x^{-1})^2 + {}^4C_3 x (x^{-1})^3 + {}^4C_4 x^0 (x^{-1})^4\}$

$= \frac{1}{2^4}\{x^4 + 4x^2 + 6 + 4x^{-2} + x^{-4}\}$

$= \frac{1}{2^4}\{(x^4 + x^{-4}) + 4(x^2 + x^{-2}) + 6\}$ $\qquad \because x^n = \cos n\theta + i\sin n\theta$

$= \frac{1}{2^4}\{2\cos 4\theta + 8\cos 2\theta + 6\}$ $\qquad x^{-n} = \cos n\theta - i\sin n\theta$

$\Rightarrow x^n + x^{-n} = 2\cos n\theta$

So, $\int \cos^4\theta\, d\theta$

$= \frac{1}{2^4}\left[\int 2\cos 4\theta\, d\theta + 4\int 2\cos 2\theta\, d\theta + 6\int d\theta\right]$

$= \frac{1}{2^4}\left[\frac{2\sin 4\theta}{4} + \frac{(4)(2)\sin 2\theta}{2} + 6\theta\right] = \frac{\sin 4\theta}{32} + \frac{\sin 2\theta}{4} + \frac{3\theta}{8}$

Example 3.11 : If p and q are roots of $x^2 - 2x + 2 = 0$, then prove that

$$p^n + q^n = 2^{\frac{n+2}{2}} \cos\left(\frac{n\pi}{4}\right).$$

Solution : Given : $x^2 - 2x + 2 = 0$.

Its roots are $\qquad x = \frac{2 \pm \sqrt{2^2 - 4(2)(1)}}{2} = 1 \pm i$

Take $p = 1 + i$, $q = 1 - i$.

If $\qquad p = 1 + i = r(\cos\theta + i\sin\theta)$, then

$\qquad r\cos\theta = 1, \ r = \sin\theta = 1 \Rightarrow r^2 = 2 \Rightarrow r = \sqrt{2}$

and $\qquad \tan\theta = 1 \Rightarrow \theta = \frac{\pi}{4}$

$$\therefore \quad p = \sqrt{2}\left(\cos\frac{\pi}{4} + i\sin\frac{\pi}{4}\right)$$

$$q = \sqrt{2}\left(\cos\frac{\pi}{4} - i\sin\frac{\pi}{4}\right)$$

$$\therefore \quad p^n + q^n = \left\{\sqrt{2}\left(\cos\frac{\pi}{4} + i\sin\frac{\pi}{4}\right)\right\}^n + \left\{\sqrt{2}\left(\cos\frac{\pi}{4} - i\sin\frac{\pi}{4}\right)\right\}^n$$

$$= 2^{n/2}\left[\cos\frac{n\pi}{4} + i\sin\frac{n\pi}{4} + \cos\frac{n\pi}{4} - i\sin\frac{n\pi}{4}\right]$$

$$= 2^{\frac{n}{2}+1}\cos\frac{n\pi}{4} = 2^{\frac{n+2}{2}}\cos\frac{n\pi}{4} = \text{R.H.S.}$$

Example 3.12 : Find all the values of $\left(\frac{1}{2} + \frac{\sqrt{3}}{2}i\right)^{3/4}$ and show that their continued product of all the values is 1.

Solution : We know that :

$$\frac{1}{2} + \frac{\sqrt{3}}{2}i = \cos\frac{\pi}{3} + i\sin\frac{\pi}{3}$$

$$= \cos\left(2k\pi + \frac{\pi}{3}\right) + i\sin\left(2k\pi + \frac{\pi}{3}\right)$$

$$= \cos\left(\frac{6k+1}{3}\right)\pi + i\sin\left(\frac{6k+1}{3}\right)\pi$$

$$\therefore \quad \left(\frac{1}{2} + \frac{\sqrt{3}}{2}i\right)^{3/4} = \left[\cos\frac{(6k+1)\pi}{3} + i\sin\frac{(6k+1)\pi}{3}\right]^{3/4}$$

$$\text{for } k = 0, 1, 2, 3$$

$$= \cos\frac{(6k+1)\pi}{4} + i\sin\frac{(6k+1)\pi}{4} \quad \text{for } k = 0, 1, 2, 3$$

Putting $k = 0, 1, 2, 3$ the different values are $\cos\frac{\pi}{4} + i\sin\frac{\pi}{4}$, $\cos\frac{7\pi}{4} + i\sin\frac{7\pi}{4}$, $\cos\frac{13\pi}{4} + i\sin\frac{13\pi}{4}$, $\cos\frac{19\pi}{4} + i\sin\frac{19\pi}{4}$.

Thus continued product of these roots

$$= \cos\left(\frac{\pi}{4} + \frac{7\pi}{4} + \frac{13\pi}{4} + \frac{19\pi}{4}\right) + i\sin\left(\frac{\pi}{4} + \frac{7\pi}{4} + \frac{13\pi}{4} + \frac{19\pi}{4}\right)$$

$$= \cos 10\pi + i\sin 10\pi$$

$$= 1$$

EXERCISE (3.2)

1. If p and q are roots of the equation $x^2 - 2\sqrt{3} + 4 = 0$, prove that $p^3 + q^3 = 0$.

2. If $a_n + ib_n = (1 + i\sqrt{3})^n$, prove that $a_{n-1} b_n - a_n b_{n-1} = 4^{n-1}\sqrt{3}$.

3. If w is a complex cube roots of unity, prove that $(1 - w)^{12} = 629$.

4. Solve $x^6 - i = 0$.

5. Solve $\left(\dfrac{1 + x}{1 - x}\right)^6 = 1$.

6. If $1 + 2i$ is a root of the equation $x^4 - 3x^3 + 8x^2 - 7x + 5 = 0$, find all other roots.

7. Find all the values of (i) $(-1)^{1/5}$, (ii) $(1)^{1/4}$, (iii) $(-i)^{1/3}$, (iv) $(1 + i)^{2/4}$, (v) $(32)^{1/5}$, (vi) $\sqrt[3]{1 + i\sqrt{3}} + \sqrt[3]{1 - i\sqrt{3}}$, (vii) $\sqrt[3]{(1 + i)/2} + \sqrt[3]{(1 - i)/2}$.

8. If one of the root of $x^4 - 6x^3 + 15x^2 - 18x + 10 = 0$ is $1 + i$ find all other roots.

9. Solve the equations :
   (i) $x^{12} - 1 = 0$, (ii) $x^7 + x^4 + x^3 + 1 = 0$, (iii) $x^7 + x^4 + ix^3 + i = 0$.

ANSWERS (3.2)

4. $\pm\left(\cos\dfrac{\pi}{12} + i\sin\dfrac{\pi}{12}\right), \pm\left(\cos\dfrac{5\pi}{12} + i\sin\dfrac{5\pi}{12}\right), \pm\left(\cos\dfrac{9\pi}{12} + i\sin\dfrac{9\pi}{12}\right)$

5. $x = \dfrac{\left(\cos\dfrac{k\pi}{3} + i\sin\dfrac{k\pi}{3}\right) - 1}{\left(\cos\dfrac{k\pi}{3} + i\sin\dfrac{k\pi}{3}\right) + 1}$ where $k = 0, 1, -1, 5$.

6. $1 - 2i, (1 \pm \sqrt{3}i)/2$

7. (i) $-1, \cos\dfrac{\pi}{5} \pm i\sin\dfrac{\pi}{5}, \cos\dfrac{3\pi}{5} \pm i\sin\dfrac{3\pi}{5}$

   (ii) $\pm 1, \pm i$ (ii) $i, \pm(\sqrt{3} - i)/2$

(iv) $2^{1/3}\left(\cos\dfrac{k\pi}{6} + i\sin\dfrac{k\pi}{6}\right)$, $k = 1, 5, 9$

(v) $2, 2\left(\cos\dfrac{k\pi}{5} \pm i\sin\dfrac{k\pi}{5}\right)$, $k = 2, 4$

(vi) $2.2^{1/3}\cos\dfrac{k\pi}{9}$, $k = 1, 7, 13$ (viii) $2\cos\dfrac{k\pi}{12}$, $k = 1, 9, 17$

8. $1 - i$, $2 \pm i$

9. (i) $\pm 1, \pm i, \pm\left(\cos\dfrac{\pi}{6} \pm i\sin\dfrac{\pi}{6}\right), \pm\left(\cos\dfrac{\pi}{3} \pm i\sin\dfrac{\pi}{3}\right)$

(ii) $\pm\dfrac{1}{\sqrt{2}}(1 \pm i)$, $\dfrac{1}{2} \pm i\dfrac{\sqrt{3}}{2}$, -1

(iii) $\pm\left(\cos\dfrac{\pi}{8} - \sin\dfrac{\pi}{8}\right), \pm\left(\cos\dfrac{5\pi}{8} - i\sin\dfrac{5\pi}{8}\right), \dfrac{1}{2} \pm i\sqrt{3}/2$, -1

3.6 EXPANSION OF cos nθ, sin nθ

By De Moivre's theorem we have,

$$\cos(n\theta) + i\sin(n\theta) = (\cos\theta + i\sin\theta)^n$$

Applying binomial theorem to right hand side, we get

$= {}^nC_0 \cos^n\theta + {}^nC_1 \cos^{n-1}\theta\,(i\sin\theta) + {}^nC_2 \cos^{n-2}\theta\,(i^2\sin^2\theta) + \ldots$

$= [{}^nC_0 \cos^n\theta - {}^nC_2 \cos^{n-2}\theta \sin^2\theta + {}^nC_4 \cos^{n-4}\theta \sin^4\theta - \ldots]$

$+ i\,[{}^nC_1 \cos^{n-1}\theta \sin\theta - {}^nC_3 \cos^{n-3}\theta \sin^3\theta + {}^nC_5 \cos^{n-5}\theta \sin^5\theta - \ldots]$

Equating real and imaginary parts on both sides, we get

$\cos n\theta = {}^nC_0 \cos^n\theta - {}^nC_2 \cos^{n-2}\theta \sin^2\theta + {}^nC_4 \cos^{n-4}\theta \sin^4\theta - \ldots$ ... (1)

$\sin n\theta = {}^nC_1 \cos^{n-1}\theta \sin\theta - {}^nC_3 \cos^{n-3}\theta \sin^3\theta + {}^nC_5 \cos^{n-5}\theta \sin^5\theta - \ldots$

... (2)

Taking division of equation (2) with (1), we get

$\tan(n\theta) = \dfrac{\sin n\theta}{\cos n\theta}$

$= \dfrac{{}^nC_1 \cos^{n-1}\theta \sin\theta - {}^nC_3 \cos^{n-3}\theta \sin^3\theta + {}^nC_5 \cos^{n-5}\theta \sin^5\theta - \ldots}{{}^nC_0 \cos^n\theta - {}^nC_2 \cos^{n-2}\theta \sin^2\theta + {}^nC_4 \cos^{n-4}\theta \sin^4\theta - \ldots}$

Dividing numerator and denominator by $\cos^n \theta$, we get

$$\tan(n\theta) = \frac{{}^nC_1 \tan\theta - {}^nC_3 \tan^3\theta + {}^nC_5 \tan^5\theta - \ldots}{1 - {}^nC_2 \tan^2\theta + {}^nC_4 \tan^4\theta - \ldots} \qquad \ldots (3)$$

Thus equation (1), (2) and (3) gives the expansion of $\cos n\theta$, $\sin(n\theta)$ and $\tan(n\theta)$.

SOLVED EXAMPLES

Example 3.13 : Express $\sin 7\theta$ and $\cos 7\theta$ in-terms of $\sin\theta$ and $\cos\theta$.

Solution : Using De Moivre's theorem.

Consider, $(\cos 7\theta + i \sin 7\theta) = (\cos\theta + i \sin\theta)^7$.

Applying binomial theorem to right hand side, we get

$$= {}^7C_0 \cos^7\theta \sin^0\theta + {}^7C_1 \cos^6\theta (i \sin\theta) + {}^7C_2 \cos^5\theta\, i^2 \sin^2\theta$$
$$+ {}^7C_3 \cos^4\theta \sin^3\theta \cdot i^3 + {}^7C_4 \cos^3\theta \cdot i^4 \sin^4\theta + {}^6C_5 \cos^2\theta\, i^5 \sin^5\theta$$
$$+ {}^7C_6 \cos\theta\, i^6 \sin^6\theta + {}^7C_7 \cos^0\theta\, i^7 \sin^7\theta$$

$$= {}^7C_0 \cos^7\theta + i \cdot 7 \cdot \cos^6\theta \sin\theta - \frac{7\cdot 6}{2}\cos^5\theta \sin^2\theta - i\cdot\frac{7\cdot 6\cdot 5}{6}\cos^4\theta \sin^3\theta$$
$$+ \frac{7\cdot 6\cdot 5\cdot 4}{4\cdot 3\cdot 2\cdot 1}\cos^3\theta \sin^4\theta + i\frac{7\cdot 6}{2}\cos^2\theta \sin^5\theta - 7\cos\theta \sin^6\theta - i\sin^7\theta$$

$$= [\cos^7\theta - 21\cos^5\theta \sin^2\theta + 35\cos^3\theta \sin^4\theta - 7\cos\theta \sin^6\theta]$$
$$+ i[7\cos^6\theta \sin\theta - 35\cos^4\theta \sin^3\theta + 21\cos^2\theta \sin^5\theta - \sin^7\theta]$$

Comparing real imaginary parts from either sides, we get

$$\cos 7\theta = \cos^7\theta - 21\cos^5\theta \sin^2\theta + 35\cos^3\theta \sin^4\theta - 7\cos\theta \sin^6\theta$$
$$\sin 7\theta = 7\cos^6\theta \sin\theta - 35\cos^4\theta \sin^3\theta + 21\cos^2\theta \sin^5\theta - \sin^7\theta$$

Example 3.14 : Evaluate (i) $\int \sin^4\theta\, d\theta$ (ii) $\int \sin^5\theta \cos^3\theta\, d\theta$.

Solution : Consider

$$x = \cos\theta + i\sin\theta$$
$$\therefore \quad \frac{1}{x} = \cos\theta - i\sin\theta$$
$$\therefore \quad 2i\sin\theta = x - \frac{1}{x}$$

$$\therefore \quad (2i\sin\theta)^4 = \left(x - \frac{1}{x}\right)^4 = \left(x + \left(\frac{-1}{x}\right)\right)^4$$

$$= {}^4C_0 x^4 \left(\frac{-1}{x}\right)^0 + {}^4C_1 x^3 \left(\frac{-1}{x}\right)^1 + {}^4C_2 x^2 \left(\frac{-1}{x}\right)^2 + {}^4C_3 x \left(\frac{-1}{x}\right)^3 + {}^4C_4 x^0 \left(\frac{-1}{x}\right)^4$$

$$= x^4 - 4x^2 + 6 - \frac{4}{x^2} + \frac{1}{x^4}$$

$$= \left(x^4 + \frac{1}{x^4}\right) - 4\left(x^2 + \frac{1}{x^2}\right) + 6 \ldots$$

$$2^4 \cdot i^4 \sin^4\theta = 2\cos(4\theta) - 4\cos(2\theta) + 6$$

$$\therefore \quad \sin^4\theta = \frac{1}{2^4}[2\cos(4\theta) - 4\cos(2\theta) + 6]$$

$$\int \sin^4\theta \, d\theta = \frac{1}{2^4} \int 2\cos 4\theta \, d\theta - \frac{4}{2^4} \int \cos 2\theta \, d\theta + \frac{6}{2^4} \int d\theta$$

$$= \frac{1}{2^3} \frac{\sin 4\theta}{4} - \frac{1}{2^2} \frac{\sin 2\theta}{2} + \frac{3\theta}{2^3}$$

$$= \frac{1}{32}\sin(4\theta) - \frac{1}{8}\sin(2\theta) + \frac{3}{8}\theta$$

(ii) $\int \sin^5\theta \cos^3\theta \, d\theta$.

Solution : Consider

$$(2i\sin\theta)^5 (\cos\theta)^3 = \left(x - \frac{1}{x}\right)^5 \left(x + \frac{1}{x}\right)^3$$

$$32i \sin^5\theta \cos^3\theta$$

$$= \left(x^5 - 5x^3 + 10x - \frac{10}{x} + \frac{5}{x^3} - \frac{1}{x^5}\right) \left(x^3 + 3x + \frac{3}{x} + \frac{1}{x^3}\right)$$

$$= \left[\left(x^5 - \frac{1}{x^5}\right) - 5\left(x^3 - \frac{1}{x^3}\right) + 10\left(x - \frac{1}{x}\right)\right]\left[\left(x^3 + \frac{1}{x^3}\right) + 3\left(x + \frac{1}{x}\right)\right]$$

$$= [2i\sin 5\theta - 5(2) i \sin 3\theta + 20i \sin\theta][2\cos(3\theta) + 3(2\cos\theta)]$$

$$\sin^5\theta \cos^3\theta$$

$$= \frac{1}{32}[4\sin 5\theta \cos 3\theta - 20\sin 3\theta \cos 3\theta - 60\sin 3\theta \cos\theta$$

$$+ 40\sin\theta \cos(3\theta) + 120\sin\theta \cos\theta]$$

$\int \sin^5 \theta \cos^3 \theta \, d\theta$

$= \dfrac{1}{8} \int \dfrac{\sin 8\theta + \sin 2\theta}{2} d\theta - \dfrac{10}{32} \int \sin(6\theta) \, d\theta$

$- \dfrac{30}{32} \int [\sin 4\theta + \sin 2\theta] \, d\theta - \dfrac{20}{32} \int [\sin 4\theta - \sin 2\theta] \, d\theta$

$+ \dfrac{60}{32} \int \sin(2\theta) \, d\theta$

$= \dfrac{1}{16} \left[\dfrac{-\cos 8\theta}{8} - \dfrac{\cos(2\theta)}{2} \right] - \dfrac{10}{32} \left[\dfrac{-\cos 6\theta}{6} \right] - \dfrac{30}{32} \left[\dfrac{-\cos 4\theta}{4} - \dfrac{\cos 2\theta}{2} \right]$

$- \dfrac{20}{32} \left[\dfrac{-\cos 4\theta}{4} + \dfrac{\cos 2\theta}{2} \right] + \dfrac{60}{32} \left[\dfrac{-\cos(2\theta)}{2} \right]$

$= -\dfrac{1}{128} \cos 8\theta - \dfrac{1}{32} \cos(2\theta) + \dfrac{5}{96} \cos(6\theta) + \dfrac{15}{64} \cos 4\theta + \dfrac{15}{32} \cos 2\theta$

$+ \dfrac{5}{32} \cos 4\theta - \dfrac{5}{16} \cos 2\theta - \dfrac{15}{16} \cos(2\theta)$

$= \dfrac{-1}{128} [\cos 8\theta + 88 \cos(2\theta) - 50 \cos 4\theta]$

Example 3.15 : Express $\cos 4\theta$ in terms of powers of $\cos \theta$.

Solution : By De Moivre's theorem, we write

$(\cos 4\theta + i \sin 4\theta) = (\cos \theta + i \sin \theta)^4$

Expand by binomial theorem,

$\therefore \quad \cos 4\theta + i \sin 4\theta = {}^4C_0 \cos^4 \theta + {}^4C_1 \cos^3 \theta \cdot i \sin \theta$
$\qquad\qquad + {}^4C_2 \cos^2 \theta \cdot (i \sin \theta)^2 + {}^4C_3 \cos \theta (i \sin \theta)^3$
$\qquad\qquad + {}^4C_4 (i \sin \theta)^4$

Noting that, $i^2 = -1$, $i^3 = -i$ and $i^4 = 1$
and ${}^4C_0 = {}^4C_4 = 1$, ${}^4C_1 = 4$, ${}^4C_2 = 6$ and ${}^4C_3 = 4$.

$\therefore \quad \cos 4\theta + i \sin 4\theta = \cos^4 \theta + 4i \cos^3 \theta \cdot \sin \theta - 6 \cos^2 \theta \sin^2 \theta$
$\qquad\qquad - i 4 \cos \theta \cdot \sin^3 \theta + \sin^4 \theta$

$\therefore \quad \cos 4\theta + i \sin 4\theta = \cos^4 \theta + 4i \cos^3 \theta \cdot \sin \theta - 6 \cos^2 \theta \sin^2 \theta$
$\qquad\qquad - 4i \cos \theta \sin^3 \theta + \sin^4 \theta$
$\qquad\qquad = \cos^4 \theta - 6 \cos^2 \theta \sin^2 \theta + \sin^4 \theta$
$\qquad\qquad + 4i (\cos^3 \theta \cdot \sin \theta - \cos \theta \sin^3 \theta)$

Equating real and imaginary parts we get,

$\cos 4\theta = \cos^4 \theta - 6 \cos^2 \theta \sin^2 \theta + \sin^4 \theta$

and $\sin 4\theta = 4 \cos^3 \theta \sin \theta - 4 \cos \theta \sin^3 \theta$

$$\therefore \quad \cos 4\theta = \cos^4\theta - 6\cos^2\theta(1-\cos^2\theta) + (1-\cos^2\theta)^2$$
$$= \cos^4\theta - 6\cos^2\theta + 6\cos^4\theta$$
$$+ 1 - 2\cos^2\theta + \cos^4\theta$$
$$= 8\cos^4\theta - 8\cos^2\theta + 1$$

is the required solution.

EXERCISE 3.3

Prove the following :

1. $\cos^7\theta = \dfrac{1}{2^6}[\cos 7\theta + 7\cos 5\theta + 21\cos 3\theta + 35\cos\theta]$
2. $\sin^8\theta = \dfrac{1}{2^7}[\cos 3\theta - 8\cos 6\theta + 28\cos 4\theta - 56\cos 2\theta + 35]$
3. $16\sin^5\theta = \sin^5\theta - 5\sin 3\theta + 10\sin\theta$
4. $32\cos^6\theta = \cos 6\theta + 6\cos 4\theta + 15\cos 2\theta + 10$
5. $2^5 \sin^4\theta \cos^2\theta = \cos 6\theta - 2\cos 4\theta - \cos 2\theta + 2$
6. $128\cos^3\theta \cdot \sin^5\theta = \sin 8\theta - 2\sin 6\theta - 2\sin 4\theta + 6\sin 2\theta$
7. $\cos 5\theta = 5\cos\theta - 20\cos^3\theta + 16\cos^5\theta$
8. $32\cos^5\theta\, d\theta = \dfrac{2}{5}\sin 5\theta + \dfrac{10}{3}\sin 3\theta + 20\sin\theta$

MISCELLANEOUS EXERCISE

I. Short questions :

1. Write -1 interms of $r\cos\theta + ir\sin\theta$.
2. Write $\sqrt{3} + i$ interms of $r\cos\theta + ir\sin\theta$.
3. State De Moivre's theorem.
4. If $x = \cos\theta + i\sin\theta$, then prove that :
$$2\cos\theta = x + \dfrac{1}{x} \text{ and } 2i\sin\theta = x - \dfrac{1}{x}.$$
5. For a complex number $x + iy$ prove that :
$$x^3 + x^{-3} = 2\cos 3\theta \text{ and } x^3 - x^{-3} = 2i\sin(3\theta).$$
6. Taking suitable value of θ show that :
$$(\sin\theta + i\cos\theta)^n \neq \sin(n\theta) + i\cos(n\theta).$$
7. Taking suitable values of θ and ϕ verify that:
$$(\cos\theta + i\sin\phi)^n \neq \cos(n\theta) + i\sin(n\phi).$$
8. Show that cube roots of unity are in G.P.

II. Numerical Problems

1. Find all the values of $(-1)^{1/5}$.
2. Find all the roots of $i^{1/4}$.
3. Find the values of $(-1+i)^7$.

4. Find the values of $(\sqrt{3} + 2i)^{3/4}$.
5. Find the continued product of the four values of $\left(\dfrac{1}{2} + \dfrac{i\sqrt{3}}{2}\right)^{3/4}$.
6. Find all values of $(\sqrt{3} - i)^{2/5}$.
7. Find all sixth roots of unity of solve $x^6 - 1 = 0$.
8. Solve $x^7 + x^4 + x^3 + 1 = 0$.
9. $z^4 - z^3 + z^2 - z + 1 = 0$.
10. Solve $(z^2 - 1)^3 = 8z^3$.
11. Let ω be the permitive 7th root of unity. then prove that :
$1 + \omega + \omega^{2n} + \omega^{3n} + \ldots + \omega^{6n} = 7$ if $n = 7m$
$\qquad\qquad\qquad\qquad\qquad\qquad\quad = 0$ if $n \ne 7m$ for any integer
12. Prove that : $z^{1/n} + z^{-1/n}$ has n real values. Hence, find the values of $\sqrt[3]{1 + i\sqrt{3}} + \sqrt[3]{1 - i\sqrt{3}}$.
13. If ω is a complex cube root of unity then show that $(1 - \omega)^5 = -27$.
14. Find the continued product of the five values of the expression $(1 + i)^{1/5}$.
15. Prove that $(1 + \sqrt{3}\, i)^8 + (1 - \sqrt{3}\, i)^8 = -256$.

III. Long Questions
(A) Theory Part :
1. State and prove De Moivre's theorem.
2. Develop the expansion of $\sin(n\theta)$, $\cos(n\theta)$ and $\tan(n\theta)$.
3. Discuss the method of qth root of $(a + ib)$.

(B) Numerical Problems :
1. Simplify :
 (i) $\dfrac{(\cos 5\theta - i\sin 5\theta)^2 (\cos 7\theta + i\sin 7\theta)^{-3}}{(\cos 4\theta - i\sin 5\theta)^9 (\cos\theta + i\sin\theta)^5}$
 (ii) $\dfrac{(\cos 3\theta + i\sin 3\theta)^{-5} (\cos 2\theta - i\sin 2\theta)^7}{(\cos 5\theta - i\sin 5\theta)^{-6} (\cos 4\theta + i\sin 4\theta)^{12}}$
2. Simplify $\dfrac{(\cos 3\theta + i\sin\theta)^5 \cdot (\cos\theta - i\sin\theta)^3}{(\cos 5\theta + i\sin 5\theta)^7 \cdot (\cos 2\theta - i\sin 2\theta)^5}$
3. Simplify
$\{(\cos p - \cos q) + i(\sin p - \sin 2)\}^n + \{(\cos p - \cos q) - i(\sin p - \sin q)\}^n$
4. If $\sin p + \sin q + \sin r = \cos p + \cos q + \cos r = 0$, prove that
$\cos 3p + \cos 3q + \cos 3r = 3\cos(p + q + r)$
and $\sin 3p + \sin 3q + \sin 3r = 3\sin(p + q + r)$.

5. If $a^2 + b^2 = 1$, prove that $\dfrac{1 + a + ib}{1 + a - ib} = a + ib$, $\dfrac{1 + b + ia}{1 + b - ia} = b + ia$.

6. If $x_n = \cos\left(\dfrac{\pi}{2^n}\right) + i \sin\left(\dfrac{\pi}{2^n}\right)$, then prove that $x_1 x_2 \ldots$ to $+\infty = -1$.

7. If p and q are the roots of $x^2 - 2x + 4 = 0$. Prove that:
$$p^n + q^n = 2^{n+2} \cos\left(\dfrac{n\pi}{3}\right).$$

8. Show that $(\sqrt{3} + i)^n + (\sqrt{3} - i)^n = 2^{n+1} \cos\left(\dfrac{n\pi}{6}\right)$, where n is any positive integer.

9. Find the values of
   (i) $1^{1/5}$, (ii) $(-1)^{1/4}$, (iii) $(8i)^{1/3}$, (iv) $(-1 + i)^7$, (v) $(\sqrt{3} + 2i)^{3/4}$.

10. Solve the following equations:
    (i) $x^9 - x^5 + x^4 - 1 = 0$ (ii) $x^6 + x^4 + x^2 + 1 = 0$ (iii) $x^{12} - 1 = 0$.

11. Prove that:
$$\cos^3 \theta \cdot \sin^5 \theta = \dfrac{1}{128} [\sin 8\theta - 2 \sin 6\theta - 2 \sin 4\theta + 6 \sin 2\theta].$$

12. If $2 \cos \theta_k = x_k + \dfrac{1}{x_k}$, $k = 1, 2, 3$, then show that
$$x_1 \cdot x_2 \cdot x_3 + \dfrac{1}{x_1 \cdot x_2 \cdot x_3} = 2 \cos (\theta_1 + \theta_2 + \theta_3).$$

IV. Multiple Choice Questions:

Select the correct alternative for each of the following with proper justification:

1. Imaginary unit $i = \ldots\ldots$
   (a) -1
   (b) $\sqrt{-1}$
   (c) $\sqrt[3]{-1}$
   (d) $\sqrt{1}$

2. For any rational number n one of the values of $(\cos \theta + i \sin \theta)^n = \cos (n\theta) + i \sin (n\theta)$. This theorem is stated by $\ldots\ldots$
   (a) Euler
   (b) Cayley-Hamilton
   (c) De Moivre's
   (d) Argand

3. Argand states that geometrical representation of complex number is a point in the $\ldots\ldots$
   (a) line
   (b) sphere
   (c) plane
   (d) pair of lines

4. For a complex number z = x + iy, imaginary part of z is ......
   (a) ix
   (b) x
   (c) iy
   (d) y

5. In a complex number z = a + ib, ib is a ......
   (a) real number
   (b) imaginary number
   (c) real part of z
   (d) imaginary part of z

6. If z = cos θ + i sin θ then $z^n + z^{-n}$ = ...
   (a) 2n cos θ
   (b) 2 cos (nθ)
   (c) cos (2nθ)
   (d) n cos (2θ)

7. If z = cos θ + i sin θ then $z^n - z^{-n}$ = ...
   (a) 2 sin (nθ)
   (b) 2i sin (nθ)
   (c) 2 sin (inθ)
   (d) i sin (2nθ)

8. If $x + \dfrac{1}{x} = 2\cos\theta$, then $x^r + \dfrac{1}{x^r}$ = ...
   (a) cos (2rθ)
   (b) 2 cos (rθ)
   (c) r cos (2θ)
   (d) 2r cos θ

9. General expression 1 + i in r (cos θ + i sin θ) is ......
   (a) $2\left(\cos\dfrac{\pi}{4} + i\sin\dfrac{\pi}{4}\right)$
   (b) $\sqrt{2}\left(\cos\dfrac{\pi}{6} + i\sin\dfrac{\pi}{6}\right)$
   (c) $\sqrt{2}\left(\cos\dfrac{\pi}{4} + i\sin\dfrac{\pi}{4}\right)$
   (d) $\sqrt{2}\left(\cos\dfrac{\pi}{3} + i\sin\dfrac{\pi}{3}\right)$

10. By De Moivre's theorem $(\sin\theta + i\cos\theta)^n$ = ...
    (a) $n\left(\cos\left(\dfrac{\pi}{2} - \theta\right) + i\sin\left(\dfrac{\pi}{2} - \theta\right)\right)$
    (b) sin (nθ) + i cos (nθ)
    (c) $\cos\left[n\left(\dfrac{\pi}{2} - \theta\right)\right] + i\sin\left[n\left(\dfrac{\pi}{2} - \theta\right)\right]$
    (d) cos (nθ) + i sin (nθ)

ANSWERS

II. (B)

1. $-1, \cos\dfrac{\pi}{5} \pm i\sin\dfrac{\pi}{5}, -\cos\dfrac{2\pi}{5} \pm i\sin\dfrac{2\pi}{5}$

2. $\pm\left(\cos\dfrac{\pi}{8} + i\sin\dfrac{\pi}{8}\right), \pm\left(\cos\dfrac{5\pi}{8} + i\sin\dfrac{5\pi}{8}\right)$

3. $-8(1 + i)$

4. $\pm 7^{3/8}\left(\cos\dfrac{3\theta}{4} + i\sin\dfrac{3\theta}{4}\right), 7^{3/8}\left(\sin\dfrac{3\theta}{4} \pm i\sin\dfrac{3\theta}{4}\right)$ where $\tan\theta = \dfrac{2}{\sqrt{13}}$.

5. 1

6. $2^{2/5}\left\{\cos\dfrac{\pi}{15}-i\sin\dfrac{\pi}{15}\right\}$, $2^{2/5}\left\{-\dfrac{4\pi}{15}+i\sin\dfrac{4\pi}{15}\right\}$,

$2^{2/5}\left\{\cos\dfrac{7\pi}{15}-i\sin\dfrac{7\pi}{15}\right\}$, $2^{2/5}\left\{\cos\dfrac{\pi}{3}+i\sin\dfrac{\pi}{3}\right\}$.

7. ± 1, $\pm\left(\dfrac{1+\sqrt{3}\,i}{2}\right)$, $\pm\left(\dfrac{-1+\sqrt{3}\,i}{2}\right)$.

8. $\dfrac{1+\sqrt{3}\,i}{2}$, -1, $\dfrac{1-\sqrt{3}\,i}{2}$, $\pm\dfrac{1+i}{\sqrt{2}}$, $\pm\dfrac{1-i}{\sqrt{2}}$

9. $\cos\dfrac{(2k+1)\pi}{5}+i\sin\dfrac{(2k+1)\pi}{5}$, $k=1,2,3,4$.

10. $1\pm\sqrt{2}$, $\dfrac{-1+\sqrt{3}\,i}{2}$, $\dfrac{-3+i}{2}$, $-\left(\dfrac{1+\sqrt{3}\,i}{2}\right)$, $\pm\left(\dfrac{\sqrt{3}+i}{2}\right)$.

11. $2^{4/3}\cos\left(\dfrac{\pi}{9}\right)$, $2^{4/3}\cos\left(\dfrac{7\pi}{9}\right)$, $2^{4/3}\cos\left(\dfrac{13\pi}{9}\right)$.

14. $1+i$.

III. (B)
1. (i) 1   (ii) $\cos(107\theta)-i\sin(107\theta)$
2. $\cos 13\theta - i\sin 13\theta$
3. $2^{n+1}\sin^n\left(\dfrac{p-q}{2}\right)\cos\left[n\left(\dfrac{\pi+p+q}{2}\right)\right]$

9. (i) 1, $\cos\left(\dfrac{2\pi}{5}\right)\pm i\sin\left(\dfrac{2\pi}{5}\right)$; $\pm\cos\left(\dfrac{\pi}{5}\right)-i\sin\left(\dfrac{\pi}{5}\right)$

(ii) $\dfrac{1\pm i}{\sqrt{2}}$, $\dfrac{-1\pm i}{\sqrt{2}}$ (iii) $\pm\sqrt{3}+i$, $-2i$ (iv) $8(1+i)$

(v) $\pm 7^{3/8}\left(\cos\dfrac{3\theta}{4}+i\sin\dfrac{3\theta}{4}\right)$, $7^{3/8}\left(\sin\dfrac{3\theta}{4}\pm i\cos\dfrac{3\theta}{4}\right)$

10. (i) $\pm i, \pm 1, -1, \cos\dfrac{3\pi}{5}\pm i\sin\dfrac{3\pi}{5}$, $\cos\dfrac{\pi}{5}\pm i\sin\dfrac{\pi}{5}$ (ii) $\pm i, \pm\dfrac{1}{\sqrt{2}}(1+i)$

(iii) $\cos\left(\dfrac{k\pi}{3}\right)+i\sin\left(\dfrac{k\pi}{3}\right)$, where $k=0,1,2,3,4,5$ and

$\cos\left[\dfrac{(2k+1)\pi}{6}\right]+i\sin\left[\dfrac{(2k+1)\pi}{6}\right]$ where $k'=0,1,2,3,4,5$.

IV.

1. (b)	2. (c)	3. (c)	4. (d)	5. (b)	6. (b)	7. (b)	8. (b)
9. (c)	10. (c)						

CHAPTER 4

TRANSCENDENTAL FUNCTIONS

Leonhard Euler (1707 to 1783) was a Swiss mathematician who made enormous contributions to a wide range of mathematics and physics including analytic geometric, trigonometry, geometry, calculus and theory.

Leonhard Euler

Euler's formula, named after Leonhard Euler, is a mathematical formula in complex analysis that establishes the fundamental relationship between the trigonometric functions and the complex exponential function. Euler's formula states that for any real number x,

$$e^{ix} = \cos x + i \sin x$$

where e is the base of the natural logarithm, i is the imaginary unit and cos and sin are the trigonometric functions cosine and sine respectively with the argument x given in radians. This complex exponential function is sometimes denoted cis (x) ("cosine plus i sine").

4.1 INTRODUCTION

We know that the functions which are expressed in terms of x only (but not in terms of log x, e^x, sin x etc.) are known as algebraic functions.

e.g. $$f(x) = \frac{(x^2 - 7x + 12)}{(x^3 + 8)}$$

Whereas some functions contains log x, sin x, $\cos^{-1} x$, e^x hyperbolic functions, which are itself an infinite series in terms of x, are known as **transcendental functions**.

For example, $f(x) = \log(x+1) + x^2 - \sin x$

Here $\log(x+1) = x - \dfrac{x^2}{2} + \dfrac{x^3}{3} - \dfrac{x^4}{4} + \ldots$

and $\sin x = x - \dfrac{x^3}{3!} + \dfrac{x^5}{5!} - \dfrac{x^7}{7!}$

In many engineering applications needs these transcendental functions. Here we study circular functions, hyperbolic functions, their inverses interms of complex number z and their periodicity.

For real x we have,

$$\left. \begin{array}{l} e^x = 1 + x + \dfrac{x^2}{2!} + \dfrac{x^3}{3!} + \ldots \\[6pt] \sin x = x - \dfrac{x^3}{3!} + \dfrac{x^5}{5!} - \dfrac{x^7}{7!} + \ldots \\[6pt] \cos x = 1 - \dfrac{x^2}{2!} + \dfrac{x^4}{4!} - \dfrac{x^6}{6!} + \ldots \end{array} \right\} \quad \ldots (4.1)$$

Similarly for complex number z we have,

$$\left. \begin{array}{l} e^z = 1 + z + \dfrac{z^2}{2!} + \dfrac{z^3}{3!} + \ldots \\[6pt] \sin z = z - \dfrac{z^3}{3!} + \dfrac{x^5}{5!} - \dfrac{z^7}{7!} + \ldots \\[6pt] \cos z = 1 - \dfrac{z^2}{2!} + \dfrac{z^4}{4!} - \dfrac{z^6}{6!} + \ldots \end{array} \right\} \quad \ldots (4.2)$$

4.2 CIRCULAR FUNCTION

sin x and cos x are circular functions of real x. Since on unit circle any point can be expressed (cos x, sin x). Similarly sin z and cos z are circular functions of complex number z.

Euler observed the following :

$$e^{iz} = 1 + (iz) + \frac{(iz)^2}{2!} + \frac{(iz)^3}{3!} + \frac{(iz)^4}{4!} + \frac{(iz)^5}{5!} + \frac{(iz)^6}{6!} + \ldots$$

$$= \left(1 - \frac{z^2}{2!} + \frac{z^4}{4!} - \frac{z^6}{6!} + \ldots\right) + i\left(z - \frac{z^3}{3!} + \frac{z^5}{5!} - \frac{z^7}{7!} + \ldots\right)$$

where $i = -1$

$$= \cos z + i \sin z$$

These series are material when these are convergent.

Hence $e^{iz} = \cos z + i \sin z$ is known as an Euler's formula. ... (4.3)

Similarly, we get

$$e^{-iz} = \cos z - i \sin z \qquad \ldots (4.4)$$

From equation (4.3) and (4.4), we get

$$\cos z = \frac{e^{iz} + e^{-iz}}{2} \qquad \ldots (4.5)$$

and $$\sin z = \frac{e^{iz} - e^{-iz}}{2i} \qquad \ldots (4.6)$$

by adding equation (4.1) with (4.2) and subtracting equation (4.1) with (4.2) respectively.

Further, we express

$$z = re^{i\theta} \qquad \ldots (4.7)$$

where, $|z| = r$ and $\arg z = \theta$.

Other relations of circular functions.

(1) $\quad \tan z = \dfrac{\sin z}{\cos z} = \dfrac{e^{iz} - e^{-iz}}{i(e^{iz} + e^{-iz})}$

$\therefore \quad \cot z = \dfrac{i(e^{iz} + e^{-iz})}{(e^{iz} - e^{-iz})}$

(2) $\quad \sec z = \dfrac{2}{e^{iz} + e^{-iz}}, \quad \text{cosec } z = \dfrac{2i}{e^{iz} - e^{-iz}}$

4.3 PERIODS OF CIRCULAR FUNCTION

A function $f(z)$ is said to be periodic with period 'p' if $f(z + p) = f(z)$, where, p is the smallest number other than zero satisfying the relation.

Period of cos z and sin z is 2π. Since

$$\cos(2\pi + z) = \cos 2\pi \cos z - \sin 2\pi \sin z = \cos z$$

$$\sin(2\pi + z) = \sin 2\pi \cos z + \cos 2\pi \sin z = \sin z$$

$$(\because \sin 2\pi = 0, \cos 2\pi = 1)$$

Period of tan z is π. Since

$$\tan(z + \pi) = \frac{\tan z + \tan \pi}{1 - \tan z \cdot \tan \pi} = \tan z \qquad (\because \tan \pi = 0)$$

SOLVED EXAMPLE

Example 4.1 : Prove that e^z is a periodic function of a period $2\pi i$.

Solution : Let $z = x + iy$ and $f(z) = e^z$

$$\therefore \quad f(z) = e^z = e^{x + iy}$$
$$= e^x \cdot e^{iy}$$
$$= e^x \{\cos y + i \sin y\}$$
$$= e^x \{\cos(y + 2n\pi) + i \sin(y + 2n\pi)\}$$
$$= e^x \cdot e^{(y + 2n\pi)i}$$
$$= e^{x + yi + 2n\pi i}$$
$$= e^{z + 2n\pi i}$$
$$= f(z + 2n\pi i)$$

$$\therefore \quad f(z) = f(z + 2n\pi i)$$

$\therefore$ f(z) is a periodic function with period $2\pi i$.

$(\because$ n is least +ve integer$)$

Periodicity of circular functions :

We know that :

$$\sin(z + 2n\pi) = \sin z \cos(2n\pi) + \cos z \sin(2n\pi)$$
$$= \sin z$$
$$\cos(z + 2n\pi) = \cos z \cos(2n\pi) - \sin z \cdot \sin(2n\pi)$$
$$= \cos z$$

From these two we conclude that sin z and cos z are periodic functions with period 2π.

Similarly, $\tan(z + \pi) = \tan z$

So that tan z is a periodic function with period π.

Example 4.2 : Show that :

$$\sin(z_1 + z_2) = \sin z_1 \cos z_2 + \cos z_1 \sin z_2 \qquad \ldots (4.5)$$

Solution :

$$\text{R.H.S.} = \sin z_1 \cos z_2 + \cos z_1 \sin z_2$$

$$= \left(\frac{e^{iz_1} - e^{-iz_1}}{2i}\right)\left(\frac{e^{iz_2} + e^{-iz_2}}{2}\right) + \left(\frac{e^{iz_1} + e^{-iz_1}}{2}\right)\left(\frac{e^{iz_2} - e^{-iz_2}}{2i}\right)$$

$$= \frac{1}{4i}\{e^{i(z_1+z_2)} + e^{i(z_1-z_2)} - e^{-i(z_1-z_2)} - e^{-i(z_1+z_2)}$$

$$\quad + e^{i(z_1+z_2)} - e^{i(z_1-z_2)} + e^{-i(z_1-z_2)} - e^{-i(z_1+z_2)}\}$$

$$= \frac{1}{4i}\left\{2\left(e^{i(z_1+z_2)} - e^{-i(z_1+z_2)}\right)\right\}$$

$$= \frac{e^{i(z_1+z_2)} - e^{-i(z_1+z_2)}}{2i}$$

$$= \sin(z_1 + z_2) \qquad \text{By definitions of } \sin z$$

$$= \text{L.H.S.}$$

Similarly, we can prove

Example 4.3 :

(i) $\quad \sin(z_1 - z_2) = \sin z_1 \cos z_2 - \cos z_1 \sin z_2$

(ii) $\quad \cos(z_1 + z_2) = \cos z_1 \cos z_2 - \sin z_1 \sin z_2 \qquad \ldots (4.6)$

(iii) $\quad \cos(z_1 - z_2) = \cos z_1 \cos z_2 + \sin z_1 \sin z_2$

$$\sin z_1 + \sin z_2 = 2 \sin\left(\frac{z_1 + z_2}{2}\right)\cos\left(\frac{z_1 - z_2}{2}\right) \qquad \ldots (4.7)$$

Solution :

$$\text{R.H.S.} = 2 \sin\left(\frac{z_1 + z_2}{2}\right)\cos\left(\frac{z_1 - z_2}{2}\right)$$

$$= 2\left[\frac{e^{i\left(\frac{z_1+z_2}{2}\right)} - e^{-i\left(\frac{z_1+z_2}{2}\right)}}{2i}\right]\left[\frac{e^{i\left(\frac{z_1-z_2}{2}\right)} + e^{-i\left(\frac{z_1-z_2}{2}\right)}}{2}\right]$$

$$= \frac{1}{2i}\left[e^{iz_1} + e^{iz_2} - e^{-iz_2} - e^{-iz_1}\right] = \frac{e^{iz_1} - e^{-iz_1}}{2i} + \frac{e^{iz_2} - e^{-iz_2}}{2i}$$

$$= \sin z_1 + \sin z_2 = \text{L.H.S.}$$

Similarly we can prove (v), (vi), (vii),

(v) $\quad \sin z_1 - \sin z_2 = 2 \sin \left(\dfrac{z_1 - z_2}{2}\right) \cos \left(\dfrac{z_1 + z_2}{2}\right)$

(vi) $\quad \cos z_1 + \cos z_2 = 2 \cos \left(\dfrac{z_1 + z_2}{2}\right) \cos \left(\dfrac{z_1 - z_2}{2}\right) \quad \ldots\ (4.8)$

(vii) $\quad \cos z_1 - \cos z_2 = -2 \sin \left(\dfrac{z_1 + z_2}{2}\right) \sin \left(\dfrac{z_1 - z_2}{2}\right)$

Example 4.4 : Separate the real and imaginary parts of

(i) e^{z^2}, (ii) $e^{[(x + iy)(a + iy)]}$.

Solution : (i) Let $z = x + iy$ then $z^2 = (x + iy)^2 = x^2 - y^2 + 2xyi$

$\therefore \quad e^{z^2} = e^{x^2 - y^2 + 2xyi}$

$\qquad = e^{x^2 - y^2} \cdot e^{2xyi}$

$\qquad = e^{x^2 - y^2} \cdot \{\cos 2xy + i \sin 2xy\}$

$\qquad = e^{(x^2 - y^2)} \cdot \cos 2xy + i\, e^{(x^2 - y^2)} \cdot \sin 2xy$

$\therefore \quad \text{Re}\,(e^{z^2}) = e^{(x^2 - y^2)} \cdot \cos (2xy)$ and

$\qquad \text{Im}\,(e^{z^2}) = e^{(x^2 - y^2)} \cdot \sin (2xy)$

(ii) $(x + iy)(a + iy) = (xa - y^2) + i(yx + ay)$

$\therefore \quad e^{(x + iy)(a + iy)} = e^{[(xa - y^2) + i(yx + ay)]}$

$\qquad = e^{(xa - y^2)} \cdot \{e^{i(yx + ay)}\}$

$\qquad = e^{(xa - y^2)} \{\cos (yx + ay) + i \sin (yx + ay)\}$

$\qquad = e^{(xa - y^2)} \cdot \cos y(x + a) + i\, e^{(xa - y^2)} \cdot \sin y(x + a)$

$\therefore \quad \text{Real part} = e^{(xa - y^2)} \cdot \cos [y(x + a)]$

$\qquad \text{Imaginary part} = e^{(xa - y^2)} \cdot \sin [y(x + a)]$

Example 4.5 : If $z = 4e^{i\pi/4}$, find $|e^{iz}|$.

Solution : $z = 4e^{i\pi/4} = 4\left\{\cos \dfrac{\pi}{4} + i \sin \dfrac{\pi}{4}\right\}$

$\qquad = 4\left(\dfrac{1}{\sqrt{2}} + i \dfrac{1}{\sqrt{2}}\right)$

$\qquad = 2\sqrt{2} + i\, 2\sqrt{2}$

$$\therefore \quad e^{iz} = e^{i(2\sqrt{2} + i2\sqrt{2})} = e^{2\sqrt{2}i - 2\sqrt{2}}$$

$$\therefore \quad = e^{-2\sqrt{2}} \cdot e^{2\sqrt{2}i}$$

$$= e^{-2\sqrt{2}} \{\cos 2\sqrt{2} + i \sin 2\sqrt{2}\}$$

$$\therefore \quad |e^{iz}| = e^{-2\sqrt{2}}$$

Example 4.6 : Using Euler's formula $e^{i\theta} = \cos\theta + i\sin\theta$ prove DeMoivre's theorem.

Solution : We know that :

$$e^{i\theta} = \cos\theta + i\sin\theta$$

Raising both sides to the power n,

$$(e^{i\theta})^n = (\cos\theta + i\sin\theta)^n$$

$$\therefore \quad (\cos\theta + i\sin\theta)^n = e^{in\theta}$$

$$= \cos n\theta + i\sin n\theta$$

$$\therefore \quad (\cos\theta + i\sin\theta)^n = \cos n\theta + i\sin\theta \qquad \text{for any n}$$

which is De Moivre's theorem.

Example 4.7 : If z is a complex number then prove the following :

(i) $\cos^2 z + \sin^2 z = 1$.

(b) $\sin z_1 + \sin z_2 = 2\sin\left(\dfrac{z_1 + z_2}{2}\right) \cdot \cos\left(\dfrac{z_1 - z_2}{2}\right)$.

Solution : We know that

$$\sin z = \frac{e^{iz} - e^{-iz}}{2i} \quad \text{and} \quad \cos z = \frac{e^{iz} + e^{-iz}}{2}$$

(a) consider :

$$\cos^2 z + \sin^2 z = \left\{\frac{e^{iz} + e^{-iz}}{2}\right\}^2 + \left\{\frac{e^{iz} - e^{-iz}}{2i}\right\}^2$$

$$= \frac{1}{4}\{e^{2iz} + 2e^{iz-iz} + e^{-2iz}\} - \frac{1}{4}\left(e^{2iz} - 2e^{iz-iz} + e^{-2iz}\right)$$

$$= \frac{1}{4}\{e^{2iz} + 2 + e^{-2iz} - e^{2iz} + 2 - e^{-2iz}\}$$

$$= \frac{1}{4}(4) = 1$$

$$\therefore \quad \cos^2 z + \sin^2 z = 1$$

(b) Consider,

$$\text{R.H.S.} = 2 \sin\left(\frac{z_1 + z_2}{2}\right) \cos\left(\frac{z_1 - z_2}{2}\right)$$

$$= 2 \left\{ \frac{e^{\left(\frac{z_1+z_2}{2}\right)i} - e^{-\left(\frac{z_1+z_2}{2}\right)i}}{2i} \right\} \left\{ \frac{e^{\left(\frac{z_1-z_2}{2}\right)i} + e^{-\left(\frac{z_1-z_2}{2}\right)i}}{2i} \right\}$$

$$= \frac{1}{2i}\{e^{z_1 i} + e^{z_2 i} - e^{-z_1 i} - e^{-z_2 i}\} = \left(\frac{e^{z_1 i} - e^{-z_1 i}}{2i}\right) + \left(\frac{e^{z_2 i} - e^{-z_2 i}}{2i}\right)$$

$$= \sin z_1 + \sin z_2 = \text{L.H.S.}$$

$$\therefore \quad \sin z_1 + \sin z_2 = 2 \sin\left(\frac{z_1 + z_2}{2}\right) \cdot \cos\left(\frac{z_1 - z_2}{2}\right)$$

EXERCISE 4.1

A. Prove the following for circular functions of complex number :
1. (a) $1 + \cos 2z = 2 \cos^2 z$ (b) $1 - \cos 2z = 2 \sin^2 z$
   (c) $\sin 3z = 3 \sin z - 4 \sin^3 z$
   (d) $\cos 3z = 4 \cos^3 z - 3 \cos z$
2. (a) $[\sin(p - q) + e^{ip} \sin q]^n = \sin^n p \cdot e^{inq}$
   (b) $[\cos(p + q) + i e^{-ip} \sin q]^n = \cos^n p \cdot e^{inq}$
3. (a) $(1 + e^{i\theta})^{-1/2} + (1 + e^{-i\theta})^{-1/2} = \sqrt{1 + \sec(\theta/2)}$
   (b) $(1 - e^{+i\theta})^{-1/2} + (1 - e^{-i\theta})^{-1/2} = \sqrt{1 + \text{cosec}(\theta/2)}$
4. (a) $\dfrac{1 + \cos p + i \sin p}{1 - \cos p + i \sin p} = \cot \dfrac{p}{2} e^{i(p - \pi/2)}$
   (b) $\left(\dfrac{1 + \sin p + i \cos p}{1 + \sin p - i \cos p}\right)^n = e^{in(\pi/2 - p)}$
   (c) $\dfrac{1 + \cos \theta + i \sin \theta}{1 - \cos \theta - i \sin \theta} = i \cos(\theta/2)$

B. Separate into real and imaginary parts of (i) $(\sqrt{i})^{\sqrt{i}}$, (ii) $\sqrt{i}$.

ANSWERS

B. (i) Real part $= e^{-\pi/4} \sqrt{2} \cdot \cos\left(\dfrac{\pi}{4\sqrt{2}}\right)$

Imaginary part $= e^{-\pi/4} \sqrt{2} \cdot \sin\left(\dfrac{\pi}{4\sqrt{2}}\right)$.

(ii) Real part $= \dfrac{1}{\sqrt{2}}$ and Imaginary part $= \dfrac{1}{\sqrt{2}}$

4.3.2 Hyperbolic Functions

Geometrically, the functions $\dfrac{(e^z + e^{-z})}{2}$ and $\dfrac{(e^z - e^{-z})}{2}$ represents hyperbola geometrically so the following hyperbolic functions are defined.

Definition 1 : Hyperbolic sine for real or complex z is defined as

$$\sinh z = \dfrac{e^z - e^{-z}}{2} \qquad \ldots (4.9)$$

Definition 2 : Hyperbolic cosine for real or complex z is defined as

$$\cosh z = \dfrac{e^z + e^{-z}}{2} \qquad \ldots (4.10)$$

Other hyperbolic functions are obtained as

$$\left. \begin{aligned} \tanh z &= \dfrac{\sinh z}{\cosh z} = \dfrac{e^z - e^{-z}}{e^z + e^{-z}} \\ \operatorname{sech} z &= \dfrac{1}{\cosh z} = \dfrac{2}{e^z + e^{-z}} \\ \coth z &= \dfrac{\cosh z}{\sinh z} = \dfrac{e^z + e^{-z}}{e^z - e^{-z}} \\ \operatorname{cosech} z &= \dfrac{1}{\sinh z} = \dfrac{2}{e^z - e^{-z}} \end{aligned} \right\} \qquad \ldots (4.11)$$

SOLVED EXAMPLES

Example 4.8 : Prove that : (1) $\cosh z + \sinh z = e^z$, (2) $\sinh(0) = 0$ (3) $\cosh\left(\dfrac{\pi}{2} i\right) = 0$ (4) $\cosh^2 z - \sinh^2 z = 1$.

Solution : We know that

$$\cosh z = \dfrac{e^z + e^{-z}}{2}, \quad \sinh z = \dfrac{e^z - e^{-z}}{2}$$

(1) Consider,

$$\cosh z + \sinh z = \dfrac{e^z + e^{-z}}{2} + \dfrac{e^z - e^{-z}}{2} = e^z$$

(2) $$\sinh(0) = \dfrac{e^0 - e^{-0}}{2} = 0$$

(3) $\quad \cosh\left(\dfrac{\pi}{2}\right)i = \dfrac{e^{\frac{\pi}{2}i} + e^{-\frac{\pi}{2}i}}{2} = \cos(\pi/2) = 0$

(4) $\quad \cosh^2 z - \sinh^2 z = \left(\dfrac{e^z + e^{-z}}{2}\right)^2 - \left(\dfrac{e^z - e^{-z}}{2}\right)^2$

$$= \dfrac{1}{4}\{(e^{2z} + e^{-2z} + 2) - (e^{2z} + e^{-2z} - 2)\}$$

$$= \dfrac{1}{4}(4)$$

$$= 1$$

$\therefore \quad \cosh^2 z - \sinh^2 z = 1$

Example 4.9 : Prove that :

$$\cosh z = 1 + \dfrac{z^2}{2!} + \dfrac{z^4}{4!} + \dfrac{z^6}{6!} + \ldots$$

$$\sinh z = z + \dfrac{z^3}{3!} + \dfrac{z^5}{5!} + \dfrac{z^7}{7!} + \ldots$$

Solution : We know that :

$$e^z = 1 + z + \dfrac{z^2}{2!} + \dfrac{z^3}{3!} + \ldots$$

$\therefore \quad e^{-z} = 1 - z + \dfrac{z^3}{2!} - \dfrac{z^3}{3!} + \ldots$

$\therefore \quad \dfrac{e^z + e^{-z}}{2} = 1 + \dfrac{z^2}{2!} + \dfrac{z^4}{4!} + \ldots$

$\therefore \quad \cosh z = 1 + \dfrac{z^2}{2!} + \dfrac{z^4}{4!} + \ldots$

Similarly, $\quad \dfrac{e^z - e^{-z}}{2} = z + \dfrac{z^3}{3!} + \dfrac{z^5}{5!} + \ldots$

$\therefore \quad \cosh z = z + \dfrac{z^3}{3!} + \dfrac{z^5}{5!} + \ldots$

Example 4.10 : $\cosh(z_1 \pm z_2) = \cosh z_1 \cosh z_2 \pm \sinh z_1 \sinh z_2$.

Solution : Consider :

R.H.S. $= \cosh z_1 \cosh z_2 + \sinh z_1 \sinh z_2$

$$= \left(\frac{e^{z_1} + e^{-z_1}}{2}\right)\left(\frac{e^{z_2} + e^{-z_2}}{2}\right) + \left(\frac{e^{z_1} - e^{-z_1}}{2}\right)\left(\frac{e^{z_2} - e^{-z_2}}{2}\right)$$

$$= \frac{1}{4}\{e^{z_1+z_2} + e^{z_1-z_2} + e^{-z_1+z_2} + e^{-z_1-z_2}\}$$

$$+ \frac{1}{4}\{e^{z_1+z_2} - e^{z_1-z_2} - e^{-z_1+z_2} + e^{-z_1-z_2}\}$$

$$= \frac{1}{4}\{2e^{z_1+z_2} + 2e^{-(z_1+z_2)}\}$$

$$= \frac{e^{(z_1+z_2)} + e^{-(z_1+z_2)}}{2}$$

$$= \cosh(z_1 + z_2)$$

$= $ L.H.S.

$\therefore \quad \cosh(z_1 + z_2) = \cosh z_1 + \cosh z_2 + \sinh z_1 \sinh z_2$

Similarly, we can prove,

$$\cosh(z_1 - z_2) = \cosh z_1 \cosh z_2 - \sinh z_1 \sinh z_2.$$

4.3.2 Relation between Circular and Hyperbolic Functions

$$\sin(iz) = \frac{e^{i(iz)} - e^{-i(iz)}}{2i} = \frac{e^{-z} - e^{z}}{2i}$$

$$= \frac{(-1)}{i}\left(\frac{e^z - e^{-z}}{2}\right) = i\left(\frac{e^z - e^{-z}}{2}\right)$$

$$= i \cdot \sinh z$$

$\therefore \qquad \sin(iz) = i \sinh z \qquad \qquad \ldots (4.13)$

Similarly, $\quad \cos(iz) = \cosh z$

$\sec(iz) = \text{sech } z$

$\tan(iz) = i \tanh z$

$\cot(iz) = -i \coth z$

$\text{cosec}(iz) = -i \text{ cosech}(z) \qquad \ldots (4.14)$

Now, $\quad \sinh(iz) = \dfrac{e^{iz} - e^{-iz}}{2} = i\left(\dfrac{e^{iz} - e^{-iz}}{2i}\right) = i \sin z$

∴ $\quad \sinh(iz) = i \sin z$ ... (4.15)

Similarly,
$$\left.\begin{array}{rcl}\cosh(iz) &=& \cos z, \\ \tanh(iz) &=& i \tan z \\ \operatorname{sech}(iz) &=& \sec z \\ \coth(iz) &=& i \cot z \\ \operatorname{cosech}(iz) &=& -\operatorname{cosec} z\end{array}\right\} \quad \ldots (4.16)$$

4.3.3 Periods of Hyperbolic Functions

Consider, $\cosh(x + iy) = \cos[i(x + iy)]$

$\qquad\qquad\qquad\qquad = \cos(ix - y)$

$\qquad\qquad\qquad\qquad = \cos(ix - y + 2\pi) \quad (\because 2\pi \text{ is period of cosine})$

$\qquad\qquad\qquad\qquad = \cos[i(x + iy - 2\pi i]$

$\qquad\qquad\qquad\qquad = \cosh[(x + iy) - 2\pi i]$

$\qquad\qquad\qquad\qquad = \cosh[(x + iy) + 2\pi i k],$

$\qquad\qquad\qquad\qquad\qquad\qquad\qquad\qquad$ where, $k = 0, \pm 1, \pm 2 \ldots$

Hence hyperbolic cosine is a periodic function with period $2\pi i$.

Similarly, hyperbolic sine is also a periodic function with period $2\pi i$.

Now, $\quad \tanh(x + iy) = \dfrac{1}{i} \tan[(x + iy)i]$

$\qquad\qquad\qquad\qquad = \dfrac{1}{i} \tan[ix - y]$

$\qquad\qquad\qquad\qquad = \dfrac{1}{i} \tan[ix - y - \pi] \qquad (\because \tan \theta \text{ has period } \pi)$

$\qquad\qquad\qquad\qquad = \dfrac{1}{i} \tan[i(x + iy + \pi i)]$

$\qquad\qquad\qquad\qquad = \tanh[(x + iy) + \pi i]$

Thus hyperbolic tangent has period πi.

SOLVED EXAMPLES

Example 4.11 : Separate real and imaginary parts of (1) sin (x + iy), (2) cos (x + iy).

Solution :

(1) $\sin(x + iy)$ = $\sin x \cos(iy) + \cos x \sin(iy)$
   = $\sin x \cdot \cosh y + \cos x \, i \sinh y$
   = $\sin x \cdot \cosh y + i \cos x \sinh y$

∴ Re {sin (x + iy)} = $\sin x \cdot \cosh y$
and Im {sin (x + iy)} = $+ \cos x \sinh y$

(2) $\cos(x + iy)$ = $\cos x \cos(iy) + \sin x \sin(iy)$
   = $\cos x \cdot \cosh y + \sin x \, i \sinh y$
   = $\cos x \cosh y + i \sin x \cdot \sinh y$

Re [cos (x + iy)} = $\cos x \cosh y$
and Im {cos (x + iy)} = $\sin x \cdot \sinh y$

Example 4.12 : If $\cos(\alpha + i\beta) = x + iy$ then prove that :

(i) $\dfrac{x^2}{\cosh^2 \beta} + \dfrac{y^2}{\sinh^2 \beta} = 1$, (ii) $\dfrac{x^2}{\cos^2 \alpha} - \dfrac{y^2}{\sin^2 \alpha} = 1$.

Solution : $x + iy$ = $\cos(\alpha + i\beta)$
   = $\cos \alpha \cos(i\beta) - \sin(\alpha) \sin(i\beta)$
   = $\cos \alpha \cosh \beta - i \sin \alpha \sinh \beta$

Equating real and imaginary parts, we get

x = $\cos \alpha \cosh \beta$
and y = $- \sin \alpha \sinh \beta$

(i) Consider :

$\dfrac{x^2}{\cosh^2 \beta} + \dfrac{y^2}{\sinh^2 \beta}$ = $\dfrac{\cos^2 \alpha \cosh^2 \beta}{\cosh^2 \beta} + \dfrac{\sin^2 \alpha \sinh^2 \beta}{\sinh^2 \beta}$
 = $\cos^2 \alpha + \sin^2 \alpha$
 = 1

∴ $\dfrac{x^2}{\cosh^2 \beta} + \dfrac{y}{\sinh^2 \beta} = 1$

(ii) Consider :

$$\frac{x^2}{\cos^2 \alpha} - \frac{y^2}{\sin^2 \alpha} = \frac{\cos^2 \alpha \cosh^2 \beta}{\cos^2 \alpha} - \frac{\sin^2 \alpha \sinh^2 \beta}{\sin^2 \alpha}$$

$$= \cosh^2 \beta - \sinh^2 \beta$$

$$= 1$$

$$\therefore \quad \frac{x^2}{\cos^2 \alpha} - \frac{y^2}{\sin^2 \alpha} = 1$$

Example 4.13 : If $\tan (\alpha + i\beta) = (x + iy)$ then prove that :

(i) $\tan 2\alpha = \dfrac{2x}{1 - x^2 - y^2}$

(ii) $\tanh 2\beta = \dfrac{2y}{1 + x^2 + y^2}$

Solution : $\tan (\alpha + i\beta) = x + iy$ so that

$$\tan (\alpha - i\beta) = x - iy$$

(i) $\tan (2\alpha) = \tan [(\alpha + i\beta) + (\alpha - i\beta)]$

$$= \frac{\tan (\alpha + i\beta) + \tan (\alpha - i\beta)}{1 - \tan (\alpha + i\beta) \tan (\alpha - i\beta)}$$

$$= \frac{x + iy + x - iy}{1 - (x + iy)(x - iy)}$$

$$= \frac{2x}{1 - (x^2 + y^2)}$$

$$\tan 2\alpha = \frac{2x}{1 - x^2 - y^2}$$

(ii) $\tan 2i\beta = \tan [(\alpha + i\beta) - (\alpha - i\beta)]$

$$= \frac{\tan (\alpha + i\beta) - \tan (\alpha - i\beta)}{1 + \tan (\alpha + i\beta) \tan (\alpha - i\beta)}$$

$$= \frac{(x + iy) - (x - iy)}{1 + (x + iy)(x - iy)}$$

$$i \tanh (2\beta) = \frac{2iy}{1 + (x^2 + y^2)}$$

$$\tanh (2\beta) = \frac{2y}{1 + x^2 + y^2}$$

Example 4.14 : By using the definitions of hyperbolic functions. Prove that : $\operatorname{cosech} z + \coth z = \coth\left(\dfrac{z}{2}\right)$.

Solution : $\operatorname{cosech} z = \dfrac{2}{e^z - e^{-z}}$

$\coth z = \dfrac{e^z + e^{-z}}{e^z - e^{-z}}$

$\therefore \quad \operatorname{cosech} z + \coth z = \dfrac{2}{e^z - e^{-z}} + \dfrac{e^z + e^{-z}}{e^z - e^{-z}} = \dfrac{e^z + e^{-z} + 2}{e^z - e^{-z}}$

$= \dfrac{(e^{z/2} + e^{-z/2})^2}{(e^{z/2} + e^{-z/2})(e^{z/2} - e^{-z/2})}$

$= \dfrac{e^{z/2} + e^{-z/2}}{e^{z/2} - e^{-z/2}}$

$= \coth\left(\dfrac{z}{2}\right)$

EXERCISE 4.2

Prove the following identities for hyperbolic functions of complex numbers :

1. (a) $\cosh^2 z - \sinh^2 z = 1$
   (b) $\operatorname{sech}^2 z + \tanh^2 z = 1$
   (c) $\coth^2 z - \operatorname{cosech}^2 z = 1$
2. (a) $\sinh(z_1 \pm z_2) = \sinh z_1 \cosh z_2 \pm \cosh z_1 \sinh z_2$
   (b) $\cosh(z_1 \pm z_2) = \cosh z_1 \cosh z_2 \pm \sinh z_1 \sinh z_2$
3. (a) $\sinh(z_1 + z_2) + \sinh(z_1 - z_2) = 2 \sinh z_1 \cosh z_2$
   (b) $\sinh(z_1 + z_2) - \sinh(z_1 - z_2) = 2 \cosh z_1 \sinh z_2$
   (c) $\cosh(z_1 + z_2) + \cosh(z_1 - z_2) = 2 \cosh z_1 \cosh z_2$
   (d) $\cosh(z_1 + z_2) - \cosh(z_1 - z_2) = 2 \sinh z_1 \sinh z_2$
4. (a) $\sinh z_1 + \sinh z_2 = 2 \sinh\left(\dfrac{z_1 + z_2}{2}\right) \cosh\left(\dfrac{z_1 - z_2}{2}\right)$
   (b) $\sinh z_1 - \sinh z_2 = 2 \cosh\left(\dfrac{z_1 + z_2}{2}\right) \sinh\left(\dfrac{z_1 - z_1}{2}\right)$
   (c) $\cosh z_1 + \cosh z_2 = 2 \cosh\left(\dfrac{z_1 + z_2}{2}\right) \cosh\left(\dfrac{z_1 - z_2}{2}\right)$
   (d) $\cosh z_1 - \cosh z_2 = 2 \sinh\left(\dfrac{z_1 + z_2}{2}\right) \sinh\left(\dfrac{z_1 - z_2}{2}\right)$

5. (a) $\sinh 2z = 2\sinh z \cosh z$
    (b) $\cosh 2z = \cosh^2 z + \sinh^2 z = 2\cosh^2 z - 1 = 1 + 2\sinh^2 z$
    (c) $\tanh 2z = \dfrac{2\tanh z}{1 + \tanh^2 z}$

6. If $u = \log_e \tan\left(\dfrac{\pi}{4} + \dfrac{\theta}{2}\right)$ prove that $\tanh \dfrac{u}{2} = \tan \dfrac{\theta}{2}$ and $\cosh u \cos \theta = 1$

7. If $\cosh z = \sec \theta$ prove that :
    $$z = \log(\sec\theta + \tan\theta) \text{ and } \theta = \dfrac{\pi}{2} - 2\tan^{-z}(e^{-z})$$

8. If $\tan\left(\dfrac{\pi}{6} + i\alpha\right) = x + iy$ prove that $x^2 + y^2 + \dfrac{2x}{\sqrt{3}} = 1$.

9. Separate real and imaginary parts of
    (i) $\sinh(x+iy)$, (ii) $\cosh(x+iy)$, (iii) $\tanh(x+iy)$, (iv) $\mathrm{sech}(x+iy)$.

ANSWERS 4.2

(i) Real part = $\sinh x \cos y$ and Imaginary part = $\cosh x \sin y$

(ii) Real part = $\cosh x \cos y$ and Imaginary part = $\sinh x \sin y$.

(iii) Real part = $\dfrac{\sinh 2x}{\cosh(2x) + \cos(2y)}$

Imaginary part = $\dfrac{\sin 2y}{\cosh(2x) + \cos(2y)}$

(iv) Real part = $\dfrac{2\cosh x \cos y}{\cosh(2x) + \cos 2y}$

Imaginary part = $-\dfrac{2\sinh x \sin y}{\cosh 2x + \cos 2y}$

4.4 INVERSE CIRCULAR FUNCTIONS

We know that circular functions are periodic and so many-one. To define its inverse we set one domain such that inverse function is defined and becomes one-one onto. We call that domain as principal domain and then generalize it.

Definition : If $x + iy = \cos(a + ib)$, then $a + ib$ is called inverse cosine of $x + iy$ and is written as $a + ib = \cos^{-1}(x + iy)$

Since $\quad x + iy = \cos(a + ib) = \cos[2n\pi \pm (a + ib)]$

where, n is an integer.

$\therefore \quad \cos^{-1}(x + iy) = 2n\pi \pm (a + ib)$ ... (4.17)

Here $\cos^{-1}(x + iy)$ is many valued function. One of the value of it is such that $(2n\pi \pm a)$ lies in $(0, \pi)$, called as the principal value. To make the sense of general and principal we take capital C in $\cos^{-1}(x + iy)$ for general and principal value as small c in $\cos^{-1}(x + iy)$.

Thus $\quad \cos^{-1}(x + iy) = 2n\pi \pm \cos^{-1}(x + iy) \quad \ldots (4.18)$

Definition : If $x + iy = \sin(a + ib)$, then $a + ib$ is called inverse sine of $x + iy$ and it is taken as $a + ib = \sin^{-1}(x + iy)$.

Since $\quad \sin(a + ib) = \sin[n\pi + (-1)^n (a + ib)] = x + iy$

$\therefore \quad \sin^{-1}(x + iy) = n\pi + (-1)^n (a + ib) \quad \ldots (4.19)$

a many valued function.

Fix the principal domain $(-\pi/2, \pi/2)$ for one-one correspondence.

Take better S capital in $\text{Sin}^{-1}(x + iy)$ for general value and small s for principal value.

$\therefore \quad \text{Sin}^{-1}(x + iy) = n\pi + (-1)^n \sin^{-1}(x + iy) \quad \ldots (4.20)$

Definition : If $(x + iy) = \tan(a + ib)$, then $a + ib$ is called inverse tangent of $x + iy$ and is shown as $a + ib = \tan^{-1}(x + iy)$.

Since, $\quad \tan(a + ib) = \tan[n\pi + (a + ib)] = x + iy$

$\tan^{-1}(x + iy) = n\pi + (a + ib) \quad \ldots (4.21)$

Take $\text{Tan}^{-1}(x + iy)$ for general value and $\tan^{-1}(x + iy)$ for principal domain $(-\pi/2, \pi/2)$.

Thus $\quad \text{Tan}^{-1}(x + iy) = n\pi + \tan^{-1}(x + iy) \quad \ldots (4.22)$

Other, inverse circular functions are

$$\left. \begin{array}{l} \text{Sec}^{-1}(x + iy) = 2n\pi \pm \sec^{-1}(x + iy) \\ \text{Cosec}^{-1}(x + iy) = n\pi + (-1)^n \text{cosec}^{-1}(x + iy) \\ \text{Cot}^{-1}(x + iy) = n\pi + \cot^{-1}(x + iy) \end{array} \right\} \quad \ldots (4.23)$$

Inverse hyperbolic functions :

Definition : If $z = \cosh \theta$ then θ is known as inverse hyperbolic cosine of z and is shown as

$$\theta = \cosh^{-1} z$$

SOLVED EXAMPLES

Example 4.15 : If z is any complex number then show that :

(1) $\sinh^{-1} z = \log\left(z + \sqrt{z^2 + 2}\right)$

(2) $\cosh^{-1} z = \log\left(z + \sqrt{z^2 - 1}\right)$

(3) $\tanh^{-1} z = \dfrac{1}{2} \log\left(\dfrac{1+z}{1-z}\right)$

Solution : (1) Let $\quad x = \sinh^{-1} z$ then $z = \sinh x$

$\therefore \quad z = \dfrac{e^x - e^{-x}}{2}$

$\therefore \quad 2z = e^x - e^{-x}$

$\therefore \quad e^{2x} - 2z e^x - 1 = 0$

which is a quadratic equation in e^x.

$\therefore \quad e^x = \dfrac{2z \pm \sqrt{4z^2 + 4}}{2}$

$\quad e^x = z \pm \sqrt{z^2 + 1}$

$\therefore$ Without loss of generality we take

$\quad e^x = z + \sqrt{z^2 + 1}$

$\quad x = \log\left(z + \sqrt{z^2 + 1}\right)$

$\therefore \quad \sinh^{-1} z = \log\left(z + \sqrt{z^2 + 1}\right)$

(2) Let $\quad y = \cosh^{-1} z$ then $z = \cosh y$

$\therefore \quad z = \dfrac{e^y + e^{-y}}{2}$

$\therefore \quad e^{2y} - 2z e^y + 1 = 0$

which is quadratic equation in e^y

$\therefore \quad e^y = \dfrac{2z \pm \sqrt{4z^2 - 4}}{2}$

$\therefore \quad e^y = z + \sqrt{z^2 - 1}$

Without loss of generality we take

$$e^y = z + \sqrt{z^2 - 1}$$

$\therefore \qquad y = \log\left(z + \sqrt{z^2 - 1}\right)$

(3) Let $\qquad w = \tanh^{-1} z$

$\therefore \qquad z = \tanh w = \dfrac{e^w - e^{-w}}{e^w + e^{-w}}$

Consider, $\qquad \dfrac{1+z}{1-z} = \dfrac{1 + \left(\dfrac{e^w - e^{-w}}{e^w + e^{-w}}\right)}{1 - \left(\dfrac{e^w - e^{-w}}{e^w + e^{-w}}\right)}$

$$= \dfrac{2e^w}{2e^{-w}}$$

$$= e^{2w}$$

$\therefore \qquad e^{2w} = \dfrac{1+z}{1-z}$

$\qquad 2w = \log\left\{\dfrac{1+z}{1-z}\right\}$

$\therefore \qquad w = \dfrac{1}{2} \log\left\{\dfrac{1+z}{1-z}\right\}$

i.e. $\qquad \tanh^{-1} z = \dfrac{1}{2} \log\left(\dfrac{1+z}{1-z}\right)$

Example 4.16 : Separate into real and imaginary parts of $\sin^{-1}(e^{i\theta})$.

Solution : Let

$$\sin^{-1}(e^{i\theta}) = x + iy$$

$\therefore \qquad \sin(x + iy) = e^{i\theta} = \cos\theta + i\sin\theta$

$\therefore \quad \sin x \cos iy + \cos x \sin(iy) = \cos\theta + i\sin\theta$

$\qquad \sin x \cosh y + i \cos x \sinh y = \cos\theta + i\sin\theta$

Equating real and imaginary parts we get,

$\qquad \cos\theta = \sin x \cosh y$

and $\qquad \sin\theta = \cos x \sinh y \qquad \Bigg\}\qquad \ldots \text{(i)}$

squaring and adding we get,

$$1 = \sin^2 x \cosh^2 y + \cos^2 x + \sinh^2 y$$
$$= \sin^2 x (1 + \sinh^2 y) + \cos^2 x \sinh^2 y$$
$$= \sin^2 x + (\sin^2 x + \cos^2 x) \sinh^2 y$$
$$= \sin^2 x + \sinh^2 y$$

$$\Rightarrow \quad 1 - \sin^2 x = \sinh^2 y$$
$$\cos^2 x = \sinh^2 y$$
$$\cos x = \sinh y \quad \ldots \text{(ii)}$$

But $\quad \cos x \sinh y = \sin \theta$

$\Rightarrow \quad \sinh^2 y = \sin \theta$

$\Rightarrow \quad \sinh y = \sqrt{\sin \theta}$

$\quad \cos^2 x = \sin \theta$

$\therefore \quad \cos x = \sqrt{\sin \theta} \quad \ldots \text{(iii)}$

$\therefore \quad x = \cos^{-1} (\sqrt{\sin \theta})$

$\therefore \quad y = \sinh^{-1} (\sqrt{\sin \theta})$
$$= \log (\sqrt{\sin \theta} + \sqrt{1 + \sin \theta}) \quad \ldots \text{(iv)}$$

Example 4.17 : Separate into real and imaginary parts of sinh (x + iy).

Solution : $\sinh (x + iy) = \dfrac{1}{i} \sin (x + iy)$

$$= \dfrac{1}{i} [\sin x \cos (iy) + \cos x \sin (iy)]$$

$$= \dfrac{1}{i} [\sin x \cosh y + i \cos x \sinh y]$$

$$= \cos x \sinh y - i \sin x \cosh y$$

$\therefore \quad$ Real part is cos x sinh y and imaginary part is – sin x cosh y.

Example 4.18 : If $\sin(p + iq) = x + iy$, then prove that :

(i) $\dfrac{x^2}{\cosh^2 q} + \dfrac{y^2}{\sinh^2 q} = 1$ (ii) $\dfrac{x^2}{\sin^2 p} - \dfrac{y^2}{\cos^2 p} = 1$.

Solution : Given :

$$x + iy = \sin(p + iq) = \sin p \cos iq + \cos p \sin iq$$
$$= \sin p \cosh q + i \cos p \sinh q$$

$\therefore \quad x = \sin p \cosh q$

and $\quad y = \cos p \sinh q \qquad \ldots (1)$

(i) $\quad$ L.H.S. $= \dfrac{x^2}{\cosh^2 q} + \dfrac{y^2}{\sinh^2 q}$

$\qquad = \dfrac{\sin^2 p \cosh^2 q}{\cosh^2 q} + \dfrac{\cos^2 p + \sinh^2 q}{\sinh^2 q}$

$\qquad = \sin^2 p + \cos^2 p = 1 =$ R.H.S.

(ii) $\quad$ L.H.S. $= \dfrac{x^2}{\sin^2 p} - \dfrac{y^2}{\cos^2 p}$

$\qquad = \dfrac{\sin^2 p \cosh^2 q}{\sin^2 p} - \dfrac{\cos^2 p \sinh^2 q}{\cos^2 p}$

$\qquad = \cosh^2 q - \sinh^2 q$

$\qquad = 1 =$ R.H.S.

Example 4.19 : Prove that $1 + \sin \log_e i^i = 0$.

Solution : We have,

$$i = 0 + 1i = \cos \dfrac{\pi}{2} + i \sin \dfrac{\pi}{2} = e^{i\pi/2}$$

$\therefore \quad i^i = (e^{i\pi/2})^i = e^{-\pi/2}$

$\Rightarrow \quad \log_e i^i = -\dfrac{\pi}{2}$

$\Rightarrow \quad \sin \log_e i^i = \sin\left(-\dfrac{\pi}{2}\right) = -\sin\left(\dfrac{\pi}{2}\right) = -1$

$\therefore \quad 1 + \sin \log_e i^i = 0$

Example 4.20 : Separate into real and imaginary parts of $\sinh^{-1}(ix)$.

Solution : Let
$$\sinh^{-1}(ix) = \alpha + i\beta$$
Then
$$ix = \sinh(\alpha + i\beta)$$
$$= \sinh\alpha \cosh(i\beta) + \cosh\alpha \sinh(i\beta)$$
$$ix = \sinh\alpha \cos\beta + i\cosh\alpha \sin\beta$$

Comparing real and imaginary parts we get,
$$0 = \sinh\alpha \cos\beta \text{ and } \cosh\alpha \sin\beta = x$$

$\sinh\alpha \cos\beta = 0$ gives $\cos\beta = 0$ and hence $\beta = \dfrac{\pi}{2}$

$$x = \cosh\alpha \sin\dfrac{\pi}{2} = \cosh\alpha$$

$\therefore \qquad \alpha = \cosh^{-1} x$

Thus, $\sinh^{-1}(ix) = \cosh^{-1} x + i\dfrac{\pi}{2}$

EXERCISE 4.3

1. Separate into real and imaginary part.
   - (a) $\cos(x + iy)$
   - (b) $\coth(x + iy)$
   - (c) $\text{sech}(x + iy)$
   - (d) $\coth[i(x + iy)]$
   - (e) $\cos(x + iy)$
   - (f) $\tan(x + iy)$
   - (g) $\cot(x + iy)$
   - (h) $\cos^{-1} e^{i\theta}$

ANSWERS 4.3

1. (a) R.P. $\cosh x \cos y$, I.P. $\sinh x \sin y$

   (b) R.P. $\dfrac{\sinh 2x}{(\cosh 2x - \cos 2y)}$ I.P. $\dfrac{-\sin 2y}{(\cosh 2x - \cos 2y)}$

(c) R.P. $\dfrac{2\cosh x \cos y}{(\cosh 2x + \cos 2y)}$ I.P. $\dfrac{-2\sinh x \sin y}{(\cosh 2x + \cos 2y)}$

(d) R.P. $\dfrac{-\sinh 2y}{(\cosh 2x - \cos 2y)}$ I.P. $\dfrac{-\sin 2x}{(\cosh 2x - \cos 2y)}$

(e) R.P. $\cos x \cosh y$ I.P. $\sin x \sinh y$

(f) R.P. $\dfrac{\sin 2x}{(\cos 2x + \cosh 2y)}$ I.P. $\dfrac{\sinh 2y}{(\cos 2x + \cosh 2y)}$

(g) R.P. $\dfrac{\sin 2x}{\cosh 2y - \cos 2x}$ I.P. $\dfrac{-\sinh 2y}{\cosh 2y - \cos 2x}$

(h) R.P. $= \sin^{-1}\sqrt{\sin\theta}$ I.P. $= \sinh^{-1}\left(-\sqrt{\sin\theta}\right)$.

MISCELLANEOUS EXERCISE

I. Short questions (2 to 3 marks) :

1. Explain how we get Euler's formula from series of $e^{i\theta}$.
2. Using Euler's formula, find the formulae of $\cos\theta$ and $\sin\theta$.
3. Using Euler's formula, prove that $\cos^2 z + \sin^2 z = 1$, where z is a complex number.
4. Define hyperbolic cosine and hyperbolic sine.
5. Prove that $\cosh z + \sinh z = e^z$.
6. Prove that $\sin(iz) = i\sinh z$.
7. Separate real and imaginary parts of $\cos(p + iq)$.
8. Prove that $\cosh^2 z - \sinh^2 z = 1$.

II. Long Questions :

(A) Theory Part :

1. Define all the circular functions and their relations. Also discuss their periods.
2. Define all the hyperbolic functions and their relations. Also discuss their periods.
3. Define all the inverse circular functions and their principal value.
4. Define all the inverse hyperbolic functions.

(B) Numerical Problems :

1. If $x = 2 \cos \theta \cosh \phi$, $y = 2 \sin \theta \sinh \phi$, show that :

   (a) $\sec(\theta + i\phi) + \sec(\theta - i\phi) = 4x/(x^2 + y^2)$

   (b) $\sec(\theta + i\phi) - \sec(\theta - i\phi) = 4iy/(x^2 + y^2)$

2. If $\tan(\theta + i\phi) = \sin(x + iy)$, then prove that

   $\coth y \sinh 2\phi = \cot x \sin(2\theta)$

3. If $\tan(x + iy) = \sin(u + iv)$, show that : $\dfrac{\sin 2x}{\sinh 2y} = \dfrac{\tan u}{\tanh(2v)}$.

4. If $\sinh^{-1} p + \sinh^{-1} q = \sinh^{-1} a$, then prove that :

   $\sqrt{a^2 + 1} = p\sqrt{1 + q^2} + q\sqrt{1 + p^2}$

5. If $\cosh^{-1} p + \cosh^{-1} q = \cosh^{-1} r$, then show that :

   $p^2 + q^2 + r^2 = 1 + 2pqr$.

6. Prove that : $\tan^{-1}\left(\dfrac{x-a}{x+a} i\right) = \dfrac{-i}{2} \log\left(\dfrac{a}{x}\right)$.

7. If $\tan(x + iy) = \alpha + i\beta$, show that :

   (i) $(\alpha^2 + \beta^2 - 1) \tan(2x) + 2\alpha = 0$

   (ii) $(\alpha^2 + \beta^2 - 1) \tan(2y) - 2\beta = 0$

8. Find the periods of (i) e^{2z}, (ii) $\sin z$, (iii) $\sinh z$.

9. Prove that following :

   (i) $\tanh^{-1}(\sin \theta) = \cosh^{-1}(\sec \theta)$

   (ii) $\tanh^{-1}(\cos \theta) = \cosh^{-1}(\csc \theta)$

   (iii) $\tanh^{-1} z = \cosh^{-1}\left(\dfrac{1}{1 - z^2}\right)$

10. Show that : $\tanh(z_1 + z_2) = \dfrac{\tanh z_1 + \tanh z_2}{1 + \tanh z_1 \tanh z_2}$.

11. Separate into real and imaginary parts of :

    (i) sec $(x + iy)$, (ii) $e^{\cos(x+iy)}$, (iii) sech $(x + iy)$.

12. Show that tanh $(\log \sqrt{3}) = \dfrac{1}{2}$.

13. Prove that : (i) $\sinh^{-1} z = -i \sin^{-1}(iz)$, (ii) $\cosh^{-1} z = -i \cos^{-1}(iz)$.

III. Multiple Choice Questions :

Select the correct alternative for each of the following with proper justification :

1. For any real θ, $\cos \theta$ is ......
   (a) $\dfrac{e^{\theta} + e^{-\theta}}{2}$
   (b) $\dfrac{e^{i\theta} + e^{-\theta}}{2}$
   (c) $\dfrac{e^{\theta} + e^{-i\theta}}{2}$
   (d) $\dfrac{e^{i\theta} + e^{-i\theta}}{2}$

2. For any real θ, $\sin \theta$ is ......
   (a) $\dfrac{e^{i\theta} + e^{-i\theta}}{2i}$
   (b) $\dfrac{e^{i\theta} - e^{-i\theta}}{2i}$
   (c) $\dfrac{e^{i\theta} - e^{-i\theta}}{2}$
   (d) $\dfrac{e^{i\theta} + e^{-i\theta}}{2}$

3. For any real θ, $e^{-i\theta}$ is ......
   (a) $\cos(-\theta) + i\sin(-\theta)$
   (b) $\cos\theta - i\sin(-\theta)$
   (c) $\cos(-\theta) - i\sin(-\theta)$
   (d) $\cos\theta + i\sin\theta$

4. For any complex number z, cosh z + sinh z is ......
   (a) e^z
   (b) e^{-z}
   (c) log z
   (d) z

5. For any complex number z, sin iz = ...
   (a) $-i \sinh z$
   (b) $i \sinh z$
   (c) $i \sinh(-z)$
   (d) none of these

6. For any complex number z, tanh (iz) ......
   (a) $-i \tan(iz)$
   (b) $\tan(iz)$
   (c) $i \tan z$
   (d) $i \tan(iz)$

7. Period of cosh z ......
   (a) 2π
   (b) 3π
   (c) $3\pi i$
   (d) $2\pi i$

8. cosh p − cosh q = ...
   (a) $2 \sinh\left(\dfrac{p+q}{2i}\right) \sinh\left(\dfrac{p-q}{2i}\right)$
   (b) $2 \sinh\left(\dfrac{p+q}{2}\right) \sinh\left(\dfrac{p-q}{2}\right)$
   (c) $2 \sinh\left(\dfrac{p+q}{2}\right) \sinh\left(\dfrac{p-q}{2i}\right)$
   (d) $2 \sinh\left(\dfrac{p+q}{2i}\right) \sinh\left(\dfrac{p-q}{2}\right)$

9. Principal value of $\sin^{-1} z$ is ......
   (a) $-\pi$ to π
   (b) $-\pi/2$ to $\pi/2$
   (c) $-3\pi/2$ to $3\pi/2$
   (d) none of these

10. If z is real, then $\cosh^{-1} z$ = ...
    (a) $\log(z + \sqrt{z^2 + 1})$
    (b) $\log(z + \sqrt{z^2 - 1})$
    (c) $\log(z - \sqrt{z^2 + 1})$
    (d) $\log(z - \sqrt{z^2 - 1})$

ANSWERS

II. (B)

11. (i) $\dfrac{2 \cos x \cosh y}{\cos 2x + \cosh 2y}$, $\dfrac{-2 \sin x + \sinh y}{\cos 2y + \cosh 2y}$

    (ii) $e^{\cos x \cosh y} \cdot \cos(\sin x \cdot \sinh y)$, $e^{\cos x \cosh y} \cdot \sin(\sin x \sin y)$

    (iii) $\dfrac{2 \cosh x \cos y}{\cosh 2x + \cos 2y}$, $\dfrac{-2 \sinh x \sin y}{\cosh 2x + \cos 2y}$

III.

1. (d)	2. (b)	3. (a)	4. (a)	5. (b)	6. (c)	7. (d)	8. (b)
9. (b)	10. (b)						

SECTION - II : CALCULUS

CHAPTER 1

DIFFERENTIATION

Although the mathematical notion of function was implicit in trigonometric and logarithmic tables, which existed in his day, Leibniz was the first, in 1692 and 1694, to employ it explicitly, to denote any of several geometric concepts derived from a curve, such as abscissa, ordinate, tangent, chord, and the perpendicular. In the 18th century, "function" lost these geometrical associations.

Gottfried Wilhelm Leibniz

Leibniz was the first to see that the coefficients of a system of linear equations could be arranged into an array, now called a matrix, which can be manipulated to find the solution of the system, if any. This method was later called Gaussian elimination. Leibniz's discoveries of Boolean algebra and of symbolic logic, also relevant to mathematics, are discussed in the preceding section. The best overview of Leibniz's writings on the calculus may be found in Bos (1974).

1.1 INTRODUCTION

We have studied the algebra of limit i.e. sum, difference, product and quotient of two functions. But these rules are not sufficient to evaluate denominator are zero.

1.2 INDETERMINATE FORMS

We know that when $x \to a$

$$\lim \frac{F(x)}{G(x)} = \frac{\lim F(x)}{\lim G(x)} \text{ if } \lim G(x) \neq 0$$

But this result fails to give any information regarding the limit of a fraction whose denominator tends to zero as its limit.

(1.1)

Now suppose denominator tends to zero as $x \to a$ and the numerator may or may not tends to zero.

If the numerator does not tends to zero. Then $\dfrac{F(x)}{G(x)}$ can not tends to a finite limit. If possible suppose it has a limit Say l, we have

$$F(x) = \dfrac{F(x)}{G(x)} G(x)$$

$$\lim F(x) = \lim \left[\dfrac{F(x)}{G(x)} G(x)\right]$$

$$= \lim \left[\dfrac{F(x)}{G(x)}\right] \lim G(x)$$

$$= l \cdot 0 = 0$$

This is a contradiction.

There are three types of fractions, may tends to $+\infty$ as or $-\infty$ or limit may not exist. For example:

(i) $\quad \lim\limits_{x \to 0} \left(\dfrac{1}{x^2}\right) = +\infty$

(ii) $\quad \lim\limits_{x \to 0} \left(\dfrac{1}{-x^2}\right) = -\infty$

The following are called indeterminate forms because they are indeterminate by usual methods.

1. The indeterminate form $\left[\dfrac{0}{0}\right]$.

    To find $\lim\limits_{x \to a} \dfrac{F(x)}{G(x)}$ if $\lim\limits_{x \to a} F(x) = 0$, $\lim\limits_{x \to 0} G(x) = 0$

2. To indeterminate form $\left[\dfrac{\infty}{\infty}\right]$.

    To find $\lim\limits_{x \to a} \dfrac{F(x)}{G(x)}$, if $\lim\limits_{x \to a} F(x) = \infty$, $\lim\limits_{x \to a} G(x) = \infty$

3. The indeterminate form $= [0, \infty]$.

    To find $\lim\limits_{x \to a} F(x) \cdot G(x)$, if $\lim\limits_{x \to a} F(x) = 0$, $\lim\limits_{x \to a} G(x) = \infty$

4. The indeterminate form $[\infty, -\infty]$.

    To find $\lim\limits_{x \to a} [F(x) - G(x)]$, if $\lim\limits_{x \to a} F(x) = \infty$, $\lim\limits_{x \to a} G(x) = \infty$

5. The indeterminate form 1^∞.

   To find $\lim\limits_{x \to a} [F(x)]^{G(x)}$, if $\lim\limits_{x \to a} F(x) = 1$ $\lim\limits_{x \to a} G(x) = \infty$

6. The indeterminate form 0^0.

   To find $\lim\limits_{x \to a} [F(x)]^{G(x)}$, if $\lim\limits_{x \to a} F(x) = 0$ $\lim\limits_{x \to a} G(x) = 0$

7. The indeterminate form ∞^0.

   To find $\lim\limits_{x \to a} [F(x)]^{G(x)}$, if $\lim\limits_{x \to a} F(x) = \infty$ $\lim\limits_{x \to a} G(x) = 0$

   These limits are evaluated by L' Hospitals Rule.

1.3 L' HOSPITAL'S RULE

If F(x) and G(x) are two functions which can be expanded by Taylor's series in the neighbourhood of x = a and F(a) = 0 = G(a), then

$$\lim_{x \to a} \frac{F(x)}{G(x)} = \lim_{x \to a} \frac{F'(x)}{G'(x)}$$ provided the later limit exists.

Proof : We have Taylor's Series,

$$F(x) = F(a) + (x - a) F'(a) + \frac{(x - a)^2}{2!} F''(a) + \ldots$$

$$G(x) = G(a) + (x - a) G'(a) + \frac{(x - a)^2}{2!} G''(a) + \ldots$$

Since, $F(a) = 0 = G(a)$

$\therefore$ $F(x) = (x - a) F'(a) + \frac{(x - a)^2}{2!} F''(a) + \ldots$

$G(x) = (x - a) G'(a) + \frac{(x - a)^2}{2!} G''(a) + \ldots$

Consider, $\lim\limits_{x \to a} \frac{F(x)}{G(x)} = \lim\limits_{x \to a} \left[\dfrac{(x - a) F'(a) + \dfrac{(x - a)^2}{2!} F''(a) + \ldots}{(x - a) G'(a) + \dfrac{(x - a)^2}{2!} G''(a) + \ldots} \right]$

Dividing numerator and denominator by $(x - a)$, we get

$$\lim_{x \to a} \frac{F(x)}{G(x)} = \lim_{x \to a} \left[\frac{F'(a) + \frac{(x-a)}{2!} F''(a) + \ldots}{G'(a) + \frac{(x-a)}{2!} G''(a) + \ldots} \right]$$

$\therefore \quad \lim_{x \to a} \frac{F(x)}{G(x)} = \frac{F'(a)}{G'(a)} = \lim_{x \to a} \frac{F'(x)}{G'(x)}$

$\therefore \quad \boxed{\lim_{x \to a} \frac{F(x)}{G(x)} = \lim_{x \to a} \frac{F'(x)}{G'(x)}}$

SOLVED EXAMPLES

Example 1.1 : $\lim_{x \to 0} \dfrac{3^x - 2^x}{x}$

Solution : $\lim_{x \to 0} \dfrac{3^x - 2^x}{x}$ $\quad \left[\dfrac{0}{0}\right]$ form

$= \lim_{x \to 0} \dfrac{3^x \log 3 - 2^x \log 2}{1}$

$= \dfrac{3^0 \log 3 - 2^0 \log 2}{1} = \dfrac{\log 3 - \log 2}{1}$

$= \log \left(\dfrac{3}{2}\right)$

Example 1.2 : $\lim_{x \to 1} \dfrac{1 + \log x - x}{1 - 2x + x^2}$

Solution : $\lim_{x \to 1} \dfrac{1 + \log x - x}{1 - 2x + x^2}$ $\quad \left[\dfrac{0}{0}\right]$ form

$= \lim_{x \to 1} \dfrac{0 + \frac{1}{x} - 1}{0 - 2 + 2x}$ $\quad \left[\dfrac{0}{0}\right]$ form

$= \lim_{x \to 1} \dfrac{\frac{-1}{x^2}}{2}$

$= \dfrac{-1}{2}$

Example 1.3: $\lim\limits_{x \to 0} \dfrac{\log(1-x^2)}{\log \cos x}$

Solution: $\lim\limits_{x \to 0} \dfrac{\log(1-x^2)}{\log \cos x}$ $\qquad \left[\dfrac{0}{0}\right]$ form

$$= \lim_{x \to 0} \dfrac{\dfrac{-2x}{(1-x^2)}}{\dfrac{-\sin x}{\cos x}} = 2 \lim_{x \to 0} \dfrac{\cos x}{1-x^2} \cdot \dfrac{x}{\sin x}$$

$$= 2 \lim_{x \to 0} \dfrac{\cos x}{1-x^2} \qquad \left[\because \lim_{x \to 0} \dfrac{x}{\sin x} = 1\right]$$

$$= 2(1)$$

$$= 2$$

Example 1.4: $\lim\limits_{x \to 0} \dfrac{e^x + \sin x - 1}{\log(x+1)}$

Solution: $\lim\limits_{x \to 0} \dfrac{e^x + \sin x - 1}{\log(x+1)}$ $\qquad \left[\dfrac{0}{0}\right]$

$$= \lim_{x \to 0} \dfrac{e^x + \cos x}{\dfrac{1}{(x+1)}} = \dfrac{2}{\dfrac{1}{1}} = 2$$

Example 1.5: $\lim\limits_{x \to 1} \dfrac{x^x - x}{x - 1 - \log x}$

Solution: $\lim\limits_{x \to 1} \dfrac{x^x - x}{x - 1 - \log x}$ $\qquad \left[\dfrac{0}{0}\right]$

$$= \lim_{x \to 1} \dfrac{x^x (1 + \log x) - 1}{1 - \dfrac{1}{x}} \qquad \left[\dfrac{0}{0}\right]$$

$$= \lim_{x \to 1} \dfrac{x^x \left(\dfrac{1}{x}\right) + (1 + \log x) x^x (1 + \log x)}{+ \dfrac{1}{x^2}}$$

$$= \lim_{x \to 1} \dfrac{x^x \left(\dfrac{1}{x}\right) + x^x (1 + \log x)^2}{\dfrac{1}{x^2}}$$

$$= \frac{1+1}{\frac{1}{1}} = 2$$

Example 1.6 : $\lim_{x \to 0} \frac{x - \tan x}{x^3}$

Solution : $\lim_{x \to 0} \frac{x - \tan x}{x^3}$ $\left[\frac{0}{0}\right]$

$$= \lim_{x \to 0} \frac{1 - \sec^2 x}{3x^2} \quad \left[\frac{0}{0}\right]$$

$$= \lim_{x \to 0} \frac{-2 \sec x (\sec x \tan x)}{6x} \quad \left[\frac{0}{0}\right]$$

$$= \lim_{x \to 0} -2 \frac{\{\sec^2 x \tan x\}}{6x} \quad \left[\frac{0}{0}\right]$$

$$= \lim_{x \to 0} -2 \frac{[\sec^2 x \cdot \sec^2 x + \tan x \cdot 2 \sec x \sec x \cdot \tan x]}{6}$$

$$= \frac{-2}{6} = \frac{-1}{3}$$

Example 1.7 : $\lim_{x \to 0} \frac{e^x - e^{\sin x}}{x - \sin x}$

Solution : $\lim_{x \to 0} \frac{e^x - e^{\sin x}}{x - \sin x}$ $\left[\frac{0}{0}\right]$

$$= \lim_{x \to 0} \frac{e^x - e^{\sin x} \cos x}{1 - \cos x} \quad \left[\frac{0}{0}\right]$$

$$= \lim_{x \to 0} \frac{e^x - (e^{\sin x} \cos^2 x - e^{\sin x} \sin x)}{\sin x} \quad \left[\frac{0}{0}\right]$$

$$= \lim_{x \to 0} e^x \frac{\{\sin x \cos^2 x \cos x + e^{\sin x} 2 \cos x (-\sin x)\} + (e^{\sin x} \cos x + e^{\sin x} \sin x \cos x)}{\cos x}$$

$$= \frac{1 - (1 - 0) + (0 + 1)}{1} = 1$$

Example 1.8 : $\lim_{x \to 0} \frac{\cos hx - \cos x}{x \sin x}$

Solution : $\lim_{x \to 0} \frac{\cos hx - \cos x}{x \sin x}$ $\left[\frac{0}{0}\right]$

$$= \lim_{x \to 0} \frac{\cos hx - \cos x}{x^2} \left(\frac{x}{\sin x}\right)$$

$$= \lim_{x \to 0} \frac{\cos hx - \cos x}{x^2} \quad \left[\frac{0}{0}\right]$$

$$= \lim_{x \to 0} \frac{\sin hx + \sin x}{2x}$$

$$= \lim_{x \to 0} \frac{\cos hx + \cos x}{2}$$

$$= \frac{1+1}{2} = 1$$

Example 1.9 : $\lim_{x \to y} \dfrac{x^y - y^x}{x^x - y^y}$

Solution : $\lim_{x \to y} \dfrac{x^y - y^x}{x^x - y^y} \left[\dfrac{0}{0}\right]$

Here y is constant

$$= \lim_{x \to y} \frac{y\, x^{y-1} - y^x \log y}{x^x (1 + \log x)}$$

$$= \frac{y\, y^{y-1} - y^y \log y}{y^y (1 + \log y)} = \frac{y^y - y^y \log y}{y^y (1 + \log y)}$$

$$= \frac{y^y (1 - \log y)}{y^y (1 + \log y)} = \frac{1 - \log y}{1 + \log y}$$

Example 1.10 : Show that $\lim_{x \to 0} \dfrac{\sin x \sin^{-1} x - x^2}{x^6} = \dfrac{1}{18}$

Solution : We use expansion of

$$\sin x = x - \frac{x^3}{3!} + \frac{x^5}{5!} + \ldots$$

$$= x - \frac{x^3}{6} + \frac{x^5}{125} + \ldots$$

$$\sin^{-1} x = x + \frac{x^3}{6} + \frac{3x^5}{40} + \ldots$$

$$\therefore \lim_{x \to 0} \frac{\sin x \sin^{-1} x - x^2}{x^6}$$

$$= \lim_{x \to 0} \frac{\left(x - \frac{x^3}{6} + \frac{x^5}{125} + \ldots\right)\left(x + \frac{x^3}{6} + \frac{3x^5}{40} + \ldots\right) - x^2}{x^6}$$

$$= \lim_{x \to 0} \frac{\left(x^2 + \left(\frac{3}{40} + \frac{1}{120} - \frac{1}{36}\right)x^6 + \ldots\right) - x^2}{x^6}$$

$$= \frac{3}{40} + \frac{1}{120} - \frac{1}{36} = \frac{1}{18}$$

Example 1.11 : Find the values of a and b if

$$\lim_{x \to 0} \frac{x(1 + a \cos x) - b \sin x}{x^3} = 1$$

Solution : Consider $\lim_{x \to 0} \dfrac{x(1 + a \cos x) - b \sin x}{x^3} \qquad \left[\dfrac{0}{0}\right]$

$$\lim_{x \to 0} \frac{x(-a \sin x) + (1 + a \cos x) - b \cos x}{3x^2} \qquad \ldots (1)$$

as $x \to 0$ the denominator tends to zero. Since the limit of fraction is finite. The numerator must also tends to zero as $x \to 0$. This gives

$$1 + a - b = 0 \qquad \therefore a - b = -1 \qquad \ldots (2)$$

$$1 = \lim_{x \to 0} \frac{x(1 + a \cos x) - b \sin x}{x^3}$$

Given limit again from (1), we get by Hospital's Rule

$$= \lim_{x \to 0} \frac{a \sin x - ax \cos x - a \sin x + b \sin x}{6x}$$

$$= \lim_{x \to 0} \frac{(b - a) \sin x - ax \cos x}{6x} \qquad \left[\frac{0}{0}\right]$$

$$= \lim_{x \to 0} \frac{(b - 2a) \cos x - [x \sin x + \cos x]}{6}$$

$$= \frac{(b - 2a) - a}{6}$$

$$= \frac{b - 3a}{6} \quad \text{But by data given value is 1}$$

$$\therefore \quad \frac{b - 3a}{6} = 1$$

∴   b − 3a = 6   ... (3)

Solve equation (2) and (3),

$$a = \frac{-5}{2}$$

$$b = \frac{-3}{2}$$

EXERCISE 1.1

1. $\lim\limits_{x \to 0} \dfrac{x \sin x}{\tan^3 x}$

2. $\lim\limits_{x \to \pi/4} \dfrac{\log \sin x}{(\pi - 2x)^2}$

3. $\lim\limits_{x \to 0} \dfrac{\log (1 + x^3)}{\sin^3 x}$

4. $\lim\limits_{x \to 0} \dfrac{e^x - e^{-x} \, 2 \log (1 + x)}{x \sin x}$

5. $\lim\limits_{x \to 0} \dfrac{\log (1 - x^2)}{\log \cos x}$

6. $\lim\limits_{x \to 0} \dfrac{\sin hx - x}{x^3}$

7. $\lim\limits_{a \to b} \dfrac{a^b - b^a}{a^a - b^b}$

8. $\lim\limits_{x \to 0} \dfrac{a^x - b^x}{c^x - d^x}$

9. $\lim\limits_{x \to 0} \dfrac{x^2 \sin \left(\dfrac{1}{x}\right)}{\tan x}$

10. $\lim\limits_{x \to 0} \dfrac{e^x \sin x - x - x^2}{x^2 + x \log (1 - x)}$

Find values of a and b such that

11. $\lim\limits_{x \to 0} \dfrac{a \sin^2 x + b \log \cos x}{x^4} = \dfrac{-1}{2}$

12. $\lim\limits_{x \to 0} \dfrac{a e^x - b \cos x + c e^{-x}}{x \sin x} = 2$

13. $\lim\limits_{x \to 0} \dfrac{a \sin hx + b \sin x}{x^3} = \dfrac{5}{3}$

14. $\lim\limits_{x \to 0} \dfrac{a \sin^2 x + b \cos \log x}{x^4} = \dfrac{1}{2}$

ANSWERS 1.1

1. $\dfrac{1}{6}$
2. $\dfrac{-1}{8}$
3. 1
4. 1
5. 2
6. $\dfrac{1}{6}$
7. $\dfrac{1 - \log b}{1 + \log b}$
8. $\dfrac{\log (a/b)}{\log (c/d)}$
9. 0
10. $\dfrac{-2}{3}$
11. $a = -1 \quad b = -2$
12. $a = 1 \quad b = 2 \quad c = 1$
13. $a = 5 \quad b = -5$
14. $a = -1 \quad b = -2$

The indeterminate from $\dfrac{\infty}{\infty}$

Theorem 1 :

If $\lim\limits_{x \to a} F(x) = \infty$, $\lim\limits_{x \to a} G(x) = \infty$ and $\lim\limits_{x \to a} \dfrac{F(x)}{G(x)} = l$ then $\lim\limits_{x \to a} \dfrac{F'(x)}{G'(x)} = l.$

Proof : (i) Let $\lim\limits_{x \to a} \dfrac{F(x)}{G(x)} = l$ where $l \neq 0$ and is finite.

$$l = \lim\limits_{x \to a} \dfrac{\dfrac{1}{G(x)}}{\dfrac{1}{F(x)}} \qquad \left[\dfrac{0}{0}\right]$$

$$= \lim\limits_{x \to a} \dfrac{-\dfrac{1}{[G(x)]^2} G'(x)}{-\dfrac{1}{[F(x)]^2} F'(x)} \qquad \text{By L' Hospital's Rule}$$

$$= \lim_{x \to a} \left[\frac{F(x)}{G(x)}\right]^2 \left[\frac{G'(x)}{F'(x)}\right]$$

$$= \lim_{x \to a} \left[\frac{F(x)}{G(x)}\right]^2 \lim_{x \to a} \left[\frac{G'(x)}{F'(x)}\right]$$

$$l = l^2 \lim_{x \to a} \left[\frac{G'(x)}{F'(x)}\right]$$

$$\therefore \quad \lim_{x \to a} \left[\frac{G'(x)}{F'(x)}\right] = \frac{1}{l}$$

$$\therefore \quad \lim_{x \to a} \left[\frac{F'(x)}{G'(x)}\right] = l$$

(ii) If $l = 0$ the above argument fails,

$$\lim_{x \to a} \frac{F(x)}{G(x)} = 0$$

Consider $\lim_{x \to a} \frac{F(x) + G(x)}{G(x)} = \lim_{x \to a} \left\{\frac{F(x)}{G(x)} + 1\right\}$

$$= 0 + 1 \qquad \left(\because \lim_{x \to a} \frac{F(x)}{G(x)} = 0\right)$$

$$= 1$$

Hence, $\quad 1 = \lim_{x \to a} \frac{F(x) + G(x)}{G(x)} = \left[\frac{\infty}{\infty}\right]$

$$1 = \lim_{x \to a} \frac{F'(x) + G'(x)}{G'(x)} \qquad \text{by Case 1}$$

$$1 = \lim_{x \to a} \frac{F'(x)}{G'(x)} + 1$$

$$\therefore \quad \lim_{x \to a} \frac{F'(x)}{G'(x)} = 0$$

$$\therefore \quad \lim_{x \to a} \frac{F(x)}{G(x)} = \lim_{x \to a} \frac{F'(x)}{G'(x)}$$

(iii) If $l = \infty$, we have $\lim_{x \to a} \frac{F(x)}{G(x)} = 0 = \lim_{x \to a} \frac{G'(x)}{f'(x)}$

∴ $\lim_{x \to a} \dfrac{F'(x)}{G'(x)} = \infty$

$\lim_{x \to a} \dfrac{F(x)}{G(x)} = \lim_{x \to a} \dfrac{F'(x)}{G'(x)}$

SOLVED EXAMPLES

Example 1.12 : Evaluate $\lim_{x \to a} \dfrac{\log(x-a)}{\log(e^x - e^a)}$

Solution : $\lim_{x \to a} \dfrac{\log(x-a)}{\log(e^x - e^a)}$ $\left[\dfrac{\infty}{\infty}\right]$

$= \lim_{x \to a} \dfrac{\dfrac{1}{x-a}}{\dfrac{e^x}{(e^x - e^a)}} = \lim_{x \to a} \dfrac{e^x - e^a}{e^x(x-a)}$ $\left[\dfrac{0}{0}\right]$

$= \lim_{x \to a} \dfrac{e^x}{e^x(x-a) + e^x} = \dfrac{e^a}{e^a(0) + e^a} = 1$

Example 1.13 : Evaluate $\lim_{x \to \infty} \dfrac{\log(1 + e^{3x})}{x}$

Solution : $\lim_{x \to \infty} \dfrac{\log(1 + e^{3x})}{x}$ $\left[\dfrac{\infty}{\infty}\right]$

$= \lim_{x \to \infty} \dfrac{\left(\dfrac{1}{1 + e^{3x}}\right) e^{3x}(3)}{1} = \lim_{x \to \infty} \left(\dfrac{e^{3x} + 1 - 1}{1 + e^{3x}}\right)(3)$

$= 3 \lim_{x \to \infty} \left[1 - \dfrac{1}{1 + e^{3x}}\right]$

$= 3\left[1 - \dfrac{1}{\infty}\right] = 3[1 - 0] = 3$

Example 1.14 : $\lim_{x \to 0} \dfrac{\log \tan 2x}{\log \tan x}$ OR $\lim_{x \to 0} \log_{\tan x} \tan 2x$

Solution : $\lim_{x \to 0} \log_{\tan x} \tan 2x$

$= \lim_{x \to 0} \dfrac{\log \tan 2x}{\log \tan x}$ $\left[\dfrac{\infty}{\infty}\right]$

$$= \lim_{x \to 0} \frac{\frac{2\sec^2 2x}{\tan 2x}}{\frac{\sec^2 x}{\tan x}}$$

$$= \lim_{x \to 0} \left(\frac{\tan x}{\tan 2x}\right)\left(\frac{\sec^2 2x}{\sec^2 x}\right)(2)$$

$$= \lim_{x \to 0} \left(\frac{\tan x}{x}\right)\left(\frac{2x}{\tan 2x}\right)\left(\frac{\sec^2 2x}{\sec^2 x}\right)$$

$$= 1$$

Example 1.15 : $\lim_{x \to \infty} \dfrac{x^n}{e^{kx}}$ (K > 0)

Solution : $\lim_{x \to \infty} \dfrac{x^n}{e^{Kx}}$ $\left[\dfrac{\infty}{\infty}\right]$

$$= \lim_{x \to \infty} \frac{n x^{n-1}}{k e^{Kx}} \quad \left[\frac{\infty}{\infty}\right]$$

$$= \lim_{x \to \infty} \frac{n(n-1) x^{n-2}}{k^2 e^{Kx}} \quad \left[\frac{\infty}{\infty}\right]$$

$$= \lim_{x \to \infty} \frac{n!}{k^n e^{Kx}} = 0$$

Example 1.16 : Evaluate $\lim_{x \to 0} \log_{\sin x} \sin 2x$

Solution : $\lim_{x \to 0} \dfrac{\log \sin 2x}{\log \sin x} \left[\dfrac{\infty}{\infty}\right] = \lim_{x \to 0} \dfrac{\dfrac{1}{\sin 2x} \cdot 2\cos 2x}{\dfrac{1}{\sin x} \cos x}$

$$= \lim_{x \to 0} \frac{\sin x}{\sin 2x} \lim_{x \to 0} \frac{2 \cos 2x}{\cos x}$$

$$= \lim_{x \to 0} \frac{\sin x}{\sin 2x} (2) = 2 \lim_{x \to 0} \frac{\sin x}{\sin 2x} \quad \left[\frac{0}{0}\right]$$

$$= 2 \lim_{x \to 0} \frac{\cos x}{2 \cos 2x}$$

$$= 2 \left(\frac{1}{2}\right) = 1$$

EXERCISE 1.2

1. $\lim_{x \to a} \dfrac{\log(x-a)}{\log(a^x - a^a)}$

2. $\lim_{x \to 0} \dfrac{\log \sin x}{\cot x}$

3. $\lim_{x \to 0} \dfrac{\log x^2}{\cot x^2}$

4. $\lim_{x \to \infty} \dfrac{\log x}{x^2}$

5. $\lim_{x \to \infty} \dfrac{(1 + e^{3x})}{x}$

6. $\lim_{x \to 0} \dfrac{\log \sin 2x}{\log \sin x}$

7. $\lim_{x \to \infty} \dfrac{1 + 2 + 3 + \ldots x}{x^2}$

8. $\lim_{x \to \infty} \dfrac{1^2 + 2^2 + 3^2 + \ldots x^2}{x^3}$

ANSWERS 1.2

1. 1
2. 0
3. 0
4. 0
5. 3
6. 1
7. $\dfrac{1}{2}$
8. $\dfrac{1}{3}$

The indeterminate forms $\infty - \infty$ AND $0 \times \infty$.

If $\lim_{x \to a} F(x) \cdot G(x)$ takes the form $0 \times \infty$

or $\lim_{x \to a} F(x) - G(x)$ takes the form $\infty - \infty$

We can reduce it to the form $\dfrac{\infty}{\infty}$ or $\dfrac{0}{0}$ and evaluate by discussed in above methods.

SOLVED EXAMPLES

Example 1.17 : Evaluate $\lim_{x \to 0} x \log \tan x$

Solution :

$L = \lim_{x \to 0} x \log \tan x$ $[0 \times \infty]$

$= \lim_{x \to 0} \dfrac{\log \tan x}{\dfrac{1}{x}}$ $\left[\dfrac{\infty}{\infty}\right]$

$$= \lim_{x \to 0} \frac{\frac{1}{\tan x} \cdot \sec^2 x}{\frac{-1}{x^2}}$$

$$= \lim_{x \to 0} \frac{-x^2}{\tan x} \lim_{x \to 0} \sec^2 x$$

$$= \lim_{x \to 0} (-x) \lim_{x \to 0} \frac{x}{\tan x} \,(1)$$

$$= 0 \times 1$$

$$= 0$$

Example 1.18 : Evaluate $\lim_{x \to 1} (x^2 - 1) \tan \frac{\pi x}{2}$

Solution : $L = \lim_{x \to 1} (x^2 - 1) \tan \frac{\pi x}{2}$ $\qquad [0 \times \infty]$

$$= \lim_{x \to 1} \frac{x^2 - 1}{\cot \frac{\pi x}{2}} \qquad \left[\frac{0}{0}\right]$$

$$= \lim_{x \to 1} \frac{2x}{\frac{-\pi}{2} \operatorname{cosec}^2 \left(\frac{\pi x}{2}\right)} = \frac{-4}{\pi}$$

Example 1.19 : $\lim_{x \to 1} \sec \frac{\pi}{2x} \log x$

Solution : $L = \lim_{x \to 1} \sec \frac{\pi}{2x} \log x$ $\qquad [0 \times \infty]$

$$= \lim_{x \to 1} \frac{\log x}{\cos \frac{\pi}{2x}} \qquad \left[\frac{0}{0}\right]$$

$$= \lim_{x \to 1} \frac{\frac{1}{x}}{\left(-\sin \frac{\pi}{2x}\right)\left(\frac{-\pi}{4x^2}(2)\right)}$$

$$= \lim_{x \to 1} \frac{\frac{1}{x}}{\sin \frac{\pi}{2x}\left(\frac{\pi}{2x^2}\right)}$$

$$= \lim_{x \to 1} \frac{2}{\pi} \frac{x}{\sin \frac{\pi}{2x}}$$

$$= \frac{2}{\pi}$$

Example 1.20 : Evaluate $\lim_{x \to 0} \left[\frac{a}{x} - \cot \frac{x}{a} \right]$

Solution : Put $\frac{x}{a} = y$ ∴ AS $x \to 0$, $y \to 0$

$$\lim_{x \to 0} \left[\frac{a}{x} - \cot \frac{x}{a} \right] = \lim_{x \to 0} \left[\frac{1}{y} - \cot y \right] \quad [\infty - \infty]$$

$$= \lim_{y \to 0} \left[\frac{1}{y} - \frac{1}{\tan y} \right] = \lim_{y \to 0} \left[\frac{\tan y - y}{y \tan y} \right] \quad \left[\frac{0}{0}\right]$$

$$= \lim_{y \to 0} \frac{\tan y - y}{y^2} \cdot \frac{y}{\tan y} = \lim_{y \to 0} \frac{\tan y - y}{y^2} \quad (1)$$

$$= \lim_{y \to 0} \frac{\tan y - y}{y^2} = \lim_{y \to 0} \frac{\sec^2 y - 1}{2y}$$

$$= \lim_{y \to 0} \frac{2 \sec^2 y \tan y}{2} = 0$$

Example 1.21 : $\lim_{x \to 0} \left[\frac{1}{x^2} - \frac{1}{\sin^2 x} \right]$

Solution : $\lim_{x \to 0} \left[\frac{1}{x^2} - \frac{1}{\sin^2 x} \right] \quad [\infty - \infty]$

$$L = \lim_{x \to 0} \left[\frac{\sin^2 x - x^2}{x^2 \sin^2 x} \right] \quad \left[\frac{0}{0}\right]$$

$$= \lim_{x \to 0} \frac{2 \sin x \cos x - 2x}{2x \sin^2 x + 2x^2 \sin x \cos x}$$

$$= \lim_{x \to 0} \frac{\sin 2x - 2x}{2x \sin^2 x + x^2 \sin 2x} \quad \left[\frac{0}{0}\right]$$

$$= \lim_{x \to 0} \frac{2 \cos 2x - 2}{2 \sin^2 x + 4x \sin x \cos x + 2x \sin 2x + 2x^2 \cos 2x}$$

$$= \lim_{x \to 0} \frac{2 \cos 2x - 2}{2 \sin^2 x + 4x \sin 2x + 2x^2 \cos 2x} \quad \left[\frac{0}{0}\right]$$

$$= \lim_{x \to 0} \frac{-4\sin 2x}{4\sin x \cos x + 4\sin 2x + 8x\cos 2x + 4x\cos 2x - 4x^2 \sin 2x}$$

$$= \lim_{x \to 0} \frac{-4\sin 2x}{6\sin 2x + 12x\cos 2x - 4x^2 \sin 2x} \quad \left[\frac{0}{0}\right]$$

$$= \lim_{x \to 0} \frac{-8\cos 2x}{12\cos 2x + 12\cos 2x - 24x\sin 2x - 8x\sin 2x - 8x^2 \cos 2x}$$

$$= \lim_{x \to 0} \frac{-8\cos 2x}{24\cos 2x - 32x\sin 2x - 8x^2 \cos 2x}$$

$$= \frac{-8}{24} = \frac{-1}{3}$$

Example 1.22 : Evaluate $\lim_{x \to 2} \left[\dfrac{1}{x-2} - \dfrac{1}{\log(x-1)} \right]$

$$L = \lim_{x \to 2} \left[\frac{1}{x-2} - \frac{1}{\log(x-1)} \right] \quad [\infty - \infty]$$

$$= \lim_{x \to 2} \frac{\log(x-1) - (x-2)}{(x-2)\log(x-1)} \quad \left[\frac{0}{0}\right]$$

$$= \lim_{x \to 2} \frac{\dfrac{1}{(x-1)} - 1}{\log(x-1) + \dfrac{(x-2)}{x-1}}$$

$$= \lim_{x \to 2} \frac{-x+2}{(x-1)\log(x-1) + (x-2)} \quad \left[\frac{0}{0}\right]$$

$$= \lim_{x \to 2} \frac{-1}{\dfrac{(x-1)}{(x-1)} + \log(x-1) + 1} = \frac{1}{-2}$$

EXERCISE 1.3

1. $\lim_{x \to a} \log\left(2 - \dfrac{x}{a}\right) \cot(x-a)$
2. $\lim_{x \to 0} \left(\dfrac{1}{x} - \dfrac{1}{e^x - 1}\right)$
3. $\lim_{x \to 1} \left[\dfrac{1}{\log x} - \dfrac{x}{x-1} \right]$
4. $\lim_{x \to 0} \left[\dfrac{1}{x^2} - \dfrac{1}{\tan^2 x} \right]$

5. $\lim_{x \to \infty} x^2 e^{-x}$

6. $\lim_{x \to \infty} (a^{1/x} - 1) \cdot x$

7. $\lim_{x \to 1} (1 + \sec x) \tan \dfrac{\pi x}{2}$

8. $\lim_{x \to 0} \left[\dfrac{1}{\sin^2 x} - \dfrac{1}{x^2} \right]$

9. $\lim_{x \to \infty} [\cos^{-1} 4x - \log x]$

10. $\lim_{x \to \pi/2} (\sec x - \tan x)$

11. $\lim_{x \to 0} \left[\cot x - \dfrac{1}{x} \right]$

12. $\lim_{x \to a} \log \left(2 - \dfrac{x}{a} \right) \cot (x - a)$

ANSWERS 1.3

1. $-\dfrac{1}{a}$

2. $\dfrac{1}{2}$

3. $\dfrac{-1}{2}$

4. $\dfrac{2}{3}$

5. $\dfrac{\pi}{4}$

6. $\log a$

7. 0

8. $\dfrac{1}{3}$

9. $\log 2$

10. 0

11. 0

12. $\dfrac{1}{2}$

The indeterminate forms 0^0, 1^∞, ∞^0

To find the limit of the function of the type $F(x)^{G(x)}$ which takes any one of the above form as $x \to a$

Let $\quad \lim_{x \to a} F(x)^{G(x)} = L$

If $F(x)$ is positive then taking log of both sides.

$$\log L = \lim_{x \to a} [G(x) \log F(x)] \qquad \ldots (1)$$

If $F(x)^{G(x)}$ is of the form 0^0, 1^∞, ∞^0 then $G(x) \log F(x)$ will take the form $0 \log 0$, $\infty \log 1$, $0 \log \infty$. Since $\log 1 = 0$, $\log \infty = \infty$ and $\log 0 = -\infty$.

$G(x) \log F(x)$ will take the form $\infty \cdot 0$ which we have learn in above.

SOLVED EXAMPLES

Example 1.23 : $\lim_{x \to a} (x-a)^{x-a}$

Solution : Let, $L = \lim_{x \to a} (x-a)^{x-a}$ $\quad 0^0$

$$\log L = \log \lim_{x \to a} (x-a)^{x-a}$$

$$= \lim_{x \to a} \log (x-a)^{x-a}$$

$$= \lim_{x \to a} (x-a) \log (x-a) \quad [0 \times \infty]$$

$$= \lim_{x \to a} \frac{\log(x-a)}{\frac{1}{(x-a)}} \qquad \left[\frac{\infty}{\infty}\right]$$

$$= \lim_{x \to a} \frac{\frac{1}{x-a}}{\frac{-1}{(x-a)^2}}$$

$$= \lim_{x \to a} -(x-a) = 0$$

$$\log L = 0$$
$$L = e^0$$
$$L = 1$$

Example 1.24 : $\lim_{x \to 0} (1 + \sin x)^{\cot x}$

Solution : Let $L = \lim_{x \to 0} (1 + \sin x)^{\cot x}$ $\qquad [1^\infty]$

$$\log L = \log \lim_{x \to 0} (1 + \sin x)^{\cot x}$$

$$= \lim_{x \to 0} \log (1 + \sin x)^{\cot x}$$

$$= \lim_{x \to 0} \cot x \log (1 + \sin x) \qquad [0 \times \infty]$$

$$= \lim_{x \to 0} \frac{\log(1 + \sin x)}{\tan x} \qquad \left[\frac{0}{0}\right]$$

$$= \lim_{x \to 0} \frac{\frac{\cos x}{1 + \sin x}}{\sec^2 x}$$

$$= 1$$

$$\log L = 1$$

$$L = e^1 = e$$

Example 1.25 : Evaluate $\lim_{x \to 0} (\cot x)^{\sin 2x}$

Solution :

$$L = \lim_{x \to 0} (\cot x)^{\sin 2x} \quad [\infty]^0$$

$$\log L = \lim_{x \to 0} \sin 2x \, \log \cot x \qquad [0 \times \infty]$$

$$= \lim_{x \to 0} \frac{\log \cot x}{\operatorname{cosec} 2x} \qquad \left[\frac{\infty}{\infty}\right]$$

$$= \lim_{x \to 0} \frac{\frac{1}{\cot x}(-\operatorname{cosec}^2 x)}{-2 \operatorname{cosec} 2x \cot 2x}$$

$$= \lim_{x \to 0} \frac{4 \sin x \cos x}{\cos 2x}$$

$$= \lim_{x \to 0} \frac{2 \sin x}{\cos 2x}$$

$$\log L = 0$$

$$L = e^0 = 1$$

Example 1.26 : Evaluate $\lim_{x \to 0} \left(\frac{a^x + b^x + c^x}{3}\right)^{1/x}$

Solution :

$$L = \lim_{x \to 0} \left(\frac{a^x + b^x + c^x}{3}\right)^{1/x}$$

$$\log L = \lim_{x \to 0} \frac{\log(a^x + b^x + c^x) - \log 3}{x} \qquad \left[\frac{0}{0}\right]$$

$$= \lim_{x \to 0} \frac{1}{a^x + b^x + c^x} \frac{[a^x \log a + b^x \log b + c^x \log c]}{1}$$

$$= \frac{1}{1 + 1 + 1} (\log a + \log b + \log c)$$

$$\log L = \frac{1}{3} \log (abc) = \log (abc)^{1/3}$$

$$L = (abc)^{1/3}$$

Example 1.27 : Evaluate $\lim_{x \to 0} \left[\dfrac{1^x + 2^x + 3^x + 4^x + 5^x}{5} \right]^{1/x}$

Solution : As above, we prove that

$$L = (1 \cdot 2 \cdot 3 \cdot 4 \cdot 5)^{1/5}$$

$$= \sqrt[5]{120}$$

Example 1.28 : Evaluate $\lim_{x \to 0} \left(\dfrac{a^{1/x} + b^{1/x} + c^{1/x}}{3} \right)^{3x}$

Solution : Put $\dfrac{1}{x} = y$ as $x \to \infty$, $y \to 0$

Given equation becomes $\lim_{y \to 0} \left(\dfrac{a^y + b^y + c^y}{3} \right)^{3/y} = L$

$\therefore \quad \log L = \lim_{y \to 0} \dfrac{3}{y} [\log (a^y + b^y + c^y) \log 3]$

$$= \lim_{y \to 0} \frac{3}{a^y + b^y + c^y} \left[\frac{a^y \log a + b^y + \log b + c^y \log c}{1} \right]$$

$$= \frac{3}{3} (\log a + \log b + \log c)$$

$$\log L = \log (abc)$$

$$L = abc$$

Example 1.29 : $\lim_{x \to 0} \left(\dfrac{\sin 4x}{x} \right)^{1/x^2}$

Solution : Let $\lim_{x \to 0} \left(\dfrac{\sin 4x}{x} \right)^{1/x^2}$ $[1^\infty]$

$$\log L = \lim_{x \to 0} \frac{\log\left(\frac{\sin 4x}{x}\right)}{x^2} \qquad \left[\frac{0}{0}\right]$$

$$= \lim_{x \to 0} \frac{\frac{1}{\left(\frac{\sin 4x}{x}\right)} \left[\frac{x \cos 4x - \sin 4x}{x^2}\right]}{2x}$$

$$= \frac{1}{4} \lim_{x \to 0} \frac{4x}{\sin 4x} \lim_{x \to 0} \frac{x \cos 4x - \sin 4x}{2x^3}$$

$$= \frac{1}{4} \lim_{x \to 0} \frac{x \cos 4x - \sin 4x}{2x^3} \qquad \left[\frac{0}{0}\right]$$

$$= \lim_{x \to 0} \frac{x \sin 4x}{6x^2} = \frac{1}{6} \lim_{x \to 0} \frac{\sin 4x}{x} = \frac{4}{6} \lim_{x \to 0} \frac{\sin 4x}{4x}$$

$$\log L = \frac{4}{6}$$

$$L = e^{4/6}$$

Example 1.30 : Evaluate $\lim_{x \to \pi/2} (\cosec x)^{\tan^2 x}$

Solution : Let, $L = \lim_{x \to \pi/2} (\cosec x)^{\tan^2 x}$

$$\log L = \lim_{x \to \pi/2} \tan^2 x \log \cosec x \qquad [\infty \times 0]$$

$$= \lim_{x \to \pi/2} \frac{\log \cosec x}{\cot^2 x} \qquad \left[\frac{0}{0}\right]$$

$$= \lim_{x \to \pi/2} \frac{-\cosec x \cdot \frac{\cot x}{\cosec x}}{-2 \cot x \cosec^2 x}$$

$$= \lim_{x \to \pi/2} \frac{\sin^2 x}{2} = \frac{1}{2}$$

$$\log L = \frac{1}{2}$$

$$L = e^{1/2}$$

Example 1.31 : Evaluate $\lim_{x \to 0} (a^x + x)^{1/x}$

Solution : $L = \lim_{x \to 0} (a^x + x)^{1/x}$

$\log L = \lim_{x \to 0} \dfrac{\log (a^x + x)}{x}$ $\left[\dfrac{0}{0}\right]$

$= \lim_{x \to 0} \dfrac{1}{a^x + x} (a^x \log a + 1)$

$= \log a + 1$

$= \log a + \log e = \log ae$

$\log L = \log ae$

$L = ae$

EXERCISE 1.4

1. $\lim_{x \to 0} x^x$

2. $\lim_{x \to 0} (\cos x)^{1/x^2}$

3. $\lim_{x \to \pi/2} (\sin x)^{\tan x}$

4. $\lim_{x \to 0} \left(\dfrac{a^x + b^x}{2}\right)^{1/x}$

5. $\lim_{x \to 0} (\cos x)^{1/x^2}$

6. $\lim_{x \to \pi/2} (\cosec x)^{\tan^2 x}$

7. $\lim_{x \to \infty} \left(\dfrac{ax + 1}{ax - 1}\right)^x$

8. $\lim_{x \to \infty} \left[\dfrac{1^{1/x} + 2^{1/x} + 3^{1/x}}{3}\right]^{3x}$

9. $\lim_{x \to 0} \left[\dfrac{3^x + 4^x + 6^x + 18^x}{4}\right]^{1/x}$

10. $\lim_{x \to 0} (\cos x)^{\cot^2 x}$

11. $\lim_{x \to \pi/4} (\tan)^{\tan 2x}$

12. $\lim_{x \to 0} (a^x + x)^{1/x}$

13. $\lim_{x \to 0} \left(\dfrac{1}{x}\right)^{\tan x}$

14. $\lim_{x \to \pi/2} (\tan x)^{\cos x}$

15. $\lim_{x \to 0} (1 + \sin x)^{\cot x}$

16. $\lim_{x \to 0} \left(\dfrac{\cos x - \sin x}{\cos x}\right)^{1/x}$

ANSWERS 1.4

1. 1
2. $e^{-1/2}$
3. 1
4. $\sqrt{ab}$
5. $e^{-1/2}$
6. $e^{1/2}$
7. $e^{2/a}$
8. $e^{-1/2}$
9. 6
10. $e^{-1/2}$
11. -1
12. ae
13. $e^{2/\pi}$
14. 1
15. e
16. $\dfrac{1}{e}$

1.4 SUCCESSIVE DIFFERENTIATION

(a) Introduction

Let $y = f(x)$ be a function of x, such that it posses a differential coefficient $f'(x)$ is called first differential coefficient of y. $f'(x)$ being itself a function of x capable of differential further. The differential coefficient of $f'(x)$ with respect to x is called second differential coefficient of y and is denoted by $f''(x)$. Similarly, the differential coefficient of $f''(x)$ is called third differential coefficient of y which is denoted by $f'''(x)$ etc.

Thus, the process of differentiating the same function again and again is called successive differentiation.

(b) Various other Notations

The following notations are used for successive differential coefficints of y. $y', y'', y''', \ldots, y^n$.

$y_1, y_2, y_3 \ldots y_n$

$f'(x), f''(x), f'''(x), \ldots f^n(x)$

$\dfrac{dy}{dx}, \dfrac{d^2y}{dx^2}, \dfrac{d^3y}{dx^3}, \ldots \dfrac{d^ny}{dx^n}$

$Dy, D^2y, D^3y, \ldots D^ny$

(c) Standard Results (The nth Derivative of some Standard Functions)

1. If $y = (ax + b)^m$ then $y_n = \dfrac{m!}{(m-n)!} a^n (ax+b)^n$ $(m > n)$

First derivative

$$y_1 = m(ax+b)^{m-1}(a) = am(ax+b)^{m-1}$$

again differentiating

$$y_2 = a^2 m(m-1)(ax+b)^{m-2}$$
$$y_3 = a^3 m(m-1)(m-2)(ax+b)^{m-3}$$

In general, $y_n = a^n m(m-1)(m-2) \ldots [m-(n-1)](ax+b)^{m-n}$

$$= a^n m(m-1)(m-2) \ldots (m-n+1)(ax+b)^{m-n}$$

$$= a^n m(m-1)(m-2) \ldots (m-n+1)$$

$$\left[\dfrac{(m-n)(m-n-1)\ldots 3.2.1}{(m-n)(m-n-1)\ldots 3.2.1}\right](ax+b)^{m-n}$$

$$= a^n \dfrac{m!}{(m-n)!}(ax+b)^{m-n} \qquad \ldots (1)$$

where, m is a positive integer greater than n.

Remarks :

1. If we have $m = n$ then result (1) becomes,

$$y_n = \dfrac{d^n(ax+b)^n}{dx^n} = \dfrac{n! \, a^n}{(n-n)!}(ax+b)^{n-n} = n! \, a^n \qquad \ldots (2)$$

2. If n is a positive integer greater than m then

$$y_n = \dfrac{d^n(ax+b)^n}{dx^n} = 0 \qquad \ldots (3)$$

Example 1 : If $y = (3x+5)^7$ then,

$$y_5 = \dfrac{7!}{(7-5)!} 3^5 (3x+5)^{7-5}$$

$$= \dfrac{7!}{2!} 3^5 (3x+5)^2$$

Now, $\quad y_7 = \dfrac{7!}{(7-7)!} 3^7 (3x+5)^{7-7}$

$$= \frac{7!}{0!} 3^7 (3x + 5)^0 = 7! \, 3^7$$

Now, $y_8 = 0$, $y_9 = y_{10} \ldots 0 = 0$ (using (3))

Example 2 : If $y = (2x + 1)^9$ then find y_7.

$$\therefore \quad y_7 = \frac{9!}{(9-7)!} (2x + 1)^{9-7}$$

$$= \frac{9!}{2!} (2x + 1)^2$$

If $y = e^{ax}$ then $y_n = a^n e^{ax}$

$y_1 = e^{ax} a$, $y_2 = a^2 e^{ax}$, $y_3 = a^3 e^{ax}$

Continue in this way $y_n = a^n e^{ax}$.

Example 3 : $y = a^{mx}$ then $y_n = m^n a^{mx} (\log a)^n$

$$y_1 = m a^{mx} (\log a)$$

$$y_2 = m^2 a^{mx} (\log a)^2$$

$$y_3 = m^3 a^{mx} (\log a)^3 \text{ etc.}$$

$$y_n = m^n a^{mx} (\log a)^n$$

Remarks :

1. If $y = e^{ax+b}$, then $y_n = a^n a^{ax+b}$
2. If $y = a^{lx+m}$, then $y_n = l^n (\log a)^n a^{lx+m}$

Example 4 : If $y = \dfrac{1}{ax+b}$ then $y_n = \dfrac{(-1)^n \, n! \, a^n}{(ax+b)^{n+1}}$.

$$y_1 = \frac{(-1) a}{(ax+b)^2}$$

$$y_2 = \frac{(-1)(-2) a^2}{(ax+b)^3} = \frac{(-1)^2 \, 2! \, a^2}{(ax+b)^3}$$

$$y_3 = \frac{(-1)(-2)(-3) a^3}{(ax+b)^4} = \frac{(-1)^3 \, 3! \, a^3}{(ax+b)^4} \ldots \text{ so on}$$

Hence, $\quad y_n = \dfrac{(-1)^n \, n! \, a^n}{(ax+b)^{n+1}}$

Example 5 : If $y = \log(ax + b)$ then $y_n = \dfrac{(-1)^n (n-1)! \, a^n}{(ax+b)^n}$

$$y_1 = \dfrac{a}{(ax+b)}$$

$$y_2 = \dfrac{(-1)\,a^2}{(ax+b)^2}$$

$$y_3 = \dfrac{(-1)(-2)\,a^3}{(ax+b)^3} = \dfrac{(-1)^2\, 2!\, a^3}{(ax+b)^3} \ldots \text{so on}$$

In general, $y_n = \dfrac{(-1)^{n-1} (n-1)! \, a^n}{(ax+b)^n}$

Example 6 : $y = \sin(ax + b)$ then $y_n = a^n \sin\left(ax + b + \dfrac{n\pi}{2}\right)$

$$y_1 = \cos(ax+b)\, a = a \sin\left(ax + b + \dfrac{\pi}{2}\right)$$

$$y_2 = a^2 \cos\left(ax + b + \dfrac{\pi}{2}\right) = a^2 \sin\left(ax + b + \dfrac{2\pi}{2}\right)$$

$$y_3 = a^3 \cos\left(ax + b + \dfrac{2\pi}{2}\right) = a^3 \sin\left(ax + b + \dfrac{3\pi}{2}\right) \ldots \text{so on}$$

In general, $y_n = a^n \sin\left(ax + b + \dfrac{n\pi}{2}\right)$

Example 7 : $y = \cos(ax + b)$ then $y_n = a^n \cos\left[(ax+b) + \dfrac{n\pi}{2}\right]$

$$y = \cos(ax+b)$$

$$y_1 = -\sin(ax+b)\cdot a = a \cos\left(ax + b + \dfrac{\pi}{2}\right)$$

$$y_2 = a^2 \sin\left(ax + b + \dfrac{\pi}{2}\right) = a^2 \cos\left(ax + b + \dfrac{2\pi}{2}\right) \ldots \text{so on}$$

In general, $y_n = a^n \cos\left(ax + b + \dfrac{n\pi}{2}\right)$

Example 8 : If $y = e^{ax} \sin(bx + c)$ then,

$$y_n = (a^2 + b^2)^{n/2}\, e^{ax} \sin\left(bx + c + \dfrac{n\pi}{2}\right)$$

Let, $\quad y = e^{ax} \sin(bx + c)$

$$y_1 = ae^{ax}\sin(bx+c) + be^{ax}\cos(bx+c)$$

Put $a = r\cos\phi$ $\qquad b = r\sin\phi$

$$a^2 + b^2 = r^2 \quad \text{and} \quad \phi = \tan^{-1}\left(\frac{b}{a}\right)$$

$$y_1 = e^{ax}[r\cos\phi\sin(bx+c) + r\sin\phi\cos(bx+c)]$$

$$= re^{ax}\sin(bx+c+\phi)$$

Similarly, $\quad y_2 = re^{ax}\{a\sin(bx+c+\phi) + b\cos(bx+\cos\phi)\}$

Using above valves,

$$y_2 = r^2 e^{ax}\{\sin(bx+c+\phi)\cos\phi + \cos(bx+c+\phi)\sin\phi\}$$

$$= r^2 e^{ax}\sin(bx+c+2\phi)$$

$$y_3 = r^3 e^{ax}\sin(bx+c+3\phi)$$

In general, $\quad y_n = r^n e^{ax}\sin(bx+c+n\phi)$

Using value s of r and ϕ

$$y_n = (a^2+b^2)^{n/2} e^{ax}\sin\left(bx+c+n\tan^{-1}\left(\frac{b}{a}\right)\right)$$

Example 9 : If $y = e^{ax}\cos(bx+c)$ then $y_n = (a^2+b^2)^{n/2}\cos\left(bx+c+n\tan^{-1}\left(\frac{b}{a}\right)\right)$

SOLVED EXAMPLES

Find n^{th} derivative of following functions :

Example 1.31 : $\dfrac{1}{x^4 - a^4}$.

Solution : Let $y = \dfrac{1}{x^4 - a^4}$

$\therefore \qquad y = \dfrac{1}{(x^2-a^2)(x^2+a^2)}$

$$= \frac{1}{2a^2}\left\{\frac{1}{(x^2-a^2)} - \frac{1}{(x^2+a^2)}\right\}$$

$$= \frac{1}{2a^2}\left\{\frac{1}{(x-a)(x+a)} - \frac{1}{(x-ai)(x+ai)}\right\}$$

$$= \frac{1}{4a^3}\left[\frac{1}{x-a} - \frac{1}{x+a}\right] - \frac{1}{4a^3 i}\left(\frac{1}{x-ai} - \frac{1}{x+ai}\right)$$

by using result (4),

$$= \frac{1}{4a^3}\left[\frac{(-1)^n n!}{(x-a)^{n+1}} - \frac{(-1)^n n!}{(x+a)^{n+1}}\right] - \frac{1}{4a^3 i}$$

$$\left[\frac{(-1)^n n!}{(x-ai)^{n+1}} - \frac{(-1)^n n!}{(x+ai)^{n+1}}\right]$$

Example 1.32 : If $y = \sin 2x \cos 3x$ find y_n

Solution : Let $y = \sin 2x \cos 3x$

$$= \frac{1}{2}[\sin 5x - \sin x]$$

$$= \frac{1}{2}\left[5^n \sin\left(5x + \frac{n\pi}{2}\right) - \sin\left(x + \frac{n\pi}{2}\right)\right]$$

Example 1.33 : $y = \log(5x + 2)$, find y_n

Solution : Let $y = \log(5x + 2)$

$$y_1 = \frac{5}{5x+2}$$

$$y_2 = \frac{-5.5}{(5x+2)^2}$$

$$y_3 = (-1)^{3-1}\frac{1.2.5^3}{(5x+2)^3}$$

$$y_n = (-1)^{4-1}\frac{1.2.3 \, 5^4}{(5x+2)^4}$$

In general, $y_n = (-1)^{n-1}\frac{(n-1)! \, 5^n}{(5x+2)^n}$

Example 1.34 : $y = \frac{x}{x^2 - a^2}$ find y_n

Solution : $y = \frac{x}{(x-a)(x+a)}$

$$= \frac{1}{2a}\left[\frac{1}{x-a} - \frac{1}{x+a}\right]$$

$$\therefore \quad y_n = \frac{1}{2a}\left[\frac{(-1)^n a^n n!}{(x-a)^{n+1}} - \frac{(-1)^n n! \, a^n}{(x+a)^{n+1}}\right]$$

Example 1.35 : $y = \dfrac{x}{x^2 + a^2}$

Solution : $y = \dfrac{x}{x^2 - (ai)^2} = \dfrac{x}{(x-ai)(x+ai)}$

$$y = \frac{1}{2}\left[\frac{1}{x-ai} + \frac{1}{x+ai}\right]$$

$$\therefore \quad y_n = \frac{1}{2}\left[\frac{(-1)^n n!}{(x-ai)^{n+1}} + \frac{(-1)^n n!}{(x^2-ai)^{n+1}}\right]$$

Example 1.36 : $y = \log[(ax+b)(cx+d)]$

Solution : $y = \log(ax+b) + \log(cx+d)$

$$y_n = \frac{d^n}{dx^n}[\log(ax+b)] + \frac{d^n}{dx^n}[\log(cx+d)]$$

$$y_n = \frac{(-1)^{n-1}(n-1)!\,a^n}{(ax+b)^n} + \frac{(-1)^{n-1}(n-1)!\,c^n}{(cx+d)^n}$$

$$= (-1)^{n-1}(n-1)!\left[\frac{a^n}{(ax+b)^n} + \frac{c^n}{(cx+d)^n}\right]$$

Example 1.37 : $y = \dfrac{1}{(1-3x)(1-2x)}$

Solution : Let $y = \dfrac{1}{(1-3x)(1-2x)}$

$$y = \left(\frac{3}{1-3x} - \frac{2}{1-2x}\right)$$

$$= \frac{3^{n+1}(n!)}{(1-3x)^{n+1}} - \frac{n!\,2^{n+1}}{(1-2x)^{n+1}}$$

Example 1.38 : If $y = \dfrac{x}{(x-1)(x-2)(x-3)}$, find n.

Solution : $y = \dfrac{x}{(x-1)(x-2)(x-3)}$

By partial fraction,

$$\frac{x}{(x-1)(x-2)(x-3)} = \frac{A}{(x-1)} + \frac{B}{(x-2)} + \frac{C}{(x-3)}$$

Put $x = 1$ in equation (1), we get

$$1 = A(-1)(-2) \Rightarrow A = \frac{1}{2}$$

Put $x = 2$ in equation (1), we get

$$2 = B(2-1)(2-3) \Rightarrow B = -2$$

Put $x = 3$ in equation (1), we get

$$3 = C(3-1)(3-2) \Rightarrow C = \frac{3}{2}$$

$$\therefore \quad y = \frac{1}{2(x-1)} - \frac{2}{(x-2)} + \frac{3}{2(x-3)}$$

$$\therefore \quad y_n = (-1)^n n! \left[\frac{1}{2(x-1)^{n+1}} - \frac{2}{(x-2)^{n+1}} + \frac{3}{2(x+3)^{n+1}} \right]$$

Example 1.39 : $y = \cos^2 x \sin x$, find y_n

Solution : Here,

$$y = \cos^2 x \sin x$$

$$= \left(\frac{1 + \cos 2x}{2} \right) \sin x = \frac{1}{2} \{\sin x + \sin x \cos 2x\}$$

$$= \frac{1}{2} \left\{ \sin x + \frac{1}{2} (\sin 3x - \sin x) \right\}$$

$$= \frac{1}{4} \{\sin x + \sin 3x\}$$

$$y_n = \frac{1}{4} \left\{ \sin \left(x + \frac{n\pi}{2} \right) + 3^n \sin \left(3x + \frac{n\pi}{2} \right) \right\}$$

Example 1.40 : Find n^{th} derivative of $\dfrac{x^4}{(x-1)(x-2)}$

Solution : Let $y = \dfrac{x^4}{(x-1)(x-2)}$

$$= \frac{x^4}{x^2 - 3x + 2}$$

Let $\dfrac{x^4}{x^2 - 3x + 2}$

By actual division method,

$$\begin{array}{r} x^2 + 3x + 7 \\ x^2 - 3x + 2 \overline{\smash{\big)}\ x^4 } \\ +x^4 - 3x^3 + 2x^2 \\ -+- \\ \overline{3x^3 - 2x^2} \\ 3x^3 - 9x^2 + 6x \\ -+- \\ \overline{7x^2 - 6x} \\ 7x^2 - 21x + 14 \\ -+- \\ \overline{15x - 14} \end{array}$$

$y = \dfrac{x^4}{x^2 - 3x + 2} = (x^2 + 3x + 7) + \dfrac{15x - 14}{x^2 - 3x + 2}$

$ = x^2 + 3x + 7 + \left[\dfrac{16}{x-2} - \dfrac{1}{(x-1)}\right]$

[By partial fraction method]

$ = x^2 + 3x + 7 + \dfrac{16}{x-2} - \dfrac{1}{(x-1)}$

∴ $y_n = 0 + 0 + 0 + 16 \dfrac{(-1)^n n!}{(x-2)^{n+1}} - \dfrac{(-1)^n n!}{(x-1)^{n+1}}$

∴ $y_n = \dfrac{16(-1)^n n!}{(x-2)^{n+1}} - \dfrac{(-1)^n n!}{(x-1)^{n+1}}$

EXERCISE 1.5

Find n^{th} derivative of :

1. $e^x \sin^4 x$
2. $\sin^3 x \cos^2 x$
3. $\dfrac{1}{x^2 - 4x + 3}$

4. $\dfrac{x+1}{x^2-4}$

5. $\log(x^2 - a^2)$

6. $y = 3^{4x+3}$

7. $y = \dfrac{1}{2-3x}$

8. $y = \dfrac{1}{1-5x+6x^2}$

9. $y = \dfrac{x^3}{(x-1)(x-2)}$ then $y_n = (-1)^n\, n!\left[\dfrac{8}{(x-2)^{n+1}} - \dfrac{1}{(x-1)^{n+1}}\right]$

10. $y = \dfrac{ax+b}{cx+d}$ then $y_n = (-1)^n\, n!\, c^{n-1}\, \dfrac{(bc-ad)}{(cx+d)^{n+1}}$

11. $y = \cos(3x+5)$ then $y_n = 3^n \cos\left(3x + 5 + \dfrac{n\pi}{2}\right)$

ANSWERS 1.5

1. $y_n = \dfrac{3}{8} e^{nx} - \dfrac{5^{n/2}}{2} e^x \cos(2x + n\tan^{-1} 2) + \dfrac{17^{n/2}}{8} e^x \cos(4x + n\tan^{-1} 4)$

2. $y_n = \dfrac{1}{16}\left[2\sin\left(x + \dfrac{n\pi}{2}\right) + 3^n \sin\left(3x + \dfrac{n\pi}{2}\right) - 5^n \sin\left(5x + \dfrac{n\pi}{2}\right)\right]$

3. $y_n = \dfrac{(-1)^n\, n!}{2!}\left[\dfrac{1}{(x-3)^{n+1}} - \dfrac{1}{(x-1)^{n+1}}\right]$

4. $\dfrac{(-1)^n\, n!}{4}\left[\dfrac{3}{(x-2)^{n+1}} + \dfrac{1}{(x+2)^{n+1}}\right]$

5. $(-1)^{n-1}(n-1)!\left[\dfrac{1}{(x-a)^n} + \dfrac{1}{(x-a)^n}\right]$

6. $y_n = 4^n (\log 3)^n\, 3^{4x+3}$

7. $y_n = \dfrac{n!\, 3^n}{(2-3x)^{n+1}}$ OR $\dfrac{(-1)^n\, n!\,(-3)^n}{(2-3x)^{n+1}}$

8. $y_n = n!\left[\dfrac{3^{n+1}}{(1-3x)^{n+1}} - \dfrac{2^{n+1}}{(1-2x)^{n+1}}\right]$

1.5 LEIBNITZ'S THEOREM

Statement :

If $y = uv$ where u and v are two functions of x possessing n^{th} order derivative then

$$y_n = (uv)_n = {}^nC_0 \, u_n v + {}^nC_1 \, u_{n-1} v_1 + {}^nC_2 \, u_{n-2} v_2 +$$
$$\ldots + \ldots + {}^nC_r \, u_{n-r} v_r + \ldots + {}^nC_n \, uv_n$$

Proof : We shall prove this theorem by principle of mathematical induction.

Step I : First, we prove that theorem is true for $n = 1, 2$.

Differentiating directly, we get

$$y_1 = (uv)_1 = u_1 v + u v_1 = {}^1C_0 \, u_1 v_0 + {}^1C_1 \, u_0 v_1$$

$$y_2 = (uv)_2 = u_2 v + u_1 v_1 + u_1 v_1 + u v_2$$

$$= u_2 v + 2 u_1 v_1 + u v_2$$

$$= {}^2C_0 \, u_2 v_0 + {}^2C_1 u_1 v_1 + {}^2C_2 \, u_0 v_2$$

Thus the theorem is true for $n = 1, 2$

Step II : Now we assume that the theorem is true for a particular value of n say m and prove that the theorem is true for $n = m + 1$.

$$y_m = (uv)_m = {}^mC_0 \, u_m v + {}^mC_1 \, u_{m-1} v_1 + {}^mC_2 \, u_{m-2} v_2 + \ldots$$
$$+ {}^mC_r \, u_{m-r} v_r + \ldots + {}^mC_{m-1} \, u_1 v_{m-1} + {}^mC_m \, uv_m \text{ differentiating both sides.}$$

$$y_m = (uv)_{m+1} = {}^mC_0 \{u_{m+1} v + u_m v_1] + {}^mC_1 [u_m v_1 + u_{m-1} v_2]$$
$$+ {}^mC_2 [u_{m-1} v_2 + u_{m-2} v_3] + \ldots + {}^mC_r$$
$$[u_{m-r+1} v_r + u_{m-r} v_{r+1}] + \ldots + {}^mC_m [u_1 v_m + uv_{m+1}]$$

Rearranging the terms, we get

$$(uv)_{m+1} = {}^mC_0 \, u_{m+1} v + ({}^mC_0 + {}^mC_1) u_m v_1 + ({}^mC_1 + {}^mC_2)$$
$$u_{m-1} v_2 + \ldots + ({}^mC_r + {}^mC_{r+1}) u_{m-r} v_{r+1} + \ldots +$$
$$({}^mC_{m-1} + {}^mC_m) u_1 v_m + {}^mC_m \, uv_{m+1}$$

Now, we use relations,
$$^mC_0 + {}^mC_1 = {}^{m+1}C_1$$
$$^mC_{r-1} + {}^mC_r = {}^{m+1}C_r$$
$$^mC_0 = m + c_0 = {}^mC_m = {}^{m+1}C_{m+1} = 1$$

Hence, above equation becomes,
$$y_{m+1} = (uv)_{m+1} = m + {}^1C_0\, u_{m+1} + m + {}^1C_1\, u_m v + m + {}^1C_2\, u_{m-1} v_2$$
$$+ \ldots + m + {}^1C_m\, u_1 v_m + m + {}^1C_{m+1}\, uv_{m+1}$$

Thus, theorem is true for $n = m + 1$, hence we say that if theorem is true for $n = m$, then it is also true for $n = m + 1$.

Step III : In step I, we proved theorem is true for $n = 1, 2$. Since it is true for $n = 2$ by step II, we conclude that it is true for $n = 2 + 1 = 3$ i.e. $n = 3$ with same reasoning, we say $n = 3$, then it is true for $n = 3 + 1 = 4$ i.e. $n = 4$ and so on. Thus, theorem is true for every value of $n = 1, 2, 3, \ldots$. Hence theorem is true by principal of mathematical induction for all positive integral value of n.

SOLVED EXAMPLES

Example 1.41 : Find n^{th} derivative of $x^3 e^x$.

Solution : Let $y = uv$ where,

$u = e^x \qquad v = x^3$
$u_1 = e^x \qquad v_1 = 3x^2$
$u_2 = e^x \qquad v_2 = 6x$
$\vdots \qquad\qquad v_3 = 6$
$u_n = e^x \qquad v_n = 0$

By Leibnnitz's theorem

$$y_n = (uv)_n = {}^nC_0\, u_n v + {}^nC_1\, u_{n-1} v_1 + {}^nC_2\, u_{n-2} v_2 + \ldots$$
$$y_n = {}^nC_0\, e^x x^3 + {}^nC_1\, e^x (3x^2) + {}^nC_2\, e^x (6x) + {}^nC_3\, e^x (6)$$
$$= (1) e^x x^3 + n e^x (3x^2) + \frac{n(n-1)}{2} e^x\, 6x + \frac{n(n-1)(n-2)}{3!} e^x (6)$$
$$= e^x x^3 + 3n e^x x^2 + 3n(n-1) e^x x + n(n-1)(n-2) e^x$$

Example 1.42 : Find n^{th} derivative $x^3 \sin 2x$.

Solution : Let $y = uv$

where, $u = \sin 2x$, $v = x^3$

$$u_n = 2\cos(2x) = 2\sin\left(2x + \frac{\pi}{2}\right), v_1 = 3x^2$$

$$u_n = 2^n \sin\left(2x + \frac{n\pi}{2}\right), v_3 = 6$$

$$y_n = (uv)n = {}^nC_0\, u_n v + {}^nC_1\, u_{n-1} v_1 + {}^nC_2\, u_{n-2} v_2 + \ldots$$

$$y_n = 2^n \sin\left(2x + \frac{n\pi}{2}\right) x^3 + n2^{n-1} \sin\left(2x + (n-1)\frac{\pi}{2}\right)(3x^2)$$

$$+ \frac{n(n-1)}{2!} 2^{n-2} \sin\left(2x + (n-2)\frac{\pi}{2}\right) 6x$$

$$+ \frac{n(n-1)(n-2)}{3!} 2^{n-3} \sin\left(2x + (n-3)\frac{\pi}{2}\right) 6$$

Example 1.43 : If $y = e^x \sin^4 x$ then $y_n = ?$

Solution : $y = e^x \sin^4 x$

$$= e^x (1 - \cos^2 x)^2 \quad [\because (\sin^2 x)^2 = [1 - \cos^2 x]^2$$

$$= e^x \left[1 - \frac{(1 + \cos 2x)}{2}\right]^2$$

$$= \frac{e^x}{4} [2 - 1 - \cos 2x]^2$$

$$= \frac{e^x}{4} [1 - \cos 2x]^2$$

$$= \frac{e^x}{4} [1 - 2\cos 2x + \cos^2 2x]$$

$$= \frac{e^x}{4} \left[1 - 2\cos 2x + \frac{(1 + \cos 4x)}{2}\right]$$

$$= \frac{e^x}{4} \left[1 - 2\cos 2x + \frac{1}{2} + \frac{\cos 4x}{2}\right]$$

$$= \frac{e^x}{4} \left[\frac{3}{2} - 2\cos 2x + \frac{\cos 4x}{2}\right]$$

$$= \frac{3}{8} e^x - \frac{e^x}{2} \cos 2x + \frac{e^x}{8} \cos 4x$$

$$= \frac{3}{8} e^{nx} - \frac{5^{n/2}}{2} e^x \cos(2x + n + \tan^{-1} 2)$$

$$+ \frac{17^{n/2}}{8} e^x \cos(4x + n + \tan^{-1} 4)$$

Example 1.44 : If $y = x^2 (ax + b)^m$ then $y_n = ?$

Solution : $y = uv$

$$u = (ax + b)^m$$

$$u_n = m(m-1)(m-2) \ldots (m-n+1) a^n (ax+b)^{m-n}$$

$v = x^2$, $v_1 = 2x$, $v_2 = 2$, $v_3 = 0$ and so on.

$$(uv)_n = {}^nC_0\, u_n v + {}^nC_1\, u_{n-1} v_1 + {}^nC_2\, u_{n-2} v_2$$

$$= 1\, m(m-1)(m-2) \ldots (m-n+1) a^n (ax+b)^{m-n} x^2$$

$$+ n\, (m(m-1) \ldots (m-n+2) a^{n-1} (ax+b)^{m-n+1} (2x)$$

$$+ \frac{n(n-1)}{2} m(m-1) \ldots (m-n+3) a^{n-2} (ax+b)^{m-n+2}$$

Example 1.45 : $y = \dfrac{\log x}{x}$ find y_5

Solution : $u = \dfrac{1}{x}$, $v = \log x$

$$u_n = (-1)^n \frac{n!}{x^{n+1}}, \quad v_1 = \frac{1}{x}, \quad v_n = (-1)^{n-1} \frac{(n-1)!}{x^n}$$

$$y_5 = u_5 v + 5 u_4 v_1 = \frac{5.4}{1.2} u_3 v_2 + \frac{5.4.3}{1.2.3} u_2 v_3 + 5 u_1 v_4 + u v_5$$

$$= \frac{-5!}{x^6} \log x + 5 \frac{(-1)^4 4!}{x^5} \left(\frac{1}{x}\right) + \frac{5.4}{1.2} (-1)^2 \frac{3!}{x^4}$$

$$+ \frac{5.4}{1.2} \frac{2!}{x^3} \left(\frac{2}{x^3}\right) - 5 \left(\frac{1}{x^2}\right)\left(\frac{-6}{x^4}\right) + \frac{1}{x}\left(\frac{24}{x^5}\right)$$

$$= \frac{-5!}{x^6} \log x + \frac{5!}{x^6} + \frac{5!}{2x^6} + \frac{5!}{3x^6} + \frac{5!}{4x^6} + \frac{5!}{5x^6}$$

$$= \frac{5!}{x^6} \left(1 + \frac{1}{2} + \frac{1}{3} + \frac{1}{4} + \frac{1}{5} - \log x\right)$$

Example 1.46 : Find n^{th} derivative of $e^x \log x$

Solution : $(uv)_n = {}^nC_0 \, u_n v + {}^nC_1 \, u_{n-1} v_1 + \ldots {}^nC_n \, u v_n$

$(e^x \log x)_n = {}^nC_0 \, e^x \log x + {}^nC_1 \, e^x \, x^{-1} + {}^nC_2 \, e^x \, (-1) x^{-2} + \ldots +$

$\qquad {}^nC_n \, e^x \dfrac{(-1)^{n-1} (n-1)!}{x^n}$

Example 1.47 : Find n^{th} derivative of $x^3 \cos x$

Solution : $(uv)_n = {}^nC_0 \, u_n v + {}^nC_1 \, u_{n-1} v_1 + {}^nC_2 \, u_{n-2} v_2 + \ldots$

Here, $u = \cos x \quad v = x^3 \Rightarrow u_n = \cos\left(x + \dfrac{n\pi}{2}\right)$, $v_1 = 3x^2$

$v_2 = 6x$, $v_3 = 6$ and $v_4 = v_5 = \ldots\ldots = v_n = 0$

$(x^3 \cos x) = {}^nC_0 \cos\left(x + \dfrac{n\pi}{4}\right) x^3 \, {}^nC_1 \cos\left(x + \dfrac{n-1}{2}\pi\right) 3x^2$

$\qquad + {}^nC_2 \cos\left(x + \dfrac{n-2}{2}\pi\right) 6x + {}^nC_3 \cos\left(x + \dfrac{n-3}{2}\pi\right) 6 + 0$

$\qquad = x^3 \cos\left(x + \dfrac{n\pi}{2}\right) + 3n x^2 \cos\left(x + \dfrac{n-1}{2}\pi\right)$

$\qquad + 3n(n-1) x \cos\left(x + \dfrac{n-2}{2}\pi\right) + n(n-1)(n-2)$

$\qquad \cos\left[x + (n-2)\dfrac{\pi}{2}\right]$

Example 1.48 : $y = x^3 \log x$ then $y_n = ?$

Solution : $u = \log x \quad v = x^3$

$u_n = (-1)^{n-1} \dfrac{(n-1)!}{x^n} \quad v_1 = 3x^2 \quad v_2 = 6x \quad v_3 = 6 \quad v_4 = 0$

$(uv)_n = u_n v + {}^nC_1 \, u_{n-1} v_1 + {}^nC_2 \, u_{n-2} v_2 + \ldots$

$(x^3 \log x)_n = \dfrac{(-1)^{n-1} (n-1)!}{x^n} x^3 + 3nx^2 \dfrac{(-1)^{n-2} (n-2)!}{x^{n-1}}$

$\qquad + 6 \dfrac{n(n-1)}{2} \times \dfrac{(-1)^{n-3} (n-3)!}{x^{n-2}}$

$\qquad + 6 \dfrac{n(n-1)(n-2) (-1)^{n-4} (n-4)!}{x^{n-3}}$

$$= \frac{(-1)^{n-4}(n-4)!}{x^{n-3}}$$

$$\{(-1)^3(n-1)(n-2)(n-3) + (-1)^2 3n(n-2)(n-3)$$
$$+ (-1) 3n(n-1)(n-3) + n(n-1)(n-2)\}$$

$$= \frac{(-1)^n (n-4)!}{x^{n-3}} \{6\} \quad \text{where } (-1)^{n-4} = (-1)^n$$

Example 1.49 : If $y = x^2 e^x \cos x$, find y_n

Solution : Let $y = uv$ where $u = e^x \cos x$, $v = x^2$

$$y_n = (uv)_n = (e^x \cos x)_n x^2 + {}^nC_1 (e^x \cos x)_{n-1} 2x + {}^nC_2 (e^x \cos x)_{n-2} (2)$$

$$= 2^{n/2} e^x \cos(x + n \tan^{-1} 1) x^2 + n2^{\left(\frac{n-1}{2}\right)}$$

$$e^x \cos[x + (n-1)\tan^{-1} 1] 2x + \frac{n(n-1)}{2!} 2^{\left(\frac{n-2}{2}\right)}$$

$$e^x \cos[x + (n-2)\tan^{-1} 1] (2)$$

$$= 2^{\frac{n-2}{2}} e^x \left[2x^2 \cos\left(x + \frac{n\pi}{4}\right) + 2^{3/2} n x \cos\left(x + (n-1)\frac{\pi}{4}\right)\right.$$
$$\left. + n(n-1) \cos\left(x + (n-2)\frac{\pi}{4}\right)\right]$$

Example 1.50 : Find n^{th} derivative of $x^3 e^x \cos^3 x$

Solution : We can write,

$$x^3 e^x \cos^3 x = x^3 e^x \left[\frac{1}{4}(3 \cos x + \cos 3x)\right]$$

$$= \frac{3}{4} x^3 e^x \cos x + \frac{1}{4} x^3 e^x \cos 3x$$

$$(x^3 e^x \cos^3 x)_n = \frac{3}{4} (x^3 e^x \cos x)_n + \frac{1}{4} (x^3 e^x \cos 3x)_n \qquad \ldots (1)$$

We use,

$$(e^{ax} \cos bx)_n = (a^2 + b^2)^{n/2} e^{ax} \cos\left[bx + c + n + \tan^{-1}\frac{b}{a}\right]$$

Now, $(x^3 e^x \cos x)_n = {}^nC_0 (e^x \cos x)_n + x^3 + {}^nC_1 (e^x \cos x)_{n-1} (3x^2)$

$\qquad + {}^nC_2 (e^x \cos x)_{n-2} (6x) + {}^nC_3 (e^x \cos x)_{n-3} (6)$

$= 2^{n/2} e^x \cos (x + n \tan^{-1} (1)) x^3 + 2^{\frac{n-1}{2}} e^x \cos$

$\qquad [x + (n-1) \tan^{-1} (1)] 3x^2 + \dfrac{n(n-1)}{2} 6x \, e^x \, 2^{\frac{n-2}{2}}$

$\qquad \cos [x + (n-2) \tan^{-1}(1)] + \dfrac{n(n-1)(n-2)}{6} 2^{\frac{n-3}{2}}$

$\qquad e^x \cos [x + (n-3) \tan^{-1}(1)] 6$

$= 2^{n/2} x^3 e^x \cos \left(x + \dfrac{n\pi}{4} \right) + 3n \, 2^{\frac{n-1}{2}} x^2 e^x \cos \left(x + \dfrac{n-1}{4} \pi \right)$

$\qquad + 3n(n-1) \, 2^{\frac{n-2}{2}} x \, e^x \cos \left(x + (n-2) \dfrac{\pi}{4} \right)$

$\qquad + n(n-1)(n-2) \, 2^{\frac{n-3}{2}} e^x \cos \left(x + (n-3) \dfrac{\pi}{4} \right)$ ... (2)

Now, $(x^3 e^x \cos 3x)_n = {}^nC_0 (e^x \cdot \cos 3x) x^3 + {}^nC_1 (e^x \cos 3x)_{n-1} (3x^2)$

$\qquad + {}^nC_2 (e^x \cos 3x)_{n-2} (6x) + {}^nC_3 (e^x \cos 3x) \, n - 3 \, (6)$

$= 10^{n/2} x^3 e^x \cos (3x + n \tan^{-1} 3) + n \, 10^{\frac{n-2}{2}}$

$\qquad 3x^2 e^x \cos [3x + (n-1) \tan^{-1} 3] + 3n(n-1) \times 10^{\frac{n-2}{2}}$

$\qquad e^x \cos [3x + (n-2) \tan^{-1} 3] + n(n-1)(n-2) \, 10^{\frac{n-3}{2}}$

$\qquad e^x \cos [3x + (n-3) \tan^{-1} 3]$ ... (3)

Put equations (2) and (3) in equation (1), we get required result.

Example 1.51 : Find n^{th} derivative of $x^2 \sin x$

Solution : Let $y = x^2 \sin x = uv$ (say)

where, $\quad u = \sin x \qquad\qquad v = x^2$

$\qquad\qquad u_n = \sin \left(x + \dfrac{n\pi}{2} \right) \qquad v_1 = 2x$

$\qquad\qquad\qquad\qquad\qquad\qquad\qquad v_2 = 2$

Differentiating n times by Leibnitz's theorem,

$$y_n = (uv)_n = {}^nC_0\, u_n v + {}^nC_1\, u_{n-1} v_1 + {}^nC_2\, u_{n-2} v_2$$

$$y_n = {}^nC_0 \sin\left(x + \frac{n\pi}{2}\right) x^2 + {}^nC_1 \sin\left(x + \frac{n-1}{2}\pi\right)(2x)$$

$$+ {}^nC_2 \sin\left(x + \frac{(n-2)}{2}\pi\right) \qquad \ldots (2)$$

$$= x^2 \sin\left(x + \frac{n\pi}{2}\right) + 2nx \sin\left(x + \frac{n-1}{2}\pi\right) + n(n-1) \sin\left(x + \frac{(n-2)\pi}{2}\right)$$

Example 1.52 : If $y = (\sin^{-1} x)^2$ then, prove that
$(1 - x^2)\, y_{n+2} - (2n + 1) \times y_{n+1} - n^2\, y_n = 0$

Solution :
$$y = (\sin^{-1} x)^2$$

differentiate w.r.t. x, $\qquad y_1 = 2 \sin^{-1} x \cdot \dfrac{1}{\sqrt{1 - x^2}}$

$$\sqrt{1 - x^2}\, y_1 = 2 \sin^{-1} x$$

Squaring on both sides,

$$(1 - x^2)\, y_1^2 = 4 (\sin^{-1} x)^2$$

$$(1 - x^2)\, y_1^2 = 4y \qquad \text{(by given)}$$

Again differentiating w.r.t. x

$$(1 - x^2)\, 2y_1 y_2 + y_1^2 (-2x) = 4y_1$$

Divide by $2y_1$, we get $(1 - x^2)\, y_2 - xy_1 = 2$

Applying Leibneitz's theorem

$$[{}^nC_0 (1 - x^2)\, y_{n+2} + {}^nC_1\, y_{n+1} (-2x) + {}^nC_2\, y_n (-2)]$$
$$- [{}^nC_0\, xy_{n+1} + {}^nC_1\, y_n(1)] = 0$$

$$\left[(1 - x^2)\, y_{n+2} + n\, y_{n+1} (-2x) + \frac{n(n-1)}{2} y_n (-2)\right] - [x\, y_{n+1} + n\, y_n (1)] = 0$$

$$(1 - x^2)\, y_{n+2} - 2nx\, y_{n+1} - n(n-1)\, y_n - xy_{n+1} - ny_n = 0$$
$$(1 - x^2)\, y_{n+2} + (-2nx - x)\, y_{n+1} + (-n^2 + n - n)\, y_n = 0$$
$$(1 - x^2)\, y_{n+2} - x(2n + 1)\, y_{n+1} - n^2 y_n = 0$$

Example 1.53 : If $y = \cos(m \sin^{-1} x)$ then prove that
$(1 + x^2) y_{n+2} - (2n + 1) x y_{n+1} + (m^2 - n^2) y_n = 0$

Solution : $y = \cos(m \sin^{-1} x)$

$$y_1 = -\sin(m \sin^{-1} x) \frac{m}{\sqrt{1 - x^2}}$$

$\therefore \left(\sqrt{1 - x^2}\right) y_1 = -m \sin(m \sin^{-1} x)$

Squaring on both sides,

$$(1 - x^2) y_1^2 = m^2 \sin^2(m \sin^{-1} x)$$

$$(1 - x^2) y_1^2 = m+2 [1 - \cos^2 m \sin^{-1} x]$$

$$(1 - x^2) y_1^2 = m^2 [1 - y^2]$$

Again differentiating w.r.t. x

$$(1 - x^2) 2y_1 y_2 + y_1^2 (-2x) = m^2 (-2yy_1) \text{ divided by } 2y_1$$

$$(1 - x^2) y_2 - x y_1 = -m^2 y$$

Apply Leibnitz's theorem,

$$[{}^nC_0 (1 - x^2) y_{n+2} + {}^nC_1 y_{n+1} (-2x) + {}^nC_2 y_n (-2)]$$
$$- [{}^nC_0 x y_{n+1} + {}^nC_1 y_n (1)] = -m^2 y_n$$

$$\left[(1 - x^2) y_{n+2} + n y_{n+1} (-2x) + \frac{n(n - 1)}{2} y_n (-2)\right]$$

$$- [x y_{n+1} + n y_n] = -m^2 y_n$$

$(1 - x^2) y_{n+2} - 2nx y_{n+1} n^2 y_n + n y_n - x y_{n+1} n y_n = -m^2 y_n$

$(1 - x^2) y_{n+2} + (2n + 1) x y_{n+1} + (m^2 - n^2) y_n = 0$

Example 1.54 : If $y = \sin(m \sin^{-1} x)$

Prove that $(1 - x^2) y_{n+2} - (2n + 1) \times y_{n+1} + (m^2 - n^2) y_n = 0$.

Solution : $y = \sin(m \sin^{-1} x)$

$$y_1 = \cos(m \sin^{-1} x) \frac{m}{\sqrt{1 - x^2}}$$

$\left(\sqrt{1 - x^2}\right) y_1 = m \cos m (\sin^{-1} x)$

Squaring on both sides,

$$(1 - x^2) y_1^2 = m^2 \cos^2 m (\sin^{-1} x)$$

$$(1 - x^2) y_1^2 = [1 - \sin^2 m (\sin^{-1} x)] m^2$$

$$(1 - x^2) y_1^2 = (1 - y^2) m^2$$

Again differentiating w.r.t. x

$$(1 - x^2) 2y_1 y_2 + y_1^2 (-2x) = [-2yy_1] m^2 \text{ divided by } 2y_1$$

$$(1 - x^2) y_2 - xy_1 = -ym^2$$

$$(1 - x^2) y_2 - xy_1 + m^2 y = 0$$

Apply Leibnitz's theorem,

$$[{}^nC_0 (1 - x^2) y_{n+2} + {}^nC_1 y_{n+1} (-2x) + {}^nC_2 y_n (-2)]$$

$$- [{}^nC_0 x y_{n+1} + {}^nC_1 y_n (1)] + m^2 y_n = 0$$

$$\left[(1 - x^2) y_{n+2} + n y_{n+1} (-2x) + \frac{n(n-1)}{2} y_n (-2) \right]$$

$$- [x y_{n+1} + n y_n] + m^2 y_n = 0$$

$$(1 - x^2) y_{n+2} + (-2nx - x) y_{n+1} + (-n^2 + n - n + m^2) y_n = 0$$

$$(1 - x^2) y_{n+2} - x(2n + 1) y_{n+1} + (m^2 - n^2) y_n = 0$$

Example 1.55 : If $y = \sin^{-1} x$

Prove that $(1 - x^2) y_{n+2} - (2n + 1) x y_{n+1} - n^2 y_n = 0$

Solution : $y = \sin^{-1} x$

Differentiating w.r.t. x $\quad y_1 = \dfrac{1}{\sqrt{1 - x^2}}$

$$\sqrt{1 - x^2} \, y_1 = 1$$

Squaring on both sides,

$$(1 - x^2) y_1^2 = 1$$

Again differentiating w.r.t. x

$$(1 - x^2) 2y_1 y_2 + y_1^2 (-2x) = 0 \text{ divided by } 2y_1,$$

we get $(1 - x^2) y_2 - xy_1 = 0$

Apply Leibnitz's theorem,

$[{}^nC_0 (1 - x^2) y_{n+2} + {}^nC_1 y_{n+1} (-2x) + {}^nC_2 y_n (-2)]$
$\quad - [{}^nC_0 x y_{n+1} + ny_n] = 0$

$\left[1(1 - x^2) y_{n+2} + n y_{n+1} (-2x) + \frac{n(n-1)}{2} y_n (-2) \right]$
$\quad - [1 xy_{n+1} + ny_n] = 0$

$(1 - x^2) y_{n+2} - 2nx y_{n+1} - n^2 y_n + ny_n - xy_{n+1} - ny_n = 0$

$(1 - x^2) y_{n+2} - (2n + 1) x y_{n+1} - n^2 y_n = 0$

Example 1.56 : If $x = \tan(\log y)$,

Prove that $(1 + x^2) y_{n+1} + (2nx - 1) y_n + n(n-1) y_{n-1} = 0$

Solution : $\quad x = \tan(\log y)$

$\log y = \tan^{-1} x$

$\therefore \quad y = e^{\tan^{-1} x}$

Differentiating w.r.t. x $\quad y_1 = e^{\tan^{-1} x} \cdot \frac{1}{1 + x^2}$

$y_1 = \frac{y}{1 + x^2}$

$(1 + x^2) y_1 = y$

Apply Leibnitz's theorem,

$[{}^nC_0 (1 + x^2) y_{n+1} + {}^nC_1 y_n (-2x) + {}^nC_2 y_{n-1} (2)] = y_n$

$\left[1(1 + x^2) y_{n+1} + ny_n (2x) + \frac{n(n-1)}{2} y_{n-1} (2) \right] = y_n$

$(1 + x^2) y_{n+1} + (2nx - 1) y_n + n(n-1) y_{n-1} = 0$

Example 1.57 : If $y = \dfrac{\sin^{-1} x}{\sqrt{1 - x^2}}$

Prove that $(1 - x^2) y_{n+1} - (2n + 1) y_n x - n^2 y_{n-1} = 0$

Solution : $\quad y = \dfrac{\sin^{-1} x}{\sqrt{1 - x^2}}$

differentiating w.r.t. x,

$$y_1 = \frac{\sqrt{1-x^2}\,\frac{1}{\sqrt{1-x^2}} - \sin^{-1}x\,\frac{1}{2\sqrt{1-x^2}}(-2x)}{\left(\sqrt{1-x^2}\right)^2}$$

$$y_1 = \frac{1 + x\left(\frac{\sin^{-1}x}{\sqrt{1-x^2}}\right)}{(1-x^2)}$$

$$y_1 = \frac{1 + xy}{1 - x^2}$$

$$(1 - x^2)y_1 = 1 + xy$$

Apply Leibnitz's theorem,

$$[{}^nC_0 (1 - x^2)\, y_{n+1} + {}^nC_1 (-2x)\, y_n + {}^nC_2 (-2)\, y_{n-1}] = xy_n + ny_{n-1}$$

$$(1 - x^2)\, y_{n+1} + n(-2x)\, y_n + \frac{n(n-1)}{2}(-2)\, y_{n-1} = xy_n + ny_{n-1}$$

$$(1 - x^2)\, y_{n+1} - x(2n+1)\, y_n - n^2\, y_{n-1} = 0$$

Example 1.58 : If $y^{1/m} + y^{-1/m} = 2x$

Prove that $(x^2 - 1)\, y_{n+2} + (2n+1)\, x\, y_{n+1} + (n^2 - m^2)\, y_n = 0$

Solution : Given :

$$y^{1/m} + y^{-1/m} = 2x$$

$$y^{1/m} + \frac{1}{y^{1/m}} = 2x$$

Let $\quad y^{1/m} = K$

$$K + \frac{1}{K} = 2x$$

$$\frac{K^2 + 1}{K} = 2x$$

$$K^2 + 1 = 2Kx$$

$$K^2 - 2Kx + 1 = 0$$

This is quadratic equation in K.

$$K = \frac{-(-2x) \pm \sqrt{(2x)^2 - 4(1)(1)}}{2(1)}$$

$$= \frac{2x \pm \sqrt{4x^2 - 4}}{2}$$

$$K = x \pm \sqrt{x^2 - 1}$$

$$\therefore \quad K = y^{1/m} = x \pm \sqrt{x^2 - 1}$$

$$y = K^m = \left(x \pm \sqrt{x^2 - 1}\right)^m$$

$$y = \left(x \pm \sqrt{x^2 - 1}\right)^m$$

$$y_1 = m\left(x \pm \sqrt{x^2 - 1}\right)^{m-1} \left(1 + \frac{1}{2\sqrt{x^2 - 1}} (2x)\right)$$

$$= m\left(x \pm \sqrt{x^2 - 1}\right)^{m-1} \left(\frac{\sqrt{x^2 - 1} + x}{\sqrt{x^2 - 1}}\right)$$

$$= \frac{m}{\sqrt{x^2 - 1}} \left(x \pm \sqrt{x^2 - 1}\right)^m$$

$$y_1 = \frac{my}{\sqrt{x^2 - 1}}$$

$$\sqrt{x^2 - 1}\, y_1 = my$$

Squaring on both side

$$(x^2 - 1)\, y_1^2 = m^2 y^2$$

Differentiating w.r.t. x

$$(x^2 - 1)\, 2y_1 y_2 + y_1^2 (2x) = m^2\, 2yy_1$$

Divided by $2y_1$

$$(x^2 - 1)\, y_2 + xy_1 = m^2 y$$

Apply Leibnitz's theorem,

$$[{}^nC_0 (x^2 - 1) y_{n+2} + {}^nC_1 (2x) y_{n+1} + {}^nC_2 (2) y_n]$$
$$+ [{}^nC_0\, xy_{n+1} + {}^nC_1\, y_n] = m^2\, y_n$$

$(x^2 - 1) y_{n+2} + n(2x) y_{n+1} + \dfrac{n(n-1)}{2} (2) y_n + x y_{n+1} + n y_n = m^2 y_n$

$(x^2 - 1) y_{n+2} + x(2n + 1) y_{n+1} + (n^2 - m^2) y_n = 0$

Example 1.59 : Solve $\cos^{-1}\left(\dfrac{y}{b}\right) = \log\left(\dfrac{x}{m}\right)$

Prove that $x^2 y_{n+2} + (2n + 1) y_{n+1} x + (m^2 + n^2) y_n = 0$

Solution : Given :

$$\cos^{-1}\left(\dfrac{y}{b}\right) = \log\left(\dfrac{x}{m}\right)^m$$

$$\cos^{-1}\left(\dfrac{y}{b}\right) = m \log\left(\dfrac{x}{m}\right)$$

$$\dfrac{y}{b} = \cos\left[m \log\left(\dfrac{x}{m}\right)\right]$$

Differentiating w.r.t. x $\quad y = -b \sin\left[m \log\left(\dfrac{x}{m}\right)\right] \dfrac{m}{\left(\dfrac{x}{m}\right)} \left(\dfrac{1}{m}\right)$

$$= -b \dfrac{m}{x} \sin\left[m \log \dfrac{x}{m}\right]$$

$$x y_1 = -b m \sin\left[m \log \dfrac{x}{m}\right]$$

Again differentiating w.r.t. x

$$x y_2 + y_1 (1) = -b m \cos\left[m \log \dfrac{x}{m}\right] \dfrac{m}{\left(\dfrac{x}{m}\right)} \left(\dfrac{1}{m}\right)$$

$$x y_2 + y_1 = -b \dfrac{m^2}{x} \cos m \log \dfrac{x}{m}$$

$$x^2 y_2 + x y_1 = -m^2 \left[b \cos m \log\left(\dfrac{x}{m}\right)\right]$$

$$x^2 y_2 + x y_1 = -m^2 y$$

Apply Leibnitz's theorem,

$[{}^nC_0 x^2 y_{n+2} + {}^nC_1 y_{n+1} (2x) + {}^nC_2 y_n(2)] + [{}^nC_0 x y_{n+1} + {}^nC_1 y_n] = -m^2 y_n$

$$x^2 y_{n+2} + n2x\, y_{n+1} + \frac{n(n-1)}{2} y_n(2) + xy_{n+1} + ny_n = -m^2 y_n$$

$$x^2 y_{n+2} + (2n+1)x\, y_{n+1} - (n^2 - n + n + m^2) y_n = 0$$

$$x^2 y_{n+2} + (2n+1)x\, y_{n+1} + (n^2 + m^2) y_n = 0$$

Example 1.60 : If $y = a \cos(\log x) + b \sin(\log x)$, show that

$$x^2 y_{n+2} + (2n+1) xy_{n+1} + (n^2 + 1) y_n = 0$$

Solution : $\qquad y = a \cos(\log x) + b \sin(\log x)$

$$y_1 = -a \frac{\sin(\log x)}{x} + b \frac{\cos(\log x)}{x}$$

$$xy_1 = -a \sin(\log x) + b \cos(\log x)$$

Again differentiating w.r.t. x

$$xy_2 + y_1 = -a \frac{\cos \log x}{x} - b \frac{\sin \log x}{x}$$

$$x^2 y_2 + xy_1 = -[a \cos \log x + b \sin \log x]$$

$$x^2 y_2 + xy_1 = -y$$

$$x^2 y_2 + xy_1 + y = 0$$

Apply Leibnitz's theorem,

$$[x^2 y_{n+2} + {}^n C_1 (2x) y_{n+1} + {}^n C_2\, 2 y_n] + [{}^n C_0\, x y_{n+1} + {}^n C_1\, y_n] + y_n = 0$$

$$x^2 y_{n+2} + (2n+1) xy_{n+1} + (n^2 + 1) y_n = 0$$

Example 1.61 : If $y = \tan^{-1} x$

Prove that $(1 + x^2) y_{n+2} + 2(n+1) x\, y_{n+1} + n(n+1) y_n = 0$

Solution : Given : $y = \tan^{-1} x$

Differentiation $\qquad y = \dfrac{1}{1 + x^2}$

$$(1 + x^2) y_1 = 0$$

Again differentiation w.r.t. x

$$(1 + x^2) y_2 + y_1 (2x) = 0$$

Apply Leibnitz's theorem,

$[^nC_0 (1 + x^2) y_{n+2} + {}^nC_1 y_{n+1} (2x) + {}^nC_2 y_n (2)] + 2[^nC_0 y_{n+1} x + {}^nC_1 y_n] = 0$

$(1 + x^2) y_{n+2} + (2n + 1) x y_{n+1} + n(n + 1) y_n = 0$

Example 1.62 : $y = \{x + \sqrt{1 + x^2}\}^m$

Prove that $(1 + x^2) y_{n+2} + (2n + 1) y_{n+1} x + (n^2 - m^2) y_n = 0$

Solution : Given : $y = \{x + \sqrt{1 + x^2}\}^m$

$$y_1 = m \{x + \sqrt{1 + x^2}\}^{m-1} \left(1 + \frac{1}{2\sqrt{1 + x^2}} (2x)\right)$$

$$= m \{x + \sqrt{1 + x^2}\}^{m-1} \left(1 + \frac{x}{2\sqrt{1 + x^2}}\right)$$

$$= m \{x + \sqrt{1 + x^2}\}^{m-1} \left(\frac{\sqrt{x^2 + 1} + x}{\sqrt{1 + x^2}}\right)$$

$$y_1 = \frac{m \{x + \sqrt{1 + x^2}\}^m}{\sqrt{1 + x^2}}$$

$$(\sqrt{1 + x^2}) y_1 = my$$

Squaring on both sides,

$$(1 + x^2) y_1^2 = m^2 y^2$$

Again differentiating w.r.t. x

$(1 + x^2) 2y_1 y_2 + y_1^2 (2x) \pm m^2 \, 2yy_1$

Divided by $2y_1$

$(1 + x^2) y_2 + xy_1 = m^2 y$

Apply Leibnitz's theorem,

$[^nC_0 (1 + x^2) y_{n+2} + {}^nC_1 (2x) y_{n+1} + {}^nC_2 (2) y_n]$
$\quad + [^nC_0 x y_{n+1} + {}^nC_1 y_n] = m^2 y_n$

$(1 + x^2) y_{n+2} \, 2nx \, y_{n+1} + n^2 y_n - ny_n + xy_{n+1} + ny_n = m^2 y_n$

$(1 + x^2) y_{n+2} (2n + 1) xy_{n+1} + (n^2 - m^2) y_n = 0$

Example 1.63 : If $y = e^{a \tan^{-1} x}$, prove that

$$(1 + x^2) y_{n+1} + (2nx - a) y_n + n(n - 1) y_{n-1} = 0$$

Solution : $\quad y = e^{a \tan^{-1} x}$

$$y_1 = e^{a \tan^{-1} x} \frac{a}{(1 + x^2)} = \frac{ay}{1 + x^2}$$

$$(1 + x^2) y_1 = ay$$

Apply Leibnitz's theorem,

$$[{}^nC_0 (1 + x^2) y_{n+1} + {}^nC_1 (2x) y_n + {}^nC_2 (2) y_{n-1} = ay_n]$$

$$(1 + x^2) y_{n+1} + 2nxy_n + \frac{n(n - 1)}{2} (2) y_{n-1} = ay_n$$

$$(1 + x^2) y_{n+1} + (2nx - a) y_n + n(n - 1) y_{n-1} = 0$$

EXERCISE 1.6

1. Find n^{th} derivative of :

   (a) $x^4 e^{3x}$ (b) $e^x \log x$

   (c) $\log (ax + x^2)$ (d) $\cos^4 x$

2. Find n^{th} derivative of :

   (a) $x^3 \log (ax + b)$ (b) $e^x (ax + b)^3$

   (c) $x^n e^x$

3. If $y = \tan (\log x)$, prove that

   $$(1 + x^2) y_{n+1} + (2nx - 1) y_n + n(n - 1) y_{n-1} = 0$$

4. If $y = e^{\tan^{-1} x}$, prove that

   $$(1 + x^2) y_{n+2} + [2(n + 1) x - 1] y_{n+1} + n(n + 1) y_n = 0$$

5. If $y = e^{m \cos^{-1} x}$, prove that

   $$(1 - x^2) y_{n+2} - (2n + 1) y_{n+1} x - (n^2 + m^2) y_n = 0$$

6. $y = e^{a \sin^{-1} x}$ prove that $(1 - x^2) y_{n+2} - (2n + 1) xy_{n+1} - n^2 y_n = 0$

7. $y = (\tan^{-1} x)^2$, prove that $(x^2 + 1)^2 y_n + 2x (n^2 + 1) y_1 = 2$

8. $y = (1 - x^2)^{1/2} \sin^{-1} x$, prove that

$$(1 - x^2) y_{n+1} - (2n - 1) xy_n - n(n - 2) y_{n-1} = 0$$

9. If $y = (x^2 - 1)^n$, prove that $(x^2 - 1) y_{n+2} + 2xy_{n+1} - n(n + 1) y_n = 0$

10. If $y = \log\left(x + \sqrt{a^2 + x^2}\right)^2$, prove that

$$(a^2 + x^2) y_{n+2} + (2n + 1) x y_{n+1} + n^2 y_n = 0$$

11. If $y = (x^2 - 1)^n$, prove that $(x^2 - 1) y_{n+2} + 2x y_{n+1} - n(n + 1) y_n = 0$

ANSWERS 1.6

1. (a) $\{81x^4 + 108x^2 n + 54 n(n - 1) x^2 + 12 n(n - 1)(n - 2) + \ldots$

$$5 n(n - 1)(n - 2)(n - 3)\} 3^{n-4} e^{3x}$$

(b) $e^x [\log x + n_{c_1} x^{-1} - n_{c_2} x^{-2} \ldots (-1)^n (n - 1)! x^{-n}]$

(c) $(-1)^{n-1} (n - 1)! \left[\dfrac{1}{x^n} + \dfrac{1}{(x + a)^n}\right]$

(d) $\dfrac{1}{2} 2^n \cos\left(2x + \dfrac{n\pi}{2}\right) + \dfrac{1}{8} 4^n \cos\left(4x + \dfrac{n\pi}{2}\right)$

2. (a) $y_n = {}^nC_0 x^3 (-1)^{n-1} (n - 1)! a^n (ax + b)^{-n}$

$\quad + {}^nC_1 3x^2 (-1)^{n-2} (n - 2)! a^{n-1} (ax + b)^{-(n-1)}$

$\quad + {}^nC_2 6x (-1)^{n-3} (n - 3)! a^{n-2} (ax + b)^{-(n-2)}$

$\quad + {}^nC_3 6 (-1)^{n-4} (n - 4)! a^{n-3} (ax + b)^{-(n-3)}$

(b) $e^x \{(ax + b)^3 + 3ax (ax + b)^2 + 3n (n - 1) a^2 (ax + b)$

$\quad + n(n - 1)(n - 2) a^3\}$

(c) $e^x \left\{x^n + \dfrac{n^2}{1!} x^{n-1} + \dfrac{n^2 (n - 1)^2}{2!} x^{n-2} + \ldots + \dfrac{n^2 (n - 1)^2 (n - 2)^2 \ldots (-1)^2}{n!}\right\}$

1.6 TAYLOR'S THEOREM AND MACLAURIN'S THEOREM (Statement Only)

(a) Taylor's Theorem :

If a function f(x) is such that (i) f(x), f'(x), f''(x) ... f^n(x) are continuous in closed interval [a, a + h]. (ii) f^n(x) exist in the open interval (a, a + h), then there exists at least one number $\theta \in (0, 1)$ such that

$$f(a + h) = f(a) + hf'(a) + \frac{h^2}{2!} f''(a) + \frac{h^3}{3!} f'''(a) + \ldots$$
$$+ \frac{h^{n-1}}{(n-1)!} f^{n-1}(a) + R_n$$

where, R_n is the remainder after n^{th} term.

Note : R_n may be in any one of the forms :

(1) $R_n = \dfrac{h^n (1-\theta)^{n-m}}{m(n-1)!} f^n(a + \theta h)$ where $0 < \theta < 1$ is called Schomilch and Roche form of remainder.

(2) $R_n = \dfrac{h^n (1-\theta)^{n-1}}{(n-1)!} f^n(a + \theta h)$ where $0 < \theta < 1$ is called Cauchy's form of remainder.

(3) $R_n = \dfrac{h^n}{n!} f^n(a + \theta h)$ where $0 < \theta < 1$ it is called Lagrange's form of remainder.

(b) Maclaurin's Theorem :

If a function $f(x)$ is such that :

(i) $f(x)$ $f'(x)$, $f''(x)$ ... $f^{n-1}(x)$ are continuous in closed interval $[0, x]$.

(ii) $f^n(x)$ exists in the open interval $(0, x)$ then there exist at least one member $\theta \in (0, 1)$, such that

$$f(x) = f(0) + xf'(0) + \frac{x^2}{2!} f''(0) + \ldots + \frac{x^n}{(n-1)!} f^{n-1}(0) + R_n$$

where, R_n is remainder after n terms R_n may be in any one of the following form

(i) $R_n = \dfrac{(1-\theta)^{n-m}}{m(n-1)!} x^n f^n(\theta x)$

Schlomilesh and Roche's form

(ii) $R_n = \dfrac{x^n}{n!} f^n(\theta x)$ Lagrange's form.

(iii) $R_n = \dfrac{(1-\theta)^{n-1}}{(n-1)!} x^n f^n(\theta x)$ Cauchy's form

(c) Taylor's Series and MacLaurin's Series (Statement Only):

Taylor series: If function f(x) is such that $f^{n-1}(x)$ is (i) continuous in [a, a + h], (ii) derivable in (a, a + h) and (iii) $\lim_{n \to \infty} R_n = 0$ where R_n is remainder then

$$f(a+h) = f(a) + hf'(a) + \frac{h^2}{2!}f''(a) + \ldots + \frac{h^n}{n!}f^n(a) + \ldots \infty.$$

This expansion is called as Tayor's series.

Maclaurin's Series: If function f(x) is such that $f^{n-1}(x)$ is (i) continuous in [0 x], (ii) derivable in (0, x) and (iii) $\lim_{n \to \infty} R_n = 0$ where R_n is remainder after n term in expansion.

$$f(x) = f(0) + xf'(0) + \frac{x^2}{2!}f''(0) + \ldots \frac{x^n}{n!}f^n(0) + \ldots \infty.$$

This expansion is called Maclaurin's series.

Series Expansions of Some Standard Functions:

SOLVED EXAMPLES

Example 1.64: Series expansion of e^{ax}.

Solution: Let $f(x) = e^{ax}$ $x \in \mathbb{R}$

$f'(x) = ae^{ax}$, $f''(x) = a^2 e^{ax}$, $f'''(x) = a^3 e^{ax}$

$f^n(x) = a^n e^{ax}$ for $\forall x \in \mathbb{R}$

Now, $f(0) = e^0 = 1$

$f'(0) = ae^0 = a$

$f''(0) = a^2 e^0 = a^2 \ldots f^n(0) = a^n e^0 = a^n$

By using Maclaurin's series expansion

$$f(x) = f(0) + xf'(0) + \frac{x^2}{2!}f''(0) + \frac{x^3}{3!}f'''(0) + \ldots$$

$$e^{ax} = 1 + ax + \frac{a^2 x^2}{2!} + \frac{a^3 x^3}{3!} + \ldots \infty$$

Example 1.65 : Expansion of cos x

Solution :
$f(x) = \cos x \qquad f(0) = 1$
$f'(x) = -\sin x \qquad f'(0) = 0$
$f''(x) = -\cos x \qquad f''(0) = -1$
$f'''(x) = \sin x \qquad f'''(0) = 0$
$f^{IV}(x) = \cos x \qquad f^{IV}(0) = 1$
and so on

Put these values in

$$f(x) = f(0) + xf'(0) + \frac{x^2}{2!}f''(0) + \ldots$$

$$= 1 + x(0) + \frac{x^2}{2!}(-1) + \frac{x^3}{3!}(0) + \frac{x^4}{4!}(1) + \ldots$$

$$\cos x = 1 - \frac{x^2}{2!} + \frac{x^4}{4!} + \frac{x^6}{6!} + \frac{x^8}{8!} + \ldots \infty$$

Example 1.66 : Expansion of sin x.

Solution : Since,
$f(x) = \sin x \qquad f(0) = 0$
$f'(x) = \cos x \qquad f'(0) = 1$
$f''(x) = -\sin x \qquad f''(0) = 0$
$f'''(x) = -\cos x \qquad f'''(0) = -1$
$f^{IV}(x) = \sin x \qquad f^{IV}(0) = 0$
and so on

Put these values in

$$f(x) = f(0) + xf'(0) + \frac{x^2}{2!}f''(0) + \frac{x^3}{3!}f'''(0) + \ldots$$

$$= 0 + x(1) + \frac{x^2}{2!}(0) + \frac{x^3}{3!}(-1) + \frac{x^4}{4!}(0) + \frac{x^5}{5!}(1) + \ldots$$

$$= x - \frac{x^3}{3!} + \frac{x^5}{5!} - \frac{x^7}{7!} + \ldots \infty$$

Example 1.67 : Expansion of log (1 + x).

Solution :
$f(x) = \log(1+x) \qquad f(0) = 0$
$f'(x) = \dfrac{1}{1+x} \qquad f'(0) = 1$

$$f''(x) = \frac{-1}{(1+x)^2} \qquad f''(0) = -1$$

$$f'''(x) = \frac{1.2}{(1+x)^3} \qquad f'''(0) = 1.2 = 2$$

$$f^{iv}(x) = \frac{1.2.3}{(1+x)^4} \qquad f^{iv}(0) = -1.2.3. = -6$$

Remainder in this case tends to zero if $-1 < x \leq 1$. Hence,

$$\log(1+x) = 0 + x(1) + \frac{x^2}{2!}(-1) + \frac{x^3}{3!}2 + \frac{x^4}{4!}(-6) + \ldots$$

$$= x - \frac{x^2}{2} + \frac{x^3}{3} - \frac{x^4}{4} + \frac{x^5}{5} \ldots \infty$$

Corollary : By changing x to $-x$, we get

$$\log(1-x) = -\left[x + \frac{x^2}{2} + \frac{x^3}{3} + \frac{x^4}{4} + \frac{x^5}{5} \ldots \infty\right]$$

Example 1.68 : Expansion of $(1+x)^m$.

Solution :

$$f(x) = (1+x)^m \qquad\qquad f(0) = 1$$

$$f'(x) = m(1+x)^{m-1} \qquad\qquad f'(0) = m$$

$$f''(x) = m(m-1)(m-1)(1+x)^{m-2} \qquad f''(0) = m(m-1)$$

$$f'''(x) = m(m-1)(m-2)(1+x)^{m-3} \qquad f'''(0) = m(m-1)(m-2)$$

If $|x| < 1$ then $R_n \to 0$ and we get

$$(1+x)^m = 1 + mx + \frac{m(m-1)}{2!}x^2 + \frac{m(m-1)(m-2)}{3!}x^3 + \ldots$$

Note : 1. If m is positive integer, we get finite number of terms

2. If $m = -1$, we get

$$\frac{1}{(1+x)} = 1 - x + x^2 - x^3 + x^4 \ldots \infty$$

3. By changing x to $-x$, we get

$$\frac{1}{1-x} = 1 + x + x^2 + x^3 + x^4 + \ldots \infty$$

Example 1.69 : Expansion of tan x.

Solution : Since,

$$y = \tan x \qquad y(0) = 0$$
$$y_1 = \sec^2 x + 1 + \tan^2 x = 1 + y^2 \qquad y_1(0) = 1$$
$$y_2 = 2yy_1 \qquad y_2(0) = 2y(0)y_1(0) = 0$$
$$y_3 = 2y_1^2 + 2yy_2 \qquad y_3(0) = 2y_1(0) + 2y(0)y_2(0) = 2$$
$$y_4 = 4y_1 y_2 + 2y_1 y_2 + 2yy_3 = 6y_1 y_2 + 2yy_3$$
$$y_4(0) = 6y_1(0) y_2(0) + 2y(0) y_3(0)$$
$$= 0$$
$$y_5 = 6y_2^2 + 6y_1 y_3 + 2y_1 y_3 + 2yy_4$$
$$= 6y_2^2 + 8y_1 y_3 + 2yy_4$$
$$y_5(0) = 6y_2^2(0) + 8y_1(0) + y_3(0) + 2y(0) y_4(0) = 16$$
$$f(x) = f(0) + xf'(0) + \frac{x^2}{2!}f''(0) + \frac{x^3}{3!}f'''(x) + \frac{x^4}{4!} + f^{IV}(0) + \dots$$
$$\tan x = \frac{x + x^3}{3!}(2) + \frac{x^5}{5!} 16 + \dots$$
$$= x + \frac{x^3}{3} + \frac{2x^5}{15} + \dots$$

EXERCISE 1.7

1. State Taylor's and Maclaurin's theorem.
2. State Maclaurin's series and hence show
$$e^x = 1 + x + \frac{x^2}{2!} + \frac{x^3}{3!} + \dots$$
3. State Maclaurin's series and hence show
$$\cos x = 1 - \frac{x^2}{2!} + \frac{x^4}{4!} - \frac{x^6}{6!}$$
$$\sin x = x - \frac{x^3}{3!} + \frac{x^5}{5!} - \frac{x^7}{7!} + \dots$$

4. Obtain the series expansion of
   (a) log (1 + x) (b) e^x
5. Find series expansion of sin x.
6. Find series expansion of log (1 − x).
7. Prove that $\dfrac{1}{1+x} = 1 - x + x^2 - x^3 + \ldots$ where $x \neq -1$.

ANSWERS 1.7

4. (a) $x - \dfrac{x^2}{2} + \dfrac{x^3}{3} - \dfrac{x^4}{4} + \ldots$ (b) $e^x = 1 + x + \dfrac{x^2}{2!} + \dfrac{x^3}{3!} + \ldots$

5. $x - \dfrac{x^3}{3!} + \dfrac{x^5}{5!} - \dfrac{x^7}{7!} + \ldots$

6. $x - \dfrac{x^2}{2} - \dfrac{x^3}{3} - \dfrac{x^4}{4} + \ldots$

MISCELLANEOUS EXERCISE

(I) Theory Questions :

1. State and prove L' Hospital's Rule.

2. If $\lim_{x \to a} F(x) = \infty$, $\lim_{x \to a} G(x) = \infty$ and $\lim_{x \to a} \dfrac{F(x)}{G(x)} = l$ then prove that $\lim_{x \to a} \dfrac{F'(x)}{G'(x)} = l$

3. If $y = \tan^{-1} x$, show that $(1 + x^2) \dfrac{d^2y}{dx^2} + 2x \dfrac{dy}{dx} = 0$.

4. If $y = \log(\sin x)$, show that $y_3 = \dfrac{2 \cos x}{\sin^3 x}$.

5. $y = \cos(\tan x)$, then $\dfrac{dy}{dx} = -\sec^2 x \sin(\tan x)$.

6. If $y = \left(x + \sqrt{1+x^2}\right)^m$, then show that $(1 + x^2) \dfrac{d^2y}{dx^2} + \dfrac{dy}{dx} - m^2 y = 0$.

7. $x = a(\cos \theta + \theta \sin \theta)$, $y = a(\sin \theta - \theta \cos \theta)$,
   then prove that $\dfrac{d^2y}{dx^2} = \dfrac{\sec^3 \theta}{a\theta}$.

8. If $y = \sin(m \sin^{-1} x)$, prove that $(1 - x^2) \dfrac{d^2y}{dx^2} - x \cdot \dfrac{dy}{dx} + m^2 y = 0$.

9. If $x = \sin\left\{\dfrac{1}{a} \log y\right\}$, then show that $(1 - x^2) y_2 - xy_1 - a^2 y = 0$.

10. If $y = (\sin^{-1} x)^2$, prove that $(1 - x^2) y_2 - xy_1 - 2 = 0$.

11. If $y = \sin^{-1} x$, prove that $(1 - x^2) y_2 - xy_1 = 0$.

12. If $y = \log\left(x + \sqrt{x^2 - a^2}\right)$, prove that $(x^2 - a^2) \dfrac{d^2 y}{dx^2} + x \cdot \dfrac{dy}{dx} = 0$.

13. If $x = a \cos\theta$, $y = b \sin\theta$, show that $\dfrac{d^2 y}{dx^2} = \dfrac{b^4}{a^2 y^3}$.

(II) Numerical Problems:

1. $\displaystyle\lim_{x \to 0} \dfrac{a^x - b^x}{\sin x}$

2. $\displaystyle\lim_{x \to 0} \dfrac{\sin x - x}{e^x - 1}$

3. $\displaystyle\lim_{x \to 1} \dfrac{1 + \log x - x}{1 - 2x + x^2}$

4. $\displaystyle\lim_{x \to 0} \dfrac{\sin ex - x}{\sin x - x \cos x}$

5. $\displaystyle\lim_{x \to 0} \dfrac{x \cos x - \log(1 + x)}{x^2}$

6. $\displaystyle\lim_{x \to 0} \dfrac{a^x - b^x}{x}$

7. $\displaystyle\lim_{x \to a} \dfrac{\log(x - a)}{\log(e^x - e^a)}$

8. $\displaystyle\lim_{x \to 0} \dfrac{\log \sin x}{\cot x}$

9. $\displaystyle\lim_{x \to 0} \dfrac{\log \tan x}{\log x}$

10. $\displaystyle\lim_{x \to 0} x \log x$

11. $\displaystyle\lim_{x \to 0} x \tan\left(\dfrac{\pi}{2} - x\right)$

12. $\displaystyle\lim_{x \to 0} \left(\dfrac{1}{x} - \dfrac{1}{e^x - 1}\right)$

13. $\displaystyle\lim_{x \to 0} \left(\dfrac{a}{x} - \cot\dfrac{x}{a}\right)$

14. $\lim\limits_{x \to \pi/2} (\sec x - \tan x)$

15. $\lim\limits_{x \to 0} (\cos x)^{1/x^2}$

16. $\lim\limits_{x \to 0} \left(\dfrac{\tan x}{x}\right)^{1/x}$

17. $\lim\limits_{x \to 1} \dfrac{1}{x^{x-1}}$

18. $\lim\limits_{x \to \pi/4} (\tan x)^{\tan 2x}$

19. $\lim\limits_{x \to 0} \left(\dfrac{\tan x}{x}\right)^{1/x^2}$

ANSWERS

1. $\log \dfrac{a}{b}$
2. 0
3. $\dfrac{-1}{2}$
4. $\dfrac{1}{2}$
5. $\dfrac{1}{2}$
6. $\log\left(\dfrac{a}{b}\right)$
7. 1
8. 0
9. 1
10. 0
11. 1
12. $\dfrac{1}{2}$
13. 0 $\left[\text{Hint}: \dfrac{\cot x}{a} = \dfrac{\cos x}{\sin x}\right]$
14. 0
15. $e^{-1/2}$
16. 1
17. e
18. $\dfrac{1}{e}$
19. $\dfrac{1}{e^3}$

(III) Multiple Choice Questions :

Choose the correct alternative for each of the following :

1. Which of the following is not an indeterminate form ?
   - (a) $\infty + \infty$
   - (b) $\infty - \infty$
   - (c) ∞ / ∞
   - (d) $0 \times \infty$

2. The indeterminate form of $\lim_{x \to 0} \dfrac{\log(1+x^2)}{\log(\sec x)}$ is .....

   (a) $\infty - \infty$ (b) $0 \times \infty$
   (c) ∞ / ∞ (d) $0/0$

3. The formula of L' Hospital's Rule is .....

   (a) $\lim_{x \to a} \left[\dfrac{F(x)}{G(x)}\right] = \lim_{x \to a}\left[\dfrac{F(x)}{G(x)}\right]$ (b) $\lim_{x \to a}\left[\dfrac{F(x)}{G(x)}\right] = \lim_{x \to a}\dfrac{F'(x)}{G'(x)}$

   (c) $\lim_{x \to a}\dfrac{F(x)}{G(x)} = \dfrac{F(a)}{G(a)}$ (d) $\lim_{x \to a}\dfrac{F(x)}{G(x)} = \dfrac{F'(a)}{G'(a)}$

4. The indeterminate form of $\lim_{x \to \pi} \dfrac{1+\cos x}{(\pi - x)^2}$ is .....

   (a) $\dfrac{1}{4}$ (b) 1
   (c) 0 (d) $\dfrac{1}{2}$

5. The indeterminate form of $\lim_{x \to 0} \dfrac{3^x - 2^x}{x}$ is .....

   (a) 0 (b) 1
   (c) $\log \dfrac{3}{2}$ (d) $\log \dfrac{2}{3}$

6. The indeterminate form of $\lim_{x \to 1} (1-x^2)^{1/\log(1-x)}$ is .....

   (a) 1^∞ (b) a^0
   (c) ∞^0 (d) None of these

7. $\lim_{x \to 0} \dfrac{\log \sin x}{\log x}$ is .....

   (a) 0 (b) 1
   (c) -1 (d) ∞

8. $\lim_{x \to 0} \dfrac{\cos 4x - \cos x}{x \sin x}$ is .....

   (a) 0 (b) -1
   (c) 1 (d) ∞

9. $\lim_{x \to 0} x \log x$ is .....

   (a) 0 (b) 1
   (c) ∞ (d) -1

10. The value of $\lim_{x \to 0} \dfrac{1 - \cos x}{3x^2}$ = ...

   (a) 3
   (b) $\dfrac{1}{3}$
   (c) $\dfrac{1}{6}$
   (d) $\dfrac{1}{9}$

11. If $y = \log(2 + 5x)$ then $y_n = ?$

   (a) $\dfrac{(-1)^n \, n! \, 5^n}{(2 + 5x)^n}$
   (b) $\dfrac{(-1)^{n-1} \, (n-1)! \, 5^n}{(2 + 5x)^n}$
   (c) $\dfrac{(-1)^n \, (n-1)!}{(2 + 5x)^n}$
   (d) None of these

12. If $y = (2x + 3)^8$ then y_5 = ...

   (a) $\dfrac{8! \, 2^5}{3!} (2x + 3)^3$
   (b) $\dfrac{8! \, 2^5}{3!} (2x + 3)^5$
   (c) $\dfrac{8}{3} 2^5 (2x + 3)^3$
   (d) None of these

13. If $y = x^m$ then y_n = ... If $n > m$
   (a) 0
   (b) $m! \, x^{m-n} (m - n)!$
   (c) $m! \, x^m (m - n)!$
   (d) None of these

14. If $y = x^m$ then y_n = ... If $n < m$
   (a) 0
   (b) $m! \, x^{m-n} (m - n)!$
   (c) $m! \, x^m (n - m)!$
   (d) None of these

15. If $y = (ax + b)^7$ then y_8 = ...

   (a) $7(ax + b)^6$
   (b) $\dfrac{7!}{a!} (ax + b)^3$
   (c) 0
   (d) None of these

16. If $y = a^{mx}$ then y_n = ...

   (a) $m^n \, a^{mx} (\log a)^n$
   (b) $m^n \, a^{mx}$
   (c) $\dfrac{m^n \, a^{mx}}{(\log a)^n}$
   (d) None of these

17. If $y = e^{ax}$ then y_7 = ...

   (a) $a^n \, e^{ax}$
   (b) $a^7 \, e^{ax}$
   (c) $\dfrac{e^{ax}}{a^7}$
   (d) None of these

18. $y = \sin(5x + 3)$ then third derivative ......

   (a) $5 \sin\left(5x + 3 + \dfrac{3\pi}{2}\right)$
   (b) $125 \cos\left(5x + 3 + \dfrac{3\pi}{2}\right)$
   (c) $125 \sin\left(5x + 3 + \dfrac{3\pi}{2}\right)$
   (d) None of these

19. If $y = \cos(ax + b)$ then $y_n = $ ......

   (a) $a^n \cos\left[(ax + b) + \dfrac{n\pi}{2}\right]$
   (b) $a^n \sin\left[(ax + b) + \dfrac{n\pi}{2}\right]$
   (c) $a \cos\left[ax + b + \dfrac{n\pi}{2}\right]$
   (d) None of these

20. $y = \sin(ax + b)$ then $y_7 = $ ......

   (a) $a^7 \sin\left[(ax + b) + \dfrac{7\pi}{2}\right]$
   (d) $a^7 \cos\left[(ax + b) + \dfrac{7\pi}{2}\right]$
   (c) $a \sin\left[(ax + b) + \dfrac{7\pi}{2}\right]$
   (d) None of these

21. If $y = (2x + 3)^5$ then $y_3 = $ ......

   (a) $480(2x + 3)$
   (b) $480(2x + 3)^2$
   (c) $\dfrac{480}{(2x + 3)}$
   (d) None of these

22. $y = \sin 3x + 2$ then $y_3 = $ ......

   (a) $3 \cos(3x + 2)$
   (b) $3^3 \cos(3x + 2)$
   (c) $3^3 \cos\left(3x + 2 + \dfrac{3\pi}{2}\right)$
   (d) None of these

23. If $y = \dfrac{1}{2 - 3x}$ then $y_n = $ ......

   (a) $\dfrac{(-1)^n \, n! \, (-3)^n}{(2 - 3x)^{n+1}}$
   (b) $\dfrac{(-1)^{n+1} \, (n+1)! \, (-3)^{n+1}}{(2 - 3x)^n}$
   (c) $\dfrac{(-1)^n \, n! \, (-3)^{n+1}}{(2 - 3x)^{n+1}}$
   (d) None of these

24. The nth term in the expansion of $f(a^{th})$ is ......

   (a) $\dfrac{1}{n!} f^n(a)$
   (b) $\dfrac{n}{n!} f^n(a)$
   (c) $\dfrac{n^n}{n!}$
   (d) None of these

25. If $\cos x - a_0 + a_1 x + a_2 x^2 + ...$ then valued $a_3 = $ ......

   (a) 0
   (b) -1
   (c) 1
   (d) $\dfrac{1}{3!}$

26. If $\sin x = a_0 + a_1 x + a_2 x^2 + ...$ then $a_2 = $ ......

   (a) 1
   (b) 0
   (c) 1
   (d) $\dfrac{1}{3!}$

27. $x - \dfrac{x^3}{3!} + \dfrac{x^5}{5!} - \dfrac{x^7}{7!} + ... \infty$ is expansion of ......

   (a) $\sin x$
   (b) $\cos x$
   (c) $\tan x$
   (d) None of these

28. Expansion of e^x is ......

   (a) $1 + x + \dfrac{x^2}{2} + \dfrac{x^3}{3} + ... \infty$
   (b) $1 + x + \dfrac{x^2}{2!} + \dfrac{x^3}{3!} + ... \infty$
   (c) $1 - x + \dfrac{x^2}{2} - \dfrac{x^3}{3!} + ... \infty$
   (d) None of these

29. Expansion of $\log(1 + x) = $ ......

   (a) $x - \dfrac{x^2}{2} + \dfrac{x^3}{3} - \dfrac{x^4}{4} + \dfrac{x^5}{5} ... \infty$
   (d) $-\left[x + \dfrac{x^2}{2} + \dfrac{x^3}{3} + ... \infty \right]$
   (c) $x + \dfrac{x^2}{2!} + \dfrac{x^3}{3} + \dfrac{x^5}{5} + ... \infty$
   (d) None of these

30. Expansion of log 2 is ......

   (a) $\log 2 = 1 + \dfrac{1}{2} + \dfrac{1}{3} + \dfrac{1}{4} + ...$
   (b) $\log 2 = 1 - \dfrac{1}{2} + \dfrac{1}{3} - \dfrac{1}{4} + ...$
   (c) $\log 2 = 1 + \dfrac{1}{2^2} + \dfrac{1}{3^2} + ...$
   (d) None of these

31. The expansion of $\dfrac{1}{1+x}$ is ......

   (a) $1 - x + x^2 - x^3 + x^4 + ...$
   (b) $1 + x + x^2 + x^3 + x^4 + ...$
   (c) $1 - x + \dfrac{x^2}{2} - \dfrac{x^3}{3} + ...$
   (d) None of these

32. The expansion of $\dfrac{1}{1-x}$ is ......

   (a) $1 - x + x^2 - x^3 - x^4 + ...$
   (b) $1 + x + x^2 + x^3 + x^4 + ...$
   (c) $1 - x + \dfrac{x^2}{2} - \dfrac{x^3}{3} + ...$
   (d) None of these

33. The expansion of tan x is ......

   (a) $x + \dfrac{x^3}{3} + \dfrac{2x^5}{15} + ...$
   (b) $x - \dfrac{x^3}{3} + \dfrac{2x^5}{15} + ...$
   (c) $1 - \dfrac{x^2}{2} + \dfrac{3x^4}{15}$
   (d) None of these

34. The expansion of sin x is ......

   (a) $1 - \dfrac{x^2}{2!} + \dfrac{x^4}{4!} - \dfrac{x^6}{6!} + ...$
   (b) $x - \dfrac{x^3}{3!} + \dfrac{x^5}{5!} - \dfrac{x^7}{7!} + \dfrac{x^9}{9!} + ... \infty$
   (c) $x + \dfrac{x^3}{3} + \dfrac{2x^5}{15} + ...$
   (d) None of these

35. The expansion of cos x is ......

   (a) $1 - \dfrac{x^2}{2!} + \dfrac{x^4}{4!} - \dfrac{x^6}{6!} + \dfrac{x^8}{8!} + ... \infty$
   (b) $x - \dfrac{x^3}{3!} + \dfrac{x^5}{5!} - \dfrac{x^7}{7!} + \dfrac{x^9}{9!} + ... \infty$
   (c) $x + \dfrac{x^3}{3} + \dfrac{2x^5}{15} + ...$
   (d) None of these

ANSWERS

1. (a)	2. (d)	3. (b)	4. (d)	5. (c)	6. (a)	7. (b)	8. (a)
9. (a)	10. (c)	11. (b)	12. (a)	13. (a)	14. (b)	15. (c)	16. (a)
17. (b)	18. (c)	19. (a)	20. (a)	21. (b)	22. (c)	23. (a)	24. (c)
25. (a)	26. (b)	27. (a)	28. (b)	29. (a)	30. (b)	31. (a)	32. (b)
33. (a)	34. (b)	35. (a)					

2
CHAPTER

FUNCTION OF TWO VARIABLES

Leonhard Euler was born on 15th April 1707 in Basel (Switzerland). It is said that if Gauss is the prince, Euler is the King. Euler's output was immense. He published more than 500 books and papers during his life-time while a further 400 appeared post humously. It has been computated that his publication during working life averaged about 800 pages a year. Hence, he was known as the most prolific Mathematician.

Leonard Euler

2.1 INTRODUCTION

In standard XI and XII, we have studied the function of one variable viz. $y = f(x)$ in space R^1. To extend this idea for R^2, R^3, ..., R^n i.e. in this chapter, we study the function of two, three, ..., n variable functions, usually these functions are defined as $y = f(x_1, x_2)$, $y = f(x_1, x_2, x_3)$, ..., $y = f(x_1, x_2, ..., x_n)$ in which the independent variables are two, three, ..., n in numbers. To differentiate such functions, we define partial derivative concept and the concept was put forward by the great Mathematician Leonhard Euler.

Definition :
1. **Cartesian Product of Two Sets :**

The set of all ordered pairs (a, b) such that a ∈ A and b ∈ B is called the Cartesian product of two non-empty sets A and B. It is denoted by A × B.

Symbolically,   A × B = {(a, b) | a ∈ A, b ∈ B}

2. Function of Two Variables :

Let X be any subset of $R \times R$ and $X' \subset R$. Then a function $f : X \to X'$ is called a real valued function of two real variables. It is denoted as $z = f(x, y)$.

e.g. $\quad z = \log(x^2 + y^2), \quad x^2 + y^2 + z^2 = c$

$\quad z = e^{x/y}, \quad x^3 y^2 z = c$ etc.

3. Neighbourhood of a Point :

Let $\delta > 0$ be any number then the set of points (x, y) such that

$$0 < |x - a| < \delta, \quad 0 < |y - b| < \delta$$

is called a δ-neighbourhood of the point (a, b).

Note : The above example represents the interior of the circle $(x - a)^2 + (y - b)^2 = \delta^2$ except the centre (a, b). So the above condition can also be written as $0 < \sqrt{(x - a)^2 + (y - b)^2} < \delta$.

4. Limit of A Function of Two Variables :

Let $f(x, y)$ be a function of two variables x and y, then the function $f(x, y)$ is said to have limit L if for every given $\epsilon > 0$, there exist $\delta > 0$. Such that $|f(x, y) - L| < \epsilon$ for all (x, y) in the neighbourhood of (a, b) i.e. for all (x, y) satisfying $0 < |x - a| < \delta, 0 < |y - b| < \delta$.

Symbolically, $\lim_{(x, y) \to (a, b)} f(x, y)$ or $\lim_{\substack{x \to a \\ y \to b}} f(x, y)$

Remark : We know that the function of one variable $y = f(x)$ approaches l as $x \to a$, if for given $\epsilon > 0, \exists\, \delta > 0$, such that $|f(x) - l| < \epsilon$ whenever $0 < |x - a| < \delta$.

Here, $\quad 0 < |x - a| < \delta$ means

$$-\delta < x - a < \delta$$

$$\Leftrightarrow a - \delta < x < a + \delta$$

```
 ←———(———|———)———→
      a−δ   a   a+δ
```

Clearly, in the interval (a − δ, a + δ) x approaches to a in two directions i.e. either from left to a or from right of a. It means that there are only two paths along which the limits must be equal. In the case of function of two variables say z = f(x, y) the point (x, y) can approach (a, b) along infinitely many ways. Since in the neighbourhood of (a, b) (x, y) can approach (a, b) in infinite ways. The limit of z = f(x, y) exist only when along all paths the limits must be equal.

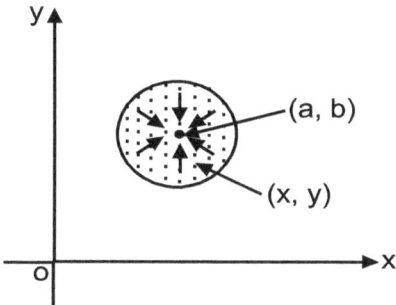

Fig. 2.1 : Infinite paths connecting two paths

Generally, we choose the following path along which (x, y) approaches (a, b).

(i) x = a, x = b, (ii) x = λy, (iii) y = λx, (iv) $x^2 = λy$, (v) $x = λy^2$,
(vi) $y = x^2 - x$ or $y = x - x^2$, (vii) $y = x^3 + x$,
(viii) $y = x - x^3$ or $y = x^3 - x$, (ix) $y = λx^3$ etc.

SOLVED EXAMPLES

Example 2.1 : Prove that $\lim_{(x, y) \to (0, 0)} f(x, y)$ does not exists,

where, $f(x, y) = \dfrac{xy^2}{x^2 + y^4}$, $(x, y) \neq (0, 0)$

$= 0,$ $(x, y) \neq (0, 0)$

Solution : Let (x, y) approaches (0, 0) along the path $y^2 = λx$

∴ $\lim_{(x, y) \to (0, 0)} f(x, y) = \lim_{x \to 0} \dfrac{x \cdot λx}{x^2 + (λx)^2}$

$= \lim_{x \to 0} \dfrac{λx^2}{x^2 + λ^2 x^2}$

$= \lim_{x \to 0} \dfrac{λx^2}{x^2(1 + λ^2)}$

$$= \frac{\lambda}{1 + \lambda^2}$$

Therefore, the limit depends upon λ i.e. the path chosen. It is different for different values of λ. Hence, $f(x, y)$ does not have a limit as $(x, y) \to (0, 0)$.

Example 2.2 : Discuss the function $f(x, y)$ for the existence of a limit at $(0, 0)$ where,

$$f(x, y) = \frac{x^2 - y^2}{x^2 + y^2}, \quad (x, y) \neq (0, 0)$$
$$= 0, \quad \text{otherwise}$$

Solution : Here, $f(x, y) = \frac{x^2 - y^2}{x^2 + y^2}, \quad (x, y) \neq (0, 0)$

Let (x, y) approaches $(0, 0)$ along the path $y = \lambda x$.

$$\lim_{(x, y) \to (0, 0)} f(x, y) = \lim_{x \to 0} \frac{x^2 - \lambda^2 x^2}{x^2 + \lambda^2 x^2}$$

$$= \lim_{x \to 0} \frac{x^2 (1 - \lambda^2)}{x^2 (1 + \lambda^2)}$$

$$= \frac{1 - \lambda^2}{1 + \lambda^2}$$

Therefore, the limit depends upon the path chosen i.e. λ. Hence $f(x, y)$ does not have a limit at $(0, 0)$.

Example 2.3 : Show that $\lim_{(x, y) \to (0, 0)} \frac{x \sin (x^2 + y^2)}{x^2 + y^2} = 0$

Solution : Since,

$$\lim_{(x, y) \to (0, 0)} \frac{x \sin (x^2 + y^2)}{x^2 + y^2} = \lim_{x \to 0} x \cdot \lim_{\substack{x \to 0 \\ y \to 0}} \frac{\sin (x^2 + y^2)}{x^2 + y^2}$$

But $x \to 0, y \to 0 \Rightarrow x^2 + y^2 \to 0$

$$\therefore \lim_{(x, y) \to (0, 0)} \frac{0 \sin (x^2 + y^2)}{x^2 + y^2} = 0(1)$$

$$\therefore \lim_{(x, y) \to (0, 0)} \frac{x \sin (x^2 + y^2)}{x^2 + y^2} = 0(1)$$

$$= 0$$

Example 2.4 : Show that $\lim_{(x, y)\to(0, 0)} xy\left(\dfrac{x^2 - y^2}{x^2 + y^2}\right) = 0$

Solution : Let $f(x, y) = xy\left(\dfrac{x^2 - y^2}{x^2 + y^2}\right)$

Changing to polar co-ordinates by the transformation $x = r\cos\theta$, $y = r\sin\theta$, we get

$$f(r\cos\theta, r\sin\theta) = r\cos\theta \cdot r\sin\theta \left(\dfrac{r^2\cos^2\theta - r^2\sin^2\theta}{r^2\cos^2\theta + r^2\sin^2\theta}\right)$$

$$= r^2\cos\theta \cdot \sin\theta \dfrac{r^2(\cos^2\theta - \sin^2\theta)}{r^2(\cos^2\theta + \sin^2\theta)}$$

$$= r^2\sin\theta\cos\theta \cdot \cos 2\theta$$

$$= \dfrac{r^2}{2}\sin 2\theta \cdot \cos 2\theta$$

$$= \dfrac{r^2}{4}\sin 4\theta \qquad \ldots (1)$$

$\therefore \qquad |f(x, y)| \leq \dfrac{r^2}{4} \quad$ since $|\sin 4\theta| \leq 1$

$\therefore \qquad |f(x, y)| \leq \dfrac{x^2 + y^2}{4} < \epsilon$

If we choose $\dfrac{x^2}{4} < \epsilon$ and $\dfrac{y^2}{4} < \epsilon$

i.e. $x < 2\sqrt{\epsilon}$ and $y < 2\sqrt{\epsilon}$

Let $\delta = 2\sqrt{\epsilon}$ then $|x - 0| < \delta$ and $|y - 0| < \delta$.

Clearly, $|f(x, y) - 0| < \epsilon$ whenever $|x| < \delta$, $|y| < \delta$.

i.e. $\lim_{(x, y)\to(0, 0)} f(x, y) = 0$

Aliter : From equation (1)

$$f(x, y) = \dfrac{r^2}{4}\sin 4\theta$$

Since $r \to 0$ as $(x, y) \to (0, 0)$, we get

$\therefore \quad \lim_{(x, y)\to(0, 0)} f(x, y) = \lim_{r\to 0} \dfrac{r^2}{4}\sin 4\theta$

$$= \frac{\sin 4\theta}{4} \cdot \lim_{r \to 0} r^2$$

$$\therefore \lim_{(x, y) \to (0, 0)} f(x, y) = 0$$

Example 2.5 : Show that the limit of the function

$$f(x, y) = y \sin \frac{1}{x} + x \sin \frac{1}{y}, \text{ exists at } (0, 0).$$

Solution : We have,

$$|f(x, y)| = \left| y \sin \frac{1}{x} + x \sin \frac{1}{y} \right|$$

$$\leq \left| y \sin \frac{1}{x} \right| + \left| x \sin \frac{1}{y} \right|$$

$$\leq |y| \left| \sin \frac{1}{x} \right| + |x| \cdot \left| \sin \frac{1}{y} \right|$$

$$\leq |y| + |x|, \qquad \because \left| \sin \frac{1}{x} \right| \leq 1, \left| \sin \frac{1}{y} \right| \leq 1$$

$\to 0$ as $(x, y) \to (0, 0)$ along any path.

Therefore, the limit of the function $f(x, y)$ exists at $(0, 0)$.

Example 2.6 : Let $A = \{(x, y) \mid 0 < x < 1, 0 < y < 1, x, y \in R\}$

Define $f : A \to R$ by

$$f(x, y) = x + y$$

Show that $\lim_{(x, y) \to (0, 1/2)} f(x, y) = \frac{1}{2}$

Solution : Let $\epsilon > 0$ be given.

Take $|x - 0| < \epsilon/2$ and $\left| y - \frac{1}{2} \right| < \epsilon/2$

Consider, $\left| f(x, y) - \frac{1}{2} \right| = \left| x + y - \frac{1}{2} \right|$

$$\leq |x| + \left|y - \frac{1}{2}\right|$$

$$< \epsilon/2 + \epsilon/2 = \epsilon$$

∴ $\left|f(x, y) - \frac{1}{2}\right| < \epsilon$ when $|x - 0| < \epsilon/2$, and $\left|y - \frac{1}{2}\right| < \epsilon/2$

If we choose $\delta = \epsilon/2$, then

$$\left|f(x, y) - \frac{1}{2}\right| < \epsilon \ \forall \ |x - 0| < \delta \text{ and } \left|y - \frac{1}{2}\right| < \delta$$

Hence, $\lim_{(x, y) \to (0, 1/2)} f(x, y) = \frac{1}{2}$

2.2 CONTINUITY OF A FUNCTION OF TWO VARIABLES

The function $f(x, y)$ is said to be continuous at (a, b) if $\lim_{(x, y) \to (a, b)} f(x, y)$ exists and is equal to $f(a, b)$.

OR

The function $f(x, y)$ is said to be continuous at (a, b) if for given $\epsilon > 0$, there exist $\delta > 0$ such that $|f(x, y) - f(a, b)| < \epsilon$

whenever $|x - a| < \delta$ and $|y - b| < \delta$

SOLVED EXAMPLES

Example 2.7 : Examine whether the function given below is continuous at $(0, 0)$

$$f(x, y) = \frac{xy}{\sqrt{x^2 + y^2}}, \text{ if } (x, y) \neq (0, 0)$$

$$= 0 \quad , \text{ if } (x, y) = (0, 0)$$

Solution : Changing to polar co-ordinates by $x = r \cos \theta$, $y = r \sin \theta$, we get

$$f(x, y) = f(r \cos \theta, r \sin \theta) = \frac{r \cos \theta \cdot r \sin \theta}{\sqrt{r^2 \cos^2 \theta + r^2 \sin^2 \theta}}$$

$$= \frac{r^2 \sin \theta \cos \theta}{r\sqrt{\cos^2 \theta + \sin^2 \theta}}$$

$$\therefore \quad f(r\cos\theta, r\sin\theta) = \frac{r}{2}\sin 2\theta$$

Now consider,

$$|f(r\cos\theta, r\sin\theta)| = \left|\frac{r}{2}\sin 2\theta\right|$$

$$= \frac{r}{2}|\sin 2\theta|$$

$$\leq \frac{r}{2}$$

$$\therefore \quad |f(x,y)| \leq \frac{\sqrt{x^2+y^2}}{2}$$

0 as (x, y) approaches to (0, 0) along any path.

Hence, $\lim\limits_{(x,y) \to (a,b)} f(x,y) = 0$

Further, $f(0, 0) = 0$

$$\therefore \quad \lim\limits_{(x,y) \to (0,0)} f(x,y) = f(0,0)$$

Therefore, f(x, y) is continuous at (0, 0)

Example 2.8 : Investigate the continuity of function

$$f(x,y) = \frac{x^3 y^2}{x^6 + y^4}, \quad (x,y) \neq (0,0)$$

$$= 0 \quad , \text{ otherwise}$$

Solution : Let (x, y) approaches to (0, 0) along the path $x^3 = \lambda y^2$

$$\therefore \quad \lim\limits_{(x,y) \to (0,0)} f(x,y) = \lim\limits_{y \to 0} \frac{\lambda y^2 \cdot y^2}{(\lambda y^2)^2 + y^4}$$

$$= \lim\limits_{y \to 0} \frac{\lambda y^4}{\lambda^2 y^4 + y^4}$$

$$= \lim\limits_{y \to 0} \frac{\lambda y^4}{y^4 (\lambda^2 + 1)}$$

$$= \frac{\lambda}{\lambda^2 + 1}$$

Since the limit depends on λ i.e. the path chosen, the limit of the function does not exists. Hence, the function f(x, y) is discontinuous at (0, 0).

Example 2.9 : Show that the function,

$$f(x, y) = \frac{x^2 + y^2}{x + y}, \text{ if } x + y \neq 0$$

$$f(0, 0) = 0$$

is not continuous at (0, 0).

Solution : Let (x, y) approaches (0, 0) along the path $y = \lambda x$.

$$\lim_{(x, y) \to (0, 0)} f(x, y) = \lim_{x \to 0} \frac{x^2 + \lambda^2 x^2}{x + \lambda x}$$

$$= \lim_{x \to 0} \frac{x^2 (1 + \lambda^2)}{x (1 + \lambda)}$$

$$= \lim_{x \to 0} x \cdot \frac{1 + \lambda^2}{1 + \lambda}$$

$$= 0$$

Now choosing the path $y = x^2 - x$

$$\therefore \lim_{(x, y) \to (0, 0)} f(x, y) = \lim_{x \to 0} \frac{x^2 + (x^2 - x)^2}{x + x^2 - x}$$

$$= \lim_{x \to 0} \frac{x^2 + x^2 (x - 1)^2}{x^2}$$

$$= \lim_{x \to 0} \frac{x^2 [1 + (x - 1)^2]}{x^2}$$

$$= \lim_{x \to 0} [1 + (x - 1)^2]$$

$$= 1 + (0 - 1)^2$$

$$= 1 + 1$$

$$= 2$$

Therefore, the limit of the function is different along different path. Hence limit of f(x, y) does not exists and the function is not continuous at (0, 0).

Example 2.10 : Discuss the continuity of

$$f(x, y) = \frac{x^4}{x^4 + y^4 - x}, \quad (x, y) \neq (0, 0)$$
$$= 0, \quad \text{otherwise}$$

at (0, 0).

Solution : Let (x, y) approaches (0, 0) along the path $y^4 = x$.

$$\therefore \lim_{(x, y) \to (0, 0)} f(x, y) = \lim_{x \to 0} \frac{x^4}{x^4 + x - x}$$

$$= \lim_{x \to 0} \frac{x^4}{x^4}$$

$$= 1$$

But $\qquad f(0, 0) = 0$

$$\therefore \lim_{(x, y) \to (0, 0)} f(x, y) \neq f(0, 0)$$

Hence, the function f(x, y) is not continuous at (0, 0).

Example 2.11 : Examine for continuity

$$f(x, y) = \frac{x^2 - y^2}{1 + x^2 + y^2}, \quad (x, y) \neq (0, 0)$$
$$= 0, \quad \text{otherwise}$$

Solution : Since, $\quad |f(x, y)| = \left| \frac{x^2 - y^2}{1 + x^2 + y^2} \right|$

$$= \left| \frac{x^2 - y^2}{1 + x^2 + y^2} \right|$$

$$\leq \frac{|x^2 - y^2|}{1} \qquad \text{as } x^2 + y^2 \geq 0$$

$$\leq |x^2| + |y^2| \to 0 \text{ as } (x, y) \to (0, 0)$$

along any path.

Hence, the function is continuous at (0, 0).

Example 2.12 : Examine the continuity of the function
$$f(x, y) = \sqrt{|xy|}$$ at the origin.

Solution : Changing to polar co-ordinates by $x = r\cos\theta$, $y = r\sin\theta$, we get

$$f(r\cos\theta, r\sin\theta) = \sqrt{|r^2 \sin\theta \cos\theta|}$$
$$= r\sqrt{|\sin\theta| \, |\cos\theta|}$$

Now consider,

$$|f(r\cos\theta, r\sin\theta) - f(0,0)| = |r\sqrt{|\sin\theta|\,|\cos\theta|} - 0|$$
$$= |r\sqrt{|\sin\theta|}\sqrt{|\cos\theta|}|$$
$$\leq |r| \qquad \because |\sin\theta| \leq 1, |\cos\theta| \leq 1$$
$$< \epsilon \text{ if } |r| < \epsilon$$

So by definition of continuity the function is continuous at the origin.

Example 2.13 : Investigate the continuity of the function.

$$f(x, y) = \frac{x^2 y^2}{x^2 y^2 + (x-y)^2}, \ (x, y) \neq (0, 0)$$

$$f(0, 0) = 0$$

Solution : Let (x, y) approaches $(0, 0)$ along the path $x - y = \lambda xy$

$$\therefore \lim_{(x,y) \to (0,0)} f(x, y) = \lim_{(x,y) \to (0,0)} \frac{x^2 y^2}{x^2 y^2 + \lambda^2 x^2 y^2}$$

$$= \lim_{(x,y) \to (0,0)} \frac{x^2 y^2}{x^2 y^2 (1 + \lambda^2)}$$

$$= \frac{1}{1 + \lambda^2}$$

Since, the limit depends on the path chosen λ, so the limit of the function does not exist. Hence, the function is not continuous at $(0, 0)$.

Example 2.14 : Show that the function

$$f(x, y) = \frac{x^3 - y^3}{x^2 + y^2}, \ x^2 + y^2 \neq 0$$

$$= 0 \qquad , \ x^2 + y^2 = 0$$

is continuous at the origin.

Solution : We see that,

$$|f(x, y)| = \left| \frac{x^3 - y^3}{x^2 + y^2} \right|$$

Changing to polar co-ordinates by $x = r \cos \theta$, $y = r \sin \theta$
where, $r = \sqrt{x^2 + y^2}$, we get

$$\therefore \quad |f(r \cos \theta, r \sin \theta)| = \left| \frac{r^3 \cos^3 \theta - r^3 \sin^3 \theta}{r^2 \cos^2 \theta + r^2 \sin^2 \theta} \right|$$

$$= \left| \frac{r^3 (\cos^3 \theta - \sin^3 \theta)}{r^2 (\cos^2 \theta + \sin^2 \theta)} \right|$$

$$= r |\cos^3 \theta - \sin^3 \theta|$$

$$= r \{|\cos^3 \theta| + |\sin^3 \theta|\}$$

$$\leq 2r \qquad \because |\cos^3 \theta| \leq 1, |\sin^3 \theta| \leq 1$$

Since $r \to 0$, as $(x, y) \to (0, 0)$ along any path.

∴ $f(x, y) \to 0$ as $(x, y) \to (0, 0)$ and $f(0, 0) = 0$

∴ $\lim\limits_{(x, y) \to (0, 0)} f(x, y) = f(0, 0)$

Hence, the function is continuous at (0, 0).

EXERCISE 2.1

1. Test the following functions for the existence of limits at (0, 0) :

   (a) $f(x, y) = \dfrac{y^2 - x^2}{y^2 + x^2}$, $y^2 + x^2 \neq 0$

   $f(0, 0) = 0$

   (b) $f(x, y) = \dfrac{2xy}{x^2 + y^2}$, $(x, y) \neq (0, 0)$

   $\qquad\qquad = 0$, $(x, y) = (0, 0)$

   (c) $f(x, y) = \dfrac{x^2 y}{x^4 + y^2}$, $(x, y) \neq (0, 0)$

   $f(0, 0) = 0$

(d) $f(x, y) = \dfrac{xy}{x^2 + y^2}$, $x^2 + y^2 \neq 0$

       $f(0, 0) = 0$

2. Show that $\lim\limits_{(x, y) \to (0, 1)} \tan^{-1}\left(\dfrac{y}{x}\right)$ does not exists.

3. Examine for continuity at (0, 0) of the following function.

(a) $f(x, y) = \dfrac{xy^3}{x^2 + y^6}$, $x \neq 0$, $y \neq 0$

       $f(0, 0) = 0$

(b) $f(x, y) = \dfrac{x^2 - y^2}{x^2 + y^2}$, $(x^2 + y^2 \neq 0)$

              $= 0$, $x^2 + y^2 = 0$

(c) $f(x, y) = \dfrac{xy^2 + x^2 y}{x^3 + y^3}$, if $(x, y) \neq (0, 0)$

              $= 0$, if $(x, y) = (0, 0)$

(d) $f(x, y) = \dfrac{x^3 + y^3}{x - y}$, $x \neq 0$, $y \neq 0$

              $= 0$, $x = 0$, $y = 0$

(e) $f(x, y) = \dfrac{x^2}{x^2 + y^2 - 2x}$, if $(x, y) \neq (0, 0)$

              $= 0$, otherwise

(f) $f(x, y) = \dfrac{xy^2}{x^3 + y^3}$, $(x, y) \neq (0, 0)$

              $= 0$, $(x, y) = (0, 0)$

(g) $f(x, y) = \dfrac{x^3 + y^3}{y - 2x}$, $y - 2x \neq 0$

              $= 0$, $y - 2x = 0$

(h) $f(x, y) = \dfrac{x^3 y^3}{x^{12} + y^4}$, $(x, y) \neq (0, 0)$

              $= 0$, otherwise

(i) $f(x, y) = \dfrac{x - y}{1 + x^2 + y^2}$, $1 + x^2 + y^2 \neq 0$

$f(0, 0) = 0$

(j) $f(x, y) = \dfrac{xy^3}{x^2 + y^6}$, $(x, y) \neq (0, 0)$

$= 0$, otherwise

(k) $f(x, y) = \dfrac{xy^2}{x^2 + y^4}$, $x^2 + y^4 \neq 0$

$= 0$, $x^2 + y^4 = 0$

4. Discuss the continuity of the following function at (1, 2)

$f(x, y) = x^2 + 4y$, if $(x, y) \neq (1, 2)$

$= 0$, if $(x, y) = (1, 2)$

5. Find the value of k such that the following function is continuous at (0, 0)

$f(x, y) = \dfrac{3y}{\sqrt{x^2 + y^2}}$, $(x, y) \neq (0, 0)$

$= k$, $(x, y) = (0, 0)$

6. Show that the function

$f(x, y) = \dfrac{xy(x^2 - y^2)}{x^2 + y^2}$, $(x, y) \neq (0, 0)$

$= 0$, $(x, y) = (0, 0)$

is continuous at the origin.

7. Show that the function $f(x, y) = xy$ is continuous at (2, 3)

ANSWERS 2.1

1. (a) $y = \lambda x$; limit does not exists.

(b) Put $y = \lambda x$, limit does not exists.

(c) $x^2 = \lambda y$; limit does not exists.

(d) Put $y = \lambda x$, limit does not exists.

3. (a) $y^3 = \lambda x$; Discontinuous

   (b) $y = \lambda x$; Discontinuous

   (c) $y = \lambda x$; Discontinuous

   (d) $y = x - x^2$, $y = x - x^3$; Discontinuous

   (e) $y^2 = 2x$; Discontinuous

   (f) $y = \lambda x$; Discontinuous

   (g) $y = 2x + x^3$; Discontinuous

   (h) $x^3 = \lambda y$; Discontinuous

   (i) $x^3 = \lambda y$; Discontinuous

   (j) $\left|\dfrac{x - y}{1 + x^2 + y^2}\right| \leq |x - y| \leq |x| + |y| \to 0$

   along any path continuous

   (k) $y = x$, $x = y^3$; Discontinuous

   (l) $y^2 = \lambda x$; Discontinuous

4. $\lim\limits_{(x, y) \to (1, 2)} f(x, y) = 9 \neq f(0, 0)$ Discontinuous

5. $k = 0$

6. **Hint :** Put $x = r \cos \theta$, $y = r \sin \theta$

   Then $r \to 0$ as $(x, y) \to (0, 0)$

7. **Hint :** $f(2, 3) = 6$; find $\delta > 0$ s.t.

   $|xy - 6| < \epsilon$ whenever $0 < \sqrt{(x - 2)^2 + (y - 3)^2} < \delta$

   $|xy - 6| = |xy - 2y + 2y - 6|$

   $= |y| \, |x - 2| + 2|y - 3|$

   Take $\delta < 1 \Rightarrow |y - 3| < \delta < 1 \Rightarrow 2 < y < 4$

   $\therefore \; |xy - 6| < 6\delta$. Then choose $\delta = \dfrac{\epsilon}{6}$

2.3 PARTIAL DERIVATIVES

Let $z = f(x, y)$ be a continuous function of two independent variables x and y. If y remains unchanged and x varies alone, then z may be treated as continuous function of x alone. Whenever this possess a derivative, then this derivative is called the partial derivative of z w.r.t. x and it is denoted by $\frac{\partial z}{\partial x}$ or $\frac{\partial f}{\partial x}$ or f_x.

Definition :

Let $z = f(x, y)$ be a differentiable function of two independent variables x and y. Suppose now x changes to $x + \delta x$, y remains constant. Then z will changes to $z + \delta z$.

$$\therefore \quad z + \delta z = f(x + \delta x, y)$$

$$\delta z = f(x + \delta x, y) - z$$

$$= f(x + \delta x, y) - f(x, y)$$

$$\therefore \quad \frac{\delta z}{\delta x} = \frac{f(x + \delta x, y) - f(x, y)}{\delta x}$$

Taking limit as $\delta x \to 0$ on both sides, we get,

$$\lim_{\delta x \to 0} \frac{\delta z}{\delta x} = \lim_{\delta x \to 0} \frac{f(x + \delta x, y) - f(x, y)}{\delta x}$$

If $\lim_{\delta x \to 0} \frac{\delta z}{\delta x}$ is exist then this limit is called partial derivative of $f(x, y)$ w.r.t. x and is denoted by f_x or $\frac{\partial f}{\partial x}$ or $\frac{\partial z}{\partial x}$.

$$\therefore \quad \frac{\partial f}{\partial x} = \lim_{\delta x \to 0} \frac{f(x + \delta x, y) - f(x, y)}{\delta x}$$

Similarly, partial derivative of z w.r.t. y is defined as

$$\lim_{\delta y \to 0} \frac{f(x, y + \delta y) - f(x, y)}{\delta y}, \text{ provided this limit exists and it is denoted}$$

by $\frac{\partial z}{\partial y}$ or $\frac{\partial f}{\partial y}$ or f_y

i.e. $\quad \frac{\partial f}{\partial y} = \lim_{\delta y \to 0} \frac{f(x, y + \delta y) - f(x, y)}{\delta y}$

$\frac{\partial z}{\partial x}, \frac{\partial z}{\partial y}$ are called the first order partial derivative of $z = f(x, y)$ with respect to x and y respectively.

Note : While differentiating z with respect to x partially treat y as a constant and while differentiating z w.r.t. y partially then treat x as a constant.

SOLVED EXAMPLES

Example 2.15 : Find $\frac{\partial z}{\partial x}$ and $\frac{\partial z}{\partial y}$ if $z = x^2 \cdot y^3$

Solution : Let $z = f(x, y) = x^2 y^3$, we know that,

$$\frac{\partial z}{\partial x} = \lim_{\delta x \to 0} \frac{f(x + \delta x, y) - f(x, y)}{\delta x}$$

$$= \lim_{\delta x \to 0} \frac{(x + \delta x)^2 y^3 - x^2 y^3}{\delta x}$$

$$= y^3 \lim_{\delta x \to 0} \frac{x^2 + 2x\delta x + \delta x^2 - x^2}{\delta x}$$

$$= y^3 \lim_{\delta x \to 0} \frac{\delta x \{2x + \delta x\}}{\delta x} \qquad \because \delta x \neq 0$$

$$= y^3 \cdot \{2x + 0\}$$

$$\frac{\partial z}{\partial x} = 2xy^3$$

and

$$\frac{\partial z}{\partial y} = \lim_{\delta y \to 0} \frac{f(x, y + \delta y) - f(x, y)}{\delta x}$$

$$= \lim_{\delta y \to 0} \frac{x^2 (y + \delta y)^3 - x^2 y^3}{\delta x}$$

$$= x^2 \lim_{\delta y \to 0} \frac{y^3 + 3y^2 y + 3y\delta y^2 + \delta y^3 - y^3}{\delta y}$$

$$= x^2 \lim_{\delta y \to 0} \frac{\delta y \{3y^2 + 3y\delta y + \delta y^2\}}{\delta y} \qquad \because \delta y \neq 0$$

$$= x^2 \{3y^2 + 0 + 0\}$$

$$\frac{\partial z}{\partial y} = 3x^2 y^2$$

Example 2.16 : If $z = e^{ax} \cdot \sin by$ find $\dfrac{\partial z}{\partial x}, \dfrac{\partial z}{\partial y}$

Solution : Let $z = f(x, y) = e^{ax} \cdot \sin by$

But, $\dfrac{\partial z}{\partial x} = \lim\limits_{\delta x \to 0} \dfrac{f(x + \delta x, y) - f(x, y)}{\delta x}$

$= \lim\limits_{\delta x \to 0} \dfrac{e^{a(x+\delta x)} \cdot \sin by - e^{ax} \cdot \sin by}{\delta x}$

$= \lim\limits_{\delta x \to 0} \dfrac{\sin by \{e^{ax} \cdot e^{a\delta x} - e^{ax}\}}{\delta x}$

$= \sin by \lim\limits_{\delta x \to 0} e^{ax} \cdot \dfrac{\{e^{a\delta x} - 1\}}{\delta x}$

$= \sin by \lim\limits_{\delta x \to 0} ae^{ax} \left\{\dfrac{e^{a\delta x} - 1}{a\delta x}\right\}$

$= \sin by \cdot ae^{ax}$ $\qquad \because \lim\limits_{h \to 0} \dfrac{e^h - 1}{n} = 1$

$\therefore \quad \dfrac{\partial z}{\partial x} = ae^{ax} \cdot \sin by$

Similarly, $\dfrac{\partial z}{\partial y} = \lim\limits_{\delta y \to 0} \dfrac{f(x, y + \delta y) - f(x, y)}{\delta y}$

$= \lim\limits_{\delta y \to 0} \dfrac{e^{ax} \sin b(y + \delta y) - e^{ax} \sin by}{\delta y}$

$= e^{ax} \lim\limits_{\delta y \to 0} \dfrac{\sin (by + b\delta y) - \sin by}{\delta y}$

$= e^{ax} \cdot \lim\limits_{\delta y \to 0} \dfrac{2 \cos\left(\dfrac{2by + b\delta y}{2}\right) \cdot \sin\left(\dfrac{b\delta y}{2}\right)}{\delta y}$

$= e^{ax} \cdot \lim\limits_{\delta y \to 0} \left[\dfrac{2 \cos\left(by + \dfrac{b}{2}\delta y\right) \cdot \sin\left(\dfrac{b \cdot \delta y}{2}\right)}{\dfrac{b\delta y}{2}}\right] \cdot \dfrac{b}{2}$

$= e^{ax} \cdot [2 \cos (by + 0)] \cdot \dfrac{b}{2}$

$\dfrac{\partial z}{\partial y} = b \, e^{ax} \cdot \cos by$

Partial derivatives of z = f(x, y) at a point (a, b) in the domain is defined as follows.

$$\left.\frac{\partial z}{\partial x}\right|_{(a,\,b)} = f_x(a,\,b) = \lim_{h \to 0} \frac{f(a+h,\,b) - f(a,\,b)}{h}, \text{ if it exists}$$

Similarly, $\left.\dfrac{\partial z}{\partial y}\right|_{(a,\,b)} = f_y(a,\,b) = \lim\limits_{k \to 0} \dfrac{f(a,\,b+k) - f(a,\,b)}{k}$, if it exists

Remark : Since the partial differentiation is the same as the ordinary differentiation when the other variables considered as constant.

Thus, all rules of the ordinary derivative holds for partial derivatives also.

For example :

1. $\dfrac{\partial}{\partial x}(u \pm v) = \dfrac{\partial u}{\partial x} \pm \dfrac{\partial v}{\partial y}$ or $\dfrac{\partial}{\partial y}(u \pm v) = \dfrac{\partial u}{\partial y} \pm \dfrac{\partial v}{\partial y}$

2. $\dfrac{\partial}{\partial x}(u \cdot v) = u\dfrac{\partial v}{\partial x} + v\dfrac{\partial u}{\partial x}$ or $\dfrac{\partial}{\partial y}(u \cdot v) = u\dfrac{\partial v}{\partial y} + v\dfrac{\partial u}{\partial y}$

3. $\dfrac{\partial}{\partial x}\left(\dfrac{u}{v}\right) = \dfrac{v\dfrac{\partial u}{\partial x} - u\dfrac{\partial u}{\partial x}}{v^2}$ or $\dfrac{\partial}{\partial y}\left(\dfrac{u}{v}\right) = \dfrac{v\dfrac{\partial u}{\partial y} - u\dfrac{\partial v}{\partial y}}{v^2}$

4. $\dfrac{\partial}{\partial x}[f(u)] = \dfrac{\partial f(u)}{\partial u} \cdot \dfrac{\partial u}{\partial x}$ or $\dfrac{\partial}{\partial y}[f(u)] = \dfrac{\partial f(u)}{\partial u} \cdot \dfrac{\partial u}{\partial y}$

2.4 PARTIAL DERIVATIVES OF HIGHER ORDER

Let z = f(x, y) and let the first order partial derivative f_x and f_y exits. They are again functions of x and y. Hence, they can be differentiated partially w.r.t. x and y. The second order partial derivatives of z w.r.t. x and y are defined below.

1. $\dfrac{\partial^2 z}{\partial x^2} = \dfrac{\partial}{\partial x}\left[\dfrac{\partial z}{\partial x}\right] = \dfrac{\partial f_x}{\partial x} = \lim\limits_{\delta x \to 0} \dfrac{f_x(x + \delta x,\,y) - f_x(x,\,y)}{\delta x}$

2. $\dfrac{\partial^2 z}{\partial y^2} = \dfrac{\partial}{\partial y}\left[\dfrac{\partial z}{\partial y}\right] = \dfrac{\partial f_y}{\partial y} = \lim\limits_{\delta y \to 0} \dfrac{f_y(x + \delta y,\,y) - f_y(x,\,y)}{\delta y}$

3. $\dfrac{\partial^2 z}{\partial x\,\partial y} = \dfrac{\partial}{\partial x}\left[\dfrac{\partial z}{\partial y}\right] = \dfrac{\partial f_y}{\partial x} = \lim\limits_{\delta x \to 0} \dfrac{f_y(x + \delta x,\,y) - f_y(x,\,y)}{\delta y}$

4. $\dfrac{\partial^2 z}{\partial y\, \partial x} = \dfrac{\partial}{\partial y}\left[\dfrac{\partial z}{\partial x}\right] = \dfrac{\partial f_x}{\partial y} = \lim_{\delta y \to 0} \dfrac{f_x(x, y + \delta y) - f_x(x, y)}{\delta y}$

Note : Generally, $\dfrac{\partial^2 y}{\partial x\, \partial y} = \dfrac{\partial^2 z}{\partial y\, \partial x}$ but need not be equal always.

SOLVED EXAMPLES

Example 2.17 : $z = f(x, y) = x^3 y^2$ then find $f_x, f_y, f_{xx}, f_{yx}, f_{yy}$ by using the definition.

Solution : Here, $f(x, y) = x^3 y^2$

$$f_x = \dfrac{\partial z}{\partial x} = \lim_{\delta x \to 0} \dfrac{f(x + \delta x, y) - f(x, y)}{\delta x}$$

$$= \lim_{\delta x \to 0} \dfrac{(x + \delta x)^3 y^2 - x^3 y^2}{\delta x}$$

$$= \lim_{\delta x \to 0} \dfrac{(x^3 + 3x^2 \delta x + 3x \delta x^2 + \delta x^3) y^2 - x^3 y^2}{\delta x}$$

$$= \lim_{\delta x \to 0} \dfrac{x^3 y^2 + 3x^2 y^2 \delta x + 3xy^2 \delta x^2 + \delta x^3 y^2 - x^3 y^2}{\delta x}$$

$$= \lim_{\delta x \to 0} \dfrac{\delta x (3x^2 y^2 + 3xy^2 \delta x + \delta x^2 y^2)}{\delta x}$$

$$= \lim_{\delta x \to 0} (3x^2 y^2 + 3xy^2 \delta x + \delta x^2 y^2)$$

$\therefore \quad f_x(x, y) = \dfrac{\partial z}{\partial x} = 3x^2 y^2$

We know that,

$$f_{xx} = \dfrac{\partial^2 z}{\partial x^2} = \lim_{\delta x \to 0} \dfrac{f_x(x + \delta x, y) - f_x(x, y)}{\delta x}$$

$$= \lim_{\delta x \to 0} \dfrac{3(x + \delta x)^2 y^2 - 3x^2 y^2}{\delta x}$$

$$= \lim_{\delta x \to 0} \dfrac{3(x^2 + 2x\delta x + \delta x^2) y^2 - 3x^2 y^2}{\delta x}$$

$$= \lim_{\delta x \to 0} \dfrac{3x^2 y^2 + 6xy^2 \delta x + 3\delta x^2 y^2 - 3x^2 y^2}{\delta x}$$

$$= \lim_{\delta x \to 0} \frac{\delta x \{6xy^2 + 3\delta xy^2\}}{\delta x}$$

$$= \lim_{\delta x \to 0} 6xy^2 + 3\delta xy^2$$

$$f_{xx}(x, y) = \frac{\partial^2 z}{\partial x^2} = 6xy^2$$

We know that,

$$f_{yx} = \frac{\partial^2 z}{\partial y\, \partial x} = \lim_{\delta y \to 0} \frac{f_x(x, y + \delta y) - f_x(x, y)}{\delta y}$$

$$= \lim_{\delta y \to 0} \frac{3x^2 (y + \delta y)^2 - 3x^2 y^2}{\delta y}$$

$$= \lim_{\delta y \to 0} \frac{3x^2 (y^2 + 2y\delta y + \delta y^2) - 3x^2 y^2}{\delta y}$$

$$= \lim_{\delta y \to 0} \frac{3x^2 y^2 + 6x^2 y \delta y + 3x^2 \delta y^2 - 3x^2 y^2}{\delta y}$$

$$= \lim_{\delta y \to 0} \frac{\delta y \{6x^2 y + 3x^2 \delta y\}}{\delta y}$$

$$= \lim_{\delta y \to 0} [6x^2 y + 3x^2\, \delta y]$$

$$f_{yx} = \frac{\partial^2 z}{\partial y\, \partial x} = 6x^2 y$$

Similarly, we get $f_{xy} = 6x^2 y$, $f_y = 2x^3 y$, $f_{yy} = 2x^3$

Example 2.18 : Without using the definition of partial derivative, find second order partial derivatives for the following functions :

(i) $x^3 + 3x^2 y^2 + 7y^3$, (ii) e^{xy}, (iii) $\log(x^2 + y^2)$

Solution : (i) Let $z = x^3 + 3x^2 y^2 + 7y^3$ then

$$\frac{\partial z}{\partial x} = 3x^2 + 6xy^2, \quad \frac{\partial^2 z}{\partial x^2} = 6x + 6y^2$$

$$\frac{\partial z}{\partial y} = 6x^2 y + 21y^2, \quad \frac{\partial^2 z}{\partial y^2} = 6x^2 + 42y$$

$$\frac{\partial^2 z}{\partial x\, \partial y} = \frac{\partial}{\partial x}\left(\frac{\partial z}{\partial y}\right) = \frac{\partial}{\partial x}(6x^2 y + 21y^2) = 12xy$$

$$\frac{\partial^2 z}{\partial y \, \partial x} = \frac{\partial}{\partial y}\left(\frac{\partial z}{\partial x}\right) = \frac{\partial}{\partial y}(3x^2 + 6xy^2) = 12xy$$

(ii) Let $z = e^{xy}$ then

$$\frac{\partial z}{\partial x} = ye^{xy}, \quad \frac{\partial^2 z}{\partial x^2} = y^2 e^{xy}$$

$$\frac{\partial z}{\partial y} = x e^{xy}, \quad \frac{\partial^2 z}{\partial y^2} = x^2 e^{xy}$$

$$\frac{\partial^2 z}{\partial x \, \partial y} = \frac{\partial}{\partial x}\left(\frac{\partial z}{\partial y}\right) = \frac{\partial}{\partial x}(x e^{xy})$$

$$= x(ye^{xy}) + e^{xy}$$

$$\frac{\partial^2 z}{\partial x \, \partial y} = (xy + 1) e^{xy}$$

$$\frac{\partial^2 z}{\partial y \, \partial x} = \frac{\partial}{\partial y}\left(\frac{\partial z}{\partial x}\right) = \frac{\partial}{\partial y}\{y e^{xy}\}$$

$$= y \cdot (xe^{xy}) + e^{xy}$$

$$\frac{\partial^2 z}{\partial y \, \partial x} = (xy + 1) e^{xy}$$

(iii) $z = \log(x^2 + y^2)$ then

$$\frac{\partial z}{\partial x} = \frac{2x}{x^2 + y^2}$$

$$\frac{\partial^2 z}{\partial x^2} = \frac{(x^2 + y^2) 2 - 2x(2x)}{(x^2 + y^2)^2}$$

$$= \frac{2x^2 + 2y^2 - 4x^2}{(x^2 + y^2)^2}$$

$$= \frac{2(y^2 - x^2)}{(x^2 + y^2)^2}$$

$$\frac{\partial z}{\partial y} = \frac{2y}{x^2 + y^2}$$

$$\frac{\partial^2 z}{\partial y^2} = \frac{(x^2 + y^2) 2 - 2y(2y)}{(x^2 + y^2)^2}$$

$$\frac{\partial^2 z}{\partial y^2} = \frac{2(x^2 - y^2)}{(x^2 + y^2)^2}$$

In this way, we can find $\dfrac{\partial^2 z}{\partial x \, \partial y}$ and $\dfrac{\partial^2 z}{\partial y \, \partial x}$

Example 2.19 : If $z = \dfrac{x^2 + y^2}{x + y}$ then show that,

$$\left(\dfrac{\partial z}{\partial x} - \dfrac{\partial z}{\partial y}\right)^2 = 4\left\{1 - \dfrac{\partial z}{\partial x} - \dfrac{\partial z}{\partial y}\right\}$$

Solution : $\dfrac{\partial z}{\partial x} = \dfrac{(x+y)\,2x - (x^2 + y^2)}{(x+y)^2} = \dfrac{x^2 + 2xy - y^2}{(x+y)^2}$

and $\dfrac{\partial z}{\partial y} = \dfrac{(x+y)\,2y - (x^2 + y^2)}{(x+y)^2} = \dfrac{y^2 + 2xy - x^2}{(x+y)^2}$

$\therefore \dfrac{\partial z}{\partial x} - \dfrac{\partial z}{\partial y} = \dfrac{x^2 + 2xy - y^2 - y^2 - 2xy + x^2}{(x+y)^2}$

$= \dfrac{2(x^2 - y^2)}{(x+y)^2}$

L.H.S $= \left(\dfrac{\partial z}{\partial x} - \dfrac{\partial z}{\partial y}\right)^2$

$\therefore \quad = \left[\dfrac{2(x^2 - y^2)}{(x+y)^2}\right]^2$

$= \dfrac{4(x^2 - y^2)^2}{(x+y)^4}$

$= \dfrac{4(x-y)^2\,(x+y)^2}{(x+y)^4}$

$= 4 \cdot \dfrac{(x-y)^2}{(x+y)^2}$

R.H.S. $= 4\left\{1 - \dfrac{\partial z}{\partial x} - \dfrac{\partial z}{\partial y}\right\}$

$= 4\left\{1 - \dfrac{x^2 + 2xy - y^2}{(x+y)^2} - \dfrac{y^2 + 2xy - x^2}{(x+y)^2}\right\}$

$= 4\left\{\dfrac{x^2 + 2xy + y^2 - x^2 - 2xy + y^2 - y^2 - 2xy + x^2}{(x+y)^2}\right\}$

$= 4\left\{\dfrac{x^2 - 2xy + y^2}{(x+y)^2}\right\}$

$= 4\,\dfrac{(x-y)^2}{(x+y)^2}$

$\therefore \quad$ L.H.S. $=$ R.H.S.

Example 2.20 : If $u = x^3 - 3xy^2$, $v = 3x^2y - y^3$, prove that :

(i) $\dfrac{\partial u}{\partial y} + \dfrac{\partial u}{\partial x} = 0$

(ii) $\dfrac{\partial u}{\partial x} - \dfrac{\partial u}{\partial y} = 0$

(iii) $\dfrac{\partial^2 v}{\partial x^2} + \dfrac{\partial^2 v}{\partial y^2} = 0$

(iv) $\dfrac{\partial^2 u}{\partial x^2} + \dfrac{\partial^2 u}{\partial y^2} = 0$

Solution : (i) $\dfrac{\partial u}{\partial y} = -6xy$, $\dfrac{\partial v}{\partial x} = 6xy$

$\therefore \quad \dfrac{\partial u}{\partial y} + \dfrac{\partial v}{\partial y} = 0$

(ii) $\dfrac{\partial u}{\partial x} = 3x^2 - 3y^2$, $\dfrac{\partial v}{\partial y} = 3x^2 - 3y^2$

$\therefore \quad \dfrac{\partial u}{\partial x} - \dfrac{\partial v}{\partial y} = (3x^2 - 3y^2) - (3x^2 - 3y^2) = 0$

(iii) $\dfrac{\partial^2 v}{\partial x^2} = \dfrac{\partial}{\partial x}\left(\dfrac{\partial v}{\partial x}\right) = \dfrac{\partial}{\partial x}(6xy) = 6y$

$\dfrac{\partial^2 v}{\partial y^2} = \dfrac{\partial}{\partial y}\left(\dfrac{\partial v}{\partial y}\right) = \dfrac{\partial}{\partial y}(3x^2 - 3y^2) = -6y$

$\therefore \quad \dfrac{\partial^2 v}{\partial x^2} + \dfrac{\partial^2 v}{\partial y^2} = 0$

(iv) $\dfrac{\partial^2 u}{\partial x^2} = \dfrac{\partial}{\partial x}(3x^2 - 3y^2) = 6x$

$\dfrac{\partial^2 u}{\partial y^2} = \dfrac{\partial}{\partial y}(-6xy) = -6x$

$\therefore \quad \dfrac{\partial^2 u}{\partial x^2} + \dfrac{\partial^2 u}{\partial y^2} = 0$

Example 2.21 : If $u = f(r)$ and $r = (x^2 + y^2)^{1/2}$, prove that

$$\dfrac{\partial^2 u}{\partial x^2} + \dfrac{\partial^2 u}{\partial y^2} = f''(r) + \dfrac{1}{r} f'(r)$$

Solution : $r^2 = x^2 + y^2$, $\quad \therefore 2r\dfrac{\partial r}{\partial x} = 2x$

$\therefore \quad \dfrac{\partial r}{\partial x} = \dfrac{x}{r}$ Similarly, $\dfrac{\partial r}{\partial y} = \dfrac{y}{r}$

$$\frac{\partial u}{\partial x} = \frac{du}{dr} \cdot \frac{\partial r}{\partial x} = f'(r) \cdot \frac{x}{r}$$

$$\therefore \quad \frac{\partial u}{\partial x} = f'(r) \cdot \frac{x}{r}$$

$$\frac{\partial^2 u}{\partial x^2} = f''(r) \cdot \frac{x}{r} \cdot \frac{\partial r}{\partial x} + f'(r) \cdot \left(\frac{-1}{r^2}\right) \cdot \frac{\partial r}{\partial x} \cdot x + f'(r) \cdot \frac{1}{r} \cdot 1$$

$$= f''(r) \cdot \frac{x}{r} \left(\frac{x}{r}\right) - f'(r) \cdot \frac{1}{r^2} \cdot \frac{x}{r} \cdot x + f'(r) \cdot \frac{1}{r}$$

$$\frac{\partial^2 u}{\partial x^2} = f''(r) \cdot \frac{x^2}{r^2} - \frac{x^2}{r^3} f'(r) + f'(r) \cdot \frac{1}{r}$$

Similarly, $\quad \dfrac{\partial^2 u}{\partial y^2} = f''(r) \cdot \dfrac{y^2}{r^2} - \dfrac{y^2}{r^3} f'(r) + f'(r) \cdot \dfrac{1}{r}$

$$\therefore \quad \frac{\partial^2 u}{\partial x^2} + \frac{\partial^2 u}{\partial y^2} = f''(r) \left\{\frac{x^2 + y^2}{r^2}\right\} - \left\{\frac{x^2 + y^2}{r^3}\right\} f'(r) + 2f'(r) \cdot \frac{1}{r}$$

But $\quad x^2 + y^2 = r^2$

$$\therefore \quad \frac{\partial^2 u}{\partial x^2} + \frac{\partial^2 u}{\partial y^2} = f''(r) - \frac{1}{r} f'(r) + 2f'(r) \cdot \frac{1}{r}$$

$$= f''(r) + \frac{1}{r} f'(r)$$

$$\therefore \quad \frac{\partial^2 u}{\partial x^2} + \frac{\partial^2 u}{\partial y^2} = f''(r) + \frac{1}{r} f'(r)$$

Example 2.22 : If $u = \log(\tan x + \tan y + \tan z)$, prove that
$$\sin 2x \frac{\partial u}{\partial x} + \sin 2y \frac{\partial u}{\partial y} + \sin 2z \frac{\partial u}{\partial z} = 2.$$

Solution : Let $v = \tan x + \tan y + \tan z \quad \therefore u = \log v$

$$\therefore \quad \frac{\partial v}{\partial x} = \sec^2 x, \quad \frac{\partial v}{\partial y} = \sec^2 y, \quad \frac{\partial v}{\partial y} = \sec^2 z$$

$$\frac{\partial u}{\partial x} = \frac{1}{v} \cdot \frac{\partial v}{\partial x} = \frac{1}{v} \cdot \sec^2 x$$

$$\frac{\partial u}{\partial y} = \frac{1}{v} \frac{\partial v}{\partial y} = \frac{1}{v} \cdot \sec^2 y$$

$$\frac{\partial u}{\partial z} = \frac{1}{v} \frac{\partial v}{\partial z} = \frac{1}{v} \cdot \sec^2 z$$

Consider, $\sin 2x \dfrac{\partial u}{\partial x} + \sin 2y \dfrac{\partial u}{\partial y} + \sin 2z \dfrac{\partial u}{\partial z}$

$$= \sin 2x \cdot \dfrac{\sec^2 x}{v} + \dfrac{\sin 2y \sec^2 y}{v} + \sin 2z \cdot \dfrac{\sec^2 z}{v}$$

But, $\quad \sin 2x = 2 \sin x \cos x$

$\therefore \quad \sin 2x \cdot \sec^2 x = 2 \cdot \tan x$

Similarly, $\sin 2y \sec^2 y = 2 \tan y$

$\sin 2z \sec^2 z = 2 \tan z$

$\therefore \quad \sin 2x \dfrac{\partial u}{\partial x} + \sin 2y \dfrac{\partial u}{\partial y} + \sin 2z \dfrac{\partial u}{\partial z}$

$$= \dfrac{2 \tan x}{v} = \dfrac{2 \tan y}{v} + \dfrac{2 \tan z}{v}$$

$$= \dfrac{2}{v} \{\tan x + \tan y + \tan z\}$$

But $\tan x + \tan y + \tan z = v$

$\therefore \quad \sin 2x \dfrac{\partial u}{\partial x} + \sin 2y \dfrac{\partial u}{\partial y} + \sin 2z \dfrac{\partial u}{\partial z} = 2$

EXERCISE 2.2

1. If $z = x\, e^{xy}$ then find $\dfrac{\partial z}{\partial x}, \dfrac{\partial z}{\partial y}, \dfrac{\partial^2 z}{\partial x\, \partial y}$ and $\dfrac{\partial^2 z}{\partial y\, \partial x}$.

2. By using the definitions of partial derivatives, find $\dfrac{\partial z}{\partial x}$ and $\dfrac{\partial z}{\partial y}$ for the following functions :

   (i) $\log x \sin y$, (ii) $e^x \cdot \cos y$, (iii) $\cos x \sin y$, (iv) $\dfrac{x^2}{y}$, (v) $\log (x + y)$

3. Find the first order partial derivatives of :

   (i) $ax^2 + by^2 + 2hxy$, (ii) $\dfrac{x}{y}$, (iii) $\dfrac{y}{x}$, (iv) $\tan^{-1}\left(\dfrac{y}{x}\right)$, (v) $(x^2 + y^2 + z^2)^{3/2}$

4. If $z = \log (x^2 + y^2)$, then show that $\dfrac{\partial^2 z}{\partial x\, \partial y} = \dfrac{\partial^2 z}{\partial y\, \partial x}$.

5. if $u = \log(x^3 + y^3 + z^3 - 3xyz)$, then show that,
$$\left(\frac{\partial}{\partial x} + \frac{\partial}{\partial y} + \frac{\partial}{\partial z}\right)^2 u = \frac{9}{(x+y+z)^2}$$

6. If $u = x^2 \tan^{-1}\left(\frac{y}{x}\right) - y^2 \tan^{-1}\left(\frac{x}{y}\right)$, then prove that $\frac{\partial^2 u}{\partial x \partial y} = \frac{\partial^2 u}{\partial y \partial x}$

7. If $u = \tan^{-1}\left(\frac{y}{x}\right)$, show that $\frac{\partial^2 u}{\partial x^2} + \frac{\partial^2 u}{\partial y^2} = 0$

8. If $u = x f\left(\frac{y}{x}\right)$, show that $x \frac{\partial u}{\partial x} + y \frac{\partial u}{\partial y} = u$.

9. If $u = xy f\left(\frac{y}{x}\right)$, show that $x \frac{\partial u}{\partial x} + y \frac{\partial u}{\partial y} = 2u$

10. If $z = \tan(y + ax) + (y - ax)^{3/2}$, prove that $\frac{\partial^2 z}{\partial x^2} = a^2 \frac{\partial^2 z}{\partial y^2}$

11. Given that $u = \frac{1}{\sqrt{x^2 + y^2 + z^2}}$, verify that $\frac{\partial^2 u}{\partial x^2} + \frac{\partial^2 u}{\partial y^2} + \frac{\partial^2 u}{\partial z^2} = 0$

12. If $u = f(x + 2y) + g(x - 2y)$, show that $4 \frac{\partial^2 u}{\partial x^2} = \frac{\partial^2 u}{\partial y^2}$

13. Examine the equality of f_{xy}, f_{yx} where, $f(x, y) = x^3 y + e^{xy^2}$

14. If $u = \log r$, $r = x^3 + y^3 - x^2 y - xy^2$, prove that $\left(\frac{\partial}{\partial x} + \frac{\partial}{\partial y}\right)^2 u = \frac{-4}{(x+y)^2}$

15. If $u = (x^2 + y^2 + z^2)^{-1/2}$, prove that $\frac{\partial^2 u}{\partial x^2} + \frac{\partial^2 u}{\partial y^2} + \frac{\partial^2 u}{\partial z^2} = 0$

ANSWERS 2.2

1. $\frac{\partial z}{\partial x} = e^{xy} + xy\, e^{xy}$, $\frac{\partial z}{\partial y} = x^2 e^{xy}$, $\frac{\partial^2 z}{\partial x \partial y} = 2x\, e^{xy} + x^2 y\, e^{xy} = \frac{\partial^2 z}{\partial y \partial x}$

2. (i) $\frac{\sin y}{x}$, $\cos y \log x$ (ii) $e^x \cos y, - e^x \sin y$

   (iii) $- \sin x \sin y, \cos x \cos y$ (iv) $\frac{2x}{y}, \frac{-x^2}{y^2}$

   (v) $\frac{1}{x+y}, \frac{1}{x+y}$

3. (i) $2ax + 2hy, 2by + 2hx$ (ii) $\dfrac{1}{y}, \dfrac{-x}{y^2}$

   (iii) $\dfrac{-y}{x^2}, \dfrac{1}{x}$ (iv) $\dfrac{-y}{x^2 + y^2}, \dfrac{x}{x^2 + y^2}$

   (v) $3x(x^2 + y^2 + z^2)^{1/2}, 3y(x^2 + y^2 + z^2)^{1/2}, 3z(x^2 + y^2 + z^2)^{1/2}$

2.5 COMPOSITE FUNCTIONS

Definition 1 : Let $z = f(x, y)$ and $x = h(t), y = g(t)$, so that z is a function of x, y and x, y are themselves a function of a single variable t. These three relations define z as a function of t. In such cases z is called a composite function of t.

Example : (i) $z = x + y$ $x = t^2$, $y = 2t$

(ii) $z = \cos(x + y)$ $x = 2\theta$, $y = 5\theta$

(iii) $z = e^x \cdot \cos y$ $x = 2t$, $y = 9t^2$

In first and third z is a composite function of t while in second z is a composite function of θ.

Definition 2 : $z = f(x, y)$ and $x = h(u, v), y = g(u, v)$, so that z is a function of x, y and x, y are themselves functions of u, v. These three relations defines z as function of u, v. Then z is called a composite function of u, v.

Example : (i) $z = x^2 + y^2$, $x = e^u + e^v$, $y = e^{-u} - e^{-v}$

(ii) $z = x + y$, $x = r\cos\theta$, $y = r\sin\theta$

(iii) $z = x^2 - y^2$, $x = 2u + 3v$, $y = 3u + 7v$

In first and third z is a composite function of u, v, while in second z is a composite function of r, θ.

2.5.1 Differentiation of Composite Functions

Theorem 1 : Let $z = f(x, y)$ possesses continuous first order partial derivatives and $x = h(t), y = g(t)$ possesses continuous first order partial derivatives then.

$$\dfrac{dz}{dt} = \dfrac{\partial z}{\partial x} \cdot \dfrac{dx}{dt} + \dfrac{\partial z}{\partial y} \cdot \dfrac{dy}{dt}$$

Proof : Let $z = f(x, y)$ and $x = h(t), y = g(t)$ then z is a composite function of t.

Let t changes to t + δt due to this change x changes to x + δx and y changes y + δy. These change effects z changes to z + δz

∴ $\quad z + \delta z = f(x, + \delta x, y + \delta y)$

∴ $\quad \delta z = f(x + \delta x, y + \delta y) - z$

$\quad \delta z = f(x + \delta x, y + \delta y) - f(x, y)$

∴ $\quad \delta z = f(x + \delta x, y + \delta y) - f(x, y + \delta y) + f(x, y + \delta y) - f(x, y)$

Then by second form of Lagranges mean value theorem for functions of two variables, we get

$$\delta z = \delta x\, f_x(x + \theta \delta x, y + \delta y) + \delta y\, f_y(x, y + \theta \delta y)$$

where, $0 < \theta < 1$

Dividing throughout by δt to above equation, we get

∴ $\quad \dfrac{\delta z}{\delta t} = \dfrac{\delta x}{\delta t} f_x(x + \theta \delta x, y + \delta y) + \dfrac{\delta y}{\delta t} f_y(x, y + \theta \delta y)$

Taking limit as $\delta t \to 0$ on both sides, so $\delta x \to 0$ and $\delta y \to 0$ also

$$\lim_{\substack{\delta t \to 0}} \dfrac{\delta z}{\delta t} = \lim_{\substack{\delta t \to 0 \\ \delta x \to 0 \\ \delta y \to 0}} \dfrac{\delta x}{\delta t} \cdot f_x(x + \theta \delta x, y + \delta y) + \lim_{\substack{\delta t \to 0 \\ \delta x \to 0 \\ \delta y \to 0}} \dfrac{\delta y}{\delta t} f_y(x, y + \theta \delta y)$$

But we know that,

$$\lim_{\delta t \to 0} \dfrac{\delta z}{\delta t} = \dfrac{\partial z}{\partial x},\ \lim_{\delta t \to 0} \dfrac{\delta x}{\delta t} = \dfrac{dx}{dt},\ \lim_{\delta t \to 0} \dfrac{\delta y}{\delta t} = \dfrac{dy}{dt}$$

and putting $\delta x = 0$ and $\delta y = 0$, we get

$$\dfrac{dz}{dt} = \dfrac{dx}{dt} \cdot f_x(x, y) + \dfrac{dy}{dt} \cdot f_y(x, y)$$

$$= \dfrac{dx}{dt} \dfrac{\partial z}{\partial x} + \dfrac{dy}{dt} \dfrac{\partial z}{\partial y}$$

∴ $\quad \dfrac{dz}{dt} = \dfrac{\partial z}{\partial x} \dfrac{dx}{dt} + \dfrac{\partial z}{\partial y} \cdot \dfrac{dy}{dt}$

Theorem 2 : Let $z = f(x, y)$ possess continuous first order partial derivatives and $x = h(u, v)$, $y = g(u, v)$ possess continuous first order partial derivatives, then

(i) $\dfrac{\partial z}{\partial u} = \dfrac{\partial z}{\partial x} \cdot \dfrac{\partial x}{\partial u} + \dfrac{\partial z}{\partial y} \dfrac{\partial y}{\partial u}$ and

(ii) $\dfrac{\partial z}{\partial v} = \dfrac{\partial z}{\partial x} \cdot \dfrac{\partial x}{\partial v} + \dfrac{\partial z}{\partial y} \dfrac{\partial y}{\partial v}$

Proof : (i) Let $z = f(x, y)$ and $x = h(u, v)$, $y = g(u, v)$ then z is a composite function of two variables u and v, let u changes $u + \delta u$ then x changes $x + \delta x$ and y changes to $y + \delta y$, these changes effects z change to $z + \delta z$.

$$\therefore \quad z + \delta z = f(x + \delta x, y + \delta y)$$

$$\delta z = f(x + \delta x, y + \delta y) - f(x, y)$$

$$\delta z = [f(x + \delta x, y + \delta y) - f(x + \delta x, y)] + [f(x + \delta x, y) - f(x, y)]$$

By using L.M.V.T., we get

$$\delta z = \delta y \cdot f_y(x + \delta x, y + \theta \delta y) + \delta x \, f_x(x + \theta \delta x, y)$$

where, $0 < \theta < 1$

Dividing throughout by δu, we get

$$\dfrac{\delta z}{\delta u} = \dfrac{\delta y}{\delta u} f_y(x + \delta x, y + \theta \delta y) + \dfrac{\delta x}{\delta u} f_x(x + \theta \delta x, y)$$

Taking limits as $\delta u \to 0$ on both sides, so $\delta x \to 0$ and $\delta y \to 0$

$$\therefore \quad \lim_{\delta u \to 0} \dfrac{\delta z}{\delta u} = \lim_{\substack{\delta u \to 0 \\ \delta x \to 0 \\ \delta y \to 0}} \dfrac{\delta x}{\delta u} \cdot f_x(x + \theta \delta x, y) + \lim_{\substack{\delta u \to 0 \\ \delta x \to 0 \\ \delta y \to 0}} \dfrac{\delta y}{\delta u} f_y(x + \delta x, y + \theta \delta y)$$

But we know that,

$$\lim_{\delta u \to 0} \dfrac{\delta z}{\delta u} = \dfrac{\partial z}{\partial u}, \; \lim_{\delta u \to 0} \dfrac{\delta y}{\delta u} = \dfrac{\partial y}{\partial u}, \; \lim_{\delta u \to 0} \dfrac{\delta x}{\delta u} = \dfrac{\partial x}{\partial u}$$

$$\therefore \quad \dfrac{\partial z}{\partial u} = \dfrac{\partial y}{\partial u} \cdot f_y(x, y) + \dfrac{\partial x}{\partial u} f_x(x, y)$$

$$\therefore \quad \frac{\partial z}{\partial u} = \frac{\partial y}{\partial u} \cdot \frac{\partial z}{\partial y} + \frac{\partial x}{\partial u} \cdot \frac{\partial z}{\partial x}$$

$$\therefore \quad \frac{\partial z}{\partial u} = \frac{\partial z}{\partial x} \cdot \frac{\partial x}{\partial u} + \frac{\partial z}{\partial y} \cdot \frac{\partial y}{\partial u}$$

Similarly, we can prove (ii).

SOLVED EXAMPLES

Example 2.23 : If $z = x^2 + y^2$, $x = at^2$, $y = 2at$, find $\frac{dz}{dt}$.

Solution : Here z is a composite function of t

$$\therefore \quad \frac{dz}{dt} = \frac{\partial z}{\partial x} \cdot \frac{dx}{dt} + \frac{\partial z}{\partial y} \cdot \frac{dy}{dt}$$

$$= (2x)(2at) + (2y)(2a)$$

$$= 4at\, x + 4ay$$

But $x = at^2$ and $y = 2at$

$$\therefore \quad \frac{dz}{dt} = 4at\,(at^2) + 4a\,(2at)$$

$$= 4a^2 t^3 + 8a^2 t$$

$$\frac{dz}{dt} = 4a^2 t\,(t^2 + 2)$$

Example 2.24 : If $z = e^{xy^2}$, $x = t \cos t$, $y = t \sin t$, compute $\frac{dz}{dt}$ at $t = \frac{\pi}{2}$

Solution : Here z is a composite function of t

$$\therefore \quad \frac{dz}{dt} = \frac{\partial z}{\partial x} \cdot \frac{dx}{dt} + \frac{\partial z}{\partial y} \cdot \frac{dy}{dt}$$

Here $\frac{\partial z}{\partial x} = y^2 e^{xy^2}$, $\frac{\partial z}{\partial y} = 2xy\, e^{xy^2}$

$$\frac{dx}{dt} = -t \sin t + \cos t, \quad \frac{dy}{dt} = t \cos t + \sin t$$

$$\therefore \quad \frac{dz}{dt} = (y^2 e^{xy^2})(\cos t - t \sin t) + 2xy\, e^{xy^2} (t \cos t + \sin t)$$

At $t = \dfrac{\pi}{2} \Rightarrow x = 0, y = \dfrac{\pi}{2}$

$$\therefore \left.\dfrac{dz}{dt}\right|_{t=\frac{\pi}{2}} = \dfrac{\pi^2}{4}\left(\dfrac{-\pi}{2}\right)$$

$$= \dfrac{-\pi^3}{8}$$

Example 2.25 : If $z = \tan^{-1}\left(\dfrac{x}{y}\right)$, $x = 2t$, $y = 1 - t^2$,

prove that $\dfrac{dz}{dt} = \dfrac{2}{1 + t^2}$

Solution : Here z is a composite function of t

$$\therefore \dfrac{dz}{dt} = \dfrac{\partial z}{\partial x}\dfrac{dx}{dt} + \dfrac{\partial z}{\partial y}\dfrac{dy}{dt}$$

$$\dfrac{\partial z}{\partial x} = \dfrac{1}{1 + \left(\dfrac{x}{y}\right)^2} \cdot \dfrac{1}{y} = \dfrac{y}{x^2 + y^2}$$

$$\dfrac{\partial z}{\partial y} = \dfrac{1}{1 + \left(\dfrac{x}{y}\right)^2} \cdot \left(\dfrac{-x}{y^2}\right) = \dfrac{-x}{x^2 + y^2}$$

$$\dfrac{dx}{dt} = 2 \text{ and } \dfrac{dy}{dt} = (-2t)$$

$$\therefore \dfrac{dz}{dt} = \dfrac{y}{x^2 + y^2}(2) + \left(\dfrac{-x}{x^2 + y^2}\right)(-2t)$$

But $x = 2t$ and $y = 1 - t^2$

$$\therefore \dfrac{dz}{dt} = \dfrac{2(1 - t^2)}{(2t)^2 + (1 - t^2)^2} + \dfrac{2t(2t)}{(2t)^2 + (1 - t^2)^2}$$

$$= \dfrac{2 - 2t^2 + 4t^2}{4t^2 + 1 - 2t^2 + t^4} = \dfrac{2t^2 + 2}{t^4 + 2t^2 + 1}$$

$$= \dfrac{2(t^2 + 1)}{(t^2 + 1)^2}$$

$$\dfrac{dz}{dt} = \dfrac{2}{t^2 + 1}$$

Example 2.26 : If $z = f(x, y)$, $x = e^u \cos v$, $y = e^u \sin v$,

prove that $x \dfrac{\partial z}{\partial v} + y \dfrac{\partial z}{\partial u} = e^{2u} \cdot \dfrac{\partial z}{\partial y}$

Solution : Here z is a composite function of two variables u and v

$$\therefore \quad \frac{\partial z}{\partial u} = \frac{\partial z}{\partial x}\frac{\partial x}{\partial u} + \frac{\partial z}{\partial y}\frac{\partial y}{\partial u}$$

and $$\frac{\partial z}{\partial v} = \frac{\partial z}{\partial x}\frac{\partial x}{\partial v} + \frac{\partial z}{\partial y} \cdot \frac{\partial y}{\partial v}$$

$$\frac{\partial z}{\partial u} = \frac{\partial z}{\partial x} \cdot \{e^u \cos v\} + \frac{\partial z}{\partial y} \{e^u \sin v\}$$

and $$\frac{\partial z}{\partial v} = \frac{\partial z}{\partial x} \{-e^u \sin v\} + \frac{\partial z}{\partial y} \{e^u \cos v\}$$

Consider,

$$x\frac{\partial z}{\partial v} + y\frac{\partial z}{\partial u} = e^u \cos v \left\{-e^u \sin v \frac{\partial z}{\partial x} + e^u \cos v \frac{\partial z}{\partial y}\right\}$$

$$+ e^u \sin v \left\{e^u \cos v \frac{\partial z}{\partial x} + e^u \sin v \frac{\partial z}{\partial y}\right\}$$

$$= -e^{2u} \sin v \cos v \frac{\partial z}{\partial x} + e^{2u} \cos^2 v \frac{\partial z}{\partial y}$$

$$+ e^{2u} \sin v \cos v \frac{\partial z}{\partial x} + e^{2u} \sin^2 v \frac{\partial z}{\partial y}$$

$$= e^{2u} \{\cos^2 v + \sin^2 v\} \frac{\partial z}{\partial y}$$

$$= e^{2u} \frac{\partial z}{\partial y}$$

$$\therefore \quad x\frac{\partial z}{\partial v} + y\frac{\partial z}{\partial u} = e^{2u} \cdot \frac{\partial z}{\partial y}$$

Example 2.27 : If $z = f(x, y)$ and $x = e^u + e^{-v}$, $y = e^{-u} - e^v$,

show that, $\dfrac{\partial z}{\partial u} - \dfrac{\partial z}{\partial v} = x\dfrac{\partial z}{\partial x} - y\dfrac{\partial z}{\partial y}$

Solution : Here z is a composite function of u and v

$$\therefore \quad \frac{\partial z}{\partial u} = \frac{\partial z}{\partial x}\frac{\partial x}{\partial u} + \frac{\partial z}{\partial y} \cdot \frac{\partial y}{\partial u}$$

and $\dfrac{\partial z}{\partial v} = \dfrac{\partial z}{\partial x} \cdot \dfrac{\partial x}{\partial v} + \dfrac{\partial z}{\partial y} \cdot \dfrac{\partial y}{\partial v}$

$\therefore \quad \dfrac{\partial z}{\partial u} = \dfrac{\partial z}{\partial x}(e^u) + \dfrac{\partial z}{\partial y}(-e^{-u})$

$\dfrac{\partial z}{\partial v} = \dfrac{\partial z}{\partial x}(-e^{-v}) + \dfrac{\partial z}{\partial y}(-e^v)$

$\therefore \quad \dfrac{\partial z}{\partial u} - \dfrac{\partial z}{\partial v} = e^u \dfrac{\partial z}{\partial x} - e^{-u}\dfrac{\partial z}{\partial y} + e^{-v}\dfrac{\partial z}{\partial x} + e^v \dfrac{\partial z}{\partial y}$

$\qquad = \{e^u + e^{-v}\}\dfrac{\partial z}{\partial x} - \{e^{-u} - e^v\}\dfrac{\partial z}{\partial y}$

$\therefore \quad \dfrac{\partial z}{\partial u} - \dfrac{\partial z}{\partial v} = x\dfrac{\partial z}{\partial x} - y\dfrac{\partial z}{\partial y}$

Example 2.28 : If $z = f(x, y)$, $x = r\cos\theta$, $y = r\sin\theta$ prove that $\left(\dfrac{\partial z}{\partial x}\right)^2 + \left(\dfrac{\partial z}{\partial y}\right)^2 = \left(\dfrac{\partial z}{\partial r}\right)^2 + \dfrac{1}{r^2}\left(\dfrac{\partial z}{\partial \theta}\right)^2$

Solution : Here z is a composite function of r and θ

$\therefore \quad \dfrac{\partial z}{\partial r} = \dfrac{\partial z}{\partial x}\dfrac{\partial x}{\partial r} + \dfrac{\partial z}{\partial y} \cdot \dfrac{\partial y}{\partial r}$

and $\dfrac{\partial z}{\partial \theta} = \dfrac{\partial z}{\partial x}\dfrac{\partial x}{\partial \theta} + \dfrac{\partial r}{\partial y} \cdot \dfrac{\partial y}{\partial \theta}$

$\therefore \quad \dfrac{\partial z}{\partial r} = \dfrac{\partial z}{\partial x}(\cos\theta) + \left(\dfrac{\partial z}{\partial y}\right)(\sin\theta) \qquad \ldots \text{(i)}$

$\dfrac{\partial z}{\partial \theta} = \dfrac{\partial z}{\partial x}(-r\sin\theta) + \dfrac{\partial z}{\partial y}(r\cos\theta) \qquad \ldots \text{(ii)}$

Consider,

$\left(\dfrac{\partial z}{\partial r}\right)^2 + \dfrac{1}{r^2}\left(\dfrac{\partial z}{\partial \theta}\right)^2 = \left\{\cos\theta\dfrac{\partial z}{\partial x} + \sin\theta\dfrac{\partial z}{\partial y}\right\}^2 + \dfrac{1}{r^2}\left\{-r\sin\theta\dfrac{\partial z}{\partial x} + r\cos\theta\dfrac{\partial z}{\partial y}\right\}^2$

$\qquad = \cos^2\theta\left(\dfrac{\partial z}{\partial x}\right)^2 + 2\sin\theta\cos\theta\dfrac{\partial z}{\partial x}\dfrac{\partial z}{\partial y} + \sin^2\theta\left(\dfrac{\partial z}{\partial y}\right)^2$

$\qquad + \dfrac{1}{r^2}\left\{r^2\sin^2\theta\left(\dfrac{\partial z}{\partial x}\right)^2 - 2r^2\sin\theta\cos\theta\dfrac{\partial z}{\partial x}\dfrac{\partial z}{\partial y} + r^2\cos^2\theta\left(\dfrac{\partial z}{\partial y}\right)^2\right\}$

$$= \{\cos^2\theta + \sin^2\theta\}\left(\frac{\partial z}{\partial x}\right)^2 + \{\sin^2\theta + \cos^2\theta\}\left(\frac{\partial z}{\partial y}\right)^2$$

$$= \left(\frac{\partial z}{\partial x}\right)^2 + \left(\frac{\partial z}{\partial y}\right)^2$$

$$\therefore \left(\frac{\partial z}{\partial x}\right)^2 + \left(\frac{\partial z}{\partial y}\right)^2 = \left(\frac{\partial z}{\partial r}\right)^2 + \frac{1}{r^2}\left(\frac{\partial z}{\partial \theta}\right)^2$$

Example 2.29 : If $x = r\cos\theta$, $y = r\sin\theta$, prove that $\dfrac{\partial^2\theta}{\partial x^2} + \dfrac{\partial^2\theta}{\partial y^2} = 0$

for $x \neq 0$, $y \neq 0$

Solution : $x = r\cos\theta$, $y = r\sin\theta$

$\therefore \quad \dfrac{y}{x} = \tan\theta$

so, $\quad \theta = \tan^{-1}\left(\dfrac{y}{x}\right)$ ... (i)

Differentiate equation (i) partially w.r.t. x, we get

$$\frac{\partial \theta}{\partial x} = \frac{1}{1 + \left(\frac{y}{x}\right)^2} \cdot \left(\frac{-y}{x^2}\right) = \frac{-y}{x^2 + y^2}$$

$\therefore \quad \dfrac{\partial^2 \theta}{\partial x^2} = \dfrac{\partial}{\partial x}\left(\dfrac{\partial \theta}{\partial x}\right)$

$$= \frac{\partial}{\partial x}\left(\frac{-y}{x^2 + y^2}\right)$$

$$= -y\frac{\partial}{\partial x}[(x^2 + y^2)^{-1}]$$

$$= -y(-2x)(x^2 + y^2)^{-2}$$

$$\frac{\partial^2 \theta}{\partial x^2} = \frac{+2xy}{(x^2 + y^2)^2} \qquad \ldots \text{(ii)}$$

Similarly, $\dfrac{\partial \theta}{\partial y} = \dfrac{1}{1 + \left(\dfrac{y}{x}\right)^2} \cdot \left(\dfrac{1}{x}\right) = \dfrac{x}{x^2 + y^2}$

$$\frac{\partial^2 \theta}{\partial y^2} = \frac{\partial}{\partial y}\left[\frac{\partial \theta}{\partial y}\right]$$

$$= \frac{\partial}{\partial y} [x (x^2 + y^2)^{-1}]$$

$$= -2xy (x^2 + y^2)^{-2}$$

$$\frac{\partial^2 \theta}{\partial y^2} = \frac{-2xy}{(x^2 + y)^2} \qquad \ldots \text{(iii)}$$

Adding equations (ii) and (iii), we get

$$\frac{\partial^2 \theta}{\partial x^2} + \frac{\partial^2 \theta}{\partial y^2} = 0 \quad \text{for } x \neq 0 \text{ and } y \neq 0$$

If $x = 0$ and $y = 0$, then $\frac{\partial^2 \theta}{\partial x^2}$ and $\frac{\partial^2 \theta}{\partial y^2}$ are indeterminate forms $\left(\frac{0}{0} \text{ form}\right)$.

EXERCISE 2.3

1. If $z = xe^y$, $x = u^2 + v^2$, $y = u^2 - v^2$, then prove that
$$\frac{\partial z}{\partial v} = 2ve^y (1 - u^2 - v^2)$$

2. If $z = \tan^{-1}\left(\frac{x}{y}\right)$, $x = 2t$, $y = 1 - t^2$, prove that $\frac{dz}{dt} = \frac{2}{1 + t^2}$

3. If $z = x + y^2$; $x = u^2 + \sin v$, $y = \log (u + v)$, find $\frac{\partial z}{\partial u}, \frac{\partial z}{\partial v}$.

4. If $z = \frac{\cos y}{x}$; $x = u^2 - v$, $y = e^v$, find $\frac{\partial z}{\partial v}$

5. If $z = \frac{2x + y}{y - 2x}$; $x = 2u - 3v$, $y = u + 2v$, find $\frac{\partial z}{\partial u}, \frac{\partial z}{\partial v}$ at $u = 2, v = 1$

6. If $z = \tan^{-1}\left(\frac{x}{y}\right)$, $x = u + v$, $y = uv$, then show that $\frac{\partial z}{\partial u} = \frac{-v^2}{(u + v)^2 + u^2v^2}$

7. If $z = f(x, y)$; $x = \log u$, $y = \log v$, prove that $\frac{\partial^2 y}{\partial x \partial y} = uv \frac{\partial^2 z}{\partial u \partial v}$.

8. If $u = f(x - y, y - z, z - x)$, prove that $\frac{\partial u}{\partial x} + \frac{\partial u}{\partial y} + \frac{\partial u}{\partial z} = 0$

9. If $z = f(u, v)$; $u = lx + my$, $v = ly - mx$,
show that $\frac{\partial^2 z}{\partial x^2} + \frac{\partial^2 z}{\partial y^2} = (l^2 + m^2) \left(\frac{\partial^2 z}{\partial u^2} + \frac{\partial^2 z}{\partial v^2}\right)$

ANSWERS 2.3

3. $2u + \dfrac{2y}{u+v}$, $\cos v + \dfrac{2y}{u+v}$
4. $\dfrac{\cos y}{x^2} - \dfrac{e^v \sin y}{x}$
5. $7, -14$

2.6 HOMOGENEOUS FUNCTIONS

Definition :

An expression in which degree of each term is same is called a homogeneous function.

Thus, $a_0 x^n + a_1 x^{n-1} y + a_2 x^{n-2} y^2 + \ldots + a_{n-1} x y^{n-1} + a_n y^n$

is a homogeneous function in x and y of degree n. This can also be written as

$$x^n \left\{ a_0 + a_1 \left(\frac{y}{x}\right) + a_2 \left(\frac{y}{x}\right)^2 + \ldots + a_{n-1} \left(\frac{y}{x}\right)^{n-1} + a_n \left(\frac{y}{x}\right)^n \right\}$$

or $x^n f\left(\dfrac{y}{x}\right)$ where $f\left(\dfrac{y}{x}\right)$ is some function of $\left(\dfrac{y}{x}\right)$

Note 1 : Let $f(x, y)$ be a homogeneous function in x and y of degree n then

$$f(x, y) = x^n F\left(\dfrac{y}{x}\right)$$

Note 2 : To test the given function $f(x, y)$ is homogeneous or not put tx for x and ty for y in it, we get

$$f(tx, ty) = t^n f(x, y)$$

Then the function is a homogeneous function of degree n; otherwise $f(x, y)$ is not a homogeneous function.

For example, $f(x, y) = x^3 + 3x^2 y + 3y^3$

$f(xt, yt) = (xt)^3 + 3(xt)^2 (yt) + 3(yt)^3$

$= t^3 \{x^3 + 3x^2 y + 3y^3\}$

$= t^3 f(x, y)$

∴ $f(xt, yt) = t^3 f(x, y)$

So $f(x, y)$ is a homogeneous function of degree 3.

Note 3 : If u is a homogeneous function in x and y of degree n then $\frac{\partial u}{\partial x}$ and $\frac{\partial u}{\partial y}$ are also homogeneous functions in x and y each being of degree (n – 1).

For example, let $z = x^4 + x^2y^2 + xy^3 + y^4$ be a homogeneous function of degree four in x and y then

$$\frac{\partial z}{\partial x} = 4x^3 + 2xy^2 + y^3 \text{ and } \frac{\partial z}{\partial y} = 2x^2y + 3xy^2 + 4y^3$$

Clearly $\frac{\partial z}{\partial x}$ and $\frac{\partial z}{\partial y}$ are both homogeneous function of degree 4 – 1 = 3.

2.6.1 Euler's Theorem on Homogeneous Functions

Statement : If u is a homogeneous function of degree n in x and y then

$$x\frac{\partial u}{\partial x} + y\frac{\partial u}{\partial y} = nu$$

Proof : Since u is a homogeneous function in x and y of degree n it can be expressed as

$$u = x^n f\left(\frac{y}{x}\right) \qquad \ldots (i)$$

Differentiating u w.r.t. x partially, we have

$$\frac{\partial u}{\partial x} = x^n f'\left(\frac{y}{x}\right) \cdot \left(\frac{-y}{x^2}\right) + n x^{n-1} f\left(\frac{y}{x}\right)$$

$$\therefore \quad x\frac{\partial u}{\partial x} = -x^{n-1} y f'\left(\frac{y}{x}\right) + n x^n f\left(\frac{y}{x}\right) \qquad \ldots (ii)$$

Again differentiating (i) w.r.t. y partially, we have

$$\frac{\partial u}{\partial y} = x^n \cdot f'\left(\frac{y}{x}\right) \cdot \frac{1}{x}$$

$$= x^{n-1} f'\left(\frac{y}{x}\right)$$

$$\therefore \quad y\frac{\partial u}{\partial y} = x^{n-1} \cdot y f'\left(\frac{y}{x}\right) \qquad \ldots (iii)$$

Adding equations (ii) and (iii), we get

$$x \frac{\partial u}{\partial x} + y \frac{\partial u}{\partial y} = n x^n f\left(\frac{y}{x}\right) \qquad \text{but } x^n f\left(\frac{y}{x}\right) = u$$

$$\therefore \quad x \frac{\partial u}{\partial x} + y \frac{\partial u}{\partial y} = nu$$

Note : Euler's theorem can be extended to homogeneous function of any number of variables.

For example, let $u = f(x, y, z)$ be a homogeneous function of degree n then

$$x \frac{\partial u}{\partial x} + y \frac{\partial u}{\partial y} + z \frac{\partial u}{\partial z} = nu.$$

SOLVED EXAMPLES

Example 2.30 : Verify Euler's theorem for

$$u = x^4 - 3x^2y^2 + 5x^3y + 4xy^3 + y^4$$

Solution : Here, u is a homogeneous function in x and y of degree 4, so by Euler's theorem

$$x \frac{\partial u}{\partial x} + y \frac{\partial u}{\partial y} = 4u \qquad \ldots \text{(i)}$$

Here, $\quad u = x^4 - 3x^2y^2 + 5x^3y + 4xy^3 + y^4$

$$\therefore \quad \frac{\partial u}{\partial x} = 4x^3 - 6xy^2 + 15x^2y + 4y^3$$

$$\therefore \quad x \frac{\partial u}{\partial x} = 4x^4 - 6x^2y^2 + 15x^3y + 4xy^3 \qquad \ldots \text{(ii)}$$

and $\quad \dfrac{\partial u}{\partial y} = -6x^2y + 5x^3 + 12xy^2 + 4y^3$

$$y \frac{\partial u}{\partial y} = -6x^2y^2 + 5x^3y + 12xy^3 + 4y^4 \qquad \ldots \text{(iii)}$$

Adding equation (ii) and (iii), we get

$$x \frac{\partial u}{\partial x} + y \frac{\partial u}{\partial y} = 4x^4 - 12x^2y^2 + 20x^3y + 16xy^3 + 4y^4$$

$$= 4 \{x^4 - 3x^2y^2 + 5x^3y + 4xy^3 + y^4\}$$

$$= 4u$$

$$\therefore \quad x\frac{\partial u}{\partial x} + y\frac{\partial u}{\partial y} = 4u \qquad \ldots \text{(iv)}$$

Thus, by equations (i) and (iv) Euler's theorem is verified.

Example 2.31 : Verify Euler's theorem for the function $u = \dfrac{x^{1/4} + y^{1/4}}{x^{1/5} + y^{1/5}}$.

Solution : Let $u = f(x, y) = \dfrac{x^{1/4} + y^{1/4}}{x^{1/5} + y^{1/5}}$

$$\therefore \quad f(xt, yt) = \frac{(xt)^{1/4} + (yt)^{1/4}}{(xt)^{1/5} + (yt)^{1/5}}$$

$$= \frac{t^{1/4}}{t^{1/5}} \left\{ \frac{x^{1/4} + y^{1/4}}{x^{1/5} + y^{1/5}} \right\}$$

$$= t^{1/20} f(x, y)$$

$\therefore$ $u = f(x, y)$ is a homogeneous function in x, y of degree $\dfrac{1}{20}$.

Here, $\quad u = \dfrac{x^{1/4} + y^{1/4}}{x^{1/4} + y^{1/4}}$

$$\log u = \log \left\{ \frac{x^{1/4} + y^{1/4}}{x^{1/4} + y^{1/4}} \right\}$$

$$\log u = \log(x^{1/4} + y^{1/4}) - \log(x^{1/5} + y^{1/5}) \qquad \ldots \text{(i)}$$

Differentiating equation (i) partially w.r.t. x

$$\frac{1}{u}\frac{\partial u}{\partial x} = \frac{\frac{1}{4}x^{-3/4}}{x^{1/4} + y^{1/4}} - \frac{\frac{1}{5}x^{-4/5}}{x^{1/5} + y^{1/5}}$$

$$\therefore \quad \frac{1}{u} x \frac{\partial u}{\partial x} = \frac{\frac{1}{4}x^{1/4}}{x^{1/4} + y^{1/4}} - \frac{\frac{1}{5}x^{1/5}}{x^{1/5} + y^{1/5}} \qquad \ldots \text{(ii)}$$

Differentiating equation (i) partially w.r.t. y

$$\frac{1}{u}\frac{\partial u}{\partial x} = \frac{\frac{1}{4}y^{-3/4}}{x^{1/4} + y^{1/4}} - \frac{\frac{1}{5}y^{-4/5}}{x^{1/5} + y^{1/5}}$$

$$\therefore \quad \frac{1}{u} y \frac{\partial u}{\partial x} = \frac{\frac{1}{4}y^{1/4}}{x^{1/4} + y^{1/4}} - \frac{\frac{1}{5}y^{1/5}}{x^{1/5} + y^{1/5}} \qquad \ldots \text{(iii)}$$

Adding equation (ii) and equation (iii), we get

$$\frac{1}{u}\left\{x\frac{\partial u}{\partial x} + y\frac{\partial u}{\partial y}\right\} = \frac{1}{4}\left\{\frac{x^{1/4} + y^{1/4}}{x^{1/4} + y^{1/4}}\right\} - \frac{1}{5}\left\{\frac{x^{1/5} + y^{1/5}}{x^{1/5} + y^{1/5}}\right\}$$

$$= \frac{1}{4} - \frac{1}{5}$$

$$= \frac{1}{20}$$

$$\therefore \quad x\frac{\partial u}{\partial x} + y\frac{\partial u}{\partial y} = \frac{1}{20}u$$

Example 2.32 : If $u = \dfrac{x + y + z}{x^2 + y^2 + z^2}$, prove that

$$x\frac{\partial u}{\partial x} + y\frac{\partial u}{\partial y} + z\frac{\partial u}{\partial z} = -u$$

Solution : Let $u = f(x, y) = \dfrac{x + y + z}{x^2 + y^2 + z^2}$

$$\therefore \quad f(xt, yt, zt) = \frac{xt + yt + zt}{(xt)^2 + (yt)^2 + (zt)^2}$$

$$= t^{-1}\left\{\frac{x + y + z}{x^2 + y^2 + z^2}\right\}$$

$$\therefore \quad f(xt, yt, zt) = t^{-1} f(x, y, z)$$

$\therefore$ $u = f(x, y, z)$ is a homogeneous function in x, y, z of degree $n = -1$ so by Euler's theorem

$$x\frac{\partial u}{\partial x} + y\frac{\partial u}{\partial y} + z\frac{\partial u}{\partial z} = nu$$

$$= -u$$

$$\therefore \quad x\frac{\partial u}{\partial x} + y\frac{\partial u}{\partial y} + z\frac{\partial u}{\partial z} = -u$$

Example 2.33 : If $z = \dfrac{1}{x^2} + \dfrac{1}{xy} - \dfrac{\log x - \log y}{x^2 + y^2}$, then show that

$$x\frac{\partial z}{\partial x} + y\frac{\partial z}{\partial y} + 2z = 0$$

Solution : Let $z = f(x, y) = \dfrac{1}{x^2} + \dfrac{1}{xy} - \dfrac{\log\left(\dfrac{x}{y}\right)}{x^2 + y^2}$

$\therefore \quad f(xt, yt) = \dfrac{1}{x^2 t^2} + \dfrac{1}{xyt^2} - \dfrac{\log\left(\dfrac{xt}{yt}\right)}{x^2 t^2 + y^2 t^2}$

$$= \dfrac{1}{t^2}\left\{\dfrac{1}{x^2} + \dfrac{1}{xy} - \dfrac{\log\left(\dfrac{x}{y}\right)}{x^2 + y^2}\right\}$$

$\therefore \quad f(xt, yt) = t^{-2} f(x, y)$

$\therefore \;\; z = f(x, y)$ is a homogeneous function in x, y of degree -2.

By Euler's theorem,

$$x \dfrac{\partial z}{\partial x} + y \dfrac{\partial z}{\partial y} = -2z$$

$\therefore \quad x \dfrac{\partial z}{\partial x} + y \dfrac{\partial z}{\partial y} + 2z = 0$

Note : In the following corollaries, we assume the equality of $\dfrac{\partial^2 f}{\partial x \, \partial y}$ and $\dfrac{\partial^2 f}{\partial y \, \partial x}$.

Corollary 1 : Let $z = F(u)$ where z is a homogeneous function in x, y of degree n then

$$x \dfrac{\partial u}{\partial x} + y \dfrac{\partial u}{\partial y} = n \dfrac{F(u)}{F'(u)}$$

Proof : Here, $z = F(u)$

$\therefore \qquad \dfrac{\partial z}{\partial x} = F'(u) \cdot \dfrac{\partial u}{\partial x}$ and $\dfrac{\partial z}{\partial y} = F'(u) \cdot \dfrac{\partial u}{\partial y}$

$\therefore \qquad x \dfrac{\partial z}{\partial x} = F'(u) \cdot x \dfrac{\partial u}{\partial x}$ and $y \dfrac{\partial z}{\partial y} = F'(u) \cdot y \dfrac{\partial u}{\partial y}$

$\therefore \qquad x \dfrac{\partial z}{\partial x} + y \dfrac{\partial z}{\partial y} = F'(u) \cdot \left\{x \dfrac{\partial u}{\partial x} + y \dfrac{\partial u}{\partial y}\right\}$

But z is a homogeneous function of degree n

∴ By Euler's theorem

$$x\frac{\partial z}{\partial x} + y\frac{\partial z}{\partial y} = nz = nF(u)$$

∴ $$nF(u) = F'(u)\left\{x\frac{\partial u}{\partial x} + y\frac{\partial u}{\partial y}\right\}$$

∴ $$x\frac{\partial u}{\partial x} + y\frac{\partial u}{\partial y} = n\frac{F(u)}{F'(u)}.$$

Corollary 2 : If $z = f(u)$ where z is a homogeneous function in x and y of degree n then

$$x^2\frac{\partial^2 u}{\partial x^2} + 2xy\frac{\partial^2 u}{\partial x\,\partial y} + y^2\frac{\partial^2 u}{\partial z^2} = G(u)\{G'(u) - 1\}$$

where, $G(u) = n\dfrac{F(u)}{F'(u)}.$

Proof : By Corollary 1, we have

$$x\frac{\partial u}{\partial x} + y\frac{\partial u}{\partial y} = n\frac{F(u)}{F'(u)} \quad \text{But } n\frac{F(u)}{F'(u)} = G(u)$$

∴ $$x\frac{\partial u}{\partial x} + y\frac{\partial u}{\partial y} = n\,G(u) \qquad \ldots \text{(i)}$$

Differentiating equation (i) partially w.r.t. x, we get

$$x\frac{\partial^2 u}{\partial x^2} + \frac{\partial u}{\partial x} + y\frac{\partial^2 u}{\partial x\,\partial y} = G'(u)\frac{\partial u}{\partial x}$$

∴ $$x^2\frac{\partial^2 u}{\partial x^2} + x\frac{\partial u}{\partial x} + xy\frac{\partial^2 u}{\partial x\,\partial y} = G'(u) \times \frac{\partial u}{\partial x} \qquad \ldots \text{(ii)}$$

Differentiating equation (i) partially w.r.t. y, we get

$$x\frac{\partial^2 u}{\partial y\,\partial x} + y\frac{\partial^2 u}{\partial y^2} + \frac{\partial u}{\partial y} = G'(u)\frac{\partial u}{\partial y}$$

∴ $$xy\frac{\partial^2 u}{\partial y\,\partial x} + y^2\frac{\partial^2 u}{\partial y^2} + y\frac{\partial u}{\partial y} = G'(u)\,y\frac{\partial u}{\partial y} \qquad \ldots \text{(iii)}$$

Adding equations (ii) and (iii) and considering $\dfrac{\partial^2 u}{\partial x\,\partial y} = \dfrac{\partial^2 u}{\partial y\,\partial x}$, we get

$$x^2\frac{\partial^2 u}{\partial x^2} + 2xy\frac{\partial^2 u}{\partial x\,\partial y} + y^2\frac{\partial^2 u}{\partial y^2} + \left(x\frac{\partial u}{\partial x} + y\frac{\partial u}{\partial y}\right) = G'(u)\left\{x\frac{\partial u}{\partial x} + y\frac{\partial u}{\partial y}\right\}$$

But $\quad x\dfrac{\partial u}{\partial x} + y\dfrac{\partial u}{\partial y} = G(u)$

$\therefore \quad \dfrac{\partial^2 u}{\partial x^2} + 2xy\dfrac{\partial^2 u}{\partial x \partial y} + y^2\dfrac{\partial^2 u}{\partial y^2} + G(u) = G'(u) \, G(u)$

$\therefore \quad x^2\dfrac{\partial^2 u}{\partial x^2} + 2xy\dfrac{\partial^2 u}{\partial x \partial y} + y^2\dfrac{\partial^2 u}{\partial y^2} = G(u)\{G'(u) - 1\}$

Corollary 3 : If $z = f(x, y)$ is a homogeneous function of degree n, then

$$x^2\dfrac{\partial^2 z}{\partial x^2} + 2xy\dfrac{\partial^2 z}{\partial x \partial y} + y^2\dfrac{\partial^2 z}{\partial y^2} = n(n-1)z.$$

Proof : Here, z is a homogeneous function in x, y of degree n so by Euler's theorem.

$$x\dfrac{\partial z}{\partial x} + y\dfrac{\partial z}{\partial y} = nz \qquad \dots \text{(i)}$$

Differentiating equation (i) w.r.t. x partially, we get

$$x\dfrac{\partial^2 z}{\partial x^2} + \dfrac{\partial z}{\partial x} + y\dfrac{\partial^2 z}{\partial x \partial y} = n\dfrac{\partial z}{\partial x} \qquad \dots \text{(ii)}$$

Differentiating equation (i) w.r.t. y partially, we get

$$x\dfrac{\partial^2 z}{\partial y \partial x} + y\dfrac{\partial^2 z}{\partial y^2} + \dfrac{\partial z}{\partial y} = n\dfrac{\partial z}{\partial y} \qquad \dots \text{(iii)}$$

Multiply equation (i) by x and equation (ii) by y and adding, we get

$$x^2\dfrac{\partial^2 z}{\partial x^2} + 2xy\dfrac{\partial^2 z}{\partial x \partial y} + y^2\dfrac{\partial^2 z}{\partial y^2} + \left(x\dfrac{\partial z}{\partial x} + y\dfrac{\partial z}{\partial y}\right) = n\left(x\dfrac{\partial z}{\partial x} + y\dfrac{\partial z}{\partial y}\right)$$

$\therefore \quad$ By equation (i), we get

$$x^2\dfrac{\partial^2 z}{\partial x^2} + 2xy\dfrac{\partial^2 z}{\partial x \partial y} + y^2\dfrac{\partial^2 z}{\partial y^2} + nz = n \cdot nz$$

$\therefore \quad x^2\dfrac{\partial^2 z}{\partial x^2} + 2xy\dfrac{\partial^2 z}{\partial x \partial y} + y^2\dfrac{\partial^2 z}{\partial y^2} = n^2 z - nz$

$\therefore \quad x^2\dfrac{\partial^2 z}{\partial x^2} + 2xy\dfrac{\partial^2 z}{\partial x \partial y} + y^2\dfrac{\partial^2 z}{\partial y^2} = n(n-1)z$

Example 2.34 : If $u = \tan^{-1}\left(\dfrac{x^3 - y^3}{x + y}\right)$, prove that $x\dfrac{\partial u}{\partial x} + y\dfrac{\partial u}{\partial y} = \sin 2u$

Solution : Here, $u = \tan^{-1}\left(\dfrac{x^3 - y^3}{x + y}\right)$ is not a homogeneous function but $\tan u = \dfrac{x^3 - y^3}{x + y}$ is a homogeneous function in x, y of degree 2. So by corollary 2.

$$x\dfrac{\partial u}{\partial x} + y\dfrac{\partial u}{\partial y} = n\dfrac{F(u)}{F'(u)}$$

But here $n = 2$, $F(u) = \tan u$ ∴ $F'(u) = \sec^2 u$

∴ $\quad x\dfrac{\partial u}{\partial x} + y\dfrac{\partial u}{\partial y} = 2 \cdot \dfrac{\tan u}{\sec^2 u}$

$$= 2 \cdot \dfrac{\sin u}{\cos u} \cdot \cos^2 u$$

$$= 2 \sin u \cos u$$

$$= \sin 2u$$

∴ $\quad x\dfrac{\partial u}{\partial x} + y\dfrac{\partial u}{\partial y} = \sin 2u$ Hence the proof.

Example 2.35 : If $u = \log\left(\dfrac{x^3 + y^3}{x^2 + y^2}\right)$, show that $x\dfrac{\partial u}{\partial x} + y\dfrac{\partial u}{\partial y} = 1$.

Solution : Here, $u = \log\left(\dfrac{x^3 + y^3}{x^2 + y^2}\right)$ is not a homogeneous function but $e^u = \dfrac{x^3 + y^3}{x^2 + y^2}$ is a homogeneous function in x, y of degree 1. So by Corollary 1 of Euler's theorem

$$x\dfrac{\partial u}{\partial x} + y\dfrac{\partial u}{\partial y} = n\dfrac{F(u)}{F'(u)}$$

But here $n = 1$, $F(u) = e^u$ ∴ $F'(u) = e^u$

∴ $\quad x\dfrac{\partial u}{\partial x} + y\dfrac{\partial u}{\partial y} = 1 \cdot \dfrac{e^u}{e^u}$

∴ $\quad x\dfrac{\partial u}{\partial x} + y\dfrac{\partial u}{\partial y} = 1$

Example 2.36 : If $u = \sec^{-1}\left(\dfrac{x^2 + y^2}{x - y}\right)$, then show that

$$x^2 \dfrac{\partial^2 u}{\partial x^2} + 2xy \dfrac{\partial^2 u}{\partial x \partial y} + y^2 \dfrac{\partial^2 u}{\partial y^2} = -\cot u\, (2 + \cot^2 u)$$

Solution : Here $u = \sec^{-1}\left(\dfrac{x^2 + y^2}{x - y}\right)$ is not a homogeneous function but $\sec u = \dfrac{x^2 + y^2}{x - y}$ is a homogeneous function in x and y of degree one. So by corollary 2 of Euler's theorem.

$$x^2 \dfrac{\partial^2 u}{\partial x^2} + 2xy \dfrac{\partial^2 u}{\partial x \partial y} + y^2 \dfrac{\partial^2 u}{\partial y^2} = G(u)\,\{G'(u) - 1\}$$

where,
$$G(u) = n\dfrac{F(u)}{F'(u)}$$

$$= 1 \cdot \dfrac{\sec u}{\sec u \tan u}$$

$$= \cot u$$

$$\therefore \qquad G'(u) = -\operatorname{cosec}^2 u$$

$$\therefore x^2 \dfrac{\partial^2 u}{\partial x^2} + 2xy \dfrac{\partial^2 u}{\partial x \partial y} + y^2 \dfrac{\partial^2 u}{\partial y^2} = \cot u\,\{-\operatorname{cosec}^2 u - 1\}$$

$$= -\cot u\,\{\operatorname{cosec}^2 u + 1\}$$

$$= -\cot u\,\{1 + \cot^2 u + 1\}$$

$$= -\cot u\,\{2 + \cot^2 u\}$$

$$\therefore x^2 \dfrac{\partial^2 u}{\partial x^2} + 2xy \dfrac{\partial^2 u}{\partial x \partial y} + y^2 \dfrac{\partial^2 u}{\partial y^2} = -\cot u\,\{2 + \cot^2 u\}$$

Example 2.37 : If $u = \tan^{-1}\left(\dfrac{x^3 - y^3}{x + y}\right)$, prove that

$$x^2 \dfrac{\partial^2 u}{\partial x^2} + 2xy \dfrac{\partial^2 u}{\partial x \partial y} + y^2 \dfrac{\partial^2 u}{\partial y^2} = 2 \sin u \cos 3u = \sin 4u - \sin 2u$$

Solution : Here $u = \tan^{-1}\left(\dfrac{x^3 - y^3}{x + y}\right)$ is not a homogeneous function but $\tan u = \dfrac{x^3 - y^3}{x + y}$ is a homogeneous function in x and y of degree 2 so by corollary 2 of Euler's theorem.

$$x^2 \frac{\partial^2 u}{\partial x^2} + 2xy \frac{\partial^2 u}{\partial x \partial y} + y^2 \frac{\partial^2 u}{\partial y^2} = G(u)\{G'(u) - 1\}$$

where, $\qquad G(u) = n\dfrac{F(u)}{F'(u)} = 2 \cdot \dfrac{\tan u}{\sec^2 u}$

$\therefore \qquad G(u) = 2 \cdot \dfrac{\tan u}{\sec^2 u}$

$\qquad\qquad\qquad = 2 \sin u \cdot \cos u$

$\qquad G'(u) = 2 \cos^2 u - 2 \sin^2 u$

$\qquad\qquad\quad = 2 \cos^2 u - 2(1 - \cos^2 u)$

$\qquad\qquad\quad = 4 \cos^2 u - 2$

$\therefore \qquad G(u)\{G'(u) - 1\} = 2 \sin u \cos u \,[4 \cos^2 u - 2 - 1]$

$\qquad\qquad\qquad = 2 \sin u \cdot \cos u \,[4 \cos^2 u - 3]$

$\qquad\qquad\qquad = 2 \sin u \,[4 \cos^3 u - 3 \cos u]$

$\qquad\qquad\qquad = 2 \sin u \cdot \cos 3u$

$\therefore x^2 \dfrac{\partial^2 u}{\partial x^2} + 2xy \dfrac{\partial^2 u}{\partial x \partial y} + y^2 \dfrac{\partial^2 u}{\partial y^2} = 2 \sin u \cos 3u$

$\qquad\qquad\qquad = 4 \sin 4u - \sin 2u$

Example 2.38 : If $u = x^2 \sin^{-1}\left(\dfrac{y}{x}\right) - y^2 \cos^{-1}\left(\dfrac{x}{y}\right)$, show that

$$x^2 \frac{\partial^2 u}{\partial x^2} + 2xy \frac{\partial^2 u}{\partial x \partial y} + y^2 \frac{\partial^2 u}{\partial y^2} = 2u$$

Solution : Here u is a homogeneous function in x, y of degree 2 so by corollary 3 of Euler's theorem.

$$x^2 \frac{\partial^2 u}{\partial x^2} + 2xy \frac{\partial^2 u}{\partial x \partial y} + y^2 \frac{\partial^2 u}{\partial y^2} = n(n-1)u$$

But here, $\qquad\qquad n = 2$

$\therefore x^2 \dfrac{\partial^2 u}{\partial x^2} + 2xy \dfrac{\partial^2 u}{\partial x \partial y} + y^2 \dfrac{\partial^2 u}{\partial y^2} = 2u$

Example 2.39 : If $u = x f\left(\dfrac{y}{x}\right) + g\left(\dfrac{y}{x}\right)$, show that

$$x^2 \dfrac{\partial^2 u}{\partial x^2} + 2xy \dfrac{\partial^2 u}{\partial x \partial y} + y^2 \dfrac{\partial^2 u}{\partial y^2} = 0$$

Solution : Let $v = x f\left(\dfrac{y}{x}\right)$ and $w = g\left(\dfrac{y}{x}\right)$, so $u = v + w$

Here v is a homogeneous function of degree 1, so by corollary 3, we get

$$x^2 \dfrac{\partial^2 v}{\partial x^2} + 2xy \dfrac{\partial^2 v}{\partial x \partial y} + y^2 \dfrac{\partial^2 v}{\partial y^2} = 1(1 - 1) u \qquad \ldots \text{(i)}$$

$$= 0$$

And, w is also a homogeneous function of degree 0, so by corollary 3 of Euler's theorem.

$$x^2 \dfrac{\partial^2 w}{\partial x^2} + 2xy \dfrac{\partial^2 w}{\partial x \partial y} + y^2 \dfrac{\partial^2 w}{\partial y^2} = 0(0 - 1) w$$

$$= 0 \qquad \ldots \text{(ii)}$$

Adding equations (i) and (ii), we get

$$x^2 \dfrac{\partial^2 (v + w)}{\partial x^2} + 2xy \dfrac{\partial^2 (v + w)}{\partial x \partial y} + y^2 \dfrac{\partial^2 (v + w)}{\partial y^2} = 0$$

But $u = v + w$

$$\therefore \quad x^2 \dfrac{\partial^2 u}{\partial x^2} + 2xy \dfrac{\partial^2 u}{\partial x \partial y} + y^2 \dfrac{\partial^2 u}{\partial y^2} = 0$$

EXERCISE 2.4

1. Verify Euler's theorem for

   (a) $z = x^n \log\left(\dfrac{y}{x}\right)$ (b) $u = \dfrac{x}{y} + \dfrac{y}{z} + \dfrac{z}{x}$

2. If $z = x^3 \log\left[\dfrac{x^{1/5} - y^{1/5}}{x^{1/5} + y^{1/5}}\right]$, prove that $x \dfrac{\partial z}{\partial x} + y \dfrac{\partial z}{\partial y} = 3z$

3. If $u = \sin^{-1}\left(\dfrac{x}{y}\right) + \cos^{-1}\left(\dfrac{y}{z}\right) + \tan^{-1}\left(\dfrac{z}{x}\right)$, prove that

   $$x \dfrac{\partial u}{\partial x} + y \dfrac{\partial u}{\partial y} + z \dfrac{\partial u}{\partial z} = 3z$$

4. If $z = \sin^{-1}\left(\dfrac{x^2 + y^2}{x + y}\right)$, prove that $x\dfrac{\partial z}{\partial x} + y\dfrac{\partial z}{\partial y} = \tan z$.

5. If $u = \log\left(\dfrac{x^5 + y^5}{x - y}\right)$, show that $x\dfrac{\partial u}{\partial x} + y\dfrac{\partial u}{\partial y} = 4$

6. If $u = \dfrac{x^3 y^2 + y^3 x^2}{x^2 + y^2}$, show that $x^2 \dfrac{\partial^2 u}{\partial x^2} + 2xy \dfrac{\partial^2 u}{\partial x \partial y} + y^2 \dfrac{\partial^2 u}{\partial y^2} = 6u$

7. If $u = \sin^{-1}\sqrt{x^2 + y^2}$, show that $x^2 \dfrac{\partial^2 u}{\partial x^2} + 2xy \dfrac{\partial^2 u}{\partial x \partial y} + y^2 \dfrac{\partial^2 u}{\partial y^2} = \tan^3 u$

8. If $u = \log(x^3 + y^3 + x^2 y + yx^2)$, show that

   (a) $x\dfrac{\partial u}{\partial x} + y\dfrac{\partial u}{\partial y} = 3$
   (b) $x^2 \dfrac{\partial^2 u}{\partial x^2} + 2xy \dfrac{\partial^2 u}{\partial x \partial y} + y^2 \dfrac{\partial^2 u}{\partial y^2} = -3$

MISCELLANEOUS EXERCISE

(I) Theory Questions :

1. If $z = f(x, y)$ then define $\dfrac{\partial z}{\partial x}$ and $\dfrac{\partial z}{\partial y}$.

2. Define homogeneous functions.

3. If $z = f(x, y)$ possesses continuous first order partial derivatives and let $x = \phi(t)$ and $y = \psi(t)$ possess continuous derivatives then prove that

$$\dfrac{dz}{dt} = \dfrac{\partial z}{\partial x} \cdot \dfrac{dx}{dt} + \dfrac{\partial z}{\partial y} \cdot \dfrac{dy}{dt}$$

4. If $z = f(x, y)$ possess continuous first order partial derivatives w.r.t. x and y and let $x = \phi(u, v)$ and $y = \psi(u, v)$ possess continuous first order partial derivative w.r.t. u and v then show that

$$\dfrac{\partial z}{\partial u} = \dfrac{\partial z}{\partial x} \dfrac{\partial x}{\partial u} + \dfrac{\partial z}{\partial y} \dfrac{\partial y}{\partial u}$$

and

$$\dfrac{\partial z}{\partial v} = \dfrac{\partial z}{\partial x} \dfrac{\partial x}{\partial v} + \dfrac{\partial z}{\partial y} \dfrac{\partial y}{\partial v}$$

5. State and prove Euler's theorem on homogeneous functions.

6. If $z = f(u)$ where z is a homogeneous function of degree n in x and y then prove that

$$x\dfrac{\partial u}{\partial x} + y\dfrac{\partial u}{\partial y} = n\dfrac{f(u)}{f'(u)}$$

7. If $z = f(u)$ where z is a homogeneous function of degree n in x and y then

$$x^2 \frac{\partial^2 u}{\partial x^2} + 2xy \frac{\partial^2 u}{\partial x \partial y} + y^2 \frac{\partial^2 u}{\partial y^2} = G(u)\{G'(u) - 1\}$$

where, $\quad G(u) = n \dfrac{f(u)}{f'(u)}$

8. If z is a homogeneous function of degree n, then prove that

$$x^2 \frac{\partial^2 z}{\partial x^2} + 2xy \frac{\partial^2 z}{\partial x \partial y} + y^2 \frac{\partial^2 z}{\partial y^2} = n(n-1)z$$

(II) Numerical Problems :

1. Examine whether the function given below is continuous or not at the origin

$$f(x, y) = \frac{x^2 y^4}{(x^2 + y^4)^2}, \text{ for } x \neq 0, y \neq 0$$

and $\quad f(0, 0) = 0$

2. Discuss the continuity of the following function at origin

$$f(x, y) = \frac{x^3 + y^3}{x - y}, \text{ when } x \neq y$$

$$= 0 \quad , \text{ for } x = 0 = y$$

3. Show that the function

$$f(x, y) = \frac{xy(x^2 - y^2)}{x^2 + y^2}, \text{ for } (x, y) \neq (0, 0)$$

and $\quad f(0, 0) = 0$

is continuous at $(0, 0)$

4. Discuss the continuity of the function

$$f(x, y) = \frac{x^2 y}{x^4 + y^2}, \text{ if } x^4 + y^2 \neq 0$$

$$= 0 \quad , \text{ if } x + y = 0$$

5. Show that the function

$$f(x, y) = \frac{xy}{\sqrt{x^2 + y^2}}, \quad (x, y) \neq (0, 0)$$
$$= 0 \quad , \quad (x, y) = (0, 0)$$

is continuous at the origin

6. Show that the function $f(x, y) = \frac{x^2 y^2}{x^2 + y^2}$, $(x, y) \neq (0, 0)$ and $f(0, 0) = 0$ is continuous at the origin.

7. If $f(x, y) = x^3 y + e^{xy^2}$, find f_x and f_y

8. Verify that $f_{xy} = f_{yx}$ for the functions

   (a) $\dfrac{2x - y}{x + y}$ (b) $x \tan(xy)$ (c) x^y

9. Given $u = e^x \cos y + e^y \sin z$, find all first order partial derivatives and verify that

$$\frac{\partial^2 u}{\partial x \, \partial y} = \frac{\partial^2 u}{\partial y \, \partial x}, \; \frac{\partial^2 u}{\partial x \, \partial z} = \frac{\partial^2 u}{\partial z \, \partial x}, \; \frac{\partial^2 u}{\partial y \, \partial z} = \frac{\partial^2 u}{\partial z \, \partial y}$$

10. If $z = \tan(y + ax) + (y - ax)^{3/2}$, find the value of $\dfrac{\partial^2 z}{\partial x^2} - a^2 \dfrac{\partial^2 z}{\partial y^2}$

11. If $u = x \, \phi\left(\dfrac{y}{x}\right) + \psi\left(\dfrac{y}{x}\right)$, prove that $x^2 \dfrac{\partial^2 u}{\partial x^2} + 2xy \dfrac{\partial^2 u}{\partial x \, \partial y} + y^2 \dfrac{\partial^2 u}{\partial y^2} = 0$.

12. If $x = r \cos \theta$, $y = r \sin \theta$, prove that $\dfrac{\partial^2 r}{\partial x^2} + \dfrac{\partial^2 r}{\partial y^2} = \dfrac{1}{r}\left[\left(\dfrac{\partial r}{\partial x}\right)^2 + \left(\dfrac{\partial r}{\partial y}\right)^2\right]$

13. If $z = x^3 - xy + y^3$, $x = r \cos \theta$, $y = r \sin \theta$, find $\dfrac{\partial z}{\partial r}, \dfrac{\partial z}{\partial \theta}$.

14. If $v = \log(x^3 + y^3 + z^3 - 3xyz)$, prove that

$$\left(\frac{\partial}{\partial x} + \frac{\partial}{\partial y} + \frac{\partial}{\partial z}\right)^2 v = \frac{-9}{(x + y + z)^2}$$

15. If $u = x^2 y + y^2 z + z^2 x$, show that

   (a) $\left(\dfrac{\partial}{\partial x} + \dfrac{\partial}{\partial y} + \dfrac{\partial}{\partial z}\right)^2 u = 6(x + y + z)$

   (b) $\dfrac{\partial^2 u}{\partial x^2} + \dfrac{\partial^2 u}{\partial y^2} + \dfrac{\partial^2 u}{\partial z^2} = 2(x + y + z)$

16. If $z = x\,f(x + y) + y\,g(x + y)$, show that $\dfrac{\partial^2 z}{\partial x^2} - 2\dfrac{\partial^2 z}{\partial x\,\partial y} + \dfrac{\partial^2 z}{\partial y^2} = 0$

17. If $z = u^2 + v^2$, $u = r\cos\theta$, $v = \sin\theta$, find $\dfrac{\partial z}{\partial r},\ \dfrac{\partial z}{\partial \theta}$

18. If $x^x\,y^y\,z^z = k$, show that when $x = y = z$, $\dfrac{\partial^2 z}{\partial x\,\partial y} = -(x\log e x)^{-1}$

19. If $u = x^3 + y^3$, where $x = a\cos\theta$, $y = b\sin\theta$, find $\dfrac{\partial u}{\partial \theta}$.

20. Verify Euler's theorem for $f(x, y) = ax^2 + 2hxy + by^2$.

21. If $u = \sin^{-1}\left\{\dfrac{x^{1/3} + y^{1/3}}{x^{1/2} - y^{1/2}}\right\}$, prove that

$$x\dfrac{\partial u}{\partial x} + y\dfrac{\partial u}{\partial y} = \dfrac{-1}{6}\tan u.$$

22. If $u = \operatorname{cosec}^{-1}\left\{\dfrac{x^{1/2} + y^{1/2}}{x^{1/3} + y^{1/3}}\right\}$, prove that

$$x^2\dfrac{\partial^2 u}{\partial x^2} + 2xy\dfrac{\partial^2 u}{\partial x\,\partial y} + y^2\dfrac{\partial^2 u}{\partial y^2} = \dfrac{\tan u}{12}\left\{\dfrac{13}{12} + \dfrac{1}{12}\tan^2 u\right\}$$

23. If $u = \log\left\{\dfrac{\sqrt{x^2 + y^2}}{x + y}\right\}$, find the value of $x^2\dfrac{\partial^2 u}{\partial x^2} + 2xy\dfrac{\partial^2 u}{\partial x\,\partial y} + y^2\dfrac{\partial^2 u}{\partial y^2}$

24. If $u = \sin^{-1}\left[\dfrac{\sqrt{x} - \sqrt{y}}{\sqrt{x} + \sqrt{y}}\right]$, prove that $x\dfrac{\partial u}{\partial x} = -y\dfrac{\partial u}{\partial y}$

25. If $u = \left(\dfrac{x}{y}\right)^{y/x}$, show that $x\dfrac{\partial u}{\partial x} + y\dfrac{\partial u}{\partial y} = 0$.

26. If $u = \log r$ and $r^2 = x^2 + y^2$, show that

$$x^2\dfrac{\partial^2 u}{\partial x^2} + 2xy\dfrac{\partial^2 u}{\partial x\,\partial y} + y^2\dfrac{\partial^2 u}{\partial y^2} = -1$$

27. If $u = \tan^{-1}\left[\dfrac{x^2 + y^2}{x - y}\right]$, show that

$$x^2\dfrac{\partial^2 u}{\partial x^2} + 2xy\dfrac{\partial^2 u}{\partial x\,\partial y} + y^2\dfrac{\partial^2 u}{\partial y^2} = -2\sin^3 u \cdot \cos u$$

28. If $u = \cos^{-1}\left[\dfrac{x + y}{\sqrt{x} + \sqrt{y}}\right]$, show that $x\dfrac{\partial u}{\partial x} + y\dfrac{\partial u}{\partial y} + \dfrac{1}{2}\cot u = 0$

29. If $u = x^2 + y^2$, $x = s + 3t$, $y = 2s - t$, find $\dfrac{\partial^2 u}{\partial s^2}$ and $\dfrac{\partial^2 u}{\partial t^2}$

ANSWERS

1. $\lim_{(x,y) \to (0,0)} f(x, y) = \dfrac{k^2}{(1 + k^2)}$ along the path $y^2 = kx$, so that $f(x, y)$ is not continuous at $(0, 0)$.

2. $\lim_{(x,y) \to (0,0)} = 0$ along $y = x - x^2$ and
$\lim_{(x,y) \to (0,0)} f(x, y) = 2$ along $y = x - x^3$
So, $f(x, y)$ is not continuous at $(0, 0)$

4. $\lim_{(x,y) \to (0,0)} f(x, y) = \dfrac{m}{1 + m^2}$ along $y = mx^2$, so it is not continuous at $(0, 0)$

7. $f_x = 3x^2 y + y^2 e^{xy^2}$, $f_y = x^3 + 2xy\, e^{xy^2}$

10. 0

13. $\dfrac{\partial z}{\partial r} = (3x^2 - y) \cos \theta + (3y^2 - x) \sin \theta$

$\dfrac{\partial z}{\partial \theta} = (3x^2 - y)(-r \sin \theta) + (3y^2 - x)\, r \cos \theta$

17. $2r, 0$
19. $3(b^3 \sin^2 \theta \cos \theta - a^3 \cos^2 \theta \sin \theta)$
23. 0
29. 10, 20

(III) Multiple Choice Questions

Choose the correct alternative for each of the following :

1. If $u = x^3 - 3xy^2$, $v = 3x^2 y - y^3$ then $\dfrac{\partial u}{\partial y} + \dfrac{\partial v}{\partial x} = \ldots\ldots$

    (a) 0 (b) 1
    (c) x (d) None of these

2. The degree of homogeneous function $f(x, y) = \dfrac{x^{1/2} + y^{1/2}}{x^{1/3} + y^{1/3}}$ is $\ldots\ldots$

    (a) $\dfrac{2}{6}$ (b) $\dfrac{1}{6}$
    (c) $\dfrac{-1}{6}$ (d) None of these

3. If z is a homogeneous function of degree n then
$$x^2 \frac{\partial^2 z}{\partial x^2} + 2xy \frac{\partial^2 z}{\partial x \partial y} + y^2 \frac{\partial^2 z}{\partial y^2} = \ldots$$

(a) nz
(b) (n − 1) z
(c) n(n − 1) z
(d) None of these

4. If $u = \frac{y}{z} + \frac{z}{x} + \frac{x}{y}$ then $x \frac{\partial u}{\partial x} + y \frac{\partial u}{\partial y} + z \frac{\partial u}{\partial z} = \ldots$

(a) u
(b) 2u
(c) −u
(d) 0

5. If $u = \tan^{-1}\left(\frac{y}{x}\right)$ then $\frac{\partial u}{\partial x} = \ldots$

(a) $\frac{y}{x^2 + y^2}$
(b) $\frac{-y}{x^2 + y^2}$
(c) $\frac{x}{x^2 + y^2}$
(d) $\frac{-yx}{x^2 + y^2}$

6. If $u = \tan^{-1}\left(\frac{y}{x}\right)$ then $\frac{\partial u}{\partial y} = \ldots$

(a) $\frac{x}{x^2 + y^2}$
(b) $\frac{-x}{x^2 + y^2}$
(c) $\frac{y}{x^2 + y^2}$
(d) $\frac{-y}{x^2 + y^2}$

7. The degree of the homogeneous function $u = \frac{x^3 + y^3}{x^2 + y^2}$ is ......

(a) 0
(b) 1
(c) −1
(d) 3

8. If u = f(x, y) where u is a homogeneous function of degree n then
$x \frac{\partial u}{\partial x} + y \frac{\partial u}{\partial y} = \ldots$ where u = F(z)

(a) F(u)
(b) $\frac{F(u)}{F'(u)}$
(c) $\frac{nF(u)}{F'(u)}$
(d) None of these

9. If $u = \log\left(\dfrac{x^5 + y^5}{x^3 + y^3}\right)$ then $x\dfrac{\partial u}{\partial x} + y\dfrac{\partial u}{\partial y} = $ ......

   (a) e^u
   (b) $2e^u$
   (c) $2u$
   (d) 2

10. If $z = \sin^{-1}\left(\dfrac{x^2 + y^2}{x + y}\right)$ then $x\dfrac{\partial z}{\partial x} + y\dfrac{\partial z}{\partial y} = $ ......

    (a) $\sin z$
    (b) $\cos z$
    (c) $\tan z$
    (d) None of these

11. If $u = f\left(\dfrac{y}{x}\right)$ then $x\dfrac{\partial u}{\partial x} + y\dfrac{\partial u}{\partial y} = $ ......

    (a) x^2
    (b) y^2
    (c) yx
    (d) 0

12. An expression in x and y is said to be homogeneous if sum the degrees of x and y in every term is ......

    (a) distinct
    (b) same
    (c) finite
    (d) none of these

13. If $z = f(x, y)$ is a homogeneous function of degree 7 then
    $x^2 \dfrac{\partial^2 z}{\partial x^2} + 2xy \dfrac{\partial^2 z}{\partial x \partial y} + y^2 \dfrac{\partial^2 z}{\partial y^2} = $ ......

    (a) $7z$
    (b) $6z$
    (c) $42z$
    (d) 0

14. If $z = f(x, y)$ then $dz = $ ......

    (a) $x\dfrac{\partial z}{\partial x} + y\dfrac{\partial z}{\partial y}$
    (b) $\dfrac{\partial z}{\partial x} dx + \dfrac{\partial z}{\partial y} dy$
    (c) 0
    (d) None of these

15. Number of independent variables in partial differentiation should be ......

    (a) 0
    (b) 1
    (c) at least 2
    (d) none of these

16. $\dfrac{\partial f}{\partial x}$ at (1, 2) for the function $f(x, y) = 2x^2 - xy + 2y^2$ is ......

   (a) 0
   (b) $\dfrac{-1}{2}$
   (c) −2
   (d) 2

17. For the function of two variables, domain is a subset of ......

   (a) R
   (b) R^2
   (c) R^3
   (d) R_n

18. If u is a function of x and y and we are differentiating partially w.r.t. x then ......

   (a) x and y are treated as a constant
   (b) y is treated as a variable
   (c) y is treated as a constant
   (d) both x and y are variables

19. A function f(x, y) is said to be homogeneous function of degree n if

   (a) $f(\lambda x, \lambda y) = \lambda^n f(x, y)$
   (b) $f(\lambda x, \lambda y) = n\lambda f(x, y)$
   (c) $f(\lambda x, \lambda y) = n(n-1)\lambda$
   (d) None of these

ANSWERS

1. (a)	2. (b)	3. (c)	4. (d)	5. (b)	6. (b)	7. (b)	8. (c)
9. (d)	10. (c)	11. (d)	12. (b)	13. (c)	14. (b)	15. (c)	16. (d)
17. (b)	18. (c)	19. (a)					

3
CHAPTER

REDUCTION FORMULAE

Georg Friedrich Bernhard Riemann (September 17, 1826 – July 20, 1866) was an influential German mathematician who made lasting contributions to analysis, number theory, and differential geometry, some of them enabling the later development of general relativity.

Bernhard Riemann

3.1 INTRODUCTION

There are many functions whose integral are reducible to one or other of standard form.

If $\sin^n x\, dx$ using method of integration by parts, we can connect $\int \sin^n x\, dx$ with $\sin^{n-2} x\, dx$. Thus, we reduce the index n to n − 2. As we reduce the index the formula, thus obtained is called reduction formula.

When n is positive integer odd or even the function $\sin^n x$ and $\cos^n x$ may be integrated using reduction formulae. If n is odd positive integer the functions $\sin^n x$ and $\cos^n x$ can be integrated by proper substitutions.

Hence, reduction formula may only employed when n is an even positive integer.

3.2 REDUCTION FORMULAE

3.2.1 Reduction Formula for $\int \sin^n x\, dx$

$\int \sin^n x\, dx = \int \sin^{n-1} x \sin x\, dx$

Integrating by parts, we get

$$I_n = \sin^{n-1} x \int \sin x\, dx - \int \frac{d}{dx}(\sin^{n-1} x)\left(\int \sin x\, dx\right) dx$$

(3.1)

$$= \sin^{n-1}x\,(-\cos x) + \int (n-1)\sin^{n-2}x \cos x\,(\cos x)\,dx$$

$$= -\cos x \sin^{n-1}x + (n-1)\int \sin^{n-2}x \cos^2 x\,dx$$

$$= -\cos x \sin^{n-1}x + (n-1)\int \sin^{n-2}x\,(1 - \sin^2 x)\,dx$$

$$= -\cos x \sin^{n-1}x + (n-1)\int \sin^{n-2}x\,dx - (n-1)\int \sin^n x\,dx$$

$$I_n = -\cos x \sin^{n-1}x + (n-1)\int \sin^{n-2}x\,dx - (n-1)I_n$$

$$I_n(1 + n - 1) = -\cos x \sin^{n-1}x\,dx + (n-1)\int \sin^{n-2}x\,dx$$

$$nI_n = -\cos x \sin^{n-1}x\,dx + (n-1)\int \sin^{n-2}x\,dx$$

$$I_n = -\frac{1}{n}\cos x \sin^{n-1}x\,dx + \frac{(n-1)}{n}\int \sin^{n-2}x\,dx$$

$$\int \sin^n x\,dx = -\frac{\sin^{n-1}x \cos x}{n} + \frac{n-1}{n}\int \sin^{n-2}x\,dx \qquad \ldots (i)$$

is reduction formula

From equation (i)

$$\int_0^{\pi/2} \sin^n x\,dx = \left[-\frac{1}{n}\sin^{n-1}x \cos x\right]_0^{\pi/2} + \frac{(n-1)}{n}\int_0^{\pi/2}\sin^{n-2}x\,dx$$

$$I_n = \frac{n-1}{n}\int_0^{\pi/2} \sin^{n-2}x\,dx$$

$$I_n = \frac{n-1}{n} I_{n-2} \qquad \ldots (ii)$$

Apply same method again from equation (ii)

$$I_n = \frac{n-1}{n} \cdot \frac{n-3}{n-2} I_{n-4} \qquad \ldots (iii)$$

Case I : If n is an even positive integer

$$I_n = \frac{n-1}{n} \cdot \frac{n-3}{n-2} \cdot \frac{n-5}{n-4} \cdots \frac{1}{2} I_0$$

where, $\quad I_0 = \int_0^{\pi/2} \sin^0 x\,dx$

$$= \int_0^{\pi/2} dx = \frac{\pi}{2}$$

$$\therefore \quad \boxed{\int_0^{\pi/2} \sin^n x \, dx = \frac{n-1}{n} \frac{n-3}{n-2} \frac{n-5}{n-4} \cdots \frac{3}{4} \frac{1}{2} \left(\frac{\pi}{2}\right)}$$

Case II : If n is an odd positive integer

$$I_n = \frac{n-1}{n} \frac{n-3}{n-2} \cdots \frac{2}{3} I_1$$

where, $\quad I_1 = \int_0^{\pi/2} \sin x \, dx = [-\cos x]_0^{\pi/2} = 1$

$$\therefore \quad \boxed{\int_0^{\pi/2} \sin^n x \, dx = \frac{n-1}{n} \frac{n-3}{n-2} \cdots \frac{2}{3} (1)}$$

SOLVED EXAMPLES

Example 3.1 : (1) $\int_0^{\pi/2} \sin^6 x \, dx = \frac{5}{6} \frac{3}{4} \frac{1}{2} \left(\frac{\pi}{2}\right) = \frac{5\pi}{32}$

(2) $\int_0^{\pi/2} \sin^5 x \, dx = \frac{4}{5} \frac{2}{3} (1) = \frac{8}{15}$

(3) $\int_0^{\pi/2} \sin^7 x \, dx = \frac{2}{7} \frac{4}{5} \frac{2}{3} (1) = \frac{16}{35}$

Find the integral of $\sin^4 x$.

Solution : $\int \sin^4 x \, dx = \int \sin x \sin^3 x \, dx = \int \sin^3 x \sin x \, dx$

$$= \sin^3 x (-\cos x) - \int (-\cos x)(3 \sin^2 x \cos x) \, dx$$

$$= -\cos x \sin^3 x + 3 \int \cos^2 x \sin^2 x \, dx$$

$$= -\cos x \sin^3 x + 3 \int (1 - \sin^2 x) \sin^2 x \, dx$$

$$= -\cos x \sin^3 x + 3 \int \sin^2 x \, dx - 3 \int \sin^4 x \, dx$$

$\therefore \quad 4 \int \sin^4 x \, dx = -\cos x \sin^3 x + 3 \int \sin^2 x \, dx$

$\therefore \quad \int \sin^4 x \, dx = \frac{-1}{4} \cos x \sin^3 x + \frac{3}{4} \int \sin^2 x \, dx \quad \ldots \text{(i)}$

Now, $\int \sin^2 x \, dx = \int \sin x \sin x \, dx$

$= \sin x (-\cos x) - \int (-\cos x) \cos x \, dx$

$= -\sin x \cos x + \int \cos^2 x \, dx$

$\int \sin^2 x \, dx = -\sin x \cos x + \int (1 - \sin^2 x) \, dx$

$2 \int \sin^2 x \, dx = -\sin x \cos x + x$

$\int \sin^2 x \, dx = \dfrac{-\sin x \cos x}{2} + \dfrac{x}{2}$ ... (ii)

From equation (i) and (ii),

$\int \sin^4 x \, dx = \dfrac{-1}{4} \cos x \sin^3 x \dfrac{-3}{8} \sin x \cos x + \dfrac{3x}{8}$

Example 3.2 : $\int \sin^5 x \, dx$

Solution : Here 5 is odd substitute $\cos x = t$

$\therefore \quad -\sin x \, dx = dt$

$\int \sin^5 x \, dx = \int (\sin^2 x)^2 \sin x \, dx$

$= \int (1 - \cos^2 x)^2 \sin x \, dx$

$= -\int (1 - t^2)^2 \, dt$

$= -\int (1 - 2t^2 + t^4) \, dt$

$= \left(-t + 2\dfrac{t^3}{3} - \dfrac{t^5}{5}\right)$

$= -\cos x + \dfrac{2}{3} \cos^3 x + \dfrac{\cos^5 x}{5}$

Example 3.3 : $\int_0^{\pi/2} \sin^{10} x \, dx$

Solution : $\int_0^{\pi/2} \sin^{10} x \, dx = \dfrac{9}{10} \dfrac{7}{8} \dfrac{5}{6} \dfrac{3}{4} \dfrac{1}{2} \left(\dfrac{\pi}{2}\right)$

$= \dfrac{63}{512} \pi$

Example 3.4 : $\int_{0}^{\pi/6} \sin^6 3x \, dx$

Solution : Put $3x = t$, $3dx = dt$

Range when $\quad x = 0 \quad\quad t = 0$

$\quad\quad\quad\quad\quad\quad x = \dfrac{\pi}{6} \quad\quad t = \dfrac{\pi}{2}$

$$\int_{0}^{\pi/6} \sin^6 3x \, dx = \int_{0}^{\pi/2} \sin^6 t \left(\dfrac{dt}{3}\right)$$

$$= \dfrac{1}{3} \int_{0}^{\pi/2} \sin^6 t \, dt$$

$$= \dfrac{1}{3} \dfrac{5}{6} \dfrac{3}{4} \dfrac{1}{2} \left(\dfrac{\pi}{2}\right)$$

$$= \dfrac{5\pi}{96}$$

Example 3.5 : $\int_{0}^{\pi} \sin\left(\dfrac{x}{2}\right) dx$

Solution : Put $\dfrac{x}{2} = t \Rightarrow dx = 2 \, dt$

Range $\quad$ when $x = 0 \quad\quad t = 0$

$\quad\quad\quad\quad\quad\quad x = \pi \quad\quad t = \dfrac{\pi}{2}$

$$\int_{0}^{\pi} \sin\left(\dfrac{x}{2}\right) dx = \int_{0}^{\pi/2} \sin t \, (2 \, dt)$$

$$= 2 \int_{0}^{\pi/2} \sin t \, dt = 2 \, [-\cos t]_{0}^{\pi/2}$$

$$= 2 \, [\cos t]_{\pi/2}^{0}$$

$$= 2 \left[\cos 0 - \cos \dfrac{\pi}{2}\right]$$

$$= 2$$

Example 3.6 : $\int_0^{\pi/4} \sin^4 2x \, dx$

Solution : Put $2x = t$, $2dx = dt$

Range $x = 0$ $t = 0$

                    $x = \dfrac{\pi}{4}$ $t = \dfrac{\pi}{2}$

$$\int_0^{\pi/4} \sin^4 2x \, dx = \int_0^{\pi/2} \sin^4 t \left(\frac{dt}{2}\right)$$

$$= \frac{1}{2} \int_0^{\pi/2} \sin^4 t \, dt$$

$$= \frac{1}{2} \left[\frac{3}{4} \cdot \frac{1}{2} \cdot \left(\frac{\pi}{2}\right) \right]$$

$$= \frac{3}{32} \pi$$

EXERCISE 3.1

1. Find integral of :
   (a) $\sin^2 x$,   (b) $\sin^3 x$ (c) $\sin^6 x$

2. Evaluate the integrals :

   (a) $\int_0^{\pi/2} \sin^5 x \, dx$

   (b) $\int_0^{\pi/2} \sin^6 x \, dx$

   (c) $\int_0^{\pi/2} \sin^7 x \, dx$

   (d) $\int_0^{\pi/4} \sin^4 2x \, dx$

(e) $\int_0^{\pi/4} \sin^7 2\theta \, d\theta$

(f) $\int_0^{\pi/2} \sin^8 x \, dx$

ANSWERS 3.1

1. (a) $\frac{1}{2}(x - \sin x \cos x)$

   (b) $-\cos x + \frac{1}{3}\cos^2 x$

   (c) $-\frac{\cos x \sin^5 x}{6} - \frac{5 \cos x - \sin^3 x}{24} - \frac{5 \cos x \sin x}{16} + \frac{5x}{16}$

2. (a) $\frac{8}{15}$ (b) $\frac{5\pi}{32}$

   (c) $\frac{16}{35}$ (d) $\frac{3\pi}{32}$

   (e) $\frac{8}{35}$ (f) $\frac{35\pi}{256}$

SOLVED EXAMPLES

Example 3.7 : Evaluate $\int_0^a (a^2 - x^2)^{5/2} \, dx$

Solution : Put $x = a \sin\theta$ Range $x = 0$ $\theta = 0$

               $dx = a \cos\theta \, d\theta$ $x = a$ $\theta = \frac{\pi}{2}$

$$I = \int_0^{\pi/2} (a^2 - a^2 \sin^2\theta)^{5/2} (a \cos\theta \, d\theta)$$

$$= \int_0^{\pi/2} (a^2)^{5/2} (1 - \sin^2\theta)^{5/2} (a \cos\theta \, d\theta)$$

$$= a^5 \int_0^{\pi/2} (\cos^2 \theta)^{5/2} \, a \cos \theta \, d\theta$$

$$= a^6 \int_0^{\pi/2} \cos^6 \theta \, d\theta$$

$$= a^6 \frac{5}{6} \frac{3}{4} \frac{1}{2} \left(\frac{\pi}{2}\right)$$

$$= \frac{5}{32} \pi a^6$$

Example 3.8 : $\int_0^a \dfrac{x^4}{\sqrt{a^2 - x^2}} dx$

Solution : $\quad I = \int_0^a \dfrac{x^4}{\sqrt{a^2 - x^2}} dx$

Put $\quad x = a \sin \theta$

$\quad dx = a \cos \theta \, d\theta$

when $\quad x = 0 \quad\quad \theta = 0$

$\quad\quad x = a \quad\quad \theta = \dfrac{\pi}{2}$

$$I = \int_0^{\pi/2} \frac{a^4 \sin^4 \theta}{\sqrt{a^2 - a^2 \sin^2 \theta}} a \cos \theta \, d\theta$$

$$= a^4 \int_0^{\pi/2} \frac{\sin^4 \theta}{a \cos \theta} a \cos \theta \, d\theta$$

$$= a^4 \int_0^{\pi/2} \sin^4 \theta \, d\theta$$

$$= a^4 \left(\frac{3}{4} \frac{1}{2} \frac{\pi}{2}\right) = \frac{3a^4 \pi}{16}$$

Example 3.9 : $I = \displaystyle\int_0^\infty \dfrac{x^2}{\sqrt{(1-x^6)^7}}\,dx$

Solution : Put $x^3 = \tan\theta$

$$3x^2\,dx = \sec^2\theta\,d\theta$$

when $\quad x = 0 \qquad\qquad \theta = 0$

$\qquad\qquad x = \infty \qquad\qquad \theta = \dfrac{\pi}{2}$

$$I = \int_0^{\pi/2} \dfrac{\sec^2\theta\,d\theta/3}{\sqrt{(1-\tan^2\theta)^7}}$$

$$= \dfrac{1}{3}\int_0^{\pi/2} \dfrac{\sec^2\theta\,d\theta}{\sec^7\theta}$$

$$= \dfrac{1}{3}\int_0^{\pi/2} \dfrac{1}{\sec^5\theta}\,d\theta = \dfrac{1}{3}\int_0^{\pi/2} \cos^5\theta\,d\theta$$

$$= \dfrac{1}{3}\left(\dfrac{4}{5}\,\dfrac{2}{3}\right) = \dfrac{8}{15}$$

Example 3.10 : $\displaystyle\int_0^{2a} \dfrac{x^{9/2}}{\sqrt{2a-x}}\,dx$

Solution : $\qquad I = \displaystyle\int_0^{2a} \dfrac{x^{9/2}}{\sqrt{2a-x}}\,dx$

Put $\qquad\qquad x = 2a\sin^2\theta$

$\qquad\qquad dx = 4a\sin\theta\cos\theta\,d\theta$

When $\quad x = 0 \qquad\qquad \theta = 0$

$\qquad\qquad x = 2a \qquad\qquad \theta = \dfrac{\pi}{2}$

$$I = \int_0^{\pi/2} \frac{(2a\sin^2\theta)^{9/2}}{\sqrt{2a - 2a\sin^2\theta}} 4a\sin\theta\cos\theta\, d\theta$$

$$= \frac{2^{9/2}}{2^{1/2}} \int_0^{\pi/2} \frac{a^{9/2}\sin^9\theta}{a^{1/2}\cos\theta} 4a\sin\theta\cos\theta\, d\theta$$

$$= 64a^5 \int_0^{\pi/2} \sin^{10}\theta\, d\theta$$

$$= 64a^5 \cdot \frac{9}{10} \cdot \frac{7}{8} \cdot \frac{5}{6} \cdot \frac{3}{4} \cdot \frac{1}{2} \left(\frac{\pi}{2}\right)$$

$$= \frac{63}{8} \pi a^5$$

Example 3.11 : $\int_0^1 x^5 \sin^{-1}x\, dx$

Solution : Put $\sin^{-1}x = \theta$ or $x = \sin\theta$

$$dx = \cos\theta\, d\theta$$

$x = 0 \qquad \theta = 0$

$x = 1 \qquad \theta = \dfrac{\pi}{2}$

$$I = \int_0^{\pi/2} \sin^5\theta \cdot \theta \cos\theta\, d\theta = \int_0^{\pi/2} \theta\, (\sin^5\theta \cos\theta)\, d\theta$$

Integrating by parts,

$$I = \left[\theta \frac{\sin^6\theta}{6}\right]_0^{\pi/2} - \int_0^{\pi/2} \frac{\sin^6\theta}{6} \cdot 1\, d\theta$$

$$= \frac{\pi}{12} - \frac{1}{6} \cdot \frac{5}{6} \cdot \frac{3}{4} \cdot \frac{1}{2} \left(\frac{\pi}{2}\right)$$

$$= \frac{\pi}{12} - \frac{5\pi}{192} = \frac{11\pi}{192}$$

Example 3.12 : Evaluate $\int_0^3 \dfrac{x^{3/2}}{(3-x)^{1/2}} dx$

Solution : $x = 3 \sin^2 \theta \qquad dx = 6 \sin \theta \cos \theta \, d\theta$

$$\int_0^3 \dfrac{x^{3/2}}{(3-x)^{1/2}} dx = \int_0^{\pi/2} \dfrac{3\sqrt{3} \sin^3 \theta}{\sqrt{3} \cos \theta} 6 \sin \theta \cos \theta \, d\theta$$

$$= 18 \int_0^{\pi/2} \sin^4 \theta \, d\theta$$

$$= 18 \left(\dfrac{3}{4} \dfrac{1}{2} \dfrac{\pi}{2}\right) = \dfrac{27}{8} \pi$$

Example 3.13 : $\int_0^{\pi} (1 - \cos \theta)^3 \, d\theta$

Solution : $\int_0^{\pi} (1 - \cos \theta)^3 \, d\theta = \int_0^{\pi} 2^3 \sin^6 \dfrac{\theta}{2} \, d\theta$

Put $\qquad \dfrac{\theta}{2} = x$

$\qquad\qquad dx = 2 \, dx$

when $\quad \theta = 0 \qquad x = 0$

$\qquad\quad \theta = \pi \qquad x = \dfrac{\pi}{2}$

$$\int_0^{\pi} (1 - \cos \theta)^3 \, d\theta = \int_0^{\pi/2} 2^3 \sin^6 x \, (2 \, dx)$$

$$= 8 \times 2 \int_0^{\pi/2} \sin^6 x \, dx$$

$$= 16 \left(\dfrac{5}{6} \dfrac{3}{4} \dfrac{1}{2} \dfrac{\pi}{2}\right)$$

$$= \dfrac{5}{2} \pi$$

Example 3.14 : $\int_0^3 \sqrt{\dfrac{x^3}{3-x}}\, dx$

Put
$$x = 3\sin^2\theta$$
$$dx = 6\sin\theta\cos\theta\, d\theta$$

$x = 0 \qquad \theta = 0$

$x = 3 \qquad \theta = \dfrac{\pi}{2}$

$$I = \int_0^{\pi/2} \sqrt{\dfrac{27\sin^6\theta}{3(1-\sin^2\theta)}}\, 6\sin\theta\cos\theta\, d\theta$$

$$= 18 \int_0^{\pi/2} \sin^4\theta\, d\theta$$

$$= 18 \left(\dfrac{3}{4}\cdot\dfrac{1}{2}\cdot\dfrac{\pi}{2}\right) = \dfrac{27\pi}{8}$$

Example 3.15 : Evaluate $\int_0^1 \dfrac{x^7}{\sqrt{1-x^4}}\, dx$

Put $x^2 = \sin\theta \quad 2x\, dx = \cos\theta\, d\theta$

$$\int_0^1 \dfrac{x^7}{\sqrt{1-x^4}}\, dx = \int_0^1 \dfrac{(x^2)^3}{\sqrt{1-(x^2)^2}}\, x\, dx$$

$$= \int_0^{\pi/2} \dfrac{\sin^3\theta}{\sqrt{1-\sin^2\theta}} \cdot \dfrac{\cos\theta\, d\theta}{2}$$

$$= \dfrac{1}{2}\int_0^{\pi/2} \sin^3\theta\, d\theta$$

$$= \dfrac{1}{2}\cdot\dfrac{2}{3} = \dfrac{1}{3}$$

Example 3.16 : $\displaystyle\int_0^\infty \dfrac{x^2}{\sqrt{(1+x^6)^7}}\,dx$

Put $\quad x^3 = \tan\theta$

$3x^2\,dx = \sec^2\theta\,d\theta$

$x^2\,dx = \dfrac{\sec^2\theta}{3}\,d\theta$

$$= \int_0^{\pi/2} \dfrac{\dfrac{\sec^2\theta}{3}\,d\theta}{\sqrt{(1+\tan^2\theta)^7}} = \int_0^{\pi/2} \dfrac{\dfrac{1}{3}\sec^2\theta\,d\theta}{\sec^7\theta}$$

$$= \dfrac{1}{3}\int_0^{\pi/2} \cos^5\theta\,d\theta$$

$$= \dfrac{1}{3}\left(\dfrac{4}{5}\cdot\dfrac{2}{3}\right) = \dfrac{8}{45}$$

Example 3.17 : Evaluate $\displaystyle\int_0^{\pi/4} \sin^7 2\theta\,d\theta$

Solution : Put $2\theta = x$

$2\,d\theta = dx$

$$= \int_0^{\pi/2} \dfrac{1}{2}\sin^7 x\,dx$$

$$= \dfrac{1}{2}\int_0^{\pi/2} \sin^7 x\,dx$$

$$= \dfrac{1}{2}\left(\dfrac{6}{7}\cdot\dfrac{4}{5}\cdot\dfrac{2}{3}\cdot 1\right)$$

$$= \dfrac{8}{35}$$

Example 3.18 : $\displaystyle\int_0^1 x^5 \sqrt{\left|\frac{1+x^2}{1-x^2}\right|}\, dx$

Solution : $\displaystyle\int_0^1 x^5 \sqrt{\frac{1+x^2}{1-x^2}}\, dx = \int_0^1 x^5 \frac{(1+x^2)}{\sqrt{1-x^4}}\, dx$

Put $\quad x^2 = \sin\theta$

$\quad 2x\, dx = \cos\theta\, d\theta$

$$I = \frac{1}{2}\int_0^{\pi/2} \sin^2\theta\, \frac{(1+\sin\theta)}{\cos\theta}\cos\theta\, d\theta$$

$$I = \frac{1}{2}\int_0^{\pi/2} (\sin^2\theta + \sin^3\theta)\, d\theta$$

$$= \frac{1}{2}\left[\frac{1}{2}\frac{\pi}{2} + \frac{2}{3}(1)\right] = \frac{1}{2}\left(\frac{\pi}{4} + \frac{2}{3}\right)$$

$$= \frac{3\pi + 8}{24}$$

Example 3.19 : Prove that $\displaystyle\int_0^1 \frac{x^{2n}}{\sqrt{1-x^2}}\, dx = \frac{(2n)!}{2^{2n}\,(n!)^2}\,\frac{\pi}{2}$

Solution : $\displaystyle\int_0^1 \frac{x^{2n}}{\sqrt{1-x^2}}\, dx$

Put $\quad x = \sin\theta$

$\quad dx = \cos\theta\, d\theta$

$$\int_0^1 \frac{x^{2n}}{\sqrt{1-x^2}}\, dx = \int_0^{\pi/2} \frac{\sin^{2n}\theta}{\cos\theta}\cos\theta\, d\theta$$

$$= \int_0^{\pi/2} \sin^{2n}\theta\, d\theta$$

$$= \frac{2n-1}{2n} \cdot \frac{2n-3}{2n-2} \cdots \frac{3}{4} \cdot \frac{1}{2} \left(\frac{\pi}{2}\right)$$

$$= \frac{2n(2n-1)(2n-2)(2n-3)(2n-4)\ldots 3.2.1}{(2n)2n(2n-2)(2n-2)\ldots 2.2} \left(\frac{\pi}{2}\right)$$

$$= \frac{(2n)!}{[2n(2n-2)(2n-4)\ldots 2]^2} \left(\frac{\pi}{2}\right)$$

$$= \frac{(2n)!}{2^{2n}(n!)^2} \left(\frac{\pi}{2}\right)$$

Example 3.20 : $\int_0^2 (4-x^2)^{7/2} \, dx$

Solution : $\quad I = \int_0^2 (4-x^2)^{7/2} \, dx$

Put $\quad x = 2\sin\theta$

$\quad dx = 2\cos\theta \, d\theta$

$x = 2 \qquad \theta = \dfrac{\pi}{2}$

$x = 0 \qquad \theta = 0$

$$I = \int_0^{\pi/2} (4 - 4\sin^2\theta)^{7/2} \, 2\cos\theta \, d\theta$$

$$= 2^8 \int_0^{\pi/2} (\cos^2\theta)^{7/2} \cos\theta \, d\theta$$

$$= 2^8 \int_0^{\pi/2} \cos^8\theta \, d\theta$$

$$= 2^8 \left[\frac{7}{8} \cdot \frac{5}{6} \cdot \frac{3}{4} \cdot \frac{1}{2} \cdot \frac{\pi}{2}\right]$$

$$= 2^8 \frac{35}{2^8} \pi$$

$$= 35\pi$$

Example 3.21 : $\int_0^1 x^2 (1 - x^2)^{7/2} dx$

Solution : $I = \int_0^1 x^2 (1 - x^2)^{7/2} dx$

Put
$$x = \sin \theta$$
$$dx = \cos \theta \, d\theta$$

$$I = \int_0^{\pi/2} \sin^2 \theta (1 - \sin^2 \theta)^{7/2} \cos \theta \, d\theta$$

$$= \int_0^{\pi/2} (1 - \cos^2 \theta) \cos^7 \theta \cos \theta \, d\theta$$

$$= \int_0^{\pi/2} (\cos^8 \theta - \cos^{10} \theta) \, d\theta$$

$$= \int_0^{\pi/2} \cos^8 \theta \, d\theta - \int_0^{\pi/2} \cos^{10} \theta \, d\theta$$

$$= \frac{7}{8} \frac{5}{6} \frac{3}{4} \frac{1}{2} \frac{\pi}{2} - \frac{9}{10} \frac{7}{8} \frac{5}{6} \frac{3}{4} \frac{1}{2} \frac{\pi}{2}$$

$$= \frac{7(5)}{256} \pi \left(\frac{1}{10}\right)$$

$$= \frac{7\pi}{512}$$

3.2.2 Reduction Formula for $\int \cos^n x \, dx$

$\int \cos^n x \, dx = \int \cos^{n-1} x \cos x \, dx$

Integrating by parts, we get

$$I_n = \cos^{n-1} x \int \cos x \, dx - \int \frac{d}{dx} (\cos^{n-1} x) \left(\int \cos x \, dx\right) dx$$

$$= \cos^{n-1} x (\sin x) - (n - 1) \int \cos^{n-2} x \sin x (- \sin x) \, dx$$

$$= \cos^{n-1} x \sin x + (n - 1) \int \cos^{n-2} x \sin^2 x \, dx$$

$$= \cos^{n-1} x \sin x + (n - 1) \int \cos^{n-2} x (1 - \cos^2 x) \, dx$$

$$= \cos^{n-1}x \sin x + (n-1) \int \cos^{n-2}x \, dx - (n-1) \int \cos^n x \, dx$$

$$= \cos^{n-1}x \sin x + (n-1) \int \cos^{n-2}x \, dx - (n-1) I$$

$$I + (n-1)I = \cos^{n-1}x \sin x + (n-1) \int \cos^{n-2}x \, dx$$

$$nI_n = \cos^{n-1}x \sin x + (n-1) \int \cos^{n-2}x \, dx$$

$$I_n = \frac{1}{n} \sin x \cos^{n-1}x + \frac{n-1}{n} I_{n-2}$$

Thus, required formula is

$$\int \cos^n x \, dx = \frac{1}{n} \sin x \cos^{n-1}x + \frac{n-1}{n} \int \cos^{n-2} x \, dx \quad \ldots \text{(i)}$$

From equation (i)

$$\int_0^{\pi/2} \cos^n x \, dx = \left[\frac{1}{n} \sin x \cos^{n-1} x \right]_0^{\pi/2} + \frac{n-1}{n} \int_0^{\pi/2} \cos^{n-2}x \, dx$$

$$I_n = 0 + \frac{n-1}{n} I_{n-2} \quad \ldots \text{(ii)}$$

Apply same method again from equation (ii),

$$I_n = \frac{n-1}{n} \left(\frac{n-3}{n-2} \right) I_{n-4} \quad \ldots \text{(iii)}$$

Case - I : If n is an even positive integer

$$I_n = \frac{n-1}{n} \cdot \frac{n-3}{n-2} \cdot \frac{n-5}{n-4} \cdots \frac{1}{2} I_0$$

where, $I_0 = \int_0^{\pi/2} \cos^0 x \, dx$

$$= \int_0^{\pi/2} dx = \frac{\pi}{2}$$

$$\therefore \quad \boxed{\int_0^{\pi/2} \cos^n x \, dx = \frac{n-1}{n} \cdot \frac{n-3}{n-2} \cdot \frac{n-5}{n-4} \cdots \frac{3}{4} \left(\frac{1}{2} \right) \frac{\pi}{2}}$$

Case - II : If n is an odd positive integer

$$I_n = \frac{n-1}{n} \frac{n-3}{n-2} \cdots \frac{2}{3} I_1$$

where, $I_1 = \int_0^{\pi/2} \cos x \, dx$

$= [\sin x]_0^{\pi/2} = 1$

$$\boxed{\int_0^{\pi/2} \cos^n x \, dx = \frac{n-1}{n} \frac{n-3}{n-2} \cdots \frac{2}{3} \quad (1)}$$

Examples : (1) $\int_0^{\pi/2} \cos^8 x \, dx = \frac{7}{8} \cdot \frac{5}{6} \cdot \frac{3}{4} \cdot \frac{1}{2} \cdot \frac{\pi}{2} = \frac{35}{256}\pi$

(2) $\int_0^{\pi/2} \cos^9 x \, dx = \frac{8}{9} \cdot \frac{6}{7} \cdot \frac{4}{5} \cdot \frac{2}{3} (1) = \frac{128}{315}$

Example 3.22 : To find $\int_0^1 \frac{x^n}{\sqrt{1-x^2}} \, dx$

Solution : Put $x = \sin\theta \quad dx = \cos\theta \, d\theta$

when $\quad x = 0 \qquad\qquad \theta = 0$

$\qquad x = 1 \qquad\qquad \theta = \dfrac{\pi}{2}$

$\int_0^1 \dfrac{x^n}{\sqrt{1-x^2}} \, dx = \int_0^{\pi/2} \dfrac{\sin^n\theta}{\sqrt{1-\sin^2\theta}} \cos\theta \, d\theta = \int_0^{\pi/2} \sin^n\theta \, d\theta$

$= \begin{cases} \dfrac{n-1}{n} \dfrac{n-3}{n-2} \cdots \dfrac{2}{3} \cdot 1 & \text{if n is odd} \\[2mm] \dfrac{n-1}{n} \dfrac{n-3}{n-2} \cdots \dfrac{1}{2} \dfrac{\pi}{2} & \text{if n is even} \end{cases}$

Example 3.23 : To find $\displaystyle\int_0^\infty \frac{dx}{(1+x^2)^{\frac{n+1}{2}}}$

Put $\quad x = \tan\theta$

$\quad dx = \sec^2\theta\, d\theta$

when $\quad x = 0 \qquad \theta = 0$

$\qquad x = \infty \qquad \theta = \dfrac{\pi}{2}$

$\displaystyle\int_0^\infty \frac{dx}{(1+x^2)^{\frac{n+1}{2}}} = \int_0^{\pi/2} \frac{\sec^2\theta\, d\theta}{\sec^{2n+1}\theta\, d\theta}$

$\qquad = \displaystyle\int_0^{\pi/2} \cos^{2n-1}\theta\, d\theta$

$\qquad = \dfrac{2n-2}{2n-1}\cdot\dfrac{2n-4}{2n-3}\cdots\dfrac{2}{3}\cdot 1$

Example 3.24 : $\displaystyle\int_0^\infty \frac{dx}{(1+x^2)^n}$

Solution : Put $\quad x = \tan\theta$

$\quad dx = \sec^2\theta\, d\theta$

when $\quad x = 0 \qquad \theta = 0$

$\qquad x = \infty \qquad \theta = \dfrac{\pi}{2}$

$\displaystyle\int_0^\infty \frac{dx}{(1+x^2)^n} = \int_0^{\pi/2} \frac{\sec^2\theta}{\sec^{2n}\theta}\, d\theta = \int_0^{\pi/2} \cos^{2n-2}\theta\, d\theta$

$\qquad = \dfrac{2n-3}{2n-2}\cdot\dfrac{2n-5}{2n-4}\cdots\dfrac{1}{2}\left(\dfrac{\pi}{2}\right)$

Example 3.25 : Evaluate $\int_0^\infty \dfrac{dx}{(1+x^2)^{9/2}}$

Solution : Put $x = \tan\theta$
$$dx = \sec^2\theta\, d\theta$$

$$I = \int_0^{\pi/2} \dfrac{\sec^2\theta}{\sec^9\theta} d\theta = \int_0^{\pi/2} \cos^5\theta\, d\theta$$

$$= \dfrac{6}{7}\dfrac{4}{5}\dfrac{2}{3}(1) = \dfrac{16}{35}$$

Example 3.26 : Evaluate $\int_0^\infty \dfrac{x^2}{(1+x^6)^{7/2}} dx$

Solution : Put $x^3 = t$
$$3x^2\, dx = dt$$

$$I = \dfrac{1}{3}\int_0^\infty \dfrac{dt}{(1+t^2)^{7/2}} \quad \text{Put } t = \tan\theta$$

$$I = \dfrac{1}{3}\int_0^{\pi/2} \dfrac{\sec^2\theta}{\sec^7\theta} d\theta = \dfrac{1}{3}\int_0^{\pi/2} \cos^5\theta\, d\theta$$

$$= \dfrac{1}{3}\dfrac{4}{5}\dfrac{2}{3}(1)$$

$$= \dfrac{8}{45}$$

Example 3.27 : $\int_0^\infty \dfrac{dx}{(1+x^2)^{7/2}}$

Solution : Put $x = \tan\theta$
$$dx = \sec^2\theta\, d\theta$$

$$I = \int_0^{\pi/2} \frac{\sec^2\theta\, d\theta}{(1+\tan^2\theta)^{7/2}}$$

$$= \int_0^{\pi/2} \frac{\sec^2\theta\, d\theta}{\sec^7\theta} = \int_0^{\pi/2} \cos^5\theta\, d\theta$$

$$= \frac{4}{5}\cdot\frac{2}{3} = \frac{8}{15}$$

Example 3.28 : $\int_0^\infty \frac{x^2}{(1+x^6)^3}\, dx$

Solution : Put $x^3 = t$

$3x^2\, dx = dt$

$$= \int_0^\infty \frac{dt/3}{(1+t^2)^3} = \frac{1}{3}\int_0^\infty \frac{dt}{(1+t^2)^3}$$

Put $t = \tan\theta$

$dt = \sec^2\theta\, d\theta$

$$= \frac{1}{3}\int_0^{\pi/2} \frac{\sec^2\theta\, d\theta}{(1+\tan^2\theta)^3} = \frac{1}{3}\int_0^{\pi/2} \frac{1}{\sec^4\theta}\, d\theta$$

$$= \frac{1}{3}\int_0^{\pi/2} \cos^4\theta\, d\theta$$

$$= \frac{1}{3}\left(\frac{3}{4}\cdot\frac{1}{2}\cdot\frac{\pi}{2}\right) = \frac{\pi}{16}$$

Example 3.29 : $\int_0^1 \frac{dx}{(x^2+1)^5}$

Solution : Put $x = \tan\theta$

$dx = \sec^2\theta\, d\theta$

$$I = \int_0^{\pi/2} \frac{\sec^2\theta \, d\theta}{(1+\tan^2\theta)^5} = \int_0^{\pi/2} \frac{\sec^2\theta \, d\theta}{\sec^{10}\theta}$$

$$= \int_0^{\pi/2} \frac{1}{\sec^8\theta} \, d\theta$$

$$= \int_0^{\pi/2} \cos^8\theta \, d\theta$$

$$= \frac{7}{8} \cdot \frac{5}{6} \cdot \frac{3}{4} \cdot \frac{1}{2} \cdot \frac{\pi}{2} = \frac{35}{256}\pi$$

EXERCISE 3.2

1. Evaluate $\displaystyle\int_0^\infty \frac{x^2}{(1+x^6)^{7/2}} \, dx$

2. Evaluate $\displaystyle\int_0^\infty \frac{dx}{(1+x^2)^5}$

3. Evaluate $\displaystyle\int_0^{\pi/2} \cos^6 x \, dx$

4. Evaluate $\displaystyle\int_0^{\pi/2} \cos^7 x \, dx$

5. Evaluate $\displaystyle\int_0^\pi \sin\left(\frac{x}{2}\right) dx$

6. Evaluate $\displaystyle\int_0^{\pi/4} \cos^7 2\theta \, d\theta$

7. Evaluate $\displaystyle\int_0^\infty \frac{dx}{(a^2+x^2)^5}$

8. Evaluate $\int_0^1 x^2 (a^2 - x^2)^{9/2} dx$

9. $\int_0^1 \dfrac{x^6}{\sqrt{1 - x^2}} dx$

10. $\int_0^\infty \dfrac{dx}{(1 + x^2)^4}$

ANSWERS 3.2

1. $\dfrac{8}{45}$
2. $\dfrac{35}{256} \pi$
3. $\dfrac{5\pi}{32}$
4. $\dfrac{16}{35}$
5. $\dfrac{16}{35}$
6. $\dfrac{8}{35}$
7. $\dfrac{35}{256} \dfrac{1}{a^9}$
8. $\dfrac{2\pi}{2048} a^{12}$
9. $\dfrac{5\pi}{32}$
10. $\dfrac{5\pi}{32}$

3.2.3 Reduction Formula for $\int \sin^m x \cos^n x\, dx$

We have $\int \sin^m x \cos^n x\, dx = \int \sin^{m-1} x (\sin x (\cos^n x)\, dx$

$$I = -\dfrac{\cos^{n+1} x \sin^{m-1} x}{n + 1} + \int \dfrac{\cos^{n+1} x (m - 1) \sin^{m-2} x}{(n + 1)} \cos x\, dx$$

$$= -\dfrac{\cos^{n+1} x \sin^{m-1} x}{n + 1} + \dfrac{m - 1}{n + 1} \int \sin^{m-2} x \cos^{n+2} x\, dx$$

$$= -\dfrac{\cos^{n+1} x \sin^{m-1} x}{n + 1} + \dfrac{m - 1}{n + 1} \int \sin^{m-2} x \cos^n x (1 - \sin^2 x)\, dx$$

$$= -\dfrac{\cos^{n+1} x \sin^{m-1} x}{n + 1} + \dfrac{m - 1}{n + 1} \int \sin^{m-2} x \cos^n x\, dx - \dfrac{(m - 1)}{(n + 1)}$$

$$\int \sin^m x \cos^n x\, dx$$

$$I = -\frac{\cos^{n+1}x \sin^{m-1}x}{n+1} + \frac{m-1}{n+1}\int \sin^{m-2}x \cos^n x\, dx - \frac{(m-1)}{(n+1)}I$$

$$\therefore \left(1 + \frac{m-1}{n+1}\right)I = -\frac{\cos^{n+1}x \sin^{m-1}x}{n+1} + \frac{m-1}{n+1}\int \sin^{m-2}x \cos^n x\, dx$$

$$\left(\frac{n+m}{n+1}\right)I = -\frac{\cos^{n+1}x \sin^{m-1}x}{n+1} + \frac{m-1}{n+1}\int \sin^{m-2}x \cos^n x\, dx$$

$$I = \left(\frac{n+1}{n+m}\right)\left(\frac{-\cos^{n+1}x \sin^{m-1}x}{n+1}\right) + \left(\frac{n+1}{n+m}\right)\left(\frac{m-1}{n+1}\right)$$
$$\int \sin^{m-2}x \cos^n x\, dx$$

$$I = -\frac{\cos^{n+1}x \sin^{m-1}x}{n+m} + \frac{m-1}{m+n}\int \sin^{m-2}x \cos^n x\, dx$$

which is required reduction formula

Similarly, we obtain

$$\int \sin^m x \cos^n x\, dx = \frac{\sin^{m+1}x \cos^{n+1}x}{m+n} + \frac{n-1}{m+n}\int \sin^m x \cos^{n-2}x\, dx$$

Remark : If m is odd positive integer, then we use the substitution cos x = t even if n is not an integer.

3.2.4 Reduction Formula for $\int_0^{\pi/2} \sin^m x \cos^n x\, dx$

where m, n are positive integers

Let $\quad I_{mn} = \int_0^{\pi/2} \sin^m x \cos^n x\, dx$

Using reduction formula above.

$$I_{mn} = \int_0^{\pi/2} \sin^m x \cos^n x\, dx$$

$$= -\left[\frac{\cos^{n+1}x \sin^{m-1}x}{m+n}\right]_0^{\pi/2} + \frac{m-1}{m+n}\int_0^{\pi/2} \sin^{m-2}x \cos^n x\, dx$$

$$= \frac{m-1}{m+n}\int_0^{\pi/2} \sin^{m-2}x \cos^n x\, dx$$

$$I_{mn} = \frac{m-1}{m+n} I_{m-2, n}$$

From this we have changing m to m − 2, m − 4, m − 6 ... and so on

$$I_{m-2, n} = \frac{m-3}{m+n-2} I_{m-4, n}$$

$$I_{m-4, n} = \frac{m-5}{m+n-4} I_{m-6, n}$$

Lastly, $\quad I_{3, n} = \dfrac{2}{3+n} I_{1, n} \qquad$ when m is odd

$$I_{2, n} = \frac{1}{2+n} I_{0, n} \qquad \text{when m is even}$$

Put all results,

$$I_{m, n} = \frac{m-1}{m+n} \frac{m-3}{m+n-2} \frac{m-5}{m+n-4} \cdots \frac{3}{n+4} \frac{1}{n+2} I_{0, n}$$

when m is even

Put all results,

$$I_{m, n} = \frac{m-1}{m+n} \frac{m-3}{m+n-2} \frac{m-5}{m+n-4} \cdots \frac{2}{3+n} I_{1, n}$$

when m is odd

Now, $\quad I_{0, n} = \displaystyle\int_0^{\pi/2} (\sin x)^0 \cos^n x\, dx$

$$= \int_0^{\pi/2} \cos^n x\, dx$$

$$= \frac{n-1}{n} \frac{n-3}{n-2} \frac{n-5}{n-4} \cdots \frac{3}{4} \frac{1}{2} \frac{\pi}{2} \qquad \text{when n is even}$$

$$= \frac{n-1}{n} \frac{n-3}{n-2} \frac{n-5}{n-4} \cdots \frac{4}{5} \frac{2}{3} \qquad \text{when n is odd}$$

Now, $\quad I_{1, n} = \displaystyle\int_0^{\pi/2} \sin x \cos^n x\, dx$

$$= \int_0^{\pi/2} \cos^n x \sin x\, dx$$

Put $\cos x = t$, $-\sin dx = dt$

$x = 0 \quad t = 1$

$x = \dfrac{\pi}{2} \quad t = 0$

$$I_{1n} = -\int_1^0 t^n \, dt = -\left(\dfrac{t^{n+1}}{n+1}\right)_1^0$$

$$= -\dfrac{1}{n+1}(0 - 1)$$

$$= \dfrac{1}{n+1}$$

$$\therefore \quad I_{mn} = \dfrac{m-1}{m+n} \dfrac{m-3}{m+n-2} \cdots \dfrac{2}{3+n} \dfrac{1}{n+1} \qquad \ldots \text{(ii)}$$

where, n may be odd or even.

When m is even and n is odd.

$$I_{mn} = \dfrac{m-1}{m+n} \dfrac{m-3}{m+n-2} \cdots \dfrac{m-5}{m+n-4} \cdots \dfrac{1}{2+n} \times \dfrac{n-1}{n} \dfrac{n-3}{n-2} \cdots \dfrac{2}{3} \cdots \text{(iii)}$$

when m is even and n is even.

$$I_{mn} = \dfrac{m-1}{m+n} \dfrac{m-3}{m+n-2} \cdots \dfrac{m-5}{m+n-4} \cdots \dfrac{1}{2+n} \times \dfrac{n-1}{n} \dfrac{n-3}{n-2} \cdots \dfrac{2}{3} \dfrac{\pi}{2}$$

$$\ldots \text{(iv)}$$

We have simple rule,

$$I_{mn} = \int_0^{\pi/2} \sin^m x \cos^n x \, dx$$

$= \dfrac{[(m-1) \times \text{factors reducing by 2 till last positive integer}}{(m+n) \times \text{factors reducing by 2 till last positive integer}}$

$\times \dfrac{[(n-1) \times \text{factors reducing by 2 till last positive integer}] \times K}{(m+n) \times \text{factors reducing by 2 till last positive integer}}$

$$\ldots \text{(v)}$$

where, $\quad K = \dfrac{\pi}{2}$; if m and n are both even

$\quad\quad\quad\quad = 1$; otherwise

SOLVED EXAMPLES

Examples 3.30 : $\int_0^{\pi/2} \sin^4 x \cos^5 x \, dx$

Solution : By using formula (iii)

$$= \frac{3 \cdot 1 \cdot 4 \cdot 2}{9 \cdot 7 \cdot 5 \cdot 3 \cdot 1} = \frac{8}{315}$$

Example 3.31 : $\int_0^{\pi/2} \sin^8 x \cos^4 x \, dx.$

Solution : Let, $I \int_0^{\pi/2} \sin^8 x \cos^4 x \, dx$

$$I = \frac{7 \cdot 5 \cdot 3 \cdot 1 \cdot 3 \cdot 1}{12 \cdot 10 \cdot 8 \cdot 6 \cdot 4 \cdot 2} \cdot \frac{\pi}{2} \qquad \text{Using formula (iv)}$$

$$= \frac{7\pi}{1024}$$

Example 3.32 : $\int_0^{\pi/2} \sin^4 x \cos^3 x \, dx$

Solution : Let, $I = \int_0^{\pi/2} \sin^4 x \cos^3 x \, dx$

$$I = \frac{3 \cdot 1 \cdot 2 \cdot 1}{7 \cdot 5 \cdot 3} = \frac{2}{35}$$

Example 3.33 : $\int_0^{\pi/6} \cos^4 3x \sin^2 6x \, dx$

Solution : Put $\quad 3x = y$
$\qquad\qquad\qquad 3dx = dy$

When $\quad x = 0 \qquad\qquad y = 0$

$\qquad\quad x = \dfrac{\pi}{6} \qquad\qquad y = \dfrac{\pi}{2}$

$$= \int_0^{\pi/2} \cos^4 y \sin^2 (2y) \frac{dy}{3}$$

$$= \frac{1}{3} \int_0^{\pi/2} \cos^4 y \, (2 \sin y \cos y)^2 \, dy$$

$$= \frac{4}{3} \int_0^{\pi/2} \cos^6 y \sin^2 y \, dy$$

$$= \frac{4}{3} \int_0^{\pi/2} \sin^2 y \cos^6 y \, dy$$

$$= \frac{4}{3} \left(\frac{1}{8} \frac{5}{6} \frac{3}{4} \frac{1}{2} \frac{\pi}{2} \right) = \frac{5}{192} \pi$$

Example 3.34 : $\int_0^{\pi} \sin^4 \frac{x}{2} \cos^3 \frac{x}{2} \, dx$

Solution : $\quad I = \int_0^{\pi} \sin^4 \frac{x}{2} \cos^3 \frac{x}{2} \, dx$

Put $\quad \frac{x}{2} = \theta \quad dx = 2d\theta$

When $\quad x = 0 \qquad \theta = 0$

$\qquad x = \pi \qquad \theta = \frac{\pi}{2}$

$$= \int_0^{\pi/2} \sin^4 \theta \cos^3 \theta \, (2 \, d\theta)$$

$$= 2 \int_0^{\pi/2} \sin^4 \theta \cos^3 \theta \, d\theta$$

$$= 2 \frac{3 \cdot 1 \cdot 2}{7 \cdot 5 \cdot 3 \cdot 1} = \frac{4}{35}$$

Example 3.35 : $\int_0^{\pi/2} \sqrt{\cos x} \sin^5 x \, dx$

Solution : $I = \int_0^{\pi/2} \sqrt{\cos x} \sin^5 x \, dx$

Put $\cos x = t$

$\therefore \qquad 1 - \cos^2 x = \sin^2 x$

$\qquad\qquad 1 - t^2 = \sin^2 x$

$\qquad\qquad -\sin x \, dx = dt$

When $x = 0$ $t = 1$
$x = \dfrac{\pi}{2}$ $t = 0$

$$\int_0^{\pi/2} \sqrt{\cos x}\,(\sin^2 x)^2\,(\sin x\,dx)$$

$$\int_1^0 \sqrt{t}\,(1 - t^2)^2\,(-dt)$$

$$= \int_0^1 t^{1/2}(1 - 2t^2 + t^4)\,dt$$

$$= \int_0^1 (t^{1/2} - 2t^{5/2} + t^{9/2})\,dt$$

$$= \left[\dfrac{t^{3/2}}{3/2} - 2\dfrac{t^{7/2}}{7/2} + \dfrac{t^{11/2}}{11/2}\right]_0^1$$

$$= \dfrac{2}{3} - \dfrac{4}{7} + \dfrac{2}{11} = \dfrac{64}{231}$$

Example 3.36 : $\displaystyle\int_0^2 x^3\sqrt{2 - x}\,dx$

Solution : $I = \displaystyle\int_0^2 x^3\sqrt{2 - x}\,dx$

Put $x = 2\sin^2\theta$
 $dx = 4\sin\theta\cos\theta\,d\theta$

When $x = 0$ $\theta = 0$
 $x = 2$ $\theta = \dfrac{\pi}{2}$

$$= \int_0^{\pi/2} (2\sin^2\theta)^3\sqrt{2 - 2\sin^2\theta}\,4\sin\theta\cos\theta\,d\theta$$

$$= 32\sqrt{2}\int_0^{\pi/2}\sin^7\theta\cos^2\theta\,d\theta = 32\sqrt{2}\,\dfrac{6\cdot 4\cdot 2}{9\cdot 7\cdot 5\cdot 3\cdot 1}$$

$$= \dfrac{512\sqrt{2}}{315}$$

Example 3.37 : $\int_0^2 x^5 (4 - x^2)^{3/2} \, dx$

Solution : $I = \int_0^2 x^5 (4 - x^2)^{3/2} \, dx$

Put $x = 2 \sin \theta$

$dx = 2 \cos \theta \, d\theta$

$x = 0 \quad \theta = 0$

$x = 2 \quad \theta = \dfrac{\pi}{2}$

$= \int_0^{\pi/2} 2^5 \sin^5 \theta \, (4 - 4 \sin^2 \theta)^{3/2} \, 2 \cos \theta \, d\theta$

$= 2^5 (4)^{3/2} \int_0^{\pi/2} \sin^5 \theta \, (\cos^2 \theta)^{3/2} \cos \theta \, d\theta$

$= 2^9 \int_0^{\pi/2} \sin^5 \theta \cos^4 \theta \, d\theta$

$= 2^9 \dfrac{4}{9} \dfrac{2}{7} \dfrac{1}{5} = \dfrac{2^{12}}{315} = \dfrac{4096}{315}$

Example 3.38 : $\int_0^{\pi/4} \sin^7 2\theta \, d\theta$

Solution : Put $2\theta = x$

$d\theta = \dfrac{dx}{2}$

When $\theta = 0 \quad x = 0$

$\theta = \dfrac{\pi}{4} \quad x = \dfrac{\pi}{2}$

$\int_0^{\pi/2} \sin^7 x \, \dfrac{dx}{2} = \dfrac{1}{2} \int_0^{\pi/2} \sin^7 x \, dx$

$= \dfrac{1}{2} \dfrac{6}{7} \dfrac{4}{5} \dfrac{2}{3} \cdot 1 = \dfrac{8}{35}$

Example 3.39 : $\int_0^\pi x \sin^4 x \cos^6 x \, dx$

Solution : $I = \int_0^\pi (\pi - x) \sin^4(\pi - x) \cos^6(\pi - x) \, dx$

$= \int_0^\pi (\pi - x) \sin^4 x \cos^6 x \, dx$

$I = \pi \int_0^\pi \sin^4 x \cos^6 x - \int_0^\pi x \sin^4 \cos^6 x \, dx$

$I = \pi \int_0^\pi \sin^4 x \cos^6 x - I$

$2I = \pi \int_0^\pi \sin^4 x \cos^6 x$

$I = \frac{\pi}{2} \int_0^\pi \sin^4 x \cos^6 x$

$2I = 2\pi \int_0^{\pi/2} \sin^4 x \cos^6 x \, dx \qquad \int_0^\pi f(x) \, dx = 2 \int_0^{\pi/2} f(x) \, dx$

$I = \pi \int_0^{\pi/2} \sin^4 x \cos^6 x \, dx$

$= \pi \left[\frac{3 \cdot 1 \cdot 5 \cdot 3 \cdot 1}{10 \cdot 8 \cdot 6 \cdot 4 \cdot 2} \frac{\pi}{2} \right] = \frac{3\pi^2}{512}$

Example 3.40 : $\int_0^\infty \frac{x^2}{(a^2 + x^2)^4} \, dx$

Solution : Put $\quad x = a \tan \theta$

$dx = a \sec^2 \theta \, d\theta$

When $\quad x = 0 \Rightarrow \theta = 0$

$$x = \infty \Rightarrow \theta = \frac{\pi}{2}$$

$$= \int_0^{\pi/2} \frac{a^2 \tan^2 \theta}{(a^2 + a^2 \tan^2 \theta)^4} \sec^2 \theta \, d\theta$$

$$= \int_0^{\pi/2} \frac{a^3 \tan^2 \theta \sec^2 \theta \, d\theta}{a^8 \sec^8 \theta}$$

$$= \frac{1}{a^5} \int_0^{\pi/2} \tan^2 \theta \cos^6 \theta \, d\theta$$

$$= \frac{1}{a^5} \int_0^{\pi/2} \sin^2 \theta \cos^4 \theta \, d\theta$$

$$= \frac{1}{a^5} \left[\frac{1}{6} \cdot \frac{3}{4} \cdot \frac{1}{2} \cdot \frac{\pi}{2} \right]$$

$$= \frac{\pi}{32 \, a^5}$$

Example 3.41 : $\int_0^{2a} x^3 (2ax - x^2)^{3/2} \, dx$

Solution : Put $x = 2a \sin^2 \theta$

$\therefore \quad dx = 4a \sin \theta \cos \theta \, d\theta$

$$= \int_0^{\pi/2} 8a^3 \sin^6\theta \, (4a^2 \sin^2\theta - 4a^2 \sin^4 \theta)^{3/2} \, 4a \sin \theta \cos \theta \, d\theta$$

$$= \int_0^{\pi/2} 256 \, a^7 \sin^9 \theta \, (1 - \sin^2 \theta)^{3/2} \sin \theta \cos \theta \, d\theta$$

$$= 256 \, a^7 \int_0^{\pi/2} \sin^{10} \theta \cos^4 \theta \, d\theta$$

$$= 256 \, a^7 \, \frac{(9 \cdot 7 \cdot 5 \cdot 3) \, 3 \cdot 1}{14 \cdot 12 \cdot 10 \cdot 8 \cdot 6 \cdot 4 \cdot 2} \cdot \frac{\pi}{2} = \frac{9}{16} \pi a^7$$

EXERCISE 3.3

1. $\int_0^{\pi/2} \sin^{15}x \cos^3x \, dx$

2. $\int_0^{\pi/2} \sin^5x \cos^6x \, dx$

3. $\int_0^{\pi/2} \sin^8x \cos^{10}x \, dx$

4. $\int_0^{\pi/2} \sin^4x \cos^3x \, dx$

5. $\int_0^{\pi/6} \sin^2 6x \cos^6 3x \, dx$

6. $\int_0^{\pi/4} \cos^3 2x \sin^4 4x \, dx$

7. $\int_0^{\pi/8} \sin^4 8x \cos^6 4x \, dx$

8. $\int_0^{\pi/6} \sin^2 6\theta \cos^4 3\theta \, d\theta$

9. $\int_0^1 x^8 \sqrt{1-x^2} \, dx$

10. $\int_0^1 x^2 (1-x)^{3/2} \, dx$

11. $\int_0^1 x^{3/2} (1-x)^{3/2} \, dx$

12. $\int_0^\infty \frac{x}{(1+x^2)^3} \, dx$

13. $\int_0^\infty \frac{x^4}{(1+x^2)^4}$

14. $\displaystyle\int_0^{2a} x^2 (2ax - x^2)^{1/2} \, dx$

15. $\displaystyle\int_0^2 x^4 \sqrt{4 - x^2} \, dx$

16. $\displaystyle\int_0^a x \sqrt{ax - x^2} \, dx$

17. $\displaystyle\int_0^\infty \frac{x^{14} - x^9}{(1 + x^5)^5} \, dx$

18. $\displaystyle\int_0^\pi \sin^5 x \cos^8 x \, dx$

19. $\displaystyle\int_0^{\pi/2} \sin^8 x \cos^4 x \, dx$

20. $\displaystyle\int_0^4 x^3 \sqrt{4x - x^2} \, dx$

21. $\displaystyle\int_0^2 x^3 \sqrt{2 - x} \, dx$

22. $\displaystyle\int_0^{2a} x^{7/2} (2a - x)^{-1/2} \, dx$

23. $\displaystyle\int_0^{2a} x^{9/2} (2a - x)^{-1/2} \, dx$

24. $\displaystyle\int_0^{\pi/2} \sin^{15} x \cos^3 x \, dx$

25. $\displaystyle\int_0^\infty \frac{x^2}{(1 + x^2)^{7/2}} \, dx$

ANSWERS 3.3

1. $\dfrac{1}{144}$
2. $\dfrac{8}{693}$
3. $\dfrac{35\pi}{2^{17}}$
4. $\dfrac{2}{35}$
5. $\dfrac{3\pi}{384}$
6. $\dfrac{128}{1155}$
7. $\dfrac{9\pi}{512}$
8. $\dfrac{5\pi}{192}$
9. $\dfrac{7\pi}{512}$
10. $\dfrac{16}{315}$
11. $\dfrac{3\pi}{128}$
12. $\dfrac{1}{4}$
13. $\dfrac{\pi}{32}$
14. $\dfrac{5\pi a^4}{8}$
15. 2π
16. $\dfrac{\pi a^3}{16}$
17. 0 [**Hint :** Put $x^5 = \tan^2 \theta$]
18. $\dfrac{4\pi}{1187}$
19. $\dfrac{3\pi}{1024}$
20. 28π [**Hint :** $x = 4 \sin^2 \theta$]
21. $\dfrac{512\sqrt{2}}{315}$ [**Hint :** $x = \sin^2 \theta$]
22. $\dfrac{35\pi a^4}{8}$
23. $\dfrac{63\pi a^5}{8}$
24. $\dfrac{1}{144}$
25. $\dfrac{2}{15}$

MISCELLANEOUS EXERCISES

(I) Theory Questions :

1. Find reduction formula for $\int \sin^n x \, dx$
2. Find reduction formula for $\int \cos^n x \, dx$
3. Find reduction formula for $\int \sin^m x \cos^n x \, dx$

4. Find reduction formula for $\int_0^{\pi/2} \sin^n x \, dx$

5. Find reduction formula for $\int_0^{\pi/2} \cos^n x \, dx$

6. Find reduction formula for $\int_0^{\pi/2} \sin^m x \cos^n x \, dx$

(II) Numerical Problems :

1. $\int_0^{\pi/2} \cos^6 x \, dx$

2. $\int_0^{\pi/2} \sin^4 2x \, dx$

3. $\int_0^{\pi/2} \sin\left(\frac{1}{2}\right) x \, dx$

4. $\int_0^{\pi/2} \sin^8 x \, dx$

5. $\int_0^1 x^5 \sin^1 x \, dx$

6. $\int_0^{\pi} \sin^4 \theta \, \dfrac{\sqrt{1 - \cos\theta}}{(1 + \cos\theta)^2} \, d\theta$

7. $\int_0^{\pi/2} \cos^4 x \sin^2 x \, dx$

8. $\int_0^{\pi/2} \sin^3 x \cos^4 x \, dx$

9. $\int_0^{\pi/2} \sin x \cos^3 x \, dx$

10. $\int_0^{\pi/2} \sin^6 x \cos^2 x \, dx$

ANSWERS

1. $\dfrac{5\pi}{32}$ 2. $\dfrac{3\pi}{32}$

3. $\dfrac{16}{25}$ 4. $\dfrac{35\pi}{256}$

5. $\dfrac{11\pi}{192}$ 6. $\dfrac{64\sqrt{2}}{15}$

7. $\dfrac{\pi}{32}$ 8. $\dfrac{2}{35}$

9. $\dfrac{1}{4}$ 10. $\dfrac{5\pi}{256}$

(III) Multiple Choice Questions :

Choose the correct alternative for each of the following :

1. $\displaystyle\int_0^{\pi/2} \sin^n x\, dx = \dfrac{(n-1)(n-3)(n-5)\ldots 2}{n(n-2)(n-4)\ldots 3}$, when n = ...

   (a) even   (b) odd
   (c) positive   (d) none of these

2. $\displaystyle\int_0^{\pi/2} \sin^n x\, dx = \dfrac{(n-1)(n-3)(n-5)\ldots 3\cdot 1}{n(n-2)(n-4)\ldots 4\cdot 2}\cdot\dfrac{\pi}{2}$ when n = ...

   (a) even   (b) odd
   (c) positive   (d) none of these

3. $\displaystyle\int_0^{\pi/2} \cos^n x\, dx = \dfrac{(n-1)(n-3)(n-5)\ldots 2}{n(n-2)(n-4)\ldots 3}\cdot 1$ when n = ...

   (a) even   (b) odd
   (c) positive   (d) none of these

4. $\displaystyle\int_0^{\pi/2} \cos^n x\, dx = \dfrac{(n-1)(n-3)(n-5)\ldots 3\cdot 1}{n(n-2)(n-4)\ldots 4\cdot 2}\dfrac{\pi}{2}$ when n = ...

   (a) even   (b) odd
   (c) positive   (d) none of these

5. $\int_0^{\pi/2} \cos^6 x \, dx$ is ......

(a) $\dfrac{5\pi}{32}$ (b) $\dfrac{5}{32}$

(c) $\dfrac{32\pi}{5}$ (d) none of these

6. $\int_0^{\pi/2} \cos^{10} x \, dx$ ......

(a) $\dfrac{63\pi}{256}$ (b) $\dfrac{63\pi}{512}$

(c) $\dfrac{63}{512}$ (d) none of these

7. $\int_0^{\pi/2} \sin^7 x \, dx = $ ......

(a) $\dfrac{16}{35}\pi$ (b) $\dfrac{35\pi}{16}$

(c) $\dfrac{16}{35}$ (d) none of these

8. $\int_0^{\pi} \sin\left(\dfrac{1}{2}x\right) dx = $ ......

(a) $\dfrac{25}{16}$ (b) $\dfrac{16}{25}$

(c) $\dfrac{16}{25}\pi$ (d) none of these

9. $\int_0^{\pi/4} \sin^7 \theta \, d\theta = $ ......

(a) $\dfrac{35}{8}$ (b) $\dfrac{8}{35}$

(c) $\dfrac{8}{35}\pi$ (d) none of these

10. $\int_0^{\pi/2} \sin^m x \cos^n x \, dx$ is, when m and n are even

   (a) $I_{m,n} = \left(\dfrac{n-1}{m+n}\right)\left(\dfrac{n-3}{m+n-2}\right) \cdots \left(\dfrac{1}{m+2}\right)\left(\dfrac{m-1}{m}\right)\left(\dfrac{m-3}{m-2}\right) \cdots \dfrac{1}{2}\dfrac{\pi}{2}$

   (b) $I_{mn} = \left(\dfrac{n-1}{m+n}\right)\left(\dfrac{n-3}{m+2-2}\right) \cdots \left(\dfrac{1}{m+2}\right)\left(\dfrac{m-1}{m}\right)\left(\dfrac{m-3}{m-2}\right)\dfrac{2}{3} \cdot 1$

   (c) $I_{mn} = \dfrac{(n-1)}{(m+n)} \dfrac{(m-3)}{(m+n-2)} \cdots \dfrac{2}{(m+3)} \dfrac{1}{m+1}$

   (d) None of these

11. When n is even and m is odd, $\int_0^{\pi/2} \sin^m x \cos^n x \, dx$ is

   (a) $I_{m,n} = \left(\dfrac{n-1}{m+n}\right)\left(\dfrac{n-3}{m+n-2}\right) \cdots \left(\dfrac{1}{m+2}\right)\left(\dfrac{m-1}{m}\right)\left(\dfrac{m-3}{m-2}\right) \cdots \dfrac{1}{2}\dfrac{\pi}{2}$

   (b) $I_{mn} = \left(\dfrac{n-1}{m+n}\right)\left(\dfrac{n-3}{m+2-2}\right) \cdots \left(\dfrac{1}{m+2}\right)\left(\dfrac{m-1}{m}\right)\left(\dfrac{m-3}{m-2}\right)\dfrac{2}{3} \cdot 1$

   (c) $I_{mn} = \dfrac{(n-1)}{(m+n)} \dfrac{(m-3)}{(m+n-2)} \cdots \dfrac{2}{(m+3)} \dfrac{1}{m+1}$

   (d) None of these

12. $\int_0^{\pi/2} \sin^4 x \cos^5 x \, dx = \ldots\ldots$

   (a) $\dfrac{15}{8}$ (b) $\dfrac{8}{15}$

   (c) $\dfrac{8}{15}\pi$ (d) none of these

13. $\int_0^{\pi/2} \sin^7 x \cos^4 x \, dx = \ldots\ldots$

   (a) $\dfrac{3}{1024}$ (b) $\dfrac{1024}{3}$

   (c) $\dfrac{3}{1024}\pi$ (d) none of these

14. $\int_0^{\pi/4} \sin^7 2\theta \, d\theta = $ ......

   (a) $\dfrac{8}{35}$ (b) $\dfrac{35}{8}$

   (c) $\dfrac{8}{35}\pi$ (d) none of these

15. $\int_0^{\pi/2} \sin^4 x \cos^3 x \, dx$ ......

   (a) $\dfrac{2}{35}$ (b) $\dfrac{35}{2}$

   (c) $\dfrac{2}{35}\pi$ (d) none of these

ANSWERS

1. (b)	2. (a)	3. (b)	4. (a)	5. (a)	6. (b)	7. (c)	8. (b)
9. (b)	10. (a)	11. (b)	12. (b)	13. (c)	14. (a)	15. (a)	

CHAPTER 4

VECTOR CALCULUS

Vector calculus or vector analysis is a branch of Mathematics concerned with differentiation and integration of vector fields, primary in three dimensional Euclidean space $\mathbb{R}^3$. The term vector calculus is some times used as a synonym for the broader subject of multivariable calculus, which includes vector calculus, as well as partial derivatives and multiple integrals. Vector calculus plays an important role in differential geometry and in the study of partial differential equations. It is used extensively in physics and engineering, especially in the fields, gravitational fields and fluid flow. Vector calculus was developed from quanternian analysis by J. Willard Gibbs and Oliver Heaviside near the end of the 19th century and most notation and terminology was established by Gibbs and Edwin Bidwell Wilson in their 1901 book vector analysis. The basic objects in the vector calculus are scalar fields (scalar-valued functions) and vector fields (vector valued functions). These are then combined or transformed under various operations and integration.

Josiah Willard Gibbs

Oliver Heaviside

4.1 INTRODUCTION

We have studied vector and their Algebra in XII standard. Also, we have discussed the applications of vectors in solid geometry and mechanics. In this chapter, first we will discuss basic definitions and then we define a vector differentiation and a new operator del (∇). From this operator, we will define gradient, divergence and curl with their properties.

Review :

    1. Scalar : A quantity having magnitude but no direction is called a scalar.

    e.g. mass, length, time, temperature, and any real number. Scalars are indicated by letters in ordinary type as in elementary algebra.

    Operations with scalars follow the same rules as in elementary algebra.

    2. Vector : A quantity having both magnitude and direction is called a vector.

    e.g. Velocity, Force, Acceleration

    Graphically vectors are indicated by an arrow (OP) defining the direction and magnitude of the vector indicated by its length. The point O is called the initial point and P is called a terminal point of a vector.

    Analytically a vector is represented by a letter with an arrow over it, as $\overline{A}$ and its magnitude by $|\overline{A}|$ or A. In printed works bold faced type such as **A** is used to indicate the vector $\overline{A}$ while $|A|$ or A indicate its magnitude.

    3. Vector Algebra :

    (a) Two vectors $\overline{A}$ and $\overline{B}$ are equal if they have same direction and magnitude.

    (b) A vector having direction opposite to that of a vector $\overline{A}$ but having same magnitude is denoted by $-\overline{A}$.

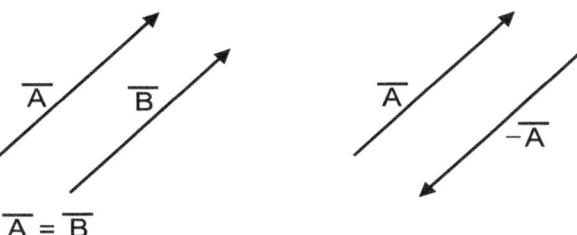

Fig. 4.1

(c) **Addition of vectors :** The sum or addition of vector $\overline{A}$ and $\overline{B}$ is a vector $\overline{C}$ formed by placing the initial point of $\overline{B}$ on the terminal point of $\overline{A}$ and then joining the initial point of $\overline{A}$ to the terminal point of $\overline{B}$. This sum is written as $\overline{C} = \overline{A} + \overline{B}$.

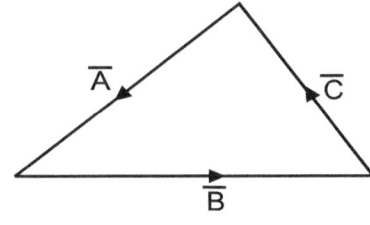

Fig. 4.2

Similarly, for addition of vectors, we use law of parallelogram.

(d) **Difference of vectors :** Sum of two vectors $\overline{A}$ and $-\overline{B}$ is called the difference of vectors $\overline{A}$ and $\overline{B}$ and it is denoted by $\overline{A} - \overline{B}$.

(e) **Multiplication of a vector by a scalar quantity :** The product of a vector $\overline{A}$ by a scalar m is a vector $m\overline{A}$ with magnitude m times the magnitude of $\overline{A}$ and with the direction same as or opposite to that of $\overline{A}$, according as m is positive or negative.

(f) **Unit vector :** A vector having magnitude unit with any direction is called a unit vector.

If $\overline{A}$ is a vector with magnitude A then $\dfrac{\overline{A}}{A}$ is a unit vector in the direction of $\overline{A}$.

(g) **Rectangular unit vectors :** Unit vectors in the positive direction of x, y, z in three dimensional co-ordinate system are denoted by $\hat{i}, \hat{j}, \hat{k}$.

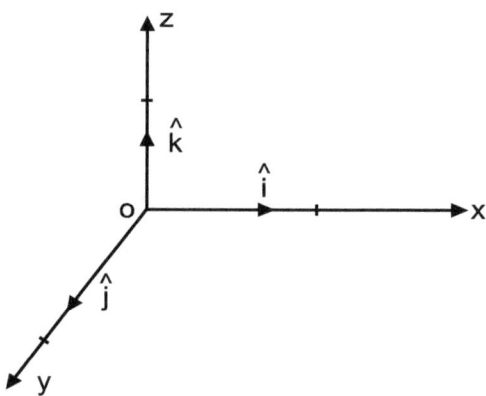

Fig. 4.3

(h) **Position vector of a point :** Let P(x, y, z) be any point in the space. Then the vector $\overline{OP}$ is called the position vector of a point P and generally a position vector of a point (x, y, z) is denoted by $\overline{r}$.

∴ $\overline{OP} = \overline{r} = x\hat{i} + y\hat{j} + z\hat{k}$ and its magnitude

$r = |\overline{OP}| = \sqrt{x^2 + y^2 + z^2}$.

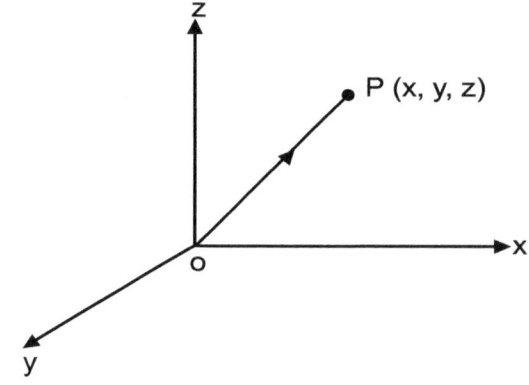

Fig. 4.4

(i) **Scalar product or a dot product of two vectors :** Let $\overline{A}$ and $\overline{B}$ are two vectors and θ be an angle between them then the scalar quantity AB cos θ is called the scalar product or dot product of vectors $\overline{A}$ and $\overline{B}$ and is denoted by $\overline{A} \cdot \overline{B}$

Thus, $\overline{A} \cdot \overline{B} = AB \cos \theta$.

From the above definition

$$\hat{i} \cdot \hat{i} = \hat{j} \cdot \hat{j} = \hat{k} \cdot \hat{k} = 1 \text{ and } \hat{i} \cdot \hat{j} = \hat{j} \cdot \hat{k} = \hat{k} \cdot \hat{i} = 0$$

(j) **Vector product or a cross product of two vectors :** If $\overline{A}$ and $\overline{B}$ be two vectors and θ be an angle between them then the vector quantity AB sin θ · $\hat{n}$, where $\hat{n}$ is a vector perpendicular to the plane $\overline{A}$ and $\overline{B}$, $\hat{n}$ form a right handed screw system is called a cross product or a vector product of $\overline{A}$ and $\overline{B}$. It is denoted by $\overline{A} \times \overline{B}$.

$$\therefore \quad \overline{A} \times \overline{B} = A \cdot B \cdot \sin \theta \cdot \hat{n}$$

From the above definition it is clear that,

$$\overline{A} \times \overline{B} = -\overline{B} \times \overline{A} \text{ and}$$

(i) $\hat{i} \times \hat{j} = \hat{k}, \hat{j} \times \hat{k} = \hat{i}, \hat{k} \times \hat{i} = \hat{j}$

(ii) $\hat{i} \times \hat{i} = \hat{j} \times \hat{j} = \hat{k} \times \hat{k} = 0$

(iii) $\hat{j} \times \hat{i} = -\hat{k}, \hat{k} \times \hat{j} = -\hat{i}, \hat{i} \times \hat{k} = -\hat{j}$

Example : If $\overline{A} = a_1\hat{i} + a_2\hat{j} + a_3\hat{k}$ and $\overline{B} = b_1\hat{i} + b_2\hat{j} + b_3\hat{k}$ then

$$\overline{A} \cdot \overline{B} = a_1b_1 + a_2b_2 + a_3b_3$$

and

$$\overline{A} \times \overline{B} = \begin{vmatrix} \hat{i} & \hat{j} & \hat{k} \\ a_1 & a_2 & a_3 \\ b_1 & b_2 & b_3 \end{vmatrix}$$

Vector Differentiation :

Consider the function $\overline{r} = f(t)$. As t changes to t + δt, f(t) changes to f(t + δt) then $\lim\limits_{\delta t \to 0} \dfrac{f(t + \delta t) - f(t)}{\delta t}$ if it exist is called the derivative f(t) and is denoted by $\dfrac{d\, f(t)}{dt}$.

$$\therefore \quad \frac{d\,f(t)}{dt} = \lim_{\delta t \to 0} \frac{f(t + \delta t) - f(t)}{\delta t}$$

Standard rules of differentiations of vectors :

1. $\dfrac{d}{dt}(\overline{F} \pm \overline{G}) = \dfrac{d\overline{F}}{dt} \pm \dfrac{d\overline{G}}{dt}$

2. $\dfrac{d}{dt}(\overline{F} \cdot \overline{G}) = \overline{F}\,\dfrac{d\overline{G}}{dt} + \overline{G}\,\dfrac{d\overline{F}}{dt}$

3. $\dfrac{d}{dt}(\overline{F} \times \overline{G}) = \dfrac{d\overline{F}}{dt} \times \overline{G} + \overline{F} \times \dfrac{d\overline{G}}{dt}$

4. $\dfrac{d}{dt}(\phi\,\overline{F}) = \dfrac{d\phi}{dt}\overline{F} + \phi\,\dfrac{d\overline{F}}{dt}$

4.2 SCALAR POINT FUNCTION

If to each point (x, y, z) of region R in space their corresponds a number of scalar $\phi(x, y, z)$, then ϕ is called a scalar point function defined in R.

Example : (i) The temperature at any point within on the earth's surface at a certain time defines a scalar field.

(ii) $\phi(x, y, z) = x^2y - z^4$ defines a scalar field.

Note : A scalar field which is independent of time is called a stationary or study state scalar field.

4.3 VECTOR POINT FUNCTION

If to each point (x, y, z) of region R in space there corresponds to a vector $\overline{V}(x, y, z)$ then $\overline{V}$ is called the vector point function defined in R.

Example :

(i) The velocity at any point (x, y, z) within a moving fluid is known at a certain time is defines a vector field.

(ii) $\overline{V}(x, y, z) = x^2y\hat{i} - y^2z^4\hat{k} + xy\hat{j}$ defines vector field.

Note : A vector field which is independent of time is called stationary or a study state vector field.

4.3.1 The Vector Differential Operator Del

We now define a new operator ∇ (read as del) by

$$\nabla = \left(\hat{i}\frac{\partial}{\partial x} + \hat{j}\frac{\partial}{\partial y} + \hat{k}\frac{\partial}{\partial z}\right)$$

This operator possesses properties analogous to those of ordinary vectors. It is useful in defining three quantities which arise in practical applications and are known as the gradient, divergence and curl. The operator ∇ is also known as **nabla.**

Note : ∇ looks like a vector but it is not a vector.

4.3.2 The Gradient

Let $\phi(x, y, z)$ be defined and differentiable at each point (x, y, z) in a certain region of space (i.e. ϕ defines a differentiable scalar field) then the gradient of ϕ, written as $\nabla\phi$ is defined by

$$\text{gradient of } \phi = \nabla\phi = \left(\hat{i}\frac{\partial}{\partial x} + \hat{j}\frac{\partial}{\partial y} + \hat{k}\frac{\partial}{\partial z}\right)\phi$$

gradient of ϕ is denoted by grad ϕ

$$\therefore \quad \text{grad } \phi = \nabla\phi = \hat{i}\frac{\partial \phi}{\partial x} + \hat{j}\frac{\partial \phi}{\partial y} + \hat{k}\frac{\partial \phi}{\partial z}$$

Note that $\nabla\phi$ is a vector field.

SOLVED EXAMPLES

Example 4.1 : If $f = 2xz^2 - 3xy - 4x$, find gradient of ϕ at $(1, -1, -2)$.

Solution :

$$\text{grad } \phi = \nabla\phi$$

$$= \left(\hat{i}\frac{\partial}{\partial x} + \hat{j}\frac{\partial}{\partial y} + \hat{k}\frac{\partial}{\partial z}\right)(2xz^2 - 3xy - 4x)$$

$$= \hat{i}\frac{\partial}{\partial x}(2xz^2 - 3xy - 4x) + \hat{j}\frac{\partial}{\partial y}(2xz^2 - 3xy - 4x)$$

$$+ \hat{k}\frac{\partial}{\partial z}(2xz^2 - 3xy - 4x)$$

$$\text{grad } \phi = \hat{i}(2z^2 - 3y - 4) + \hat{j}(-3x) + \hat{k}(4xz)$$

$\therefore$ grad $\phi|_{(1, -1, -2)} = \hat{i}(7) + \hat{j}(-3) + \hat{k}(-8)$

$\therefore$ grad $\phi|_{(1, -1, -2)} = 7\hat{i} - 3\hat{j} - 8\hat{k}$

Example 4.2 : If $\phi(x, y, z) = 3x^2y - y^3z^2$, find $\nabla\phi$ (or grad ϕ) at the point $(1, -2, -1)$.

Solution :
$$\nabla\phi = \left(\hat{i}\frac{\partial}{\partial x} + \hat{j}\frac{\partial}{\partial y} + \hat{k}\frac{\partial}{\partial z}\right)(3x^2y - y^3z^2)$$

$$= \hat{i}\frac{\partial}{\partial x}(3x^2y - y^3z^2) + \hat{j}\frac{\partial}{\partial y}(3x^2y - y^3z^2)$$

$$+ \hat{k}\frac{\partial}{\partial z}(3x^2y - y^3z^2)$$

$$= 6xy\hat{i} + (3x^2 - 3y^2z^2)\hat{j} + (-2y^3z)$$

$$\nabla\phi|_{(1, -2, -1)} = 6(1)(-2)\hat{i} + [3(1)^2 - 3(-2)^2(-1)^2]\hat{j}$$

$$+ [-2(-2)^3(-1)]\hat{k}$$

$\therefore \quad \nabla\phi|_{(1, -2, -1)} = -12\hat{i} - 9\hat{j} - 16\hat{k}$

Example 4.3 : Show that $\nabla r^n = nr^{n-2}\bar{r}$

Solution : We know that, $\bar{r} = x\hat{i} + y\hat{j} + z\hat{k}$

$\therefore \quad r = \sqrt{x^2 + y^2 + z^2}$ i.e. $r = (x^2 + y^2 + z^2)^{1/2}$

$\therefore \quad r^n = (x^2 + y^2 + z^2)^{n/2}$

$\therefore \quad \nabla r^n = \left(\hat{i}\frac{\partial}{\partial x} + \hat{j}\frac{\partial}{\partial y} + \hat{k}\frac{\partial}{\partial z}\right)(x^2 + y^2 + z^2)^{n/2}$

$$= \hat{i}\frac{\partial}{\partial x}(x^2 + y^2 + z^2)^{n/2} + \hat{j}\frac{\partial}{\partial y}(x^2 + y^2 + z^2)^{n/2}$$

$$+ \hat{k}\frac{\partial}{\partial z}(x^2 + y^2 + z^2)^{n/2}$$

$$= \frac{n}{2}(x^2 + y^2 + z^2)^{\frac{n}{2} - 1}(2x)\hat{i} + \frac{n}{2}(x^2 + y^2 + z^2)^{\frac{n}{2} - 1}$$

$$(2y)\hat{j} + \frac{n}{2}(x^2 + y^2 + z^2)^{\frac{n}{2} - 1}(2z)\hat{k}$$

$$= nx(x^2+y^2+z^2)^{\frac{n}{2}-1}\hat{i} + ny(x^2+y^2+z^2)^{\frac{n}{2}-1}\hat{j}$$

$$+ nz(x^2+y^2+z^2)^{\frac{n}{2}-1}\hat{k}$$

$$= n(x^2+y^2+z^2)^{\frac{n}{2}-1} \cdot \{x\hat{i} + y\hat{j} + z\hat{k}\}$$

But $x^2 + y^2 + z^2 = r^2$

$\therefore \quad \nabla r^n = n \cdot (r^2)^{\frac{n}{2}-1} \bar{r}$

$\therefore \quad \nabla r^n = n \cdot r^{n-2} \cdot \bar{r}$

4.4 GEOMETRICAL MEANING OF $\nabla \phi$

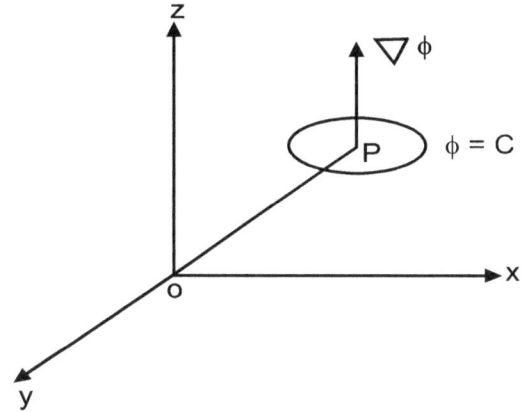

Fig. 4.5

Consider a scalar point function ϕ and let $\bar{r} = x\hat{i} + y\hat{j} + z\hat{k}$ be a position vector of a point P on the surface $\phi(x, y, z) = c$ and also we know that a surface for which the value of the function is constant is called a level surface. Here $\phi(x, y, z) = c$ is a level surface.

Now, $\quad d\bar{r} = dx\hat{i} + dy\hat{j} + dz\hat{k}$

it lies in the plane tangential to the surface $\phi(x, y, z) = c$.

Also we know that by theory of partial derivatives that

$$d\phi = \frac{\partial \phi}{\partial x}dx + \frac{\partial \phi}{\partial y}dy + \frac{\partial \phi}{\partial z}dz$$

Since $\phi(x, y, z) = c$, $d\phi = 0$

$$\therefore \quad 0 = \frac{\partial \phi}{\partial x} dx + \frac{\partial \phi}{\partial y} dy + \frac{\partial \phi}{\partial z} dz \qquad \ldots (i)$$

Consider
$$\nabla \phi \cdot d\bar{r} = \left(\hat{i} \frac{\partial \phi}{\partial x} + \hat{j} \frac{\partial \phi}{\partial y} + \hat{k} \frac{\partial \phi}{\partial z}\right) \cdot (dx\hat{i} + dy\hat{j} + dz\hat{k})$$

$$= \frac{\partial \phi}{\partial y} dx + \frac{\partial \phi}{\partial y} dy + \frac{\partial \phi}{\partial z} dz$$

$$= 0 \qquad \ldots \text{by (i)}$$

$\therefore \quad \nabla \phi \cdot d\bar{r} = 0$

Thus $\nabla \phi$ is perpendicular to a vector $d\bar{r}$.

But $d\bar{r}$ lies in the tangent plane, so $\nabla \phi$ is a vector perpendicular to the tangent plane to the surface $\phi(x, y, z) = c$ at the point (x, y, z).

4.5 DIRECTIONAL DERIVATIVE

The resolved part of $\nabla \phi$ in the direction of a given unit vector is called directional derivative of ϕ in the given direction.

Thus, directional derivative of ϕ in the direction of a vector $\bar{A}$ is $\nabla \phi \cdot \dfrac{\bar{A}}{|\bar{A}|}$.

Remark : Since the resolve part of any vector is maximum in its own direction, the directional derivative is maximum in the direction of $\nabla \phi$.

4.6 PROPERTIES OF GRADIENT

If u and v are scalar point functions then

1. grad $(u \pm v)$ = grad u $\pm$ grad v.

2. grad $(u \cdot v)$ = u $\cdot$ grad v + v grad u.

3. grad $\left(\dfrac{u}{v}\right) = \dfrac{v \text{ grad } u - u \text{ grad } v}{v^2}$

4. grad $f(u) = f'(u)$ grad u.

Proof :

1. $\text{grad}(u \pm v) = \nabla(u \pm v)$

$$= \left(\hat{i}\frac{\partial}{\partial x} + \hat{j}\frac{\partial}{\partial y} + \hat{k}\frac{\partial}{\partial z}\right)(u \pm v)$$

$$= \hat{i}\frac{\partial}{\partial x}(u \pm v) + \hat{j}\frac{\partial}{\partial y}(u \pm v) + \hat{k}\frac{\partial}{\partial z}(u \pm v)$$

$$= \hat{i}\left\{\frac{\partial u}{\partial x} \pm \frac{\partial v}{\partial x}\right\} + \hat{j}\left\{\frac{\partial u}{\partial y} \pm \frac{\partial v}{\partial z}\right\} + \hat{k}\left\{\frac{\partial u}{\partial z} \pm \frac{\partial v}{\partial z}\right\}$$

$$= \left\{\hat{i}\frac{\partial u}{\partial x} + \hat{j}\frac{\partial u}{\partial y} + \hat{k}\frac{\partial u}{\partial z}\right\} \pm \left\{\hat{i}\frac{\partial v}{\partial x} + \hat{j}\frac{\partial v}{\partial y} + \hat{k}\frac{\partial v}{\partial z}\right\}$$

$$= \left\{\hat{i}\frac{\partial}{\partial x} + \hat{j}\frac{\partial}{\partial y} + \hat{k}\frac{\partial}{\partial z}\right\}u \pm \left\{\hat{i}\frac{\partial}{\partial x} + \hat{j}\frac{\partial}{\partial y} + \hat{k}\frac{\partial}{\partial z}\right\}v$$

$$= \nabla \cdot u \pm \nabla v$$

$$= \text{grad } u \pm \text{grad } v$$

∴ $\text{grad}(u \pm v) = \text{grad } u \pm \text{grad } v$

2. $\text{grad}(u \cdot v) = \nabla \cdot (u \cdot v)$

$$= \left(\hat{i}\frac{\partial}{\partial x} + \hat{j}\frac{\partial}{\partial y} + \hat{k}\frac{\partial}{\partial z}\right)(u \cdot v)$$

$$= \hat{i}\frac{\partial}{\partial x}(uv) + \hat{j}\frac{\partial}{\partial y}(uv) + \hat{k}\frac{\partial}{\partial z}(uv)$$

$$= \hat{i}\left\{u\frac{\partial v}{\partial x} \pm v\frac{\partial u}{\partial x}\right\} + \hat{j}\left\{u\frac{\partial v}{\partial y} + v\frac{\partial u}{\partial y}\right\} + \hat{k}\left\{u\frac{\partial v}{\partial z} \pm v\frac{\partial u}{\partial z}\right\}$$

$$= u\left\{\hat{i}\frac{\partial v}{\partial x} + \hat{j}\frac{\partial v}{\partial y} + \hat{k}\frac{\partial v}{\partial z}\right\} + v\left\{\hat{i}\frac{\partial u}{\partial x} + \hat{j}\frac{\partial u}{\partial y} + \hat{k}\frac{\partial u}{\partial z}\right\}$$

$$= u\left\{\hat{i}\frac{\partial}{\partial x} + \hat{j}\frac{\partial}{\partial y} + \hat{k}\frac{\partial}{\partial z}\right\}v + v\left\{\hat{i}\frac{\partial}{\partial x} + \hat{j}\frac{\partial}{\partial y} + \hat{k}\frac{\partial}{\partial z}\right\}u$$

$$= u\nabla \cdot v + v\nabla \cdot u$$

$$= u \text{ grad } v + v \text{ grad } u$$

∴ $\text{grad}(u \cdot v) = u \cdot \text{grad } v + v \text{ grad } u$

3. $\text{grad}\left(\dfrac{u}{v}\right) = \nabla\left(\dfrac{u}{v}\right)$

$$= \left(\hat{i}\frac{\partial}{\partial x} + \hat{j}\frac{\partial}{\partial y} + \hat{k}\frac{\partial}{\partial z}\right)\left(\frac{u}{v}\right)$$

$$= \hat{i}\frac{\partial}{\partial x}\left(\frac{u}{v}\right) + \hat{j}\frac{\partial}{\partial y}\left(\frac{u}{v}\right) + \hat{k}\frac{\partial}{\partial z}\left(\frac{u}{v}\right)$$

$$= \hat{i}\left\{\frac{v\frac{\partial u}{\partial x} - u\frac{\partial v}{\partial x}}{v^2}\right\} + \hat{j}\left\{\frac{v\frac{\partial u}{\partial y} - u\frac{\partial v}{\partial y}}{v^2}\right\} + \hat{k}\left\{\frac{v\frac{\partial u}{\partial z} - u\frac{\partial v}{\partial z}}{v^2}\right\}$$

$$= \frac{v\left\{\hat{i}\frac{\partial u}{\partial x} + \hat{j}\frac{\partial u}{\partial y} + \hat{k}\frac{\partial u}{\partial z}\right\} - u\left\{\hat{i}\frac{\partial v}{\partial x} + \hat{j}\frac{\partial v}{\partial y} + \hat{k}\frac{\partial v}{\partial z}\right\}}{v^2}$$

$$= \frac{v\left\{\hat{i}\frac{\partial}{\partial x} + \hat{j}\frac{\partial}{\partial y} + \hat{k}\frac{\partial}{\partial z}\right\}u - u\left\{\hat{i}\frac{\partial}{\partial x} + \hat{j}\frac{\partial}{\partial y} + \hat{k}\frac{\partial}{\partial z}\right\}}{v^2}$$

$$= \frac{v\,\nabla u - u\,\nabla v}{v^2}$$

$$= \frac{v\,\text{grad}\,u - u\,\text{grad}\,v}{v^2}$$

$$\therefore \quad \text{grad}\left(\frac{u}{v}\right) = \frac{v\,\text{grad}\,u - u\,\text{grad}\,v}{v^2}$$

4. $\quad \text{grad}\,f(u) = \nabla \cdot f(u)$

$$= \left(\hat{i}\frac{\partial}{\partial x} + \hat{j}\frac{\partial}{\partial y} + \hat{k}\frac{\partial}{\partial z}\right)f(u)$$

$$= \hat{i}\frac{\partial}{\partial x}[f(u)] + \hat{j}\frac{\partial}{\partial y}[f(u)] + \hat{k}\frac{\partial}{\partial z}[f(u)]$$

$$= \hat{i}\frac{\partial}{\partial u}[f(u)]\frac{\partial u}{\partial x} + \hat{j}\frac{\partial}{\partial u}[f(u)]\frac{\partial u}{\partial y} + \hat{k}\frac{\partial}{\partial u}[f(u)]\frac{\partial u}{\partial z}$$

$$= \hat{i}\,f'(u)\cdot\frac{\partial u}{\partial x} + \hat{j}\,f'(u)\frac{\partial u}{\partial y} + \hat{k}\,f'(u)\frac{\partial u}{\partial z}$$

$$= f'(u)\left\{\hat{i}\frac{\partial u}{\partial x} + \hat{j}\frac{\partial u}{\partial y} + \hat{k}\frac{\partial u}{\partial z}\right\}$$

$$= f'(u)\left\{\hat{i}\frac{\partial}{\partial x} + \hat{j}\frac{\partial}{\partial y} + \hat{k}\frac{\partial}{\partial z}\right\}u$$

$$= f'(u)\,\nabla \cdot u$$

$$= f'(u) \text{ grad } u$$

Thus, $\quad \text{grad } f(u) = f'(u) \text{ grad } u$

SOLVED EXAMPLES

Example 4.4 : Find a unit normal to the surface $x^2y + 2xz = 4$ at the point $(2, -2, 3)$.

Solution : Let $\phi = x^2y + 2xz - 4 = 0$

$$\nabla\phi = \left(\hat{i}\frac{\partial}{\partial x} + \hat{j}\frac{\partial}{\partial y} + \hat{k}\frac{\partial}{\partial z}\right)(x^2y + 2xz - 4)$$

$$= \hat{i}\frac{\partial}{\partial x}(x^2y + 2xz - 4) + \hat{j}\frac{\partial}{\partial y}(x^2y + 2xz - 4) + \hat{k}\frac{\partial}{\partial z}(x^2y + 2xz - 4)$$

$$= \hat{i}(2xy + 2z) + \hat{j}(x^2) + \hat{k}(2x)$$

$$\nabla\phi|_{(2, -2, 3)} = \hat{i}\{2(2)(-2) + 2(3)\} + \hat{j}\{(2)^2\} + \hat{k}\{2(2)\}$$

$$= -2\hat{i} + 4\hat{j} + 4\hat{k}$$

is a vector normal to the surface ϕ at $(2, -2, 3)$.

Then unit normal to the surface at given point is

$$\nabla\phi|_{(2, -2, 3)} = \frac{-2\hat{i} + 4\hat{j} + 4\hat{k}}{\sqrt{4 + 16 + 16}}$$

$$\nabla\phi|_{(2, -2, 3)} = -\frac{1}{3}\hat{i} + \frac{2}{3}\hat{j} + \frac{2}{3}\hat{k}$$

Another unit normal is $\frac{1}{3}\hat{i} - \frac{2}{3}\hat{j} - \frac{2}{3}\hat{k}$ having direction opposite to that above.

Example 4.5 : Find the angle between the normals to the surface $xy = z^2$ at $(1, 4, 2)$ and $(-3, -3, 3)$

Solution : L:et $\phi = xy - z^2$

$$\therefore \quad \nabla\phi = \left(\hat{i}\frac{\partial}{\partial x} + \hat{j}\frac{\partial}{\partial y} + \hat{k}\frac{\partial}{\partial z}\right)(xy - z^2)$$

$$= \hat{i}(y) + \hat{j}(x) + \hat{k}(-2z)$$

At (1, 4, 2), $\nabla\phi = 4\hat{i} + \hat{j} - 4\hat{k}$

At (−3, −3, 3) $\nabla\phi = -3\hat{i} - 3\hat{j} - 6\hat{k}$

Let $\nabla\phi$ at (1, 4, 2) = $\bar{A}$ and $\nabla\phi$ at (−3, −3, 3) = $\bar{B}$, then we know that if θ is an angle between them, then

$$\bar{A} \cdot \bar{B} = A \cdot B \cdot \cos\theta$$

∴ $\quad A = \sqrt{16 + 1 + 16} = \sqrt{33}$

and $\quad B = \sqrt{9 + 9 + 36} = \sqrt{54}$

$$\bar{A} \cdot \bar{B} = A \cdot B \cdot \cos\theta$$

$(4\hat{i} + \hat{j} - 4\hat{k}) \cdot (-3\hat{i} - 3\hat{j} - 6\hat{k}) = \sqrt{33} \cdot \sqrt{54} \cdot \cos\theta$

$-12 - 3 + 24 = \sqrt{33} \cdot \sqrt{54} \cos\theta$

$$\cos\theta = \frac{9}{\sqrt{33}\sqrt{54}}$$

∴ $\quad \theta = \cos^{-1}\left\{\frac{9}{\sqrt{33}\sqrt{54}}\right\}$

Example 4.6 : If $\phi_1 = x + y + z$, $\phi_2 = x + y$, $\phi_3 = 2xz + 2yz + z^2$, then show that $\nabla\phi_1 \cdot [\nabla\phi_2 \times \nabla\phi_3] = 0$.

Solution : $\nabla\phi_1 = \left(\hat{i}\frac{\partial}{\partial x} + \hat{j}\frac{\partial}{\partial y} + \hat{k}\frac{\partial}{\partial z}\right)(x + y + z)$

$\nabla\phi_1 = \hat{i} + \hat{j} + \hat{k}$

$\nabla\phi_2 = \left(\hat{i}\frac{\partial}{\partial x} + \hat{j}\frac{\partial}{\partial y} + \hat{k}\frac{\partial}{\partial z}\right)(x + y)$

$\nabla\phi_2 = \hat{i} + \hat{j}$

$\nabla\phi_3 = \left(\hat{i}\frac{\partial}{\partial x} + \hat{j}\frac{\partial}{\partial y} + \hat{k}\frac{\partial}{\partial z}\right)(2xz + 2yz + z^2)$

$\nabla\phi_3 = 2z\hat{i} + 2z\hat{j} + (2x + 2y + 2z)\hat{k}$

Consider,

$\nabla\phi_2 \times \nabla\phi_3 = (\hat{i} + \hat{j}) \times [2z\hat{i} + 2z\hat{j} + (2x + 2y + 2z)\hat{k}]$

$$= \begin{vmatrix} \hat{i} & \hat{j} & \hat{k} \\ 1 & 1 & 0 \\ 2z & 2z & 2x + 2y + 2z \end{vmatrix}$$

$$= \hat{i}\{2x + 2y + 2z\} - \hat{j}\{2x + 2y + 2z\} + \hat{k}\{2z - 2z\}$$

$$\nabla\phi_2 \times \nabla\phi_3 = 2(x + y + z)\hat{i} - 2(x + y + z)\hat{j} + 0\hat{k}$$

Then consider,

$$\nabla\phi_1 \cdot [\nabla\phi_2 \times \nabla\phi_3] = [\hat{i} + \hat{j} + \hat{k}] \cdot [2(x + y + z)\hat{i} - 2(x + y + z)\hat{j} + 0\hat{k}]$$

$$= 2(x + y + z) - 2(x + y + z)$$

$$= 0$$

$\therefore \quad \nabla\phi_1 \cdot [\nabla\phi_2 \times \nabla\phi_3] = 0$

Example 4.7 : If $F = x^2z + e^{y/x}$ and $G = 2x^2y - xy^2$, find,

(a) grad $(F + G)$ and (b) grad (FG) at $(1, 0, -2)$.

Solution : (a) $F + G = x^2z + e^{y/x} + 2x^2y - xy^2$

$\therefore \quad$ grad $(F + G) = \nabla(F + G)$

$$= \left(\hat{i}\frac{\partial}{\partial x} + \hat{j}\frac{\partial}{\partial y} + \hat{k}\frac{\partial}{\partial z}\right)(x^2z + e^{y/x} + 2x^2y - xy^2)$$

$$= \hat{i}\{2xz + e^{y/x}\left(\frac{-y}{x^2}\right) + 4xy - y^2\}$$

$$+ \hat{j}\{e^{y/x}\left(\frac{1}{x}\right) + 2x^2 - 2xy\} + \hat{k}\{x^2\}$$

At $(1, 0, -2)$,

$$\text{grad }(F + G) = \hat{i}\{-4\} + \hat{j}\{1 + 2\} + \hat{k}\{1\}$$

$$\text{grad }(F + G) = -4\hat{i} + 3\hat{j} + \hat{k}$$

(b) $\quad F \cdot G = (x^2z + e^{y/x}) \cdot (2x^2y - xy^2)$

We know that,

$$\text{grad }(FG) = F \cdot \text{grad } G + G \cdot \text{grad } F$$

$$= (x^2z + e^{y/x}) \left(\hat{i} \frac{\partial}{\partial x} + \hat{j} \frac{\partial}{\partial y} + \hat{k} \frac{\partial}{\partial z} \right) \cdot (2x^2y - xy^2)$$

$$+ (2x^2y - xy^2) \left(\hat{i} \frac{\partial}{\partial x} + \hat{j} \frac{\partial}{\partial y} + \hat{k} \frac{\partial}{\partial z} \right) (x^2z + e^{y/x})$$

$$= (x^2z + e^{y/x}) \{ \hat{i}(4xy - y^2) + \hat{j}(2x^2 - 2xy) + \hat{k}(0) \}$$

$$+ (2x^2y - xy^2) \left\{ \hat{i} \left[2xz + e^{y/x} \left(\frac{-y}{x^2} \right) \right] + \hat{j} \left(e^{y/x} \cdot \frac{1}{x} \right) + \hat{k}(x^2) \right\}$$

At (1, 0, −2)

$$\text{grad (FG)} = [-2 + 1] \{ \hat{i}(0) + \hat{j}(2) + \hat{k}(0) \} + 0$$

$$\text{grad (FG)} = -2\hat{j} \text{ at } (1, 0, -2)$$

Example 4.8 : Find the directional derivative of $\phi = x^2yz + 4xz^2$ at (1, −2, −1) in the direction $2\hat{i} - \hat{j} - 2\hat{k}$.

Solution :
$$\nabla \phi = \left(\hat{i} \frac{\partial}{\partial x} + \hat{j} \frac{\partial}{\partial y} + \hat{k} \frac{\partial}{\partial z} \right) (x^2yz + 4xz^2)$$

$$= \hat{i} \{ 2xyz + 4z^2 \} + \hat{j} \{ x^2z \} + \hat{k} \{ x^2y + 8xz \}$$

At (1, −2, −1),

$$\nabla \phi = \hat{i} \{ 2(1)(-2)(-1) + 4(-1)^2 \} + \hat{j} \{ (1)^2 (-1) \}$$

$$+ \hat{k} \{ (1)^2 (-2) + 8(1)(-1) \}$$

$$= \hat{i} \{ 8 \} - \hat{j} + \hat{k} \{ -10 \}$$

$$= 8\hat{i} - \hat{j} - 10\hat{k}$$

Let $\bar{A} = 2\hat{i} - \hat{j} - 2\hat{k}$

∴ $A = \sqrt{4 + 1 + 4} = 3$

∴ Directional derivative of ϕ at (1, −2, −1) in the direction of $\bar{A}$

$$= \nabla \phi \cdot \frac{\bar{A}}{A}$$

$$= (8\hat{i} - \hat{j} - 10\hat{k}) \cdot \frac{(2\hat{i} - \hat{j} - 2\hat{k})}{3}$$

$$= \frac{16 + 1 + 20}{3}$$

$$= \frac{37}{3}$$

Since, this is positive, ϕ is increasing in this direction.

Example 4.9 : (a) In what direction from the point $(2, 1, -1)$ is the directional derivative of $\phi = x^2yz^3$ a maximum ?

(b) What is the magnitude of this maximum ?

Solution : $\nabla\phi = \left(\hat{i}\dfrac{\partial}{\partial x} + \hat{j}\dfrac{\partial}{\partial y} + \hat{k}\dfrac{\partial}{\partial z}\right)(x^2yz^3)$

$$= \hat{i}\{2xyz^3\} + \hat{j}\{x^2z^3\} + \hat{k}\{3x^2yz^2\}$$

At the point $(2, 1, -1)$,

$$\nabla\phi = \hat{i}\{2(2)(1)(-1)^3\} + \hat{j}\{(2)^2(-1)^3\} + \hat{k}\{3(2)^2(1)(-1)^2\}$$

$$\nabla\phi = -4\hat{i} - 4\hat{j} + 12\hat{k}$$

But we know that, the directional derivative is always maximum in the direction of $\nabla\phi$, so :

(a) Directional derivative of $\phi = x^2yz$ at $(-2, 1, -1)$ is maximum in the direction of the vector $-4\hat{i} - 4\hat{j} + 12\hat{k}$.

(b) Magnitude of this vector

$$= \sqrt{16 + 16 + 144}$$
$$= \sqrt{176}$$
$$= 4\sqrt{11}$$

Example 4.10 : Find the rate of change of

$\phi = xy + yz + zx$ at $(1, -1, 2)$ in the direction of normal to the surface $x^2 + y^2 = z + 4$.

Solution : $\nabla\phi = \left(\hat{i}\dfrac{\partial}{\partial x} + \hat{j}\dfrac{\partial}{\partial y} + \hat{k}\dfrac{\partial}{\partial z}\right)(xy + yz + zx)$

$$= \hat{i}(y + z) + \hat{j}(x + z) + \hat{k}(y + x)$$

At the point $(1, -1, 2)$

$$\nabla \phi = \hat{i} + 3\hat{j} + 0\hat{k}$$

Let $\psi = x^2 + y^2 - z - 4 = 0$

Then the vector normal to this surface is

$$\nabla \psi = \left(\hat{i}\frac{\partial}{\partial x} + \hat{j}\frac{\partial}{\partial y} + \hat{k}\frac{\partial}{\partial z}\right)(x^2 + y^2 - z - 4)$$

$$= 2x\hat{i} + 2\hat{j} - \hat{k}$$

At the point $(1, -1, 2)$,

$$\nabla \psi = 2\hat{i} - 2\hat{j} - \hat{k}$$

Now we have find the rate of change i.e. directional derivative of ϕ in the direction $2\hat{i} - 2\hat{j} - \hat{k} = \nabla \psi$.

∴ Directional derivative of ϕ at $(1, -1, 2)$ in the direction of $\nabla \psi$

$$= \nabla \phi \cdot \frac{\nabla \psi}{|\nabla \psi|}$$

$$= (\hat{i} + 3\hat{j} + 0\hat{k}) \cdot \frac{(2\hat{i} - 2\hat{j} - \hat{k})}{\sqrt{4 + 4 + 1}}$$

$$= \frac{2 - 6}{3}$$

$$= \frac{-4}{3}$$

EXERCISE 4.1

1. If $\bar{a}$ is any constant vector, then show that grad $(\bar{r} \cdot \bar{a}) = \bar{a}$.

2. Find the unit vector normal to the surface $x^2 + y^2 - z = 1$ at $(1, 1, 1)$.

3. Find the equations of the tangent plane and normal to the surface $xy + yz + zx = 7$ at $(1, 1, 3)$.

4. Find the angle between the surfaces
   $x^2y + z = 3$ and $x \log z - y^2 + 4 = 0$ at the point $(-1, 2, 1)$.

5. Find grad ϕ if (i) $\phi = x^2 + yz$ (ii) $\phi = \log(x^2 + y^2 + z^2)$.

6. Find the values of a and b if the surfaces $ax^2 - byz = (a + 2)x$ and $4x^2y + z^3 = 4$ are orthogonal at the point $(1, -1, 2)$.

7. Find the directional derivative of $f(x, y, z) = 2xy + z^2$ at the point $(1, -1, 3)$ in the direction of the vector $\hat{i} + 2\hat{j} + 2\hat{k}$.

8. In what direction from $(3, 1, -2)$ is the directional derivative of $\phi = x^2y^2z^4$ maximum ? Find also the magnitude of this maximum.

9. Find the directional derivative of $\phi = x^2y + xz^2 - 2$ at $(1, 1, -1)$ along $\overline{AB}$ where B is the point $(2, -1, 3)$.

ANSWERS 4.1

2. $\dfrac{1}{3}(2\hat{i} + 2\hat{j} - \hat{k})$

3. Equation of tangent surface is $2x + 2y + z - 7 = 0$.
   Equation of normal surface is $\dfrac{x - 1}{2} = \dfrac{y - 1}{2} = \dfrac{z - 3}{1}$

4. $\theta = \cos^{-1}\left(\dfrac{3}{\sqrt{130}}\right)$.

5. (i) $2x\hat{i} + z\hat{j} + y\hat{k}$ (ii) $\dfrac{2(x\hat{i} + y\hat{j} + z\hat{k})}{(x^2 + y^2 + z^2)}$

6. $a = \dfrac{5}{4}$, $b = 1$

7. $\dfrac{14}{3}$

8. $\dfrac{1}{13}(4\hat{i} + 3\hat{j} - 12\hat{k})$

9. $-\sqrt{\dfrac{7}{3}}$

4.7 DIVERGENCE AND CURL

In previous article, we discussed that when ∇ operates on a scalar point function the resulting quantity is a vector and it is called gradient. In this article, we operate ∇ on vector by two ways.

1. **Definition :** Let $\bar{f} = f_1\hat{i} + f_2\hat{j} + f_3\hat{k}$ be defined and differentiable at each point (x, y, z) in a certain region R of a space (i.e. $\bar{f}$ defines a differentiable vector field) then

$$\nabla \cdot \bar{f} = \left(\hat{i}\frac{\partial}{\partial x} + \hat{j}\frac{\partial}{\partial y} + \hat{k}\frac{\partial}{\partial z}\right) \cdot (f_1\hat{i} + f_2\hat{j} + f_3\hat{k})$$

$$= \frac{\partial f_1}{\partial x} + \frac{\partial f_2}{\partial y} + \frac{\partial f_3}{\partial z}$$

Is called the divergence of a vector $\bar{f}$ and is denoted by div $\bar{f}$

$$\therefore \quad \text{div } \bar{f} = \nabla \cdot \bar{f} = \frac{\partial f_1}{\partial x} + \frac{\partial f_2}{\partial y} + \frac{\partial f_3}{\partial z}$$

Then clearly divergence of a vector point function is a scalar point function.

Note : If $\bar{f}$ is a vector point function such that div. $\bar{f} = \nabla \cdot \bar{f} = 0$ then $\bar{f}$ is called a **solenoidal**.

2. **Definition :** Let $\bar{f} = f_1\hat{i} + f_2\hat{j} + f_3\hat{k}$ is a differentiable vector point function then

$$\nabla \times \bar{f} = \left(\hat{i}\frac{\partial}{\partial x} + \hat{j}\frac{\partial}{\partial y} + \hat{k}\frac{\partial}{\partial z}\right) \times (f_1\hat{i} + f_2\hat{j} + f_3\hat{k})$$

$$= \begin{vmatrix} \hat{i} & \hat{j} & \hat{k} \\ \frac{\partial}{\partial x} & \frac{\partial}{\partial y} & \frac{\partial}{\partial z} \\ f_1 & f_2 & f_3 \end{vmatrix}$$

is called curl of a vector $\bar{f}$ and it is denoted by curl $\bar{f}$.

$$\therefore \quad \text{Curl } \overline{f} = \nabla \times \overline{f} = \begin{vmatrix} \hat{i} & \hat{j} & \hat{k} \\ \dfrac{\partial}{\partial x} & \dfrac{\partial}{\partial y} & \dfrac{\partial}{\partial z} \\ f_1 & f_2 & f_3 \end{vmatrix}$$

Clearly curl of a vector is vector point function.

Note : If $\overline{f}$ is a vector point function such that curl $\overline{f} = \nabla \times \overline{f} = 0$, then $\overline{f}$ is called a **conservative** or **irrotational**.

Example 4.11 : If $\overline{A} = xz^3\hat{i} - 2x^2yz\hat{j} + 2yz^4\hat{k}$, then find div $\overline{A}$ and curl $\overline{A}$ at $(1, -1, 1)$.

Solution : div $\overline{A} = \nabla \cdot \overline{A}$

$$= \left(\hat{i}\dfrac{\partial}{\partial x} + \hat{j}\dfrac{\partial}{\partial y} + \hat{k}\dfrac{\partial}{\partial z} \right) \cdot (xz^3\hat{i} - 2x^2yz\hat{j} + 2yz^4\hat{k})$$

$$= \dfrac{\partial}{\partial x}(xz^3) + \dfrac{\partial}{\partial y}(-2x^2yz) + \dfrac{\partial}{\partial z}(2yz^4)$$

div $\overline{A} = z^3 - 2x^2z + 8yz^3$

At $(1, -1, 1)$

div $\overline{A} = (1)^3 - 2(1)^2(1) + 8(-1)(1)^3$

$= 1 - 2 - 8$

div $\overline{A} = -9$ at $(1, -1, 1)$

$$\text{Curl } \overline{A} = \begin{vmatrix} \hat{i} & \hat{j} & \hat{k} \\ \dfrac{\partial}{\partial x} & \dfrac{\partial}{\partial y} & \dfrac{\partial}{\partial z} \\ xz^3 & -2x^2yz & 2yz^4 \end{vmatrix}$$

$= \hat{i}\{2z^4 + 2x^2y\} - \hat{j}\{0 - 3xz^2\} + \hat{k}\{-4xyz - 0\}$

$= \hat{i}\{2z^4 + 2x^2y\} + \hat{j}\{3xz^2\} - \hat{k}\{4xyz\}$

At the point $(1, -1, 1)$,

$$\text{Curl } \bar{A} = \hat{i}\{2(1)^4 + 2(1)^2(-1)\} + \hat{j}\{3(1)(1)^2\} - \hat{k}\{4(1)(-1)(1)\}$$
$$= \hat{i}\{2-2\} + \hat{j}\{3\} + \hat{k}(4)$$
$$\text{Curl } \bar{A} = 3\hat{j} + 4\hat{k} \text{ at } (1, -1, 1)$$

Example 4.12 : If $\bar{A} = 2yz\hat{i} - x^2y\hat{j} + xz^2\hat{k}$ and $\phi = 2x^2yz^3$, then show that $(\bar{A} \cdot \nabla)\phi = \bar{A} \cdot \nabla\phi$.

Solution : Consider,

$$(\bar{A} \cdot \nabla)\phi = \left[(2yz\hat{i} - x^2y\hat{j} + xz^2\hat{k}) \cdot \left(\hat{i}\frac{\partial}{\partial x} + \hat{j}\frac{\partial}{\partial y} + \hat{k}\frac{\partial}{\partial z}\right)\right] 2x^2yz^3$$

$$= \left(2yz\frac{\partial}{\partial x} - x^2y\frac{\partial}{\partial y} + xz^2\frac{\partial}{\partial z}\right)(2x^2yz^3)$$

$$= 2yz\frac{\partial}{\partial x}(2x^2yz^3) - x^2y\frac{\partial}{\partial y}(2x^2yz^3) + xz^2\frac{\partial}{\partial z}(2x^2yz^3)$$

$$= 2yz(4xyz^3) - x^2y(2x^2z^3) + xz^2(6x^2yz^2)$$

$$(\bar{A} \cdot \nabla\phi) = 8xy^2z^4 - 2x^4yz^3 + 6x^3yz^4 \qquad \ldots (1)$$

Consider,

$$\bar{A} \cdot \nabla\phi = (2yz\hat{i} - x^2y\hat{j} + xz^2\hat{k}) \cdot \left[\left(\hat{i}\frac{\partial}{\partial x} + \hat{j}\frac{\partial}{\partial y} + \hat{k}\frac{\partial}{\partial z}\right)(2x^2yz^3)\right]$$

$$= (2yz\hat{i} - x^2y\hat{j} + xz^2\hat{k})(4xyz^3\hat{i} + 2x^2z^3\hat{j} + 6x^2yz^2\hat{k})$$

$$= (2yz)(4xyz^3) - (x^2y)(2x^2z^3) + (xz^2)(6x^2yz^2)$$

$$\bar{A} \cdot \nabla\phi = 8xy^2z^4 - 2x^4yz^3 + 6x^3yz^4 \qquad \ldots (2)$$

By equation (1) and (2), we get

$$(\bar{A} \cdot \nabla)\phi = \bar{A} \cdot (\nabla\phi)$$

Example 4.13 : If $\bar{F} = (y + z)\hat{i} + (z + x)\hat{j} + (x + y)\hat{k}$, then show that $\bar{F}$ is a solenoidal.

Solution : We know that, a vector $\bar{f}$ is a solenoidal if div. $\bar{f} = 0$. So consider,

$$\text{div. } \bar{F} = \nabla \cdot \bar{f} = \left(\hat{i}\frac{\partial}{\partial x} + \hat{j}\frac{\partial}{\partial y} + \hat{k}\frac{\partial}{\partial z}\right) \cdot \{(y+z)\hat{i} + (x+z)\hat{j} + (x+y)\hat{k}\}$$

$$= \frac{\partial}{\partial x}(y+z) + \frac{\partial}{\partial y}(x+z) + \frac{\partial}{\partial z}(x+y)$$

$$= 0 + 0 + 0$$

$$= 0$$

Thus, div. $\bar{F} = 0$, so $\bar{F}$ is a solenoidal.

Example 4.14 : Show that the vector $\bar{F} = \dfrac{-y\hat{i} + x\hat{j}}{x^2 + y^2}$ is irrotational.

Solution : We know that a vector $\bar{A}$ is irrotational if curl $\bar{A} = 0$.

So consider,

$$\text{Curl } \bar{F} = \nabla \times \bar{F}$$

$$= \left(\hat{i}\frac{\partial}{\partial x} + \hat{j}\frac{\partial}{\partial y} + \hat{k}\frac{\partial}{\partial z}\right) \times \left(\frac{-y\hat{i}}{x^2+y^2} + \frac{x}{x^2+y^2}\hat{j} + 0\hat{k}\right)$$

$$= \begin{vmatrix} \hat{i} & \hat{j} & \hat{k} \\ \dfrac{\partial}{\partial x} & \dfrac{\partial}{\partial y} & \dfrac{\partial}{\partial z} \\ \dfrac{-y}{x^2+y^2} & \dfrac{x}{x^2+y^2} & 0 \end{vmatrix}$$

$$= \hat{i}\{0-0\} - \hat{j}\{0-0\} + \hat{k}\left\{\frac{\partial}{\partial x}\left(\frac{x}{x^2+y^2}\right) + \frac{\partial}{\partial y}\left(\frac{y}{x^2+y^2}\right)\right\}$$

$$= \hat{k}\left\{\frac{-x^2+y^2}{(x^2+y^2)^2} + \frac{x^2-y^2}{(x^2+y^2)^2}\right\}$$

$$= \bar{0}$$

∴ Curl $\bar{F} = \bar{0}$, so $\bar{F}$ is irrotational or conservative vector.

4.8 PROPERTIES OF DIVERGENCE AND CURL

1. div. $\bar{a} = 0$ and curl $\bar{a} = \bar{0}$, where $\bar{a}$ is a constant vector.
2. div. $(\bar{f} \pm \bar{g}) = $ div $\bar{f} \pm $ div $\bar{g}$.
3. curl $(\bar{f} \pm \bar{g}) = $ curl $\bar{f} \pm $ curl $\bar{g}$.
4. div. $(\phi \bar{f}) = \phi$ div $\bar{f} + $ grad $\phi \cdot \bar{f}$, where ϕ is a scalar point function and $\bar{f}$ is a vector point function.
5. curl $(\phi \bar{f}) = $ grad $\phi \times \bar{f} + \phi$ curl $\bar{f}$.
6. div (grad. ϕ) $= \dfrac{\partial^2 \phi}{\partial x^2} + \dfrac{\partial^2 \phi}{\partial y^2} + \dfrac{\partial^2 \phi}{\partial z^2}$
7. curl (grad. ϕ) $= \bar{0}$
8. div. (curl $\bar{f}$) $= 0$.

Proof :

1. Let $\bar{a}$ be a constant vector then $\bar{a} = a_1\hat{i} + a_2\hat{j} + a_3\hat{k}$, where a_1, a_2, a_3 are all constants.

   $\therefore$ div. $\bar{a} = \nabla \cdot \bar{a}$

   $= \left(\hat{i}\dfrac{\partial}{\partial x} + \hat{j}\dfrac{\partial}{\partial y} + \hat{k}\dfrac{\partial}{\partial z} \right)(a_1\hat{i} + a_2\hat{j} + a_3\hat{k})$

   $= \dfrac{\partial a_1}{\partial x} + \dfrac{\partial a_2}{\partial y} + \dfrac{\partial a_3}{\partial z}$

   $= 0 + 0 + 0$ as a_1, a_2, a_3 are constants

   $= 0$

   $\therefore$ div $\bar{a} = 0$

   Consider, curl $\bar{a} = \nabla \times \bar{a}$

   $= \left(\hat{i}\dfrac{\partial}{\partial x} + \hat{j}\dfrac{\partial}{\partial y} + \hat{k}\dfrac{\partial}{\partial z} \right) \times (a_1\hat{i} + a_2\hat{j} + a_3\hat{k})$

   $= \begin{vmatrix} \hat{i} & \hat{j} & \hat{k} \\ \dfrac{\partial}{\partial x} & \dfrac{\partial}{\partial y} & \dfrac{\partial}{\partial z} \\ a_1 & a_2 & a_3 \end{vmatrix}$

$$= \hat{i}\{0-0\} - \hat{j}\{0-0\} + \hat{k}\{0-0\}$$

$$= \overline{0}$$

∴ curl $\overline{a} = \overline{0}$

2. Let $\overline{f} = f_1\hat{i} + f_2\hat{j} + f_3\hat{k}$ and $\overline{g} = g_1\hat{i} + g_2\hat{j} + g_3\hat{k}$

∴ $\overline{f} \pm \overline{g} = (f_1 \pm g_1)\hat{i} + (f_2 \pm g_2)\hat{j} + (f_3 \pm g_3)\hat{k}$

∴ div $(\overline{f} \pm \overline{g}) = \nabla \cdot (\overline{f} \pm \overline{g})$

$$= \left(\hat{i}\frac{\partial}{\partial x} + \hat{j}\frac{\partial}{\partial y} + \hat{k}\frac{\partial}{\partial z}\right) \cdot [(f_1 \pm g_1)\hat{i} + (f_2 \pm g_2)\hat{j} + (f_3 \pm g_3)\hat{k}]$$

$$= \frac{\partial}{\partial x}(f_1 \pm g_1) + \frac{\partial}{\partial y}(f_2 \pm g_2) + \frac{\partial}{\partial z}(f_3 \pm g_3)$$

$$= \left(\frac{\partial f_1}{\partial x} + \frac{\partial f_2}{\partial y} + \frac{\partial f_3}{\partial z}\right) \pm \left(\frac{\partial g_1}{\partial x} + \frac{\partial g_2}{\partial y} + \frac{\partial g_3}{\partial z}\right)$$

$$= \nabla \cdot \overline{f} \pm \nabla \cdot \overline{g}$$

$$= \text{div. } \overline{f} \pm \text{div } \overline{g}$$

Thus, div. $(\overline{f} \pm \overline{g}) = $ div. $\overline{f} \pm $ div $\overline{g}$

3. curl $(\overline{f} \pm \overline{g}) = \nabla \times (\overline{f} \pm \overline{g})$

$$= \left(\hat{i}\frac{\partial}{\partial x} + \hat{j}\frac{\partial}{\partial y} + \hat{k}\frac{\partial}{\partial z}\right)[(f_1 \pm g_1)\hat{i} \pm (f_2 \pm g_2)\hat{j} + (f_3 \pm g_3)\hat{k}]$$

$$= \begin{vmatrix} \hat{i} & \hat{j} & \hat{k} \\ \frac{\partial}{\partial x} & \frac{\partial}{\partial y} & \frac{\partial}{\partial z} \\ f_1 \pm g_1 & f_2 \pm g_2 & f_3 \pm g_3 \end{vmatrix}$$

$$= \begin{vmatrix} \hat{i} & \hat{j} & \hat{k} \\ \dfrac{\partial}{\partial x} & \dfrac{\partial}{\partial y} & \dfrac{\partial}{\partial z} \\ f_1 & f_2 & f_3 \end{vmatrix} \pm \begin{vmatrix} \hat{i} & \hat{j} & \hat{k} \\ \dfrac{\partial}{\partial x} & \dfrac{\partial}{\partial y} & \dfrac{\partial}{\partial z} \\ g_1 & g_2 & g_3 \end{vmatrix}$$

$$= \nabla \times \overline{f} \pm \nabla \times \overline{g}$$

$$\therefore \quad \mathrm{curl}\,(\overline{f} \pm \overline{g}) = \mathrm{curl}\,\overline{f} \pm \mathrm{curl}\,\overline{g}$$

4. $\quad \phi \overline{f} = \phi(f_1 \hat{i} + f_2 \hat{j} + f_3 \hat{k}) = \phi f_1 \hat{i} + \phi f_2 \hat{j} + \phi f_3 \hat{k}$

Consider,

$$\mathrm{div.}\,(\phi\,f) = \nabla \cdot (\phi\,f)$$

$$= \left(\hat{i}\dfrac{\partial}{\partial x} + \hat{j}\dfrac{\partial}{\partial y} + \hat{k}\dfrac{\partial}{\partial z} \right) \cdot (\phi f_1 \hat{i} + \phi f_2 \hat{j} + \phi f_3 \hat{k})$$

$$= \dfrac{\partial}{\partial x}(\phi f_1) + \dfrac{\partial}{\partial y}(\phi f_2) + \dfrac{\partial}{\partial z}(\phi f_3)$$

$$= \phi \left(\dfrac{\partial f_1}{\partial x} + \dfrac{\partial f_2}{\partial y} + \dfrac{\partial f_3}{\partial z} \right) + \left(f_1 \dfrac{\partial \phi}{\partial x} + f_2 \dfrac{\partial \phi}{\partial y} + f_3 \dfrac{\partial \phi}{\partial z} \right)$$

$$= \phi \left(\hat{i}\dfrac{\partial}{\partial x} + \hat{j}\dfrac{\partial}{\partial y} + \hat{k}\dfrac{\partial}{\partial z} \right) \cdot (f_1 \hat{i} + f_2 \hat{j} + f_3 \hat{k})$$

$$+ (f_1 \hat{i} + f_2 \hat{j} + f_3 \hat{k}) \cdot \left(\hat{i}\dfrac{\partial}{\partial x} + \hat{j}\dfrac{\partial}{\partial y} + \hat{k}\dfrac{\partial}{\partial z} \right) \phi$$

$$= \phi \cdot \nabla \cdot \overline{f} + \overline{f} \cdot \nabla \phi = \phi\,\mathrm{div}\,\overline{f} + \overline{f} \cdot \mathrm{grad}\,\phi$$

Thus, $\mathrm{div.}\,(\phi\,\overline{f}) = \phi\,\mathrm{div.}\,\overline{f} + \mathrm{grad}\,\phi \cdot \overline{f}$.

5. $\mathrm{curl}\,(\phi\,\overline{f}) = \nabla \times (\phi f_1 \hat{i} + \phi f_2 \hat{j} + \phi f_3 \hat{k})$

$$= \left(\hat{i}\dfrac{\partial}{\partial x} + \hat{j}\dfrac{\partial}{\partial y} + \hat{k}\dfrac{\partial}{\partial z} \right) \times (\phi f_1 \hat{i} + \phi f_2 \hat{j} + \phi f_3 \hat{k})$$

$$= \begin{vmatrix} \hat{i} & \hat{j} & \hat{k} \\ \dfrac{\partial}{\partial x} & \dfrac{\partial}{\partial y} & \dfrac{\partial}{\partial z} \\ \phi f_1 & \phi f_2 & \phi f_3 \end{vmatrix}$$

$$= \hat{i}\left\{\phi\frac{\partial f_3}{\partial y} + f_3\frac{\partial \phi}{\partial y} - \phi\frac{\partial f_2}{\partial z} - f_2\frac{\partial \phi}{\partial z}\right\} - \hat{j}\left\{\phi\frac{\partial f_3}{\partial x} + f_3\frac{\partial \phi}{\partial x} - \phi\frac{\partial f_1}{\partial z} - f_1\frac{\partial \phi}{\partial z}\right\}$$

$$+ \hat{k}\left\{\phi\frac{\partial f_2}{\partial x} + f_2\frac{\partial \phi}{\partial x} - \phi\frac{\partial f_1}{\partial y} - f_1\frac{\partial \phi}{\partial y}\right\}$$

$$= \begin{vmatrix} \hat{i} & \hat{j} & \hat{k} \\ \frac{\partial \phi}{\partial x} & \frac{\partial \phi}{\partial y} & \frac{\partial \phi}{\partial z} \\ f_1 & f_2 & f_3 \end{vmatrix} + \phi \begin{vmatrix} \hat{i} & \hat{j} & \hat{k} \\ \frac{\partial}{\partial x} & \frac{\partial}{\partial y} & \frac{\partial}{\partial z} \\ f_1 & f_2 & f_3 \end{vmatrix}$$

$$= \text{grad } \phi \times \overline{f} + \phi \text{ curl } \overline{f}$$

$\therefore$ curl $(\phi \overline{f}) = \text{grad } \phi \times \overline{f} + \phi \text{ curl } \overline{f}$.

6. Consider, div. grad ϕ = div. $\left(\hat{i}\frac{\partial \phi}{\partial x} + \hat{j}\frac{\partial \phi}{\partial y} + \hat{k}\frac{\partial \phi}{\partial z}\right)$

$$= \left(\hat{i}\frac{\partial}{\partial x} + \hat{j}\frac{\partial}{\partial y} + \hat{k}\frac{\partial}{\partial z}\right) \cdot \left(\hat{i}\frac{\partial \phi}{\partial x} + \hat{j}\frac{\partial \phi}{\partial y} + \hat{k}\frac{\partial \phi}{\partial z}\right)$$

$$= \frac{\partial}{\partial x}\left(\frac{\partial \phi}{\partial x}\right) + \frac{\partial}{\partial y}\left(\frac{\partial \phi}{\partial y}\right) + \frac{\partial}{\partial z}\left(\frac{\partial \phi}{\partial z}\right)$$

$$= \frac{\partial^2 \phi}{\partial x^2} + \frac{\partial^2 \phi}{\partial y^2} + \frac{\partial^2 \phi}{\partial z^2}$$

$\therefore$ div. [grad ϕ] = $\left(\frac{\partial^2}{\partial x^2} + \frac{\partial^2}{\partial y^2} + \frac{\partial^2}{\partial z^2}\right)\phi$

7. Consider grad $\phi = \hat{i}\frac{\partial \phi}{\partial x} + \hat{j}\frac{\partial \phi}{\partial y} + \hat{k}\frac{\partial \phi}{\partial z}$

$\therefore$ curl grad $\phi = \nabla \times \text{grad } \phi$

$$= \left(\hat{i}\frac{\partial}{\partial x} + \hat{j}\frac{\partial}{\partial y} + \hat{k}\frac{\partial}{\partial z}\right) \times \left(\hat{i}\frac{\partial \phi}{\partial x} + \hat{j}\frac{\partial \phi}{\partial y} + \hat{k}\frac{\partial \phi}{\partial z}\right)$$

$$= \begin{vmatrix} \hat{i} & \hat{j} & \hat{k} \\ \frac{\partial}{\partial x} & \frac{\partial}{\partial y} & \frac{\partial}{\partial z} \\ \frac{\partial \phi}{\partial x} & \frac{\partial \phi}{\partial y} & \frac{\partial \phi}{\partial z} \end{vmatrix}$$

$$= \hat{i}\left\{\frac{\partial^2 \phi}{\partial y \partial z} - \frac{\partial^2 \phi}{\partial y \partial z}\right\} - \hat{j}\left\{\frac{\partial^2 \phi}{\partial x \partial z} - \frac{\partial^2 \phi}{\partial z \partial x}\right\}$$
$$+ \hat{k}\left\{\frac{\partial^2 \phi}{\partial x \partial y} - \frac{\partial^2 \phi}{\partial y \partial x}\right\}$$

But generally know that $\dfrac{\partial^2 z}{\partial x \partial y} = \dfrac{\partial^2 z}{\partial y \partial x}$

$\therefore\ \hat{i}(0) + \hat{j}(0) + \hat{k}(0)$

$\therefore\quad$ curl [grad ϕ] $= \overline{0}$

8.$\quad$ curl $\overline{f} = \nabla \times \overline{f}$

$$= \left(\hat{i}\frac{\partial}{\partial x} + \hat{j}\frac{\partial}{\partial y} + \hat{k}\frac{\partial}{\partial z}\right) \times (f_1\hat{i} + f_2\hat{j} + f_3\hat{k})$$

$$= \begin{vmatrix} \hat{i} & \hat{j} & \hat{k} \\ \dfrac{\partial}{\partial x} & \dfrac{\partial}{\partial y} & \dfrac{\partial}{\partial z} \\ f_1 & f_2 & f_3 \end{vmatrix}$$

$$= \hat{i}\left\{\frac{\partial f_3}{\partial y} - \frac{\partial f_2}{\partial z}\right\} - \hat{j}\left\{\frac{\partial f_3}{\partial x} - \frac{\partial f_1}{\partial z}\right\} + \hat{k}\left\{\frac{\partial f_2}{\partial x} - \frac{\partial f_1}{\partial y}\right\}$$

Consider div (curl $\overline{f}$) = $\nabla \cdot$ curl $\overline{f}$

$$= \left(\hat{i}\frac{\partial}{\partial x} + \hat{j}\frac{\partial}{\partial y} + \hat{k}\frac{\partial}{\partial z}\right)\left\{\hat{i}\left(\frac{\partial f_3}{\partial y} - \frac{\partial f_2}{\partial z}\right) - \hat{j}\left(\frac{\partial f_3}{\partial x} - \frac{\partial f_1}{\partial z}\right) + \hat{k}\left(\frac{\partial f_2}{\partial x} - \frac{\partial f_1}{\partial y}\right)\right\}$$

$$= \frac{\partial}{\partial x}\left\{\frac{\partial f_3}{\partial y} - \frac{\partial f_2}{\partial z}\right\} - \frac{\partial}{\partial y}\left\{\frac{\partial f_3}{\partial x} - \frac{\partial f_1}{\partial z}\right\} + \frac{\partial}{\partial z}\left\{\frac{\partial f_2}{\partial x} - \frac{\partial f_1}{\partial y}\right\}$$

$$= \frac{\partial^2 f_3}{\partial x \partial y} - \frac{\partial^2 f_2}{\partial x \partial z} - \frac{\partial^2 f_3}{\partial y \partial x} + \frac{\partial^2 f_1}{\partial y \partial z} + \frac{\partial^2 f_2}{\partial z \partial x} - \frac{\partial^2 f_1}{\partial z \partial y}$$

$= 0$

$\therefore\ $ div (curl $\overline{f}$) = 0

SOLVED EXAMPLES

Example 4.15 : If $u = x^2 + y^2 + z^2$, prove that curl grad u = 0

Solution : $u = x^2 + y^2 + z^2$ then

$$\text{grad } u = \nabla \cdot u$$

$$= \hat{i}\frac{\partial}{\partial x}(x^2 + y^2 + z^2) + \hat{j}\frac{\partial}{\partial y}(x^2 + y^2 + z^2) + \hat{k}\frac{\partial}{\partial z}(x^2 + y^2 + z^2)$$

$$\text{grad } u = 2x\hat{i} + 2y\hat{j} + 2z\hat{k}$$

$$\text{curl grad } u = \nabla \times \text{grad } u$$

$$= \left(\hat{i}\frac{\partial}{\partial x} + \hat{j}\frac{\partial}{\partial y} + \hat{k}\frac{\partial}{\partial z}\right)(2x\hat{i} + 2y\hat{j} + 2z\hat{k})$$

$$= \begin{vmatrix} \hat{i} & \hat{j} & \hat{k} \\ \dfrac{\partial}{\partial x} & \dfrac{\partial}{\partial y} & \dfrac{\partial}{\partial z} \\ 2x & 2y & 2z \end{vmatrix}$$

$$= \hat{i}\{0 - 0\} - \hat{j}\{0 - 0\} + \hat{k}\{0 - 0\}$$

$$= \overline{0}$$

$$\therefore \text{ curl grad } u = \overline{0}$$

Example 4.16 : Prove that $\nabla \cdot (r\nabla r^{-n}) = \dfrac{n(n-2)}{r^{n+1}}$

Solution : $r^{-n} = (x^2 + y^2 + z^2)^{\frac{-n}{2}}$

$$\nabla\left(\frac{1}{r^n}\right) = \hat{i}\frac{\partial}{\partial x}(x^2 + y^2 + z^2)^{\frac{-n}{2}} + \hat{j}\frac{\partial}{\partial y}(x^2 + y^2 + z^2)^{\frac{-n}{2}}$$

$$+ \hat{k}\frac{\partial}{\partial z}(x^2 + y^2 + z^2)^{\frac{-n}{2}}$$

$$= \hat{i}\left[\frac{-n}{2}(2x)(x^2 + y^2 + z^2)^{-\frac{n}{2}-1}\right] + \hat{j}\left[\frac{-n}{2}(x^2 + y^2 + z^2)^{-\frac{n}{2}-1}(2y)\right]$$

$$+ \hat{k}\left[\frac{-n}{2}(x^2 + y^2 + z^2)^{-\frac{n}{2}-1}(2z)\right]$$

$$= \frac{-n}{2}(2)(x^2 + y^2 + z^2)^{-\frac{n}{2}-1}[x\hat{i} + y\hat{j} + z\hat{k}]$$

$$= -n(r^2)^{-\frac{n}{2}-1} \cdot \bar{r}$$

$$= -n\, r^{-n-2} \cdot \bar{r}$$

$$= -n\, r^{-n-2}\{x\hat{i} + y\hat{j} + z\hat{k}\}$$

$$r\nabla r^{-n} = r\{-n\, r^{-n-2}\}\{x\hat{i} + y\hat{j} + z\hat{k}\}$$

$$= -n\, r^{-n-1}\{x\hat{i} + y\hat{j} + z\hat{k}\}$$

Consider,

$$\nabla\{r\nabla \cdot r^{-n}\} = \left\{\hat{i}\frac{\partial}{\partial x} + \hat{j}\frac{\partial}{\partial y} + \hat{k}\frac{\partial}{\partial z}\right\}\{-nr^{-n-1}(x\hat{i} + y\hat{j} + z\hat{k})\}$$

$$= -n\frac{\partial}{\partial x}(r^{-n-1}x) - n\frac{\partial}{\partial y}(r^{-n-1}\cdot y) - n\frac{\partial}{\partial z}(r^{-n-1}z)$$

$$= -n\left[(-n-1)x\, p^{-n-2}\frac{\partial r}{\partial x} + r^{-n-1}\right] + [\ldots\ldots] + [\ldots\ldots]$$

$$= -n\left[-\frac{n+1}{r^{n+3}}\cdot(x^2+y^2+z^2) + \frac{3}{r^{n+1}}\right]$$

$$= -n\left[\frac{-n-1}{r^{n+1}} + \frac{3}{r^{n+1}}\right]$$

$$= -n\left[\frac{-n-1+3}{r^{n+1}}\right]$$

$$= -n\left[\frac{-n+2}{r^{n+1}}\right]$$

$$= \frac{n(n-2)}{r^{n+1}}$$

Example 4.17 : Prove that curl $\dfrac{\bar{r}}{r^2} = 0$

Solution : $\dfrac{\bar{r}}{r^2} = \dfrac{x\hat{i} + y\hat{j} + z\hat{k}}{x^2 + y^2 + z^2}$

$$= \frac{x}{x^2+y^2+z^2}\hat{i} + \frac{y}{x^2+y^2+z^2}\hat{j} + \frac{z}{x^2+y^2+z^2}\hat{k}$$

$$\text{Curl}\,\frac{\bar{r}}{r^2} = \nabla \times \frac{\bar{r}}{r^2}$$

$$= \begin{vmatrix} \hat{i} & \hat{j} & \hat{k} \\ \dfrac{\partial}{\partial x} & \dfrac{\partial}{\partial y} & \dfrac{\partial}{\partial z} \\ \dfrac{x}{x^2+y^2+z^2} & \dfrac{y}{x^2+y^2+z^2} & \dfrac{z}{x^2+y^2+z^2} \end{vmatrix}$$

$$= \hat{i}\{-2yz(x^2+y^2+z^2)^{-2} + 2yz(x^2+y^2+z^2)^{-2}\} - \hat{j}\{-2xz(x^2+y^2+z^2)^{-2}$$
$$+ 2xz(x^2+y^2+z^2)^{-2}\} + \hat{k}\{-2xy(x^2+y^2+z^2)^{-2} + 2xy(x^2+y^2+z^2)^{-2}\}$$

$$= 0\hat{i} + 0\hat{j} + 0\hat{k} = \bar{0}$$

$\therefore \qquad \text{curl}\,\dfrac{\bar{r}}{r^2} = 0$

4.9 DIVERGENCE OF GRADIENT OF ϕ OR $\nabla^2 \phi$

We shall consider the operation ∇^2 because it has many applications. We know that,

$$\text{grad}\,\phi = \hat{i}\frac{\partial \phi}{\partial x} + \hat{j}\frac{\partial \phi}{\partial y} + \hat{k}\frac{\partial \phi}{\partial z}$$

$\therefore \qquad$ div. grad $\phi = \nabla \cdot \text{grad}\,\phi$

$$\nabla \cdot \nabla\phi = \left\{\hat{i}\frac{\partial}{\partial x} + \hat{j}\frac{\partial}{\partial y} + \hat{k}\frac{\partial}{\partial z}\right\}\left\{\hat{i}\frac{\partial \phi}{\partial x} + \hat{j}\frac{\partial \phi}{\partial y} + \hat{k}\frac{\partial \phi}{\partial z}\right\}$$

$$= \frac{\partial}{\partial x}\left\{\frac{\partial \phi}{\partial x}\right\} + \frac{\partial}{\partial y}\left\{\frac{\partial \phi}{\partial y}\right\} + \frac{\partial}{\partial z}\left\{\frac{\partial \phi}{\partial z}\right\}$$

$$= \frac{\partial^2 \phi}{\partial x^2} + \frac{\partial^2 \phi}{\partial y^2} + \frac{\partial^2 \phi}{\partial z^2}$$

$$\nabla^2 \phi = \left\{\frac{\partial^2}{\partial x^2} + \frac{\partial^2}{\partial y^2} + \frac{\partial^2}{\partial z^2}\right\}\phi$$

The operator is denoted by ∇^2 and is called Laplacian. Thus, Laplacian ∇^2 is

$$\nabla^2 = \frac{\partial^2}{\partial x^2} + \frac{\partial^2}{\partial y^2} + \frac{\partial^2}{\partial z^2}$$

The equation, $\nabla^2 \phi = 0$ i.e. $\dfrac{\partial^2 \phi}{\partial x^2} + \dfrac{\partial^2 \phi}{\partial y^2} + \dfrac{\partial^2 \phi}{\partial z^2} = 0$

is known as Laplacian equation.

SOLVED EXAMPLES

Example 4.18 : Prove that $\nabla^2 (\log r) = \dfrac{1}{r^2}$

Solution :

$$\nabla^2 (\log r) = \left\{ \dfrac{\partial^2}{\partial x^2} + \dfrac{\partial^2}{\partial y^2} + \dfrac{\partial^2}{\partial z^2} \right\} (\log r)$$

$$= \dfrac{\partial^2}{\partial x^2} (\log r) + \dfrac{\partial^2}{\partial y^2} (\log r) + \dfrac{\partial^2}{\partial z^2} (\log r)$$

We know that,

$$\dfrac{\partial}{\partial x} (\log r) = \dfrac{1}{r} \dfrac{\partial r}{\partial x}$$

$$= \dfrac{1}{r} \cdot \dfrac{x}{r} \qquad \text{As } r = (x^2 + y^2 + z^2)^{1/2}$$

$$= \dfrac{x}{r^2}$$

$$\dfrac{\partial^2}{\partial x^2} (\log r) = \dfrac{\partial}{\partial x} \left\{ \dfrac{x}{r^2} \right\}$$

$$= \dfrac{r^2 - (x)(2r)\dfrac{\partial r}{\partial x}}{r^4}$$

$$= \dfrac{r^2 - 2xr \cdot \dfrac{x}{r}}{r^4} \qquad \because \dfrac{\partial r}{\partial x} = \dfrac{x}{r}$$

$$\dfrac{\partial^2}{\partial x^2} (\log r) = \dfrac{r^2 - 2x^2}{r^4}$$

Similarly, $\dfrac{\partial^2}{\partial y^2} (\log r) = \dfrac{r^2 - 2y^2}{r^4}$

and $\dfrac{\partial^2}{\partial z^2} (\log r) = \dfrac{r^2 - 2z^2}{r^4}$

$\therefore \nabla^2 \log r = \dfrac{\partial^2}{\partial x^2} (\log r) + \dfrac{\partial^2}{\partial y^2} (\log r) + \dfrac{\partial^2}{\partial z^2} (\log r)$

$$= \frac{3r^2 - 2(x^2 + y^2 + z^2)}{r^4}$$

$$= \frac{3r^2 - 2r^2}{r^4}$$

$$= \frac{r^2}{r^4}$$

$$= \frac{1}{r^2}$$

∴ $\boxed{\nabla^2 (\log r) = \frac{1}{r^2}}$

Example 4.19 : Prove that, $\nabla^2 \left(\frac{1}{r}\right) = 0$

Solution : We know that, $r = (x^2 + y^2 + z^2)^{1/2}$

$$\frac{1}{r} = (x^2 + y^2 + z^2)^{-1/2}$$

$$\frac{\partial}{\partial x}\left(\frac{1}{r}\right) = -x(x^2 + y^2 + z^2)^{-3/2}$$

$$\frac{\partial^2}{\partial x^2}\left(\frac{1}{r}\right) = 3x^2(x^2 + y^2 + z^2)^{-5/2} - (x^2 + y^2 + z^2)^{-3/2}$$

$$= \frac{2x^2 - y^2 - z^2}{(x^2 + y^2 + z^2)^{5/2}}$$

Similarly, $\dfrac{\partial^2}{\partial y^2}\left(\dfrac{1}{r}\right) = \dfrac{2y^2 - x^2 - z^2}{x^2 + y^2 + z^2}$

and $\dfrac{\partial^2}{\partial z^2}\left(\dfrac{1}{r}\right) = \dfrac{2z^2 - y^2 - x^2}{x^2 + y^2 + z^2}$

∴ $\nabla^2\left(\dfrac{1}{r}\right) = \dfrac{\partial^2}{\partial x^2}\left(\dfrac{1}{r}\right) + \dfrac{\partial^2}{\partial y^2}\left(\dfrac{1}{r}\right) + \dfrac{\partial^2}{\partial z^2}\left(\dfrac{1}{r}\right)$

$$= \frac{2x^2 - y^2 - z^2}{(x^2 + y^2 + z^2)^{5/2}} + \frac{2y^2 - x^2 - z^2}{(x^2 + y^2 + z^2)^{5/2}}$$

$$+ \frac{2z^2 - x^2 - y^2}{(x^2 + y^2 + z^2)^{5/2}}$$

$$= 0$$

∴ $\nabla^2 \left(\dfrac{1}{r}\right) = 0$

Example 4.20 : Prove that $\nabla^2 f(r) = \dfrac{\partial^2 f}{\partial r^2} + \dfrac{2}{r}\dfrac{df}{dr} = f''(r) + \dfrac{2}{r}f'(r)$

Solution : $r = (x^2 + y^2 + z^2)^{1/2}$

$\therefore \quad \dfrac{\partial}{\partial x}[f(r)] = \dfrac{\partial}{\partial r}[f(r)] \dfrac{\partial r}{\partial x}$

$= f'(r) \cdot \dfrac{x}{r}$

$\dfrac{\partial^2}{\partial x^2}[f'(r)] = \dfrac{\partial}{\partial x}\left[f'(r) \cdot \dfrac{x}{r}\right]$

$= f'(r)\left[\dfrac{r - x\dfrac{\partial r}{\partial x}}{r^2}\right] + \dfrac{x}{r} \cdot f''(r)\dfrac{\partial r}{\partial x}$

$= f'(r)\left[\dfrac{r - \dfrac{x^2}{r}}{r^2}\right] + \dfrac{x^2}{r^2}f''(r)$

$= f'(r)\left[\dfrac{r^2 - x^2}{r^3}\right] + \dfrac{x^2}{r^2}f''(r)$

Similarly, $\dfrac{\partial^2}{\partial y^2}[f(r)] = f'(r)\left[\dfrac{r^2 - y^2}{r^3}\right] + \dfrac{y^2}{r^2}f''(r)$

and $\dfrac{\partial^2}{\partial z^2}[f(r)] = f'(r)\left[\dfrac{r^2 - z^2}{r^3}\right] + \dfrac{z^2}{r^2}f''(r)$

Consider, $\nabla^2[f(r)] = \dfrac{\partial^2}{\partial x^2}[f(r)] + \dfrac{\partial^2}{\partial y^2}[f(r)] + \dfrac{\partial^2}{\partial z^2}[f(r)]$

$= f'(r)\left[\dfrac{3r^2 - (x^2 + y^2 + z^2)}{r^3}\right] + \dfrac{f''(r)}{r^2}(x^2 + y^2 + z^2)$

$= f'(r)\left[\dfrac{3r^2 - r^2}{r^3}\right] + \dfrac{f''(r)}{r^2} \cdot r^2$

$= f'(r)\dfrac{(2)}{r} + f''(r)$

$= \dfrac{2}{r}f'(r) + f''(r)$

$\nabla^2[f(r)] = \dfrac{2}{r}f'(r) + f''(r)$

EXERCISE 4.2

1. If $\bar{r} = x\hat{i} + y\hat{j} + z\hat{k}$ and $r = |\bar{r}|$ find: (i) div. $\bar{r}$, (ii) curl $\bar{r}$, (iii) div $(r^m \cdot \bar{r})$, (iv) curl $(r^m \cdot \bar{r})$.

2. If $\bar{f} = (x + y + 1)\hat{i} + \hat{j} + (-x - y)\hat{k}$, then prove that $\bar{f} \cdot \text{curl } \bar{f} = 0$

3. Prove that $r^n \cdot \bar{r}$ is irrotational. Find n when it is solonoidal.

4. If $\bar{f} = x^2z\hat{i} - 2y^3z^2\hat{j} + xzy^2\hat{k}$, find div $\bar{f}$ and curl $\bar{f}$ at $(1, -1, 1)$.

5. If $\bar{F} = \text{grad } (x^3 + y^3 + z^3 - 3xyz)$, find div $\bar{F}$ and curl $\bar{F}$.

6. If $\bar{f} = (y + \sin z)\hat{i} + x\hat{j} + (x \cos z)\hat{k}$, show that $\bar{f}$ is irrotational and find ϕ such that $\nabla\phi = \bar{f}$.

7. If $\bar{a} = 3xy\hat{i} + x^2z\hat{j} + y^2e^{2z}\hat{k}$, show that at the point $(1, 2, 0)$, div $\bar{a} = -2$ and curl $\bar{a} = 5\hat{i} + 3\hat{k}$.

8. If $\bar{a} = x^2\hat{i} + 5\hat{j} + 3\hat{k}$ and $\phi = xy^2$, find div $(\phi\bar{a})$.

9. If $\bar{f} = (x^2 - y^2)\hat{i} + 2xy\hat{j} + (y^2 - 2xy)\hat{k}$, find div $\bar{f}$, curl $\bar{f}$, grad (div $\bar{f}$).

10. If $\bar{f} = x^2y\hat{i} + xz\hat{j} + 2yz\hat{k}$, show that div (curl $\bar{f}$) = 0.

11. Let $\phi = x^3 + y^3 + z^3 + 3xyz$ and $\bar{v} = x^2\hat{i} + y^2\hat{j} + z^2\hat{k}$, verify that curl (grad ϕ) = $\bar{0}$ and div $(\phi\bar{v})$ = (grad ϕ) $\cdot \bar{v}$ div $(\bar{v})$

12. Prove that $\nabla^2 u = 0$ if $u = y^2 - z^2$.

13. With usual notation prove that, $\nabla^2 (r^n) = n(n + 1) r^{n-2}$.

14. Show that, curl (grad r^n) = 0

15. If $\bar{A} yz^2\hat{i} + zx^2\hat{j} + xy^2\hat{k}$, prove that, $\bar{A} \cdot \text{curl } \bar{A} = xyz (xy + yz + zx)$.

ANSWERS 4.2

1. (i) div $\bar{r}$ = 3, (ii) curl $\bar{r} = \bar{0}$, (iii) div $(r^m \cdot \bar{r}) = (3 + m) r^m$.

    (iv) curl $(r^m \cdot \bar{r}) = \bar{0}$

2. n = −3

4. $\operatorname{div} \bar{f} = -3$ and $\operatorname{curl} \bar{f} = -6\hat{i}$

6. $\phi = (y + \sin z)x + c$

8. $3x^2y^2 + 4xy^2$

9. $(2x + 2y)$, $2(y-x)\hat{i} + 2y\hat{j} + 4y\hat{k}$, $2\hat{i} + 2\hat{j}$

MISCELLANEOUS EXERCISE

(I) Theory Questions :

1. Define gradient, divergence and curl of a point functions.
2. Prove that grad ϕ is a vector normal to the surface $\phi(x, y, z) = k$.
3. If u and v are scalar point functions then prove that

    (i) $\operatorname{grad}(u \pm v) = \operatorname{grad} u \pm \operatorname{grad} v$

    (ii) $\operatorname{grad}(u \cdot v) = u \operatorname{grad} v + v \operatorname{grad} u$

    (iii) $\operatorname{grad}\left(\dfrac{u}{v}\right) = \dfrac{v \operatorname{grad} u - u \operatorname{grad} v}{v^2}$

    (iv) $\operatorname{grad} f(u) = f'(u) \cdot \operatorname{grad} u$

4. Define directional derivative.
5. If $\bar{a}$ is any constant vector then show that

    $\operatorname{div} \bar{a} = 0$ and $\operatorname{curl} \bar{a} = \bar{0}$

6. If $\bar{f}$ and $\bar{g}$ are any vector point functions and ϕ is any scalar then, show that :

    (i) $\operatorname{div}(\bar{f} \pm \bar{g}) = \operatorname{div} \bar{f} \pm \operatorname{div} \bar{g}$.

    (ii) $\operatorname{curl}(\bar{f} \pm \bar{g}) = \operatorname{curl} \bar{f} \pm \operatorname{curl} \bar{g}$.

    (iii) $\operatorname{div}(\phi \bar{f}) = \phi \operatorname{div} \bar{f} + (\operatorname{grad} \phi) \cdot \bar{f}$.

    (iv) $\operatorname{div}(\operatorname{grad} \phi) = \dfrac{\partial^2 \phi}{\partial x^2} + \dfrac{\partial^2 \phi}{\partial y^2} + \dfrac{\partial^2 \phi}{\partial z^2} = \nabla^2 \phi$.

    (v) $\operatorname{curl}(\operatorname{grad} \phi) = \bar{0}$.

    (vi) $\operatorname{div}(\operatorname{curl} \bar{f}) = 0$.

7. Define solenoidal and irrotatinal of a vector.

8. If $\bar{f}$ is a vector point function and ϕ is a scalar function, prove that

$$\text{curl } (\phi \bar{f}) = \text{grad } \phi \times \bar{f} + \phi \cdot \text{curl } \bar{f}$$

(II) Numerical Questions

1. If $\phi = 3x^2y - y^3z$, find the grad ϕ at the point $(1, -2, -1)$.

2. If $\bar{A} = 2x^2\hat{i} - 3yz\hat{j} + xz^2\hat{k}$ and $\phi = 2z - x^3y$, find $\bar{A} \cdot \nabla\phi$ and $\bar{A} \times \nabla\phi$ at the point $(1, -1, 1)$.

3. If $\phi = 2xz^4 - x^2y$, find grad ϕ and grad ϕ at the point $(2, -2, -1)$.

4. Find the unit outward drawn normal to the surface

$$(x - 1)^2 + y^2 + (3 + 2)^2 = g \text{ at the point } (3, 1, -4).$$

5. Prove that grad $\left(\dfrac{1}{r}\right) = \dfrac{-\bar{r}}{r^3}$

6. If $\phi = x^2yz$ find grad ϕ at $(2, 3, 1)$.

7. Find the unit normal vector at $(3, -2, 0)$ to the level surface of $\phi(x, y, z) = x^2 + 2y^2 - x \cos yz$

8. Find the angle between the normals to the surface $xy = z^2$ at $(1, 4, 2)$ and $(-3, -3, 3)$.

9. Find the directional derivative of $\phi(x, y, z) = xy^2 + yz^3$ at the point $(2, -1, 1)$ in the direction of vector $\hat{i} + 2\hat{j} + 2\hat{k}$.

10. Find the directional derivative of $\phi = xy + yz + zx$ at $(1, 2, 3)$ in the direction of $3\hat{i} + 4\hat{j} + 5\hat{k}$.

11. Find the directional derivative of $\phi = xy^2 + yz^2$ at $(2, -1, 1)$ in the direction of vector $\hat{i} + 2\hat{j} - 2\hat{k}$.

12. Find the directional derivative of $\phi = x^3yz + 4z^2$ at $(1, -2, -1)$ in the direction of $2\hat{i} - \hat{j} - \hat{k}$.

13. In what direction from the point $A(2, 1, -1)$ is the directional derivative of $\phi = x^3yz^3$ a maximum and find its magnitude.

14. In what direction is the directional derivative of $\phi = 2xz - y^2$ at (1, 3, 2) maximum ? Find its magnitude.

15. If $\bar{r} = x\hat{i} + y\hat{j} + z\hat{k}$ find (a) grad r, (b) div. $\bar{r}$ (c) curl $\bar{r}$.

16. If $\bar{a}$ is a constant vector, prove that curl $(\bar{r} \times \bar{a}) = -2\bar{a}$

17. If $\phi = x^3 + y^3 + z^3 - 3xyz$, and $\bar{F} = \nabla\phi$, then find div $\bar{F}$ and curl $\bar{F}$.

18. If $\bar{f} = (x + y + 1)\hat{i} + \hat{j} + (x - y)\hat{k}$, then find curl $\bar{f}$ and div $\bar{f}$.

19. If $\phi = x^3 + y^3 + z^3 - 3xyz$, then find div grad ϕ and curl grad ϕ.

20. If $\bar{u} = x^2y\,\hat{i} + y^2x^3\,\hat{j} - 3x^2z^2\,\hat{k}$ and

$\bar{v} = 2xz^2\,\hat{i} - yz\hat{i} + x^2y^3\,\hat{k}$, find div $(\bar{u} \times \bar{v})$ at (1, 2, 1)

21. If $\bar{A} = yz^2\,\hat{i} + zx^2\,\hat{j} + xy^2\,\hat{k}$, prove that $\bar{A} \cdot$ curl $\bar{A} = xyz(xy + yz + zx)$.

22. If $u = x^2 + y^2 + z^2$, prove that curl grad $u = \bar{0}$.

23. Show that the vector $\bar{F} = (3 + \sin y)\hat{i} + (x\cos y - z)\hat{j} + (x - y)\hat{k}$ is solenoidal.

24. Show that the vector $\bar{F} = yz\hat{i} + zx\hat{j} + xy\hat{k}$ is solenoidal.

25. Show that the vector $\bar{F} = \dfrac{-y\hat{i} + x\hat{j}}{x^2 + y^2}$ is irrotational.

26. Prove that, $\nabla^2 (r^2 e^r) = (r^2 + 4r + 2)\,e^r$.

27. Prove that, $\nabla^2 (r^2 \log r) = 5 + 6 \log r$.

ANSWERS

1. $-12\hat{i} - 9\hat{j} - 16\hat{k}$
2. $5;\ 7\hat{i} - \hat{j} - 11\hat{k}$
3. $10\hat{i} - 4\hat{j} - 16\hat{k};\ 2\sqrt{93}$
4. $\dfrac{2}{3}\hat{i} + \dfrac{1}{3}\hat{j} - \dfrac{2}{3}\hat{k}$
6. $12\hat{i} + 4\hat{j} + 12\hat{k}$
7. $\dfrac{5\hat{i} - 8\hat{j}}{\sqrt{89}}$
8. $\cos\theta = \dfrac{1}{\sqrt{22}}$
9. $\dfrac{-11}{3}$

10. $\dfrac{46}{5\sqrt{6}}$
11. -3
12. $\dfrac{37}{3}$
13. $-4\hat{i} - 4\hat{j} + 12\hat{k};\ 4\sqrt{11}$
14. $4\hat{i} - 6\hat{j} + 2\hat{k};\ 2\sqrt{15}$
15. (a) $\dfrac{\bar{r}}{r}$ (b) 3   (c) 0
17. $6(x + y + z);\ \bar{0}$
18. $-\hat{i} - \hat{j} - \hat{k};\ 1$
19. $6(x + y + z);\ \bar{0}$
20. 96

(III) Multiple Choice Questions :

Choose the correct alternative for each of the following :

1. If $\phi = x^2 + y^2 + z^2$, then the value of grad ϕ is ……
   (a) $x\hat{i} + y\hat{i} + 2\hat{k}$
   (b) $2x\hat{i} + 2y\hat{j} + 2\hat{k}$
   (c) $2x + 2y + 2z$
   (d) $2x^2\hat{i} + 2y^2\hat{j} + 2z^2\hat{k}$

2. If $\phi = x + y + z$ then $\nabla\phi$ is ……
   (a) $\hat{i} + \hat{j} + \hat{k}$
   (b) $\hat{i} - \hat{j} + \hat{k}$
   (c) $\hat{i} + \hat{j} - \hat{k}$
   (d) $-\hat{i} - \hat{j} - \hat{k}$

3. If $\phi(x, y, z) = 3x^2 y - y^3 z^2$ then $\nabla\phi$ at $(1, 1, 1)$ is ……
   (a) $6\hat{i} - \hat{j} + \hat{k}$
   (b) $6\hat{i} - 2\hat{j}$
   (c) $6\hat{i} + 2\hat{j} + \hat{k}$
   (d) $6\hat{i} + \hat{j} + \hat{k}$

4. If ϕ is a constant, then $\nabla\phi$ is ……
   (a) 0
   (b) positive
   (c) negative
   (d) none of these

5. If ϕ is a scalar field then grad is ……
   (a) 0
   (b) scalar field
   (c) vector field
   (d) none of these

6. If $\bar{F} = 2x^2 z\hat{i} - xy^2 z\hat{j} + 3yz^2 \hat{k}$, then value of div $\bar{F}$ is ......

   (a) $4xz - 2xyz + 6y^2$

   (b) $4x^2 - 2xz + 6yz$

   (c) $2xz + 2xyz + 6yz$

   (d) none of these

7. If $\bar{F} = 2xy\hat{i} + 3yz\hat{j} + 4zx\hat{k}$, then $\nabla\bar{F}$ at point (1, 2, 3) is ...... units.

   (a) 20 (b) 17

   (c) 25 (d) none of these

8. If $\bar{F} = x\hat{i} + y\hat{j} + z\hat{k}$, then div $\bar{F}$ = ... units.

   (a) -3 (b) $\hat{i} + \hat{j} + \hat{k}$

   (c) 0 (d) 3

9. If $\bar{F} = x\hat{i} + xy\hat{j} + xyz\hat{k}$, then div. $\bar{F}$ at the point (0, 0, 0) is ...... units.

   (a) 0 (b) -1

   (c) 1 (d) 3

10. $(\nabla\phi)\bar{F} + \phi(\nabla\bar{F})$ = ...

    (a) $\nabla(\phi \cdot \bar{F})$ (b) $\nabla(\phi \times \bar{F})$

    (c) $\nabla(\phi\bar{F})$ (d) none of these

11. If $\bar{F} = x\hat{i} + y\hat{j} + z\hat{k}$ then curl $\bar{F}$ is ......

    (a) $x\hat{i} - y\hat{j} + z\hat{k}$ (b) $x\hat{i} + y\hat{j} - z\hat{k}$

    (c) $\bar{0}$ (d) none of these

12. If $\bar{F} = xy\hat{i} + yz\hat{j} + zx\hat{k}$, then $\nabla \times \bar{F}$ ......

    (a) $-y\hat{i} - z\hat{j} - x\hat{k}$

    (b) $y\hat{i} + z\hat{j} + x\hat{k}$

    (c) $z\hat{i} + x\hat{j} + y\hat{k}$

    (d) none of these

13. If $\bar{F} = z\hat{i} + x\hat{j} + y\hat{k}$, then curl $\bar{F}$ = ... units.

    (a) 0
    (b) $x\hat{i} + y\hat{j} + z\hat{k}$
    (c) $z\hat{i} + x\hat{j} + y\hat{k}$
    (d) none of these

14. If $\phi = x^2\hat{i} + y^2\hat{j} + z^2\hat{k}$ then $\nabla \cdot \nabla\phi$ = ...

    (a) 0
    (b) 4
    (c) 5
    (d) 6

15. The vector $\bar{F}$ is called irrational if ......

    (a) $\bar{F} = \bar{0}$
    (b) curl $\bar{F} = \bar{0}$
    (c) div $\bar{F} = 0$
    (d) curl $[\phi \bar{F}] = \bar{0}$

16. If $\bar{F} = x^2y^2z^2\hat{i} + x^3y^3z^3\hat{j} + x^4y^4z^4\hat{k}$, the value of div. curl $\bar{F}$ = ...

    (a) $\nabla \cdot \bar{F}$
    (b) $\nabla \times \bar{F}$
    (c) 0
    (d) none of these

17. If $\phi = x + y + z$ then curl grad ϕ = ...

    (a) 0
    (b) grad curl ϕ
    (c) $\nabla \phi$
    (d) none of these

18. If $\phi(x, y, z) = x^3 + y^3 + z^3 - 3xyz$ then div. grad ϕ = ...

    (a) 0
    (b) $6(x + y + z)$
    (c) $x + y + z$
    (d) none of these

19. If $\phi(x, y, z) = x^3 + y^3 + z^3 - 3xyz$ the curl grad ϕ = ...

    (a) 0
    (b) $3x^2 + 3y^2 + 3z^2$
    (c) $6(x + y + z)$
    (d) none of these

20. If $\bar{F} = y(x + z)\hat{i} + z(x + y)\hat{j} + x(y + z)\hat{k}$, then $\nabla \times \bar{F}$ = ...

    (a) $y\hat{i} + z\hat{j} + x\hat{k}$
    (b) $-(y\hat{i} + z\hat{j} + x\hat{k})$
    (c) $\bar{0}$
    (d) none of these

ANSWERS

1. (b)	2. (a)	3. (b)	4. (a)	5. (c)	6. (a)	7. (b)	8. (d)
9. (c)	10. (c)	11. (c)	12. (a)	13. (a)	14. (d)	15. (b)	16. (c)
17. (a)	18. (b)	19. (a)	20. (b)				

www.ingramcontent.com/pod-product-compliance
Lightning Source LLC
Chambersburg PA
CBHW081345230426
43667CB00017B/2730